THE WORLD CRISIS IN EDUCATION

THE WORLD CRISIS
IN EDUCATION

THE VIEW FROM THE EIGHTIES

Philip H. Coombs

New York   Oxford
OXFORD UNIVERSITY PRESS
1985

Oxford University Press

Oxford London New York Toronto
Delhi Bombay Calcutta Madras Karachi
Kuala Lumpur Singapore Hong Kong Tokyo
Nairobi Dar es Salaam Cape Town
Melbourne Auckland

and associated companies in
Beirut Berlin Ibadan Mexico City Nicosia

Copyright © 1985 by Philip H. Coombs

Published by
OXFORD UNIVERSITY PRESS
200 MADISON AVENUE
NEW YORK, NEW YORK 10016

LIBRARY OF CONGRESS CATALOGING IN PUBLICATION DATA
Coombs, Philip Hall, 1915–
  The world crisis in education.
  1. Education. I. Title.
LA132.C64 1985   370   84-5713
ISBN 0-19-503502-X
ISBN 0-19-503503-8 (pbk.)

Printing (last digit): 9 8 7 6 5 4 3 2
Printed in the United States of America

ACKNOWLEDGMENT

The trustees of the International Council for Educational Development express their gratitude to the following organizations, whose financial support made this study possible. We wish to emphasize, however, that they share no responsibility for the views expressed in this report.

U.S. Agency for International Development
U.S. Department of State, Bureau of Educational and Cultural Affairs
Edward W. Hazen Foundation
Minister of Cooperation, The Netherlands
U.S. National Center for Educational Statistics
National Endowment for the Humanities
U.K. Overseas Development Administration
World Bank, Education Department

PREFACE

This book presents the findings of a worldwide assessment of recent major trends and changes in education and the critical problems and opportunities likely to confront educational systems throughout the world in coming years. A brief genealogical note will help explain its background and purpose.

As some readers will recognize, this book is a descendant of an earlier book, entitled *The World Educational Crisis: A Systems Analysis* (Oxford University Press, 1968), which I wrote near the end of my term as the first director of the International Institute for Educational Planning (IIEP) founded in Paris by UNESCO in 1963. The book's jarring thesis, that there was an emerging crisis in world education, came at a time of widespread educational euphoria. It shocked the international educational community and stirred widespread discussion and debate.

Since then great changes have taken place all around the world, in both education and its economic, social, and political environment. As a consequence, during my visits to various countries in recent years, I have repeatedly been asked the same two questions: "What has happened to that educational crisis you wrote about in the late 1960s, where does it stand now? What do you see as the most critical common issues likely to face education around the world over the next ten years or so?"

These are obviously important and timely questions, but not ones that can be answered off the top of one's head. In hopes of shedding greater light on them, my colleagues and I at the International Council for Educational Development (ICED),* after consulting a variety of well-informed people, undertook a wide-ranging reassessment of the world educational crisis. It fell to my lot to direct this study and write this book. As its author, I accept full responsibility for all the views expressed in it.

---

*The ICED is an independent, nonprofit research and analytical organization concerned with problems of educational development common to many countries. It enjoys the cooperation of a worldwide network comprised of experienced individuals and organizations that share these concerns.

The study could not have been accomplished, however, without the generous help of many others. To all of them, collectively, I want to acknowledge my deep indebtedness and sincere gratitude, including the organizations listed earlier, which contributed financial support; the innumerable organizations and individuals around the world who provided all sorts of valuable information, ideas, and suggestions; and several distinguished scholars who prepared special background papers for the study.

Most of these contributors are cited by name in the text and reference notes of the report itself. Here, however, I want to acknowledge my special thanks to several colleagues who had a direct and important hand in the enterprise. These include *Sydney Hyman,* whose talented editorial hand removed many rough edges from the draft report; my two able and indefatigable research associates, *Julie Fisher* and *Krashruzzaman Choudhury,* who mined and smelted many valuable nuggets from an imposing mountain of documentation; *Leo Dubbeldam,* who was generously donated by CESO (the Centre for the Study of Education in Developing Countries in The Hague) to work with me for a year, and whose rich knowledge of the educational and cultural conditions in many African and Asian countries added greatly to the study; and not least of all, my versatile and tireless administrative assistant, *Frances O'Dell,* who kept the complex logistical details of the project on track from beginning to end. In addition, I want to thank *Leo Fernig* for his wise counsel during the planning phase of the study, and our three bright and energetic ICED summer research interns—*Rezan Benitar* (Turkey), *Jennie Hay Woo* (United States), and *Joel Momanyi* (Kenya)—who helped early in the project to sift and synthesize pertinent information from a great variety of sources. Most important of all, I want to express my deep indebtedness and gratitude to the lady whose infinite patience and encouragement nurtured this book from beginning to end—my wife, Helen.

As a final cautionary word, readers of this book should not expect to find ready-made solutions to the formidable problems it explores. Its more modest aim is to provide a comparative international perspective that may help planners and policymakers in individual countries to see their own country's educational problems and opportunities more clearly as they seek to formulate policies and actions appropriate to its particular goals and circumstances.

P.H.C.

Essex, Connecticut
November, 1984

CONTENTS

FIGURES AND TABLES   *xii*

ABBREVIATIONS   *2*

CHAPTER 1. A NEW LOOK AT AN OLD CRISIS   *3*

In Retrospect   3
Summarization of the Earlier Thesis   4
Present Purpose   8
Recent Changes in Education's Environment   9
Changes in Development Thinking and Policies   14
Changes in Educational Thought   20
The Analytical Approach   27

*CHAPTER 2. THE RAPID GROWTH
             OF LEARNING NEEDS*   *33*

Supply and Demand: The 1968 Appraisal   33
Population Growth   36
Migration and Urbanization   44
Conditions and Learning Needs in Rural Areas   49
Impact of Development on Learning Needs   57
Adding It All Up   61

*CHAPTER 3. QUANTITATIVE GROWTH
             ON THE SUPPLY SIDE*   *66*

National Agendas, Priorities, and Strategies   66
Education's New Look by 1980   71
The Slowdown in the 1970s   80
The Outlook for Formal Education   83
The Upsurge in Nonformal Education   86
The Enrichment of Informal Education   92
Some Preliminary Conclusions   95

*CHAPTER 4. THE CHANGING QUALITATIVE
            DIMENSIONS*   105

Getting the Subject in Focus   106
Impact of Environmental Changes   110
Changes in the Schools and Colleges   113
Changes in Objectives and Curriculum   114
The Changing Supply and Roles of Teachers   117
Educational Technologies   125
The Balance Sheet and Outlook   131

CHAPTER 5. THE GROWING FINANCIAL SQUEEZE   136

Prediction   136
Trends in Public Educational Expenditures: 1960–79   139
The Impact of Inflation   143
Rising Real Educational Costs   145
Responses of Education Systems to the Squeeze   154
The Future?   160
Ways to Combat the Squeeze   165

CHAPTER 6. EDUCATION AND EMPLOYMENT   171

Background   171
The Turn of Events in the 1970s   179
Caveats about Employment Statistics   183
Growth of Youth Unemployment in OECD Countries   184
The Case of the European Socialist Countries   190
The Case of Developing Countries   194
Looking to the Future   200

CHAPTER 7. DISPARITIES AND INEQUALITIES   211

The Ideal Versus the Real   211
Voices of Criticism   215
Focusing Questions   217
Geographic Disparities   218
Sex Disparities   224
Socioeconomic Disparities   230
Possible Ways to Reduce Inequalities   233

*CHAPTER 8. EDUCATION, CULTURE, SCIENCE,
            AND LANGUAGE*   243

Directional Signal   243
Education and Cultural Upheavals   244

Impact of Science on Education   246
The Ambiguous Issue of Moral Education   250
The Language Dilemma   255
Prospects   263

CHAPTER 9. THE TARNISHED LITERACY MYTH   *265*

The Literacy Balance Sheet   266
Historical Roots   270
More Recent Experiences   271
Lessons of a Major UNESCO Experimental Program   272
Putting the Lessons to Good Use   276
Ambiguities   279
Critical Questions for Future Strategy   281

CHAPTER 10. INTERNATIONAL COOPERATION (I): EDUCATIONAL DEVELOPMENT ASSISTANCE   *285*

The Altered Climate of Cooperation   287
Changes in Educational Development Assistance   289
The New Directions   300
The Future of Educational Assistance   305

CHAPTER 11. INTERNATIONAL COOPERATION (II): PEOPLE, IDEAS, AND KNOWLEDGE   *314*

Changes in Foreign Student Flows and Policies   314
The Exchange of Teachers, Scholars, and Research   329
The Worrisome Decline in International Studies   331

INDEX   *341*

FIGURES AND TABLES

FIGURES

2.1 The expanding world of learners.   39
2.2 Distribution of the world's learners by age group, 1980.   39
2.3 Actual and projected enrollment increments, 1960–80 versus
     1980–2000.   43
2.4 Projected growth of rural and urban populations, 1970–2000.   50
2.5 Percentage of landless and near-landless rural labor force.   52

3.1 Distribution of world enrollment growth between developed and
     developing countries (not including China) at all levels, 1960–80. 74
3.2 Past and projected enrollment ratios by age groups, 1960–2000.   85

5.1 Public expenditure on education in the world, 1970, 1975, 1979.   140
5.2 Public expenditure on education as a percentage of the GNP.   141
5.3 Public expenditures per student as a percentage of national per
     capita income, circa 1975.   159
5.4 Comparative expenditure per student in high- and low-income
     countries, circa 1975.   160

6.1 The growing employment gap in OECD countries, 1960–82.   185

9.1 Estimates and projections of number of literate people (age 15
     and older), 1970, 1980, 1990.   267
9.2 Estimates and projections of number of illiterate people, by
     selected regions (age 15 and older), 1970, 1980, 1990.   268

10.1 Sources of external aid to education, 1970 and 1975.   295

11.1 Increases in numbers of foreign students by region of origin.   315
11.2 Foreign students: where they came from; where they studied.   316
11.3 Distribution of U.S. foreign students by major fields of study,
     1969–70 versus 1981–82.   320

TABLES

3.1 Trends in Gross Enrollment Ratios, 1960–80.   76
3.2 Comparison of Different Enrollment Ratios, 1980.   80

4.1 Worldwide Growth of Teaching Staff, 1965–80.   117

5.1 Trends in Ratio of Public Expenditures on Education to Total
     Government Expenditures, 1970–79.   144

5.2 Comparison of Public Expenditures on Elementary and Higher
     Education per Student, 1976.   158

7.1 Growth in Percentage of Females in Total Enrollments, 1965–80. 225

9.1 Growth in the Percent of Literates (age 15 and older), 1970–90. 267

10.1 Official Development Assistance in Real Terms, 1970–82.   293

10.2 Technical Assistance Exchanges Under Bilateral Programs of
      OECD/DAC Countries, 1969 and 1975.   296

APPENDIX TABLES

2.1 The Expanding World of Learners, 1950–2000.   63
2.2 Trends in School Age Populations, 1960–2000.   63
2.3 Projected Adjusted Gross Enrollment Ratios by Regions and
     Levels, 1980–2000.   64
2.4 Basic Health Indicators.   64
2.5 Increasing Female Participation in the Labor Force in Eight
     OECD Countries.   65

3.1 Growth of Enrollments by Levels and Regions, 1960–80.   99
3.2 Growth of Enrollment Ratios by Age Groups, 1960, 1970, and
     1980.   100
3.3 Annual Percentage Rates of Enrollment Growth by Levels and
     Regions, 1960–80.   101
3.4 Enrollment Increments by Five-Year Periods, by Regions and
     Education Levels, 1960–80.   102
3.5 World Book Production by Regions, 1960–80.   102
3.6 Daily Newspapers by Region, 1965 and 1979.   103
3.7 Movie Theaters and Seating Capacity by Region, 1965, 1970, and
     1978.   103
3.8 Radio Broadcasting Transmitters and Receivers by Region, 1965,
     1979, and 1980.   103
3.9 Television Transmitters and Receivers by Region, 1965, 1979,
     and 1980.   104

5.1 Worldwide Trends in Public Expenditure on Education, 1970–79.   167
5.2 Public Expenditure on Education per Inhabitant, 1970–79.   168
5.3 Inflation in 117 Countries, 1960–81.   168
5.4 Sweden: Increasing Cost per Student in Stockholm
     Comprehensive Schools, 1963–75.   169
5.5 Canada: Trends in Real Cost per Student, 1960–74.   169

5.6 United States: Total and Current Expenditures per Pupil in Average Daily Attendance, 1929–30 to 1979–80. 170

5.7 Past and Projected Growth of Gross Domestic Product, 1960–95. 170

6.1 Ratio of Youth to Adult Unemployment Rates in Selected OECD Countries, 1970–82. 206

6.2 Eastern Socialist Countries: Higher Education Enrollments and Graduates, 1960–77. 207

6.3 Higher Education Enrollments in the Union of Soviet Socialist Republics by Type of Students, 1950–80. 208

6.4 Trends in Higher Education Graduates Employed in Six Socialist Economies, 1960–75. 208

6.5 First-Year Enrollments in Higher Education in the Union of Soviet Socialist Republics, 1950–80. 209

6.6 First-Year Enrollments of Day Students Only, Eastern European Socialist Countries, 1960–77. 210

7.1 Public Expenditure on Education per Child by Income Groups: A Composite Profile of 19 Latin American Countries (ca. 1970). 242

10.1 World Bank Lending for Education and Training, 1970–82. 311

10.2 OECD/DAC Bilateral Allocations to Education Sector, 1975–81. 311

10.3 Percentage of Total Bilateral Aid Allocated to Education Sector by OECD/DAC Members. 312

10.4 Distribution of World Bank Lending for Education Sector, 1963–82. 313

11.1 Foreign Students: Major Countries of Origin in 1980–81. 336

11.2 Foreign Students: Major Host Countries, in 1970 and 1980. 336

11.3 Percentage Distribution of Foreign Students from Major World Regions among Leading Host Countries, 1978. 337

11.4 15 Leading Countries of Origin of All Foreign Students in the United States in 1981–82, Compared to Their Ranks in 1969–70. 338

11.5 Countries with More than 1,000 Students in the United Kingdom, 1969–70 and 1978–79. 338

11.6 Distribution of Overseas Students in the United Kingdom by Subject Fields, 1977–78. 339

11.7 Minimum Recommended Fees for Overseas Students in the United Kingdom, effective 1980–81. 339

THE WORLD CRISIS IN EDUCATION

ABBREVIATIONS

ACPO	Accion Cultural Popular
CERI	OECD's Centre for Educational Research and Innovation
CESO	Center for the Study of Education in Developing Countries
CMEA	Council for Mutual Economic Assistance
DAC	OECD's Development Assistance Committee
EEC	European Economic Community
EWLP	Experimental World Literacy Program
FAO	United Nations Food and Agricultural Organization
GER	Gross Enrollment Ratio
GNP	Gross National Product
IBRD	International Bank for Reconstruction and Development
ICED	International Council for Educational Development
IDA	International Development Association of the World Bank
IDRC	International Development Research Centre
IIEP	International Institute for Educational Planning
ILO	International Labour Office
IUT	Instituts Universitaires de Technologie
MPATI	Midwest Program of Airborne Television Instruction
NUFFIC	Netherlands University Foundation for International Cooperation
ODA	Official Development Assistance
OECD	Organization for Economic Cooperation and Development
OPEC	Organization of Petroleum Exporting Countries
PEE	Public Expenditure on Education
SAREC	Swedish Agency for Research Cooperation
TPB	Total Public Budget
U.K.	United Kingdom
UNDP	United Nations Development Programme
UNESCO	United Nations Educational, Scientific & Cultural Organization
UNICEF	United National Children's Fund
USAID	United States Agency for International Development
WHO	World Health Organization

CHAPTER 1

A NEW LOOK AT AN OLD CRISIS

IN RETROSPECT

RALPH WALDO Emerson, the nineteenth century American philosopher, laid down the rule that friends who meet after a time apart should greet each other by asking one question: Has anything become clear to you since we were last together? The question is uniquely applicable to this book, whose pages revisit—and take off from—themes of a book published in 1968, *The World Educational Crisis: A Systems Analysis.*

This earlier book jolted the international educational community, not unlike a fire bell in the night, by warning that a world educational crisis, long in the making, was everywhere gathering force. In a seeming paradox, the warning was sounded amid the greatest worldwide educational expansion in all of human history—an expansion fueled by hopes and expectations that followed the end of World War II. To countless new nations born from the old colonial empires, educational expansion was a cause, a war cry, a catalyst for economic development, a leveler of hard-set social inequalities. It was the same for industrially advanced countries, all of whose governments had pledged to democratize educational opportunity as an essential step toward improving the quality of life for their peoples.

Immense consequences followed. By the mid-1960s student enrollments in educational systems had doubled in many countries; expenditures on education had risen even faster, and education had emerged as the largest local industry. The graphic aspects of the physical expansion could be seen on all sides, and the statistics of the process could be proudly broadcast for domestic consumption and from the rostrums of international organizations. It was taken as an article of faith that swift

3

educational progress would continue, unchecked, until all of its great aims had been attained. But then . . .

In October 1967 a noted group of educators and economists from all over the world came together in Williamsburg, Virginia, to assess the current state of world education and its prospects. Unlike other conferences where papers rival each other for attention, this conference's discussion focused on a single basic working paper sent to the participants before their arrival in Williamsburg. This text drew a picture in which two sets of realities, one bright and the other ominous, were entwined. The first showed the valiant efforts many governments made to carry their people over the hump of mass illiteracy, to level gross educational inequalities, and to widen access to education at successively higher levels of instruction. The second showed how and why the conditions for a profound crisis were encroaching on educational systems everywhere and already held many of them in an iron grip.

The conferees at Williamsburg, after discussing the working paper in the light of evolving educational conditions in their own countries and regions, agreed that the world educational crisis sketched in the document was real and merited urgent attention. On returning home, they joined in amplifying the warning—each in his or her own national tongue—about what was in store for world education. Subsequently, the text of what had been prepared for the Williamsburg Conference was refined and buttressed in details and published in 1968. Because that book—and its dozen or so foreign-language editions—serves as the point of departure for the present book, it is important to recall briefly its basic message.

SUMMARIZATION OF THE EARLIER THESIS

The report asserted that the crisis in view went well beyond the common kind that had been experienced episodically by many local education systems. In the precise sense of the word, it was a *world* crisis, the first of its kind, and, though it varied in form and severity from one place to the next, it had been precipitated by a combination of factors common to virtually all countries: "Its inner lines of force appear in all nations alike, whether they are old or new, rich or poor, whether they have stable institutions or are struggling to build them in defiance of heavy odds." The interrelations between three words—change, adaptation, and disparity—lay at the heart of the crisis, as is expressed in the following exerpt from the report:

Since 1945, all countries have undergone fantastically swift environmental changes, brought about by a number of concurrent worldwide revolutions—in science and technology, in economic and political affairs, in demographic and social structures. Educational systems have also grown and changed more rapidly than ever before. But they have adapted all too slowly in relation to the faster pace of events on the move all around them. The consequent disparity—taking many forms—between educational systems and their environments is the essence of the worldwide crisis in education.

Among the disparities alluded to was the growing obsolescence of the old curriculum content in relation to the advancing state of knowledge and the realistic learning needs of students. Another was the misfit between education and the development needs of societies. Yet another entailed the growing imbalances and maladjustments between education and employment, as well as serious educational inequalities between various social groups. There was also the growing gap between the rising costs of education and the funds countries would be able and willing to invest in it.

In focusing on the causes for disparities, the report touched particularly on four: first, the sharp increase in popular aspirations for education; second, the acute scarcity of resources; third, the inherent inertia of educational systems, "which caused them to respond too sluggishly in adapting their internal affairs to new external necessities, even when resources have not been the main obstacle to adaptation"; and fourth, the inertia of societies themselves—"the heavy weight of traditional attitudes, religious customs, prestige and incentive patterns, and institutional structures—which has blocked them from making the optimum use of education and of educated manpower to foster national development."

Against this diagnostic background, the report argued that educators could not be expected by themselves to set right everything that was out of joint in their educational systems, because the crisis encompassed the whole of society and the economy, not education alone. This being the case, any attempts to resolve the crisis plainly called for "a substantial mutual adjustment and adaptation by *both* education and society." Otherwise, the "growing disparity between education and society [would] inevitably crack the frame of educational systems—and, in some cases, the frame of their respective societies." But if educational systems were to play their part in meeting the crisis, the report continued, they would need help from every sector of domestic life. In many cases, they would also need much additional help from sources beyond their national boundaries.

They would need a larger share of the nation's best human resources, not merely to carry forward the current work of education, but to raise its quality, efficiency, relevance, and productivity. They would need more money to buy essential physical facilities and equipment, more and better teaching materials, and, in some instances, food for hungry pupils to put them in a condition to learn. Above all, educational systems would need what money alone could not buy—"ideas and courage, determination, and a new will for self-appraisal, reinforced by a will for adventure and change." Precisely on this account the report trained its strongest fire on the inertia of educational systems themselves:

> An educational system can lose the power to see itself clearly. If it clings to conventional practices merely because they are traditional, if it lashes itself to inherited dogmas in order to stay afloat in a sea of uncertainty, if it invests folklore with the dignity of science and exalts inertia to the plane of first principles—that system is a satire on education itself. Individuals showing authentic gifts may still emerge from such a system. But they will not have been produced by it; they will merely have survived it. Moreover, from the standpoint of society, the resources invested in perpetuating such a system are misused resources—misused because a high proportion of its students will emerge ill-fitted to serve well either themselves or their society.

The report concluded by strongly urging the managers of educational systems to reconsider the implications of the simplistic strategy virtually all countries had pursued since the early 1950s, namely, the linear expansion of existing or inherited educational systems. Judged by its own limited objectives and criteria, such a strategy had been remarkably successful. But preoccupation with increasing the statistics of enrollments as fast as possible at all levels was having serious consequences. Especially serious was that educational system managers were busily expanding the wrong systems for their new circumstances; in an era of rapid change education's imperative was not simply "more of the same" but a need for fresh approaches that would adapt it to the evolving demands of a much larger and more diversified group of learners. Meanwhile, the effects of a mechanistic preoccupation with the linear expansion led to the erosion of quality and relevance and to the diversion of energies from the qualitative changes that could help raise the internal efficiency and external productivity of educational systems.

The report noted how newly developing countries in particular placed themselves at a double disadvantage when they imported foreign educational systems designed to fit quite different aims and circumstances. The imports were largely elitist academic structures that had served remarkably well in earlier times in their countries of origin but had become increasingly obsolete in the greatly changed postwar environment. Under no circumstances could they fit the fundamentally different needs and circumstances, not to mention the thin pocketbooks, of newly independent developing countries.

They had helped create elite cadres to run new governmental ministries and to work in the small urban/modern sector of the economy, but they were ill-suited to develop the vast human and other resources of the traditional rural sector where most of the people still lived. In fact, they deprived rural areas of their best potential development leaders by draining bright and ambitious young people away from the countryside into the cities.

The report was widely read throughout the world. In the fashion of the time, it focused largely on formal education, though it did contain what proved to be a provocative and prophetic chapter calling attention to the potential importance of what it called "nonformal education." Further, the mold of a system analysis, in which the structure of the report was cast, had its own appeal. It offered what was at the time a fresh way of looking at formal educational systems—with their inputs, internal process and outputs, and the interactions between these and the surrounding society.

If the report had appeared five or ten years earlier, most educators and many others might well have rejected or ignored it. Coming when it did, however, it was generally well received. More to the point, it helped to precipitate a widespread debate over and reexamination of previously accepted educational orthodoxies and to stimulate the search for alternative approaches.

The report, however, was not spared criticism. On the one extreme, several "new left" academics, especially in the United States, charged the author with being a progressivist and evolutionist who favored patching up an essentially "exploitive capitalistic educational system" rather than a radical structuralist who favored up-ending the entire system and replacing it with some unspecified radical alternative. From dead center, an embittered reviewer of a London newspaper, who clearly had not taken time to read the book but had noted its many statistical tables, dismissed it out of hand as just one more example of a narrow quantitative view of education that ignored its crucial qualitative dimensions.

Milder criticisms, not of the book's content but of its title, came initially from a few Western European educators. They readily agreed that the developing world faced a profound educational crisis, but not *their* particular countries, though admittedly each did have some "serious problems." That criticism quickly evaporated in the spring of 1968, when the universities of the Western world were overwhelmed by an unprecedented wave of student protests which produced daily local headlines about the educational crisis. Soviet educational authorities, though complimenting the report itself, also objected to the title. They quickly agreed that both the developing countries and the Western capitalist societies had a real educational crisis. But socialist systems such as their own had a built-in natural immunity to crisis. In the end, the Soviet publisher of the Russian language edition of the report solved this semantic problem with a minor tour de force—he translated the title as *The Educational Crisis in the World,* thus leaving a loophole for exemption of socialist societies.

PRESENT PURPOSE

The issue of nomenclature need not delay us here, for the crisis, by whatever name, is still serious. The question of central importance to the present book is how the world of education looks from the vantage point of the mid-1980s, compared to how it looked from the earlier perspective of 1968. As will be seen in a moment, the many economic, social, and political changes that have occurred in the ecology of education worldwide—all of which carry extensive implications for education proper—also define the main questions that demand attention. Among them are these: What has happened to the world educational crisis since it first surfaced in 1968? Did it turn out to be a false alarm? Did it diminish or worsen? More important, in the light of recent trends and new developments, what can be said about the critical issues that are likely to besiege education around the world in the 1980s and 1990s? And what steps might countries take, individually and collectively, to resolve these critical issues?

The aim of the present book is to try to shed instructive light on these and related questions. Its data and ideas are rooted in a wide-ranging reassessment of the world educational crisis conducted over the past three years by the staff of the International Council for Educational Development (ICED), along with its consultants, research interns, and many cooperative friends. In addition, the present book draws on a host of sources from around the world—from international and regional organizations such as the United Nations Educational, Scientific and Cultural Organization (UNESCO) and its International Institute for Educational Planning (IIEP), the World Bank, and the Organization for Economic Cooperation and Development (OECD); from the American, British, Dutch, and other bilateral assistance agencies; from various research institutions and numerous voluntary agencies active in education and development;

and from able observers in both governmental and nongovernmental agencies in all regions of the world, by correspondence, seminars, and individual discussions.

Once the pages lay bare the evidence assembled for this report, along with the caveats attached to its conclusions, it will become apparent to the reader that the early warnings of a world educational crisis were no false alarm. Not only has the crisis been intensified by growing maladjustments between education systems and the rapidly changing world all around them, but it has also acquired new dimensions in the 1970s and early 1980s. Of these new dimensions, the most significant is that *there is now a crisis of confidence in education itself.*

The implications, however, should not automatically be pressed too hard and too far. It should not be assumed that nothing is beyond redemption before educational systems are overwhelmed with ruin. The evidence does not support any such cataclysmic forecast. Moreover, we have a positive duty, as a simple matter of morale, to remind ourselves that, despite many formidable obstacles and shortcomings, the educational progress made throughout the world over the past three decades has been substantially greater than most forecasters would have dared predict in the early 1950s. The task is to grasp the nature of the critical problems that have enveloped the world of education and move to overcome them by altering their underlying causes. To that end it may be useful next to offer a quick overview of some of the major changes that have occurred during the past decade in the educational environment.

RECENT CHANGES IN EDUCATION'S ENVIRONMENT

The strengths and weaknesses of any educational enterprise cannot be properly assessed, nor can education's future be rationally planned unless one takes into account the major forces in the world that strongly impinge on education and are already shaping its future. Some of these forces have only domestic roots; others are international in scope and as such have implications for education in many countries. What follows is an overview of the changing worldwide environmental factors that have left their mark on education between the late 1960s and the early 1980s. Most of the matters to be touched on will be discussed more fully later in connection with specific educational issues.

Economic Changes

Four economic changes during the 1970s had, and will continue to have, a far reaching impact on education. The first is the jolting transition made in the early 1970s by most national economies around the world from an era of pervasive educated manpower shortages to one of manpower surpluses. The time inevitably arrived when the rapidly increasing output of educational systems everywhere, particularly at the secondary and postsecondary levels, finally caught up with the backlog of postwar and postindependence manpower demands and began to outstrip the creation of new jobs by the economy. The resulting phenomenon of educated unemployed soon spread from country to country, creating widespread anxieties and frustrations among students and their families and worrisome political and psychological problems for governments and educational systems.

The second change, growing out of the first, is a major shift in the pattern of international manpower flows and a marked decline in the 1970s in the brain drain from developing to developed countries. European and North American countries that had earlier welcomed educated talent from the developing world began to stiffen their immigration restrictions and, in some instances, expelled "guest workers" and even imposed measures to stem the rapidly increasing inflow of foreign students. At the same time, however, a brisk new market opened up in the oil-rich countries, especially in the Middle East, for technical experts, teachers, and skilled workers from such countries as India, Pakistan, Bangladesh, and the Republic of Korea. The governments viewed this transfer not as a brain drain but as a lucrative form of export—negotiated on a government-to-government basis in some instances. It resulted in valuable remittances in hard currency and also helped lessen the politically volatile problem of the educated unemployed at home.

The third important economic change, which had a severe impact on education virtually everywhere and intensified the problem of the educated unemployed, is the sharp rise in oil prices and the severe worldwide recession and accelerated inflation that began in 1973 and continued through the decade and into the 1980s. The widespread slowdown of economic growth rates, in both industrialized and developing countries, created highly disruptive changes in international trade, capital flows, and exchange rates and threatened the integrity of the world's monetary system. This stagflation affected educational systems in two important ways: first by contracting employment openings for new graduates and, second, by raising hob with educational costs and budgets. It was a traumatic experience for most developed countries, especially those in Europe that had been rapidly converting their former elitist educational systems into mass systems. But the impact was far more severe in most developing countries. Their export earnings declined, their terms of trade worsened, their oil import costs skyrocketed, unemployment mounted, and extreme poverty spread to an ever-increasing number of families. Their public budgets, already heavily burdened with a large accumulation of external debt, became seriously overstrained. Educational systems, whose budgets had by now become a much higher percentage of the Gross National Product (GNP) and the total public budget, inevitably bore a sizable share of the consequences.

The fourth economic factor—with the greatest long-term consequences for education and employment—is the advancing technologies and changing economic structures in both developed and developing countries. In the case of the developed countries, the industrial component of the GNP, whose vigorous growth had previously been the prime mover of overall national economic growth, stagnated in the 1970s, whereas the service sector experienced unprecedented growth. The net effect was to increase the segmentation of the job market between a limited number of high-paying high-tech jobs in industry, requiring advanced specialized training, and the increasing availability of low-paying, low-skill jobs in such expanding service areas as fast-food counters, supermarkets and discount department stores.

Most developing countries also experienced a further segmentation of their labor markets in the 1970s. Although agriculture's previous dominant percentage share of the GNP continued to decline, the heavy proportion of the national labor force attached to low-productivity, low-income employment in agriculture failed to decline correspondingly. Meanwhile the share of the GNP accounted for by the urban modern sector, with its capital-intensive technologies and much higher productivity and wages, grew substantially but without a corresponding growth in its share of the national labor force. As a result young people with a modern education found it increasingly difficult to secure a good paying and stable and secure job in the modern sector. Added to this was the spread of new communications media whose messages whetted the aspirations of people for a better life, including greater access to education.

Political Instability and Eruptions

The turbulent political changes that accompanied the worldwide economic changes in the 1970s and early 1980s also left their mark on education. Some of these changes were peaceful and positive, but a distressing number involved tragic military conflicts, both within and between nations. It was a time when established institutions and power alignments were being stoutly challenged; when newer nations were striving to achieve political stability and older nations to keep theirs from crumbling; when heightened nationalism, insecurity, economic rivalries, and cultural collisions precipitated a rash of internal and external conflicts; and when a rising wave of protests against repression and of popular demands for participation and greater equality swept across the world.

In the developing nations students and teachers were frequently in the vanguard of these protest movements, including outright civil wars and revolutions. Numerous examples spring to mind, among them Pakistan and Bangladesh, Ethiopia, Iran, Poland, Chile, Nicaragua, and El Salvador.

The developed nations, though far less wracked by outright military conflict and physical violence than Indochina and the Middle East, for example, nevertheless had their fill of internal political turmoil and even a shocking dose of terrorism that left many of their old institutions fragile and vulnerable. Many of these internal conflicts arose from historic cultural, linguistic, religious, and ethnic divisions that grew wider and sharper and louder in the 1970s. The classic example, of course, is Northern Ireland; but similar if less dramatic examples can be cited in Belgium, Canada, Holland, Spain, and the decaying inner cities of the United States and England, now heavily populated by disadvantaged racial and ethnic minorities.

The schools and higher educational institutions were invariably in the middle of such socioeconomic and political disruptions. They were often charged with being part of the problem or with having failed to avert it. Society also saddled them with a disporportionate responsibility for curing whatever was wrong.

Another worldwide political phenomenon of this recent period that has placed great burdens on the schools of many countries is the unprecedented flood of refugees and other migrants. The host countries not only must provide these refugees and migrants with food, shelter, and other basic amenities and with jobs to enable them to support themselves, but they must also meet the urgent educational needs of their children. Typically, however, the children start off as cultural and linguistic misfits and the schools find it extremely difficult to adapt to the immigrant children and at the same time keep up with the needs of native-born children. Most surprising, perhaps, is that the process of mutual adaptation has progressed as well as it has in many places—perhaps because children and teachers are more adaptable than most adults.

Possibly the single most significant political development of the 1970s was the reemergence of China from relative isolation, especially from the West. For without the active involvement of this giant society, containing one quarter of the world's total population, all international efforts to secure permanent peace and to iron out gross inequities within and between nations could be fatally handicapped. China's new "opening to the West" has already had extensive educational ramifications. It quickly led to mutually beneficial exchanges of knowledge. The rest of the world, for example, acquired valuable lessons from China's own development experience, particularly as it involved the integration of nonformal education and community-based efforts to improve food production, health, family planning, and other basic human necessities. China, for its part, benefited by sending its students and specialists abroad to tap the latest knowledge of Western scientists, technologists, and others.

Demographic Changes

Demographic factors constitute yet another set of powerful forces that impinged heavily on education in the 1970s, forces that moved in opposite directions in the industrialized countries and the developing countries.

The extent of the postwar population explosion had been grossly underestimated by those who, in the early 1960s, had computed ambitious educational expansion targets over the next two decades for each of the developing regions. In fact, the educational systems in these regions soon found it difficult simply to maintain their existing school participation rates in the face of their rapidly growing school-age populations and harder yet to make a little headway toward their adopted school participation targets. This race between education and population growth continued at a hectic pace throughout the 1970s, with little let-up in sight for the next two decades.

In sharp contrast, the postwar baby boom in the industrialized countries, which had crowded their educational systems in the 1950s and 1960s, unexpectedly collapsed around the mid-1960s, causing absolute reductions in enrolments by the mid-1970s, initially at the primary level and then successively at secondary and tertiary levels.

This demographic turnaround removed the earlier popular pressure for substantial educational expansion that had dominated educational policy in the industrialized countries for more than 20 years. In principle, it gave their educational systems a much needed chance to catch their breath and shift the focus from quantitative expansion to qualitative improvement. Yet, paradoxically, it seemed more difficult to cope with the new problems and controversies arising from enrollment stagnation than with those that arose from the earlier great expansion. A basic reason for this paradox was the altered public and official mood and attitude toward education, resulting in part from the growing burden of educational costs on overstrained public budgets and tax structures and in part from the mounting criticism of the performance of the schools. The aura of euphoria that had surrounded all things educational in the earlier Age of Innocence had by now been transmuted into a Crisis of Confidence.

Everything said so far adds up to the following propositions. The economic, political, and demographic world that enveloped education as it entered the decade of the 1980s differed fundamentally from that existing at the start of the 1960s and 1970s. Overall it was a more complex, divided, and dangerous world, yet in some respects a more hopeful one. This combination has created unprecedented challenges and responsibilities for education of every kind and at every level in every nation. And there is no reason to suppose that the economic, social, political, and demographic ecology of education throughout the world will not continue to change at a rapid rate over the next two decades, creating still greater educational challenges for humankind. Ever since the late 1960s, the situation has had, and will continue to have as far ahead as the mind's eye can see, all the attributes of a *continuing* crisis. (This makes one wonder whether "crisis" is technically the right word, yet it is difficult to find a more apt one.)

CHANGES IN DEVELOPMENT THINKING AND POLICIES

While these tumultuous economic and political changes were taking place in the 1970s, educational thought and policies were also undergoing radical changes. More of this in a moment. First, however, we need to understand the way the changes in education flowed from and ran concurrently with fundamental changes in what had been the governing conventional theories about national development.

The Initial Theories

Before World War II economists had paid little attention to the process of what later came to be called national development. As a result the new concepts and theories of development they began to spin shortly after the war lacked strong empirical foundations. The new concepts were the outgrowth of the immediate postwar reconstruction experience of Western Europe and Japan. New forms of economic planning and cooperation among countries, reinforced by large infusions of U.S. capital, technology, and management practices under the Marshall Plan, put these wartorn economies back on their feet far more swiftly than anyone had dared hope. More than this, they also launched these countries into an era of lusty technological advance and economic growth.

A few years later, in a daring leap of logic, many Western economists and political leaders assumed that a similar formula was applicable to developing countries as well. They assumed, that is, that large capital infusions plus the transfer of modern technology—this time from the West's industrialized nations to newly independent agrarian nations of Asia and Africa and to the older independent nations of Latin America—would enable these countries' struggling economies to take off into a self-sustaining process of economic development and modernization, at a far faster pace than in the industrialized nations of the West. It soon became evident, however, that the analogy between the Marshall Plan countries and the newly developing countries was flawed. The war-torn European countries and Japan needed mainly to replace their devastated physical facilities and to update their managerial and research and development capacities, for they still retained a strong economic and administrative infrastructure, abundant industrial know-how, and a well-educated modern labor force. The developing countries, however, lacked all of these requisites for rapid economic growth.

Thus, modified economic growth theories and models were created that described the process of accelerated modernization in less developed countries and provided the intellectual underpinnings of new national development strategies and new bilateral and multilateral aid policies and programs designed to support them. Under these modified theories, development came to be defined as "economic growth," measured statistically by increases in a nation's GNP—the economist's loftiest aggregate.

The educational development strategy that evolved in the 1950s soon became the handmaiden of this GNP-centered strategy of development. The latter called for the initial concentration of development efforts on modernizing and industrializing the urban centers of developing countries, the theory being that, once the new modern sector in the cities began to grow, its dynamic impulses would spread across the vast countryside, where most of the population and labor force lived and worked. Here it would trigger a spontaneous, self-sustaining process of rural development (perceived mainly as increased commercial agricultural production for urban and export markets), thus steadily narrowing the urban-rural gap.

Education and training fitted neatly into this development theory and strategy. Economists generally agreed that the rapid expansion of the modern sector would require, in addition to a large infusion of physical capital and modern technologies, a greatly increased supply of educated manpower and modern skills. These, however, were in exceedingly short supply in the developing countries at the time and hence created a major bottleneck to economic growth. The obvious solution was to import and rapidly expand the modern educational and training models that had proved their worth in the industrially advanced countries. Along this line of reasoning, many development economists argued strongly for increased education budgets as a high-yielding investment in economic development. Educational leaders naturally welcomed this strategically important support of the economists in their quest for steadily expanding educational budgets, though, imbued with a more humanistic philosophy of education and its loftier purposes, they cringed at the economists' crassly materialistic view of education and especially resented their treatment of schools and colleges as manpower factories. Such concerns and invectives were common fare, for example, in the IIEP seminars in the 1960s that brought educational leaders and economists together to exchange views.

The alliance between economists and educators, reinforced by broad popular and political support for rapid educational expansion, held together until the early 1970s. But then, a flush of disturbing facts and critical analyses about what was actually happening in the real world of development called sharply into question the validity and viability of the conventional theories, doctrines, and strategies on which the alliance was based.

These new facts reaffirmed that a majority of developing countries had indeed made impressive progress, measured by the statistical growth of both their GNP and their educational enrollments and participation rates. But the facts also revealed a shockingly lopsided and inequitable pattern of both economic and educational development. Among other things the urban–rural gap, far from narrowing, had widened. Robert McNamara, president of the World Bank, took the lead in sounding the alarm in his landmark address in Nairobi in October 1973 to the annual conference of the world's financial leaders. He shocked his audience and the entire development community by asserting that 800 million people in the developing world—40 percent of the total—were living in absolute poverty. By this he meant that they were not just relatively poor, but living on the ragged edge of sheer survival. And their number was growing rapidly.[1]

New rural surveys by other agencies and institutions reinforced McNamara's point. They revealed staggering proportions of landless and near-landless rural families in developing countries; spreading unemployment and underemployment; and atrociously poor health, water supply, sanitation, and nutritional conditions, coupled with high infant mortality rates. Underlying and intensifying all these problems was a high rate of rural population growth, which, despite the heavy migration to towns and cities, promised to enlarge the rural population very substantially in most low-income countries by the year 2000.

The rural schools, at close examination, contrasted sharply with the glowing impressions of progress conveyed by the upward-trending statistics of nationwide enrollments for individual countries found in UNESCO's *Statistical Yearbooks*. Concealed behind a facade of inflated numbers were thinly spread and often incomplete rural primary schools, shockingly high dropout and absentee rates, and deteriorating classroom buildings staffed by poorly qualified teachers and lacking textbooks and other basic supplies. In many rural areas, less than 10 percent of the school-age boys and even fewer girls were actually completing the primary cycle, and no more than 10 to 15 percent of these were able to move on to the secondary cycle in the nearest large town or city. To compound the problem, the highly academic, urban, and modern-sector-oriented curriculum of these schools did not realistically fit the learning needs and life prospects of most rural youngsters. Moreover, these imported educational models alienated the brightest and most motivated children from their rural environment and whetted their appetite for migrating to the city, not for remaining in the countryside and developing their own community.

If the rural areas were in bad shape, the cities were frequently not much better. To be sure, their modern sector had blossomed impressively with modern factories, government buildings, schools and colleges, hospitals, and apartments, as well as trucks, buses, paved roads, airports, traffic jams, movie theaters, bright lights, and the ubiquitous whiff of freshly poured concrete. But this booming modern sector (dubbed by many economists the "formal sector"), with its educated labor force, capital intensity, and high wage levels, still constituted only a fraction of the whole urban economy. The great majority of the burgeoning urban labor force, including many recent migrants from small towns and villages, were working (if they could find work, which was becoming increasingly difficult) mostly at miscellaneous low-paid jobs in the so-called informal sector. The physical and economic capacities of dozens of capital cities, such as Bangkok, Manila, New Delhi, Nairobi, Cairo, and Mexico City, to absorb, house, and employ their exploding populations had become saturated, and urban poverty no less extreme than in the villages was increasing rapidly. Besides, the new modern urban industries were beginning to lose their momentum because of the absence of sufficiently expanding rural purchasing power and markets at home and trade barriers to new markets abroad in industrial countries.

The educational situation in the cities, however, was strikingly better than in the countryside, especially for the children of middle- and upper-class parents in the modern sector. Primary schools were much more abundant, better equipped, and better staffed (except in the slum areas and peripheral shantytowns) and had far higher participation rates and lower dropout rates than in the rural areas. Since most of the nation's numerous new secondary schools and virtually all of its greatly expanded postsecondary institutions were concentrated in the cities, the statistical probabilities for an able urban youngster to climb the academic ladder were vastly better than for his or her equally able rural counterpart. Moreover, the imported modern school curriculum was considerably more relevant in the rapidly modernizing urban environment, where reading and writing in a colonial language and sophisticated computational skills played a much larger and more essential role in one's daily life and in getting ahead.

Still, this picture of the imbalances and inequities of the development progress in developing countries that emerged in the early 1970s should not be overdrawn, for there were also many bright spots that held hope for the future. Though unemployment and underemployment were mounting, many new and more rewarding jobs had been created, and living conditions had improved—for a sizable minority if not for the poorer majority. Moreover, for all their shortcomings, the expanded educational systems had opened up new opportunities for millions of disadvantaged young people and given them a new upward mobility. They had also, in less than two decades, dramatically increased the earlier meager domestic reservoir of middle- and high-level educated manpower essential to moving these developing countries much further ahead in coming years.

In short, many of the real gains that had been made by the early 1970s exceeded even the most optimistic forecasts of the early 1950s. But precisely because of these gains and because the distribution of the benefits had been so exceedingly lopsided, with the comparatively well-off becoming even better off while the masses of the poor became poorer, the enormous magnitude of the unfinished business of development that had now come into clearer focus created deep moral indignation and political anxieties.

The New Concepts and Priorities

Recognition of these ugly realities spurred a critical reexamination of conventional development concepts, theories, and practices, and prompted a great debate over how they should be revised. One of the most important and far-reaching results was the rise and wide acceptance of a much broader, people-oriented notion of the nature and objectives of development, along with a broader view of education and its diverse roles in developing both individuals and the society.

The basic objective of development, as perceived anew, was to improve people's quality of life—not just of some people but of *all* the people, with special emphasis on the poorest and most disadvantaged who had thus far been bypassed by the development process. Economic growth based on increased productivity was still viewed as being of fundamental importance. But the broader end now in view was not simply a rise in the GNP. It was growth with equity, which militated against human exploitation and ensured a fair distribution of the fruits of development. Greater emphasis on more equitable distribution, the economists now argued, was not only a moral imperative but an imperative for healthy economic growth and future political stability. The new concept also rejected the old theoretical notion that economic and social development were distinct and separate processes and that the first must precede the second. Instead, the new thinking recognized that the two were inseparable and must go forward hand-in-hand. Half-sick farmers could hardly be expected to have the stamina to boost their productivity, just as half-starved children were in no condition to learn the intricacies of reading, writing, and arithmetic.

The new strategies and priorities that grew out of this broadened concept called for a greatly increased emphasis on rural development, broadly perceived by some as the thoroughgoing social, economic, and political transformation of backward rural societies. The enlarged aim now was to increase rural productivity, employment, and income, and to "meet the basic needs" of all rural people—including education, food, family planning, shelter, clothing, and, especially, rewarding jobs. Special emphasis was given to improving the status of the two most vulnerable groups—women and young children. These new strategies, as articulated in the early 1970s by numerous bilateral and multinational agencies and increasingly by leaders of the developing countries, also called for a *more integrated and community-based* approach to rural development, in sharp contrast with the prevailing top-down and fragmented sector-by-sector approach.

It was recognized that all this would require encouragement, guidance, and practical assistance from national governments and external agencies. Even more important, it would require a major and sustained effort by rural communities to make their own plans and to mobilize local resources and energies to carry out those plans. For, in the last analysis, the rural people themselves must be the ultimate change agents.

By the end of the 1970s the rhetoric of this new consensus on rural development and other aspects of this humanized concept of development had become the common coin the world over. Many promising starts had been made on innovative programs to give expression to the ideas central to the new consensus. Yet the greater part of the immense task of converting rhetoric into concrete deeds entered the 1980s in a very unfinished state.

CHANGES IN EDUCATIONAL THOUGHT

Against this background of the radical changes in development thinking in the 1970s, we can now turn directly to the closely related and equally radical changes in educational thought.

Central to these changes was a sweeping redefinition of education itself. Up to the 1970s, education had been popularly equated with "schooling"—with the familiar formal educational system, ranging from the first grade of primary school to the highest reaches of the university. By this definition, a person's education was measured by years of classroom exposure and by the type and level of educational credentials earned. It had become increasingly evident by the early 1970s, however, that this view of education was not only much too narrow and artificial to fit the realities of life, but that it was standing in the way of much needed attention to other modes of learning and also doing a disservice to formal education itself. Taken literally, this institution-bound, age-bound concept of education implied three things that simply did not square with everyday experience: (1) that schools, and *only* schools, could meet all of the essential learning needs of individuals; (2) that this could be accomplished, once and for all, during an individual's school-age years; and (3) that anyone who lacked proper schooling was ipso facto uneducated (that is, ignorant).

The much wider view that emerged in the early 1970s, and that soon gained wide acceptance, equated education broadly with *learning,* regardless of where, how, or at what age the learning occurred. It also viewed education as a *lifelong* process, spanning all of the years from earliest infancy to life's end.

This enlarged concept of education in no way lessened the importance of formal education systems; it simply reflected a belated recognition that formal schools and higher institutions, though well-suited to meeting certain types of important learning needs, particularly those of school-age children and youth, could not possibly be expected to meet the full spectrum of important lifetime learning needs of all age groups in the population. The inherent limitations of formal education, and the importance of viewing education as a lifetime process, were emphasized by the landmark 1972 report of UNESCO's International Commission on the Development of Education (Faure Commission), *Learning to Be.*[2] The report stated point blank that "the schools' importance in relation to other means of education . . . is not increasing, but diminishing."

In saying this, the commission clearly had no intention of belittling the importance of formal education. On the contrary, its report included many suggestions for strengthening formal education, some of them radical. Its basic point was that in a fast-changing world characterized by rapidly growing and changing learning needs, and also by unacceptable gross inequalities, it was essential to give attention also to strengthening other modes of education. These other modes of learning (to be discussed later) soon came to be called nonformal and informal education. The upsurge of interest in these other modes opened new horizons for educational research and action and for a much broader and more direct role for education in national development.

Overhauling and Updating Formal Education

The widely read and respected Faure Commission report, echoing a central theme of the earlier World Educational Crisis report, emphasized that existing formal education systems everywhere were growing increasingly obsolete and maladjusted in relation to their rapidly changing societies. Hence it argued strongly that all these systems required major changes and innovations—not simply on a one-shot basis but as a continuing process. The report particularly stressed the grave problems faced by developing countries because of their ill-fitting imported educational models.

The time was ripe in the early 1970s for this critical theme to get a sympathetic hearing and response. Only a few years earlier the term innovation had been viewed with deep suspicion by educators in many countries, for it implied criticism of the established educational order and of the way schools were being run. Like evaluation, it was a threatening term. During the 1970s, however, it became generally accepted throughout the world educational community that many conventional arrangements and practices were indeed obsolete and inefficient and required substantial change. In this altered atmosphere, the term innovation suddenly acquired high status—so much so that representatives at many international gatherings vied to report proudly on their country's latest innovations. During the decade an unprecedented number and variety of innovations were introduced in all levels and types of education, in both developing and developed countries.

It must be said in retrospect, however, that most of these innovations were limited in their scope and impact. Most involved changes in a certain piece of curriculum, or the introduction on a limited scale of some new teaching method or aid—new at any rate in that particular educational milieu. Few involved fundamental changes in the framework of the system, its logistics, and its conventional modes of operation. Still, important lessons about managing changes in tradition-bound education systems had emerged by the end of the 1970s, and a new spirit and momentum of educational change had taken hold. There was reason to hope that this momentum would gather strength in the coming decade, resulting in much more far-reaching and fundamental changes and innovations.

The Rise of Nonformal Education

The new interest in nonformal education that arose in the 1970s was prompted especially by the newly proclaimed strategies calling for a stronger, more integrated, and more community-based approach to rural development and to meeting the basic needs of the poor. It was evident that if a real dent was to be made in these basic needs, millions of people of all ages and walks of life would have to learn many new things. Those engaged in delivering various technical advisory services and material assistance to individual communities, ranging from top managers and specialists at the national level down to local extension workers, would all require special and continuing training, and the masses of local recipients of such services would have to learn how to make the best use of them and how to take command of their futures. The formal education system could help in these matters, but even if it were more fully developed and widely accessible, it could not be expected to serve more than a fraction of this great melange of learning needs and learners. Clearly, a wide variety of nonformal education activities would also be required, especially to serve out-of-school youth and adults.

But here a series of insistent questions begged for answers: What is nonformal education? What does it look like? How does it work? Whom should it serve? How is it organized, managed, and financed? What is its relation to formal education and to the ministry of education? These were among the questions being asked by educators and by development authorities as this awkward and unfamiliar new term made its way into the international lexicon of education in the early 1970s.

Not surprisingly, the term nonformal education (which translated into various languages with different overtones) soon became shrouded in confusion and misunderstanding as different people and organizations, viewing it from their own special vantage points, interpreted it differently. Many occupants of ministries of education in developing countries equated nonformal education with adult education, which in turn they equated with adult literacy classes. Others, not yet fully aware of the vast variety of learners, learning objectives, and types of specialized knowledge and skills encompassed by nonformal education, immediately assumed that, since it wore an education label, it should be brought promptly within the jurisdiction of the ministry of education. This view was fueled by the recently declared willingness of leading development assistance agencies such as the World Bank, the United Nations Children's Fund (UNICEF), and the U.S. Agency for International Development (USAID) to support nonformal education. Still other guardians of the schools, however, feared the growing popularity of nonformal education, seeing it as a competing alternative system that would siphon much-needed resources away from the formal system.

Ironically, some of the strongest critics of formal education, including the "de-schoolers" inspired by Ivan Illich, saw nonformal education in the same light but welcomed it as a means of breaking the monopoly of the formal system.[3] Ironically, also, the new left critics, who had roundly condemned Western-style formal education as a conspiracy of capitalists to retain their power by training docile and obedient workers who could be exploited, now condemned nonformal education as a hoax designed to delude the poor into thinking they were getting "the real thing."

Although much of this confusion has since dissipated, enough lingers on to warrant a brief pause to clarify what nonformal education is and what it is not.[4]

Nonformal education, contrary impressions notwithstanding, does not constitute a distinct and separate educational system, parallel to the formal education system. Nonformal education is simply a handy generic label covering:

> any organized, systematic, educational activity, carried on outside the framework of the formal system, to provide selected types of learning to particular subgroups in the population, adults as well as children. Thus defined nonformal education includes, for example, agricultural extension and farmer training programs, adult literacy programs, occupational skill training given outside the formal system, youth clubs with substantial educational purposes, and various community programs of instruction in health, nutrition, family planning, cooperatives, and the like.[5]

Unlike nonformal education, formal education is a "true" system in the sense that all of its parts, at least in principle, are interconnected and mutually supporting. Various nonformal educational activities, on the other hand, are generally independent of each other, though some are integral parts of particular development systems, such as agricultural, health, industrial, or integrated community development systems. In some instances (though only a minority), they are closely related to formal education, as in the case of adult literacy programs or "second chance" school-type programs for out-of-school youth (an interesting example of a hybrid of formal and nonformal education).

To clarify the terminology, the third basic mode of education—namely, informal education—sounds like nonformal education but is actually quite different. Informal education refers to

> The life-long process by which every person acquires and accumulates knowledge, skills, attitudes and insights from daily experiences and exposure to the environment—at home, at work, at play; from the example and attitudes of family and friends; from travel, reading newspapers and books; or by listening to the radio or viewing films or television. Generally, informal education is unorganized, unsystematic and even unintentional at times, yet it accounts for the great bulk of any person's total lifetime learning—including that of even a highly"schooled" person.[6]

What an individual learns from informal education, however, is limited to whatever his or her personal environment happens to offer.

Formal and nonformal education are similar in some respects. Both have been organized by various societies "to augment and improve upon the informal learning process—in other words, to promote and facilitate certain valued types of learning that individuals cannot as readily or quickly acquire through exposure to the environment."[7] On the other hand, formal and nonformal education generally differ significantly in their sponsorship and institutional arrangements, in their educational objectives and content, and in the groups they serve. Also, formal education generally involves full-time, sequential study extending over a period of years, within the framework of a relatively fixed curriculum. By contrast, nonformal programs tend to be part time and of shorter duration, to focus on more limited, specific, practical types of knowledge and skills of fairly immediate utility to particular learners, and to have the inherent flexibility to respond quickly to new learning needs as they arise.

Formal education, being in principle a coherent, integrated system, lends itself to centralized planning, management, and financing.* Nonformal education is quite the opposite in this respect. It has many different sponsors and managers and sources of support, including almost all

---

*Many observers currently believe, however, that the centralization has gone too far in many countries and that a larger share of these planning, management, and financing responsibilities should be devolved to lower administrative echelons, closer to the scene of action.

government ministries and departments, and a wide assortment of non-governmental agencies. It is not unusual even to find individual communities, and groups within them, running their own nonformal educational activities. Thus, any dream of tying all these disparate educational activities, *plus* formal education, into some neat and tidy organized package—with the aim of keeping everything well coordinated, well planned, and under control—can never be more than a dream.

Before concluding this discussion, two other misconceptions about nonformal education should also be set right. The first is the notion that nonformal education is meant solely for the poor and suitable only for developing countries. The truth is that the most highly industrialized nations have a bewildering variety of nonformal educational programs and activities, without which their social, economic, and technological progress would come to a grinding halt. Nonformal education (though rarely called by that name) is widely used, for example, to familiarize progressive farmers, factory workers, bank clerks, and many others, including consumers, with new technologies and new products (such as computers). It is a major means by which many well-educated people continue their education in all sorts of directions. Not least important, nonformal education in these advanced countries enables highly trained specialists, such as physicians, engineers, and scientists, and top government and business managers, to keep abreast of the rapidly advancing frontiers of knowledge in their respective fields.

The other misconception is that nonformal education is less costly than formal education, that it is inherently more efficient and can be purchased on the cheap.[8] First, although it is undoubtedly true that many nonformal educational activities have a lower cost per learner than formal education, it is meaningless to compare the costs of formal and nonformal education except in those rare cases in which both are pursuing identical specific learning objectives and serving comparable groups of learners and where the learning achievements can also be compared. Second, the costs of different nonformal educational programs and activities vary enormously. Some have impressively low costs for the learning results achieved. At the other extreme, one can find instances of absurdly high costs, accompanied by disappointing results. Nonformal education has no inherent magical power to ensure low cost or efficient learning. Like formal education, it can be highly efficient in some situations and shockingly inefficient in others.

One unique economic advantage that many nonformal education programs do have—one that should calm the fears of educators that it will divert large sums from formal education—is the capacity to draw support from a wide variety of sources not ordinarily available to formal education. They may draw funds, for example, from numerous ministries (apart from the education ministry), use borrowed facilities and voluntary personnel, and receive payments and contributions in kind from the learners themselves.

The Shift in Educational Priorities in the 1970s

The major changes in development strategies in the early 1970s discussed earlier were accompanied by corresponding shifts in educational strategies and priorities on the part of most external assistance agencies and many developing countries. The basic thrust of these changes was toward alleviating poverty and gross socioeconomic inequalities, at the same time facilitating increased productivity and employment. This does not mean, of course, a monolithic set of priorities for all countries imposed by external assistance agencies. On the contrary, as a World Bank educational policy statement emphasized at the time (reflecting the views of other external assistance agencies as well):

> In attempting to discuss educational policies, account should be taken of the variety of conditions observed in different developing societies, including countries with yearly per capita incomes ranging from $70 to $1,500, with populations ranging from less than one million to 500 million, and with literacy rates varying from 5% to over 90%. These countries also differ in social stratification, cultural and political traditions, and physical resources.[9]

The revised policies placed a heavy new emphasis on "basic education," including primary schooling for children and appropriate nonformal education for out-of-school youth and adults, and a reduced priority for secondary and higher education. Heavy new emphasis was also given to improving the quality of education and the relevance of the content; to needed reforms and innovations in the formal system, including the design and testing of more affordable alternative approaches; and to strengthening educational management, internal efficiency, and external productivity. No one familiar with the prevailing conditions of education and development in the developing world in the early 1970s could seriously challenge the logic and rightness of these new policy directions.

A huge problem remained, however: how to translate these new policies into action, a topic examined in later chapters. Before we draw this introductory chapter to a close, however, we must explain to the reader the analytical perspective and framework of the study that underlies this report, set forth a few caveats about the limitations of its findings, and outline the structure of the book.

THE ANALYTICAL APPROACH

The magnitude and complexity of undertaking a worldwide appraisal of the educational scene makes it essential at the outset to adopt an appropriate analytical framework and perspective to guide the selection of evidence and the manner in which it is examined. In the 1968 report on the world educational crisis, this need was met by adopting a systems-analysis perspective and framework. Such a framework was both appropriate and timely, first, because that report focused on *formal* education systems (which, as noted earlier, are true systems), and second, because the application of a broad systems-analysis method to education was novel at the time and merited explicit demonstration.

In planning the analytical approach to the present study, however, we ruled out the old systems-analysis framework as a possibility for two reasons. First, the unique advantages of viewing any educational situation through the wide-angle lens of a systems analysis are now well established. It is done intuitively every day by many educational analysts, planners, and administrators. Second, and more decisively, the present study intends to take a considerably broader view of the world's educational scene than the earlier one—a view that will encompass not only formal education but also informal and nonformal education. These highly diversified educational activities, by their very nature, cannot be compressed into the mold of a single systems-analysis framework.

To accommodate this much wider range of educational activities and to make our analysis conform to the real world of education, we have adopted as our basic intellectual framework the notion of a nationwide "learning network." This broad and flexible concept has several important advantages not only for a worldwide study such as this one but also for assessing the overall educational situation and prospects in individual countries.

The first advantage is that this concept dovetails with the view of education as a lifelong process. The basic objective and function of such a learning network, as we perceive it here, is to accommodate, as fully as feasible at any particular time, the highly diverse and constantly growing and changing learning needs and interests of all members of the population, from their earliest infancy to their old age. Such a network can also respond to the growing and changing learning needs and human resource requirements of a whole society.

A second advantage is that this network concept accords with the world of education as it really is. Every country, whether rich or poor, already possesses many elements of such a network. They include a wide range and variety of educational forms and modes—informal, formal, and nonformal. None of these alone can meet all the important lifetime learning needs of an individual, much less of a whole society. All are needed, and no one of them can properly claim superiority of rank, value, or effectiveness over all the others; each has its peculiar strengths and limitations. They are complementary and supplementary and mutually reinforcing.

Viewed in this light, the overarching educational challenge of any nation is first to size up the learning network it already possesses, assessing both its strengths and shortcomings; and then to proceed, step by step, to broaden and strengthen the network to fit the nation's present and evolving needs and circumstances more fully and effectively. To make it function as a real network, of course, all the different members must become familiar with the idea and feel and act like members of a cooperative team with a common purpose. This in itself is a major educational task for the leaders of the country, for it cannot be accomplished simply by executive fiat, even in a strongly authoritarian country, much less in a free and open society.

As a third advantage, this learning network concept provides all those concerned with education in any country with a broader and more integrated view of the total national educational effort and helps them ask the right questions about how better to plan, organize, and manage this effort. It can help steer them away from the mischievous illusion that there can be a big technocratic blueprint providing for everything to be planned, coordinated, and controlled by some top-level bureaucracy—an inoperable approach that, if seriously tried, could only frustrate all members of the network and inhibit their creativity, efficiency, and effectiveness.

Finally, and not least important, this concept invites all educational planners, researchers, and analysts to embark on fresh lines of investigation and thinking that could yield important new insights on ways for policymakers and program managers to improve the network.

One thing that this network concept cannot do is to eliminate the need for certain caveats in a report of this sort. Several important ones that apply to all the chapters that follow must be stated.

Caveats

The first caveat is that any survey that takes the whole world of education as the object of its attention must inevitably frame many of its findings in broad terms that, though basically valid as generalizations, will not conform to the detailed realities of every individual country. Nor can such a broad-gauged international diagnosis be an adequate substitute for the more detailed diagnosis each country must make of its own educational situation and prospects. It can, however, help individual countries in making their own diagnoses by broadening their perspective to take account of important international trends, forces, changes, and prospects likely to impinge on and be mirrored in their particular educational needs and problems.

The second caveat concerns the adequacy and reliability of the statistical material and other evidence used in this report. Although the available supply of international data on various aspects of education has improved considerably since the writing of the 1968 book about the world educational crisis, the present supply still has major gaps and other serious shortcomings and must be interpreted with caution, as will be noted at appropriate points in the text. It should also be emphasized that some of the most important aspects of the educational changes that have, or have not, taken place in recent years are qualitative and do not lend themselves to statistical measurement. This report does not shy away from drawing conclusions about these qualitative changes, based on the best evidence available. Personal judgment, however, obviously comes into play here much more than with the quantifiable dimensions.

The third caveat grows out of the second and relates especially to nonformal education, on which there is literally no comprehensive and systematic international evidence available. This is only partly because no international agency has taken responsibility for collecting such evidence across a broad range of activities. A more fundamental reason has been stressed in other connections—namely, that because nonformal education programs are so diverse, not only between countries but within each one, they defy systematic measurement and comparison by any standard yardstick. Nor is it likely to be feasible to collect systematic data on nonformal education programs comparable to what is regularly collected on formal education. The widely varying characteristics of these programs—in terms, for example, of their objectives and intended audience, their relationship to various development programs, the frequency and duration of their meetings, the methods and materials used, and the great differences in their cultural and socioeconomic environment—militates against collecting reliable and comparable statistics on such indicators as enrollments, expenditures, dropouts, and completers, not to mention actual learning achievements.

Fortunately, however, because of the greatly increased interest in nonformal education since the early 1970s, there is by now a substantial accumulation of significant information about such activities from a wide variety of countries, including numerous case studies by ICED and other research groups and reports by innumerable public and private organizations. This scattered material plus direct field observations by the author and his colleagues in a number of countries are the principal basis for this report's conclusions about nonformal education.

Structure

In beginning our analysis from the perspective of the learning network concept, it soon became evident that several critical educational issues, already serious and likely to become more so, would be of paramount concern in the future to most if not all countries and thus to most readers of this report. We therefore decided to structure the chapters of the report around several of these issues. All of them in reality are woven together like a tapestry, but for analytical and editorial convenience we have dealt with them here in separate chapters. As will be seen, however, the chapters frequently echo each other, bringing out important relationships between these various issues. In this sense, it could be said that we have employed systems-analysis thinking.

The next three chapters explore in succession the dynamic changes taking place on both sides of the world's educational equation, the demand side (Chapter 2), where a virtual explosion of learning needs is in process, and the supply side, where the key problem is to achieve adequate quantitative growth (Chapter 3) and appropriate qualitative changes (Chapter 4) to balance the evolving learning needs on the demand side.

Chapter 5 follows the demand-supply discussion with an examination of the finance and cost squeeze on education that has grown much tighter since the earlier crisis report and promises to grow even more acute. Chapter 6 pursues another important connection, or maladjustment, between education and the economy, namely, the relationship between education and the world of work.

The next two chapters reach well beyond the economic aspects of education into the politically charged issue of educational disparities and inequalities (Chapter 7), and the complex relationships between education and culture, science, and language (Chapter 8). Chapter 9, an offshoot of Chapter 8, examines the reasons the highly promoted "Literacy Doctrine" has run afoul of the realities and offers suggestions for a more effective approach to advancing literacy.

Chapters 10 and 11 come full circle back to the fundamental question of international cooperation and its potentialities for helping all countries to cope more effectively with the critical educational needs and problems they all share. These final chapters also seek to draw together, in an international perspective, the main strands of the previous chapters.

Three additional cross-cutting critical issues are so entwined in all the others that it would have been too artificial to treat them in isolation. Foremost among these is the vital matter of teachers—the preeminent leaders, catalysts, and orchestrators of almost all organized learning processes. The second is the important and much discussed matter of educational technologies, which by nature permeate every sort of educational activity. The third is the ever-present, interconnected set of issues relating to educational planning, management, governance, and—not to duck the issue—politics. All of these issues will crop up repeatedly in the various chapters.

Point of View

One final point to complete this introduction concerns the author's point of view on the matters under discussion and how he perceives the purpose of this book. Along with most other people, the author attaches profound importance to education as an indispensible element for achieving a fuller development of the potential of individuals and whole societies and for attaining a progressively more creative, secure, peaceful, and rewarding existence for all people and nations. To say this, however, is not to assert that education is a cure-all for the world's ills. It clearly is not; it is but one of the essential requisites for humankind's continued advancement toward a more peaceful and equitable world. Nor does it suggest that all is right with the world of education, which is also clearly not the case. Thus, to be faithful to the aim of this book, the author has endeavored, in the spirit of constructive criticism, to point out some things that are not right with education (along with others that are), to explore the causes of these maladies, and where possible to suggest ways to set them right.

However, the reader is neither asked nor expected to accept the author's views blindly but, on the contrary, is urged to make his or her own interpretations and judgments on the basis of the evidence presented here and in the light of his or her own values and view of the world. In other words, the aim of this book is not to be a bible with all the answers, but to provoke and contribute to a broad discussion of these critical and complex educational issues.

NOTES

1. Robert S. McNamara, *Address to Board of Governors,* World Bank Group, Nairobi, Kenya, Sept. 24, 1973 (Washington, D.C.: The World Bank, 1973), p. 7.

2. Report of the International Commission for the Development of Education, *Learning to Be: The World of Education Today and Tommorrow* (Paris: UNESCO, 1972). The chairman of the Commission was Edgar Faure, a former prime minister of France.

3. Ivan Illich, *Deschooling Society* (New York: Harper & Row, 1970).

4. Based largely on ICED's extensive field research on the subject in the early 1970s. P. H. Coombs, R. C. Prosser, and M. Ahmed, *New Paths to Learning: For Rural Children and Youth* (Essex, Conn.: ICED, 1973), a report to UNICEF; and Philip H. Coombs and Manzoor Ahmed, *Attacking Rural Poverty: How Nonformal Education Can Help* (Baltimore: Johns Hopkins University Press, 1974), a report to the World Bank.

5. Coombs and Ahmed, *Attacking Rural Poverty,* p. 8.

6. Ibid., p. 8.

7. Coombs, Prosser, and Ahmed, *New Paths to Learning,* p. 12.

8. For a useful discussion of the economics of nonformal education see Manzoor Ahmed, *The Economics of Nonformal Education: Resources, Costs and Benefits* (New York: Praeger, 1975).

9. World Bank, *Education Sector Working Paper* (Washington, D.C.: The World Bank, December 1974), p. 16.

CHAPTER 2

THE RAPID GROWTH OF
LEARNING NEEDS

WINSTON CHURCHILL's oft-repeated remark, "The further back you look, the further forward you can see," has direct relevance to our aim in this chapter, which is twofold. First, we intend to assess, in the light of past trends, the current and prospective extent of world educational needs. Second, we will lay the basis for an inquiry into the question of whether and how societies can actually meet their basic needs for education. In keeping with what was said previously, we will equate education with *learning*—a wider concept than formal schooling alone, and one that in turn has an obvious corollary: all human beings, starting at birth, have diverse learning needs whose form, substance, and utility evolve over the course of a lifetime.* By extension, whole societies also have evolving learning needs, many of which extend well beyond the lifetime of any one individual.

SUPPLY AND DEMAND: THE 1968 APPRAISAL

The 1968 report on the world educational crisis drew attention to a gap, dating from the end of World War II, between expanding learning needs and the capacity of various societies to meet them. These learning needs

---

*A useful analytical distinction was made in the Club of Rome's Report, *No Limits to Learning* (New-York: Pergamon Press, 1979), by James W. Botkin, M. Elmandjra, and M. Malitza, between two broad classes of human learning needs. Of the two, the one called "maintenance learning" enables individuals to function effectively in an existing social system or established way of life. The other, called "innovative learning" enables individuals to anticipate and make timely adaptations to important changes in the world around them. A third, "learning by shock," is what happens when full reliance is placed on maintenance education unaccompanied by innovative learning.

translate into educational demands, but the two terms are not synony-
mous. Often the needs exceed the visible social demand—as, for example, when the children of poverty-stricken rural parents fail to attend
school, even if one is available. Conversely, the social demand for education at times exceeds felt learning needs, as when young people vie for
entry into the university not primarily to satisfy their yearning to learn
but to obtain a diploma that has special prestige and market value. One
of the tasks of educational planners and policymakers is to pay attention
to needy and disadvantaged people whose essential learning needs are not
reflected in the day-to-day social demand for education.

The 1968 report advanced the thesis that the gap, visible in both the
developed and developing countries, though at different levels of their
respective educational structures, was bound to widen further. Of the
three reasons cited on the demand side of the equation, the first was the
"mounting educational aspirations of parents and their children." The
second was the "new stress of public policy everywhere on educational
development as a pre-condition for overall national development, and
the parallel stress on the democratic imperative of increasing 'educational
participation rates'"—which means sending a higher proportion of each
age group to school and for more years. The third reason was "the population explosion which acts as a quantitative multiplier of the social
demand." Here the report paused to make the following observation:

> Educational demand, feeding on itself, creates its own dynamic. A population
> that suddenly starts getting more education soon wants still more. An African
> child of illiterate parents who learns to read and do sums in primary school
> wants to go on to secondary school; and from there, he wants to go on to the
> university if he can make it. But even if he gets no further than primary
> school, he will insist that *his* children do better. Thus the social demand for
> education is inexorably compounded, regardless of what may be happening
> to the economy and to the resources available to education.

Were there any reasons to believe that the boom in educational
demand would subside in the years ahead so that the existing quantitative
mismatch between the social demand for education and the means for
meeting it would be corrected? The report's answer was "twice no." First,
"the signs indicate that the forces of the recent past which account for the
increased social demand for education will not only continue but may
even accelerate." Second, "the signs say that the intensity of human pressures embraced by these forces will undergo a kind of 'quantum jump' in
the case of developing countries—this, because of the extraordinarily
high rate of increase in their youth population." In short, virtually every-

where more and more students would be knocking on education's door each year. In the industrialized countries the pressures would be greatest beyond the secondary level; in the developing countries they would be great at all levels.

These observations from the report focused mainly on quantitative aspects of the educational gap. But elsewhere it placed even heavier emphasis on the qualitative aspects, asserting that the growing disparities and maladjustments between what students are being taught in the schools and colleges and their actual priority learning needs lay at the very heart of the crisis.

In assessing the causes of these serious and growing qualitative maladjustments, the report singled out two of the primary culprits. One was the rigidity of educational systems that allowed their curriculum and content to become progressively obsolete while the world of knowledge and action all around them continued to change at an ever more rapid clip. The other culprit was the widespread practice of transplanting from industrialized to developing countries education models that often grotesquely misfit the countries' actual needs, circumstances, and resources.

What has happened to these quantitative and qualitative gaps—as seen in the late 1960s—between the demand and supply side of the educational equation? Have they narrowed or widened? Have the learning needs and social demands on the one side of the equation continued to proliferate, and how well have educational provisions on the supply side kept pace with them? Do existing educational provisions, formal and nonformal, meet the full range of human learning needs? If the educational gaps actually widened as the 1970s wore on, are they likely to widen even further during the 1980s and beyond?

In connection with these questions, we are reminded of Aristotle's caution that no subject should have any more precision imposed on it than the subject itself warrants. Learning needs, being so diverse and changeable by nature, cannot be measured with mathematical precision as if distinctive groups of people in distinctive contexts were like piles of lumber cut to a specified size in a lumberyard. Still, noting what cannot be done is not saying that it is impossible to make informed judgments on the subject. The basis for such judgments can be established by focusing on those forces that define the learning needs of individuals and societies, create new ones, or outstrip the existing educational arrangements of a given society.

Some of the most important of these powerful forces are population growth and migration, urbanization, advances in knowledge and technologies, social and economic changes, and, not least, national development strategies and growing international interdependence. These forces criss-cross, overlap, and reinforce each other. Together they have generated, and will continue to generate, an explosive worldwide growth of learning needs affecting people in all places and of all ages, sexes, and stations in life. Though the forces are tightly fused and inseparable, for analytical convenience they are examined more or less separately here, together with their educational implications.

POPULATION GROWTH

The most obvious of these forces is the growth in the sheer number of learners in the world, or in other words, the growth of the world's population, each member of which is viewed here as a lifetime "learner."

A key difference between the demographic position of industrially advanced countries, on the one side, and that of developing countries on the other is that in most industrially advanced countries, contrary to earlier general expectations, birth rates declined sharply after the mid-1960s—in many instances down to the so-called replacement level or below by the mid-1970s. Their death rates have also dropped to levels about as low as they can go without breakthroughs in conquering chronic diseases that strike mostly in old age—heart attack, cancer, and stroke. Their overall populations are still growing, but because of these low birth rates, future schooling requirements of new cohorts of children can be met without staggering increases in required resources. This does not mean, however, that learning needs and educational demands in industrially advanced countries will cease to grow. On the contrary, converging forces, apart from population growth, are constantly creating new learning needs for limitless millions of people in industrially advanced as well as developing countries.

The developing countries, for their part, present a strikingly different picture of recent and prospective trends in the number of learners. Taking the Third World as a whole, birth rates, with the exception of those observed in Africa, are also now declining. In fact, in certain places the rate of decline has exceeded what demographers concerned with population control thought was possible in the early 1970s. Yet because of the extraordinarily high levels from which the decline began, the developing world will be the great nursery for most of the massive global population growth in the foreseeable future. The facts here translate into equally massive numbers of learners and learning needs in the very areas of the world least capable of supporting their costs—areas most urgently in need of food, dwellings, schools, health care, employment opportunities, resources for development, and an infrastructure for development.

Public concern over the great population explosion in recent decades has been marked by an anxious debate about whether a world inhabited by 6 billion people in the year 2000 will be more frightening than one now inhabited by 4 billion, or whether any further increases in population—up to possibly 11 billion in the next century—will catastrophically overshoot the carrying capacity of the earth's resources. These are urgent issues with a clear claim to detailed attention. Yet public concern with this overall global expansion can obscure other dynamic factors in the population picture that may be as important as, if not more important than, the gross total.

Some of these other factors are the differential rates at which population is growing in different places and the way people are being redistributed geographically within and between regions, countries, and urban/rural districts. Another factor is the changes taking place in the age structure of national populations—in the relative size of the preschool and school-age cohort, the child-bearing cohort, the active labor force, and the elderly. Also included are factors bearing on how population increases are positioned at points of connection or disconnection with employment opportunities, technology, arable land, water, other natural resources, transportation networks, and other such matters related to the productive process.

Before examining their educational implications we should view these churning demographic changes from longer-range perspective, both backward and forward.

The Proliferating Human Species

No country has as yet declared war on another because of its birth rate. Yet many governments, societies, and individuals throughout the world are now increasingly threatened by both the pace and the size of the dynamic demographic changes sweeping through and over them. These recent and prospective changes seem even more awesome when viewed from the perspective of humanity's long development as a species. Recently, anthropologists and demographers have made the following observations:

> During the hundreds of thousands of years of the Old Stone Age when *homo sapiens* was a hunter and food-gatherer, the world population probably never exceeded 10 million. Somewhere about 8,000–6,000 B.C., humans learned how to grow food and create settlements and eventually cities. The shift from food gathering to food growing was a momentous change; far larger numbers could be supported.[1]

From then on the pace of demographic growth accelerated. By the time of Jesus of Nazareth, the world population had grown to about 300 million, and by 1650 A.D. it had reached an estimated 500 million. It was not until about 1800 A.D., however—some 2 million to 5 million years after the appearance of the first humanlike creatures—that the world's population reached the 1 billion mark. Adding the second billion took only 130 years, to 1930. The third billion was reached after only 30 years, in 1960, and the fourth after 15 years, in 1975. The world's rate of population growth peaked in the mid-1960s at about 2 percent annually—a rate at which numbers double in 35 years. That growth rate has now fallen slightly and is expected to continue to decline gradually. Given the built-in momentum, however, world population is projected to top 6 billion by the year 2000, when the numbers being added each year could be well over 90 million. Demographers now speculate that the level at which humankind's total numbers will ultimately peak, perhaps late in the twenty-first century, could be as high as 11 billion, depending on a range of variables from the depletion of resources and degradation of the environment to natural disasters or extermination in man-made holocausts.[2]

Uneven Geographic and Age Distribution

The great bulk of this rapid growth, as noted earlier, is taking place in the less developed regions. Their combined share of the total world population rose from 66 percent in 1950 to 75 percent in 1975, and according to the medium variant of the most recently revised United Nations population projections, will reach about 80 percent by 2000 (see Figure 2.1 and Appendix Table 2.1).* Leon Tabah, the chief United Nations demographer, was being not romantic but dryly factual when he remarked that "today's developing world will be the grand reservoir of mankind tomorrow."[3]

Because the populations of the developing countries are younger than those of the developed regions, their share of the world's total school-age population is even larger. In 1980, as can be seen in Figure 2.2, nearly 40 percent of the total population of the developing world was under 15 years of age, compared to only 23 percent in the more developed world. The data on *Trends in School Age Populations* shown in Appendix Table 2.2 reveal that in 2000, six out of every seven primary-school-age chil-

---

*Throughout this book the medium variant, lying between the low and high variants, of the United Nations population projections is used. UNESCO follows the same practice.

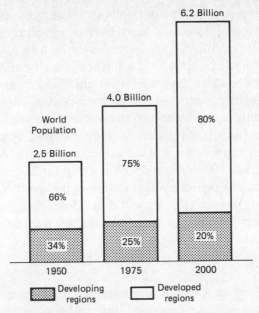

Figure 2.1. The expanding world of learners. [Source: United Nations, *Population Estimates and Projections, 1980 Assessment* (New York: Department of International Economic and Social Affairs, United Nations, 1981.)]

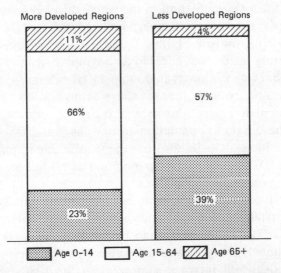

Figure 2.2. Distribution of the world's learners by age groups, 1980. [Source: United Nations, *Selected Demographic Indicators by Country, 1950–2000* (New York: United Nations, 1980), p. 18.]

dren in the world (age 6–11) will be in developing countries. Again, this means that the huge educational burdens resulting from this global demographic growth are falling largely on the countries least able to bear them. These age distribution figures have a further ironic twist. They show that the developing countries have a much higher "child dependency ratio" than the developed countries—that is, their population of children (age 0–14) is much higher in relation to the working-age population (age 15–64) that has to support them than in the developed countries. In 1980 this dependency ratio in the less developed regions was 69 to 100, compared to only 35 to 100 in more developed regions.[4]

Not all regions or countries in the developing world will grow at the same rate. Their respective cases will differ depending on the speed and duration of their mortality and fertility decline and on the size of the wedge between these two dimensions. But subject to all of these variables, the United Nations medium projections look like this:

- The population of Africa, now the fastest growing region and the only one, as noted earlier, whose birth rate had not yet begun to taper off by the late 1970s, will be double its 1975 size by the end of this century, having risen from 406 million people in 1975 to 828 million in 2000. And if present longer-range projections prove out, Africa will have grown to 2.7 billion by the year 2100—more than five times the 1975 population of Europe (excluding the U.S.S.R), and almost as large as the total population in the whole developing world in 1975.
- South Asia, already heavily overpopulated with its 1.26 billion people in 1975, will grow to 2.2 billion by 2000. Latin America, another rapidly growing region, was equal in demographic size to North America in 1950 but will be more than double the latter's size by the year 2000. As for China, with its present share of one quarter of the world's entire population, a combination of favorable conditions may enable it to achieve a stable population around the year 2025. But this statement, standing alone, hides what the word stable implies, that in the year 2025, China will have a population of 1.4 billion—a 64 percent increase over its 1975 population.[5]
- The developed nations, by contrast, are moving rapidly toward population stabilization by the end of this century. Their postwar baby boom subsided in the 1960s and by the 1970s their fertility rates, as already noted, plunged to or below the replacement level. The number of births will increase somewhat in the 1980s when the now mature postwar babies are at the height of their reproductive years. But because of the all-time low level of current birth rates, this secondary boom will be smaller than its predecessor and is likely to be

a relatively short-lived blip on the long-term demographic curve of the developed world.

Educational Implications of Population Trends

The foregoing population trends carry very different implications for future educational needs and demands in developed and developing countries.

In developed countries, the bumper crops of postwar babies have already passed through primary schools, leaving behind empty classrooms and teacher surpluses. They peaked in the secondary schools in the early 1980s and will crest through the colleges and universities by the mid-1980s. Soon thereafter, in the late 1980s, the secondary baby boom (the children of the previous boom) will be entering the primary schools in increased numbers and, later, the secondary schools and higher institutions. Although not of the tidal wave proportions of the earlier boom, this boom will nevertheless have an important impact on educational costs and expenditures and could cause some troublesome shortages of teachers and classrooms if it is not adequately planned for.

But as emphasized earlier, this is not the whole of the future story of educational needs for developed countries. Although their population slowdown will have eliminated the heavy postwar pressures on the schools to expand, these countries, because of dynamic changes, will continue to experience sizable increases in overall learning needs far into the future. New learning needs affecting the entire population of industrial countries will come to the forefront in direct consequence of the infusion of new technologies, the altered character of jobs and job classifications, increased geographic and employment mobility, increased employment of women and their improved status, changing life-styles within and outside the home, the shortening of the work week, and the commensurate increase in leisure time.

Again, the developing countries, with their relatively lower enrollment ratios at all levels and their continuing strong population pressures for educational expansion, present a markedly different outlook. To keep pace with their demographic growth and at the same time keep raising their enrollment ratios will require a continuing high annual rate of educational expansion. In addition to these quantitative increases, of course, the schools and colleges of these countries face the formidable task of improving the quality and fitness of their programs and steadily adapting them to the changing environment and realistic development needs of their students and their society.

Beyond all this, the developing countries must massively expand and adapt nonformal education to serve the population's vast and diversified learning needs that lie beyond the scope and capabilities of formal education. Like the developed countries, they will experience great increases in learning needs resulting from widespread changes in technology, economic structures and markets, and other dynamic changes to be examined later.

Some Startling Projections

No one can forecast precisely what various developing countries will actually be able to accomplish along these lines, but some recent UNESCO projections provide the basis for a rough idea of the magnitude of their task, at least for formal education. The purpose of these projections (they are not predictions) is to show what would happen, country by country and region by region, if the main lines of enrollment trends observed between 1960 and 1980 were to continue until the year 2000, taking into account future changes in the size of the school-age population.[6] The UNESCO projections are presented here in two forms. The first, displayed in Appendix Table 2.3, shows what would happen (under the preceding assumptions) to gross enrollment ratios (GERs) between 1980 and 2000, at each educational level in each developing region. The second, in Figure 2.3, shows the numerical enrollment increments (all levels combined) that would have to be achieved between 1980 and 2000 to meet these projected enrollment ratios.

In the case of the African region, for example, the GER would rise from 78 percent in 1980 to 93 percent in 2000 at the primary level; from 21 to 43 percent at the secondary level and from 3 to 6 percent at the postsecondary level. These GER, however, for reasons explained in the next chapter, must be treated with extreme caution because they tend to convey an exaggerated and misleading impression.

A more direct way of viewing the magnitude of the task is provided by the projected numerical enrollment increases (shown in Figure 2.3) that would be achieved between 1980 and 2000 under the foregoing assumptions. They are truly formidable in size, especially when compared to the observed increments achieved during the preceding 20-year period, from 1960 to 1980. The African region would have to increase total enrollments by 116 million between 1980 and 2000, compared to only 55 million added (with enormous effort and sacrifice) between 1960 and 1980. Latin America and South Asia would both have to add about the same number between 1980 and 2000 as was added between 1960 and 1980, but the addition of each succeding thousand or million becomes harder than the previous one. In striking contrast, northern America would have

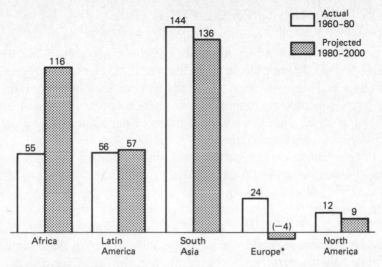

Figure 2.3. Actual and projected enrollment increments, 1960–80 versus 1980–2000. [Source: *Trends and Projections of Enrolments (as assessed in 1982)* (Paris: UNESCO, Division of Statistics on Education, March 1983).]

to add only another 9 million to the 12 million added between 1960 and 1980 and Europe would shrink its 1980 total by 4 million.

These towering figures underscore the enormous impact that high birth rates are having on educational requirements in developing countries. UNESCO statisticians have calculated that about 50 percent of all the primary level enrollment increases in these countries between 1960 and 1980 were offset by population growth, meaning that only half of their total educational development effort went into increasing the proportion of children attending school. Put differently, the education systems of developing countries have to run fast just to stand still in relation to their existing participation ratios and faster yet to gain new ground.

Undoubtedly, most developing countries, faced with continuing strong pressures of population growth and popular demand for education, and still relatively low enrollment ratios, would like very much to maintain a high rate of expansion and will try hard to do so. Unfortunately, however, that aspiration has a dark underside. It seems highly improbable that most of these countries will be able to repeat their impressive educational growth record of earlier years, except those countries with rich oil assets or other special economic advantages. The reasons for their general inability in the matter are discussed in Chapter 5, which examines the outlook for educational costs and finance.

MIGRATION AND URBANIZATION

The immediately preceding discussion focused mainly on the drastic increase in the number of learners in the world, their increasingly uneven geographic and age distribution, and the implications of these trends for education. A different demographic phenomenon affecting learning needs—the speeded-up worldwide process of population migration and urbanization—is discussed next.

In the past three decades, untold millions of families, far more than in any equivalent period of history, pulled up stakes and moved to strange new locations, most often within their own country but in many cases in another country. The great bulk of these migrants, especially in developing countries, moved from a rural to an urban area or from a small town to a big city, pushed by joblessness and poverty in the countryside and pulled by the perceived opportunities in the "urb" for a better life. Many of those who migrated across national borders, sometimes halfway across the world, were refugees—more than 10 million of them as of 1982—who had been uprooted from their original habitat by wars, droughts, or political repression.[7] Millions of others, driven by poverty and the quest for a better life, entered a more promising land illegally as undocumented workers.

All this moving about has had, and will continue to have, far-reaching educational implications. When a family uproots itself, or is uprooted by others, and moves to a new and unfamiliar location with a different socio-economic and cultural environment, all its members are immediately confronted by a host of new learning needs. Villagers in developing countries, for example, who come to the large already packed cities as squatters and settlers must learn how to survive in a setting unlike any they had ever known before. In their new cash environment, they can neither grow their own food nor barter such goods as they have in surplus for the goods they need. Instead, they must learn how to earn cash in order to get food, clothing, and shelter. But here, again, they face a novel problem. In their previous rural setting, oral instruction and informational material were often sufficient for their daily routine. In the urban setting, however, literacy is essential to the most elemental aspects of their daily life. They cannot readily move about without knowing how to read road signs and signs on public transportation systems. They cannot readily look for available jobs unless they know how to read want ads in newspapers. They cannot readily embrace the ways and means of better hygiene or better family planning unless they can read at least the simple printed instructions they receive at clinics. Nor can they hope even to gain access to public housing unless they know how to fill in the requisite governmental forms.

Those who migrate to a different country quickly find themselves with even more complex learning needs, often including learning a new language in order to communicate beyond the family circle. Even for well-educated and sophisticated urban people, such a plunge into a strange culture can be a traumatic experience.

Yesterday's and Tomorrow's Cities

All this moving about is also changing the face of the world's cities. By the year 2000, over half the world's population is expected to be living in towns and cities—up from one fifth in 1925 and two fifths in 1975. This process of urbanization is occurring far more rapidly in the developing countries than it ever did earlier in today's industrialized countries. It is occurring against a background of higher population growth, lower incomes, massive rural populations, and fewer opportunities for international migration. Vast numbers of people are involved. Specifically, between 1950 and 1975, the urban population of developing countries grew by some 500 million people. Between 1975 and 2000, the expected increase will be close to 1.3 billion.[8]

The problem is intensified by the concentration of urban dwellers in giant cities. Back in 1950, only one city in the developing world—greater Buenos Aires—had a population of more than 5 million, compared to five such cities in the industrialized countries. By the year 2000, according to World Bank projections, the developing world will have about 40 cities this size, and the developed world 12. Moreover, as of that time, the huge urban conglomerates within the developing world will be of a sprawling magnitude never encountered in the industrialized world. Current projections, for example, envision Mexico City with 31 million, Sao Paulo with 26 million, Shanghai and Peking with 22 million, Rio de Janeiro with 19 million, and Bombay and Calcutta both with 20 million.[9] For comparison, New York City's population in 1980 was 7 million; in 1970 the population of metropolitan Paris was 9 million and that of greater London was 11 million.

There are other points of contrast between the developed and developing countries. That the giant cities in the developing countries are growing far faster than those in the developed countries reflects the historical trends continuing to this day and the different roles played by the major cities in the two groups of countries. Unlike the spontaneous economic evolution in the industrialized countries, most urban concentrations in the developing world spring from institutional structures established under colonial administrations, at a time when the capitals served as a link between the bourgeoisie and the outside world, often directed toward foreign markets. Yet today, because of this heritage, many of the major cities of the developing world do not serve well as the vanguard of their national economies. Those people not integrated into the urban economy often dominate the urban landscape, giving a rural cast to increased areas of the cities.

The cities are growing not only in size but in the complexity of their socioeconomic composition. The urb in the developing world is not a single social, economic, or political piece. It subdivides into different geographic, economic, and ethnic sectors, each occupied by people with very different backgrounds, education levels, types of employment, and economic status. They occupy dwellings in different neighborhoods ranging from mansions to impoverished shanties. Typically, more than half the entire population lives in slums and squatter settlements, and between one third and one half has no access to safe water supply or sanitary waste disposal facilities. Those with an education and salaried position or regular wage-paying job in the modern sector make up a relatively small minority. The great majority ekes out a living in a vast variety of ways in the informal sector—running small shops, doing domestic work, running errands, operating pedicabs, and picking up any odd job that will bring in a little cash.

Most of urban growth in the developing world has been fueled by the migration of rural people, but increasingly, urban growth is being fueled by a different factor—natural increases within the cities, that is, an increase of local births over deaths. In the case of Latin America, for example, where half the population lived in cities and towns by 1975, the projected growth of urban dwellers to three quarters of the region's population by 2000 will mainly entail such natural increases. For sheer magnitude, however, the urban populations of Latin America are dwarfed by those of Southeast Asia. India alone, though still much more rural, had an urban population in 1975 greater than the combined urban population of Latin America's three most populous countries—Argentina, Brazil, and Mexico.

Migration Patterns in the Developed World

Since World War II, the cities and rural areas of the more developed world have also undergone extensive transformation, similar to that of the developing world in some respects but very different in other respects.

By and large, rural populations and the agricultural labor force contin-

ued to decline while urban populations increased.* This trend was especially marked in countries of Southern and Eastern Europe and in the
U.S.S.R., which still had large rural populations at the end of World War
II, but it was also apparent in the most industrialized countries. In the
Federal Republic of Germany in 1950, 5 million people were employed
in agriculture, and less than 2 million by 1975. In the Netherlands, agricultural workers dropped from 17 percent of the total labor force in 1950
to 6 percent by 1978. In the United Kingdom, concomitant with rapid
agricultural mechanization and farm consolidation following World War
II, the agricultural labor force tumbled to only 3.1 percent of all workers
by 1968, and still further to 2.7 percent in 1975. Nearly one third of the
Italian labor force was engaged in agriculture in 1961, whereas ten years
later this proportion had shrunk to one fifth.[10]

Many developed countries, among them some of the most highly
industrialized ones, also experienced major waves of internal migration
involving urban as well as rural people. Like a magnet, the more dynamic
economic growth areas drew people from the slow growth and declining
areas. In the United States, for example, the large migration from the old
industrial cities of the Northeast and Midwest to the Sunbelt states of the
South and Southwest between 1960 and 1980 drastically altered both the
demographic and the economic and political map of the nation.

These same industrialized countries have also attracted many people
from less developed countries into their urban economies—for the most
part less educated, unskilled workers. During the 1950s and 1960s, "guest
workers" (and often their families) flooded into West Germany, France,
the United Kingdom, Switzerland, Belgium, and Holland to meet their
manpower needs, from such countries as Turkey, Greece, Yugoslavia,
Italy, Spain, Portugal, and Algeria. The flow of immigrants, both legal
and illegal, into the United States in recent years has been at an all-time
high. Legal newcomers have arrived at the rate of 4 million per decade,
with only 7 percent coming from Northern and Western Europe, which
provided 95 percent of America's earlier immigration. The number of
immigrants to the United States from Asia, including 567,000 Indo-
chinese refugees up to the end of 1981, has increased by leaps and
bounds, and the flow from the Soviet Union and Eastern Europe has also
increased. But by all odds the greatest increase has been of Hispanic peo-

---

*In the United States and in some Western European countries, a reverse
migration from the city to the countryside has set in recently, for the first time in
history and with far-reaching implications for the schools and other social institutions as well as for the urban economies, which are losing middle- and upper-
income families and drawing in more low-income families.

ple from Mexico and Central America, including a high proportion of undocumented workers seeking employment and better wages. In 1980 alone, at least 3 million are estimated to have entered illegally from Mexico.

Educational Implications

These internal migrations and foreign influxes since World War II into Western Europe and North America, and also Australia and New Zealand, have greatly altered the sociological chemistry of their cities and in turn created difficult challenges for their schools. They have clearly had an enormous impact on the learning needs of everyone involved, children and adults alike, whether native born or foreign. They have all had to learn to adapt to their new multicultural surroundings, new types of employment, new kinds of schools, and a very new way of life. Many of the newcomers have also had (or still need) to learn a new language to cope effectively in their new environment.

In the United States it is difficult enough for a small-town New England family, for example, to adapt to its new home in Houston, Texas. But it is obviously far more difficult for a Latin American or Vietnamese or Korean family of rural origin to adjust to whatever U.S. city or town it happens to end up in. Other matters may further complicate the situation. Those who began their lives under dictatorial regimes may, within a democratic haven, have learning needs that are as much political as cultural and occupational. Moreover, as a result of the chaotic national situations that uprooted them and subsequent years spent in refugee camps, some may have psychological problems in dealing with their new environment that are incorrectly diagnosed as learning disabilities.

At stake here is the education of parents as well as children, as in the case of parents who fear that if they sign documents to allow their children to go on a school-sponsored trip they may never see them again. Also at stake is the reeducation of teachers in the country of refuge in the language and culture of the new class of children they will be teaching. The magnitude of the problem can be seen vividly in many European cities such as Amsterdam, Rotterdam, Liverpool, and Paris, and in cities all across the United States and Canada. In 1980 alone, the New York City school system experienced an increase of up to 50,000 immigrant school children, primarily from Cuba, Haiti, and elsewhere "south of the border" and from Southeast Asia and the Soviet Union. In Miami and Los Angeles, children of Spanish-speaking families are fast becoming a majority of the school population, with consequences that intensify both the needs of education and the problems of bilingual education.

In facing such problems, educational administrators are in a painful bind. They understand the folly of interpreting the aim of bilingual education as one of maintaining the non-English language rather than pushing for the faster mastery of English. They know that most parents want their children to enter successfully into the English-speaking mainstream. Yet they are under heavy counterpressure by those who view the "Americanization" of these children as a threat to their own political power or who are genuinely concerned about the loss of ethnic values and cultural identity.

The heritage of these urban educational problems generated by large-scale internal migrations and immigration from other countries will linger in the developed countries for many years to come, even if this great geographic transfer of people slows down.

CONDITIONS AND LEARNING NEEDS IN RURAL AREAS

What effect is the great urbanization in developing countries having on their rural populations, and in turn on the learning needs of rural people? One might suppose, as a matter of simple arithmetic, that as more rural people are drained off to the cities, following the historical pattern of most developing countries today, there would be a progressive easing of the pressure on land and health and school facilities and thus a reversal of the growth of rural poverty. Paradoxically, however, the trend is in the opposite direction. Despite the large migration to the cities, the rural population in most of the developing world is expected to be substantially larger by the end of the century than at present; this because of the especially high birth rates in rural areas. United Nations demographers estimate that between 1980 and 2000 the total rural population of the less developed regions will grow from 2276 million to 2774 million, an increase of 22 percent. Figure 2.4 tells the story graphically by regions. In Africa, the urban portion of the total population is projected to rise from 26 percent in 1980 to 42 percent in 2000, but at the same time the number of rural people is projected to increase from 349 million to 478 million. The number of rural dwellers in South Asia is expected to increase from 1069 million to 1387 million between 1980 and 2000—and even in more urbanized Latin America from 130 million to 151 million.

Increasing Poverty

This means, unhappily, that the already deep and extensive rural poverty is likely to spread, especially in the already overcrowded countries of Asia

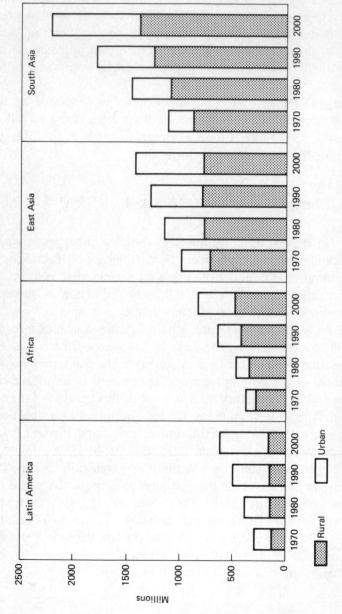

Figure 2.4. Projected growth of rural and urban populations, 1970–2000. [Source: UN Population Assessment (1978).]

and parts of Africa and the Middle East. Here the pressures of people against arable land, educational facilities, water supplies, health provisions, transportation, and other essential household and community services are destined to increase. This will make their respective populations, particularly the women and children of the poorest families, painfully vulnerable to crop failures, devastating floods, epidemics, and other natural and man-made disasters.

It is a sobering fact, for example, that per capita food production has already declined to dangerous levels in many of the poorest countries. Out of the 33 developing countries classified by the World Bank in 1982 as low income (with per capita annual incomes ranging from $80 to $410 U.S. 1980 dollars), 19, located mainly in Africa and Asia, experienced a decline in per capita food production of 5 to 59 percent in the years between 1969–71 and 1978–80.[11] In many developing countries, both middle-income and low-income, the great majority of rural families are either totally landless or have too little land to feed themselves adequately, as illustrated in Figure 2.5. Some of these people, of course, work seasonally on other people's land, some are self-employed in small businesses, and some find occasional work in the nearest town. But the large majority are in the poverty category and have only part-time employment at best.

The health status of many people in these lower income countries—reflecting inadequate nutrition, lack of access to safe water, unsanitary conditions, and poor child and maternal care—is strikingly bad. It is true that, for their populations as a whole, infant and child mortality rates have declined significantly over the past 20 years, and life expectancy has risen. Yet the situation still stands in shocking contrast to that of higher income nations, as shown by the comparative figures in Appendix Table 2.4. These group averages, weighted by population size, conceal even worse conditions in some of the poorest countries. For example, the average rate of infant mortality is 124 deaths per 1000 for the 34 lowest income countries, but the rates in Afghanistan, Sierra Leone, and Upper Volta in 1981 exceeded 200 per 1000. On the other hand, to illustrate what is possible even under poor economic conditions, another member of this low-income group, Sri Lanka, managed to reduce its infant mortality rate to 43 per 1000 by 1981. Similar variations exist with respect to other health indicators, such as the percentage of the population with access to safe water, daily calorie supply, and the ratio of medical doctors to population.

These health indicators are frequently only rough estimates, and none by itself tells the whole story. In combination, however, they make it abundantly clear that there is an enormous need for effective primary health care services in the rural areas of all developing countries. Better

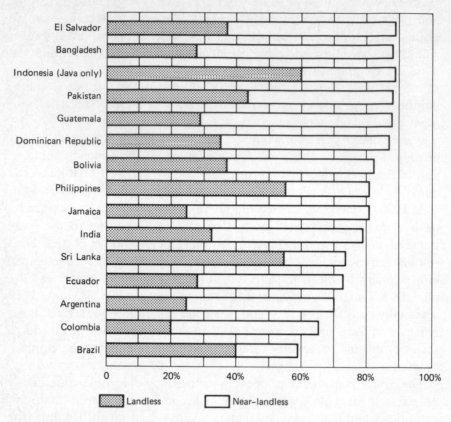

Figure 2.5. Percentage of landless and near-landless rural labor force. [Source: Milton J. Esman et al., *The Landless and Near Landless in Developing Countries* (Ithaca, N.Y.: Cornell University, Center for International Studies, 1978).]

health is a major objective in its own right, but it is more than that. It is an essential requirement for raising the productivity of rural people, which in turn holds the key to a reduction of widespread rural poverty. Better health and nutrition are also prerequisites to better learning by children.

Against this background of adverse conditions under which a substantial majority of rural people is living in lower income countries, attention can now be focused on how these conditions translate into everyday learning needs.

New Rural Learning Needs

The barrage of new learning needs greeting rural people who move to the city is matched by the great array of new learning needs facing those left behind in the countryside. Their learning needs are closely tied, in the first instance, to their basic survival needs. These include such things as health and nutrition, household improvements and employment. Their needs for survival may also include literacy, if they are in an environment in which written communication and media are available to a considerable extent and literacy has a frequent practical use in their daily lives (which is not yet the case in many rural areas).

Obviously these rural people will require many forms of outside help to improve their conditions of life. Yet without their own extensive participation and effort, outside help can prove sterile. To improve the family's health, for example, they must learn and apply new practices in nutrition, the use of uncontaminated water, sanitation, family planning, and child and maternal care. It is not enough simply to train the outside professional and paraprofessional deliverers of health services to a village; the villagers themselves must learn to protect and improve their own family's and their community's health status. To improve their farming productivity they must learn about new seed varieties and improved agricultural practices, about using fertilizer and credit, and about crop protection, storage, and marketing. This involves much more than simply listening to, and following the advice of, an agricultural extension worker. All too often that advice has been wrong for the situation. The farmer must understand why, and be convinced by logic and experimentation that a new practice will yield better (and safer) results than old ones.

The occupational learning needs of rural people differ widely from group to group, according to local ecological conditions, the size and character of their land holdings, their access to water and markets, and so on. The rice farmer's learning needs, for example, are quite different from those of the maize farmer, the local carpenter or metal worker, or the fisherman. What the small subsistence farmer needs to learn to take the next step forward is different from what the large commercial farmer needs to learn to increase yields and net profit.

Rural children and youth, of course, also have many essential learning needs. For them, learning reading, writing, and arithmetic—the "three Rs"—is especially important and can stand them in good stead throughout their lifetime, wherever they end up. They can learn these at school, if they are lucky enough to get there and stay long enough. But to prevent their new literacy skills from evaporating, they must keep using and improving them, and this can happen only if they have continuous access to relevant, useful, and interesting things to read, which they often do not. The three Rs alone, however, are much too thin a diet, and many of the other things they need to learn are beyond the scope of the school. By way of illustration, the authors of an earlier ICED report ventured to list a number of "minimum essential learning needs" of children and teenagers growing up in a rural environment, recognizing, of course, that the details would differ and would have to be defined in terms adapted to local conditions.[12] The list included the following:

1. *Positive attitudes,* toward cooperation with one's family and fellow human beings, toward work and community and national development, and, not least of all, toward continued learning.
2. *Functional literacy and numeracy,* sufficient (*a*) to read with comprehension a national newspaper or magazine, useful agricultural, health, and other "how-to" bulletins or manufacturers' instruction sheets; (*b*) to write a legible letter to, for example, a friend or to a government bureau requesting information; and (*c*) to handle important common computations, such as the measurement of land and buildings, agricultural input costs and revenues, and interest charges on credit, and rental rates on land.
3. *A scientific outlook and an elementary understanding of the processes of nature* in the particular area, as they pertain, for example, to health and sanitation, raising crops and animals, nutrition, food storage and preparation, and the environment and its protection.
4. *Functional knowledge and skills for raising a family and operating a household,* including the essential elements of protecting family health, family planning where appropriate, good child care, nutrition and sanitation; cultural activities and recreation; care of the injured and sick; intelligent shopping and use of money; making clothes and other consumption goods, house repairs, and environmental improvements; and growing and preserving food for family consumption.
5. *Functional knowledge and skills for earning a living,* including not only the skills required for a particular local occupation, but also knowledge of a variety of locally useful common skills for agriculture and nonfarm use.
6. *Functional knowledge and skills for civic participation,* including some knowledge of national and local history and ideology; an understanding of one's society; awareness of government structure and functions; taxes and public expenditures; available social services; rights and obligations of individual citizens; and principles, aims, and functioning of cooperatives and local voluntary associations.

The report made two practical suggestions about meeting these minimum essential learning needs. First, be quite clear about their specific nature.

However these essential learning needs are defined within a particular society, it is important that they be stated in operationally meaningful terms so as to provide a clear guide to instruction and learning and a practical basis for measuring achievement. Vaguely defined objectives, such as "giving every child a good basic education" (often defined as four to six or more years of formal schooling) are of little practical help in these matters.

The second suggestion concerns various ways of meeting these needs.

Fortunately, countries have wide latitude in the choice of means and methods for pursuing the learning objectives listed above; varieties and combinations of formal, nonformal and informal education can be designed and fitted to the circumstances. What is clear from this list of minimum learning needs is that *no one mode or institution of education ... is capable by itself of meeting all these minimum essential learning needs.*

Rural Learning Needs in Developed Countries

Thus far the focus has been on the conditions and learning needs of rural dwellers in developing countries. But what about the people still living in the rural areas of developed countries? They generally have a quite different mix and level of learning needs from rural people in developing countries. The reasons are themselves mixed. Their agricultural ecology and technologies, for example, are different. Their socioeconomic environment and infrastructure are more developed and, with some exceptions, generally offer much better income and employment opportunities.

Still, much of what has been said about the learning needs of rural people in poorer countries is relevant for those in richer ones. Granted the great differences in their specific circumstances, rural people everywhere have to fend for themselves in different ways from urban people. They need different and broader occupational skills and somewhat different family and community skills. They must be highly self-reliant in virtually all aspects of life, for they live much closer to nature and its elements and must learn to cooperate and cope with their natural environment. It is no accident that rural people everywhere tend to be more religious than urban people, living as they do surrounded by powerful and awesome natural forces.

It is true that today the majority of rural families in Western Europe and North America, in contrast to earlier times, have access to most of the amenities of urban life, such as automobiles, radio and television, indoor plumbing, and modern education. It does not follow, however, that the learning needs of rural young people, and hence the specific kinds of education they require, are identical to those of young people growing up in cities. And here lies the heart of the problem. In most developed countries, as in most developing countries, national education authorities impose a strongly urban-oriented curriculum on rural school-goers, as if the chief aim of the schools was to prepare them for migrating to the city. Actually, of course, many thousands of rural young people in these countries did move to the city in the post-World War II period, in search of better paying jobs and what they perceived as a more exciting life, leaving the "old folks" behind to run the family farm as best they could with the help of a versatile labor-saving tractor and other mechanical equipment. But what about those who aspired to rural careers? How suitable was an urban-biased education for them? And what does all this mean in the longer run for the integrity of the agricultural sector of these countries and for the special advantages and cherished values of rural living?

This question has come forcibly to the fore in recent years in conferences of the OECD in Paris and elsewhere, of the Arkleton Trust based in the United Kingdom, and in other official and unofficial forums. Rural education and learning needs have inevitably dominated the discussion, not simply in terms of technical training in agriculture, which has generally been strong in these countries, but in terms of general education for rural children and youth, suited to their environment and way of life.

Lately the matter has been moving from the rhetorical stage into action. To cite but one example, in the 1970s the civic leaders and educational officials in the Scottish Outer Hebrides, having finally been granted administrative control over their own schools, moved with dispatch to recast their curriculum, giving a larger place to the uniqueness of their own special culture, language, history, and economy. The results are already having a salutory effect on the perceptions, morale, and attitudes of children and adults alike. Similar new educational steps are being taken in the sparsely settled but highly important rural settlements of other OECD countries—for example, in portions of Canada, in the Scandinavian countries, in the Australian outback, and in many rural areas in the United States.

This is not to say that special modes of rural education have been totally ignored in the past in these countries. On the contrary, in most of them the training of agricultural specialists at the postsecondary level has made great advances over the past 50 years. Significantly, many agricultural college graduates in the United States and England, for example, end up managing their own family farm or some other sizable farm, and many keep returning to the colleges and universities to catch up on the latest research and new technologies. This is in striking contrast to the typical situation in developing countries, where agricultural college graduates—if they stick to an agricultural career, which many do not—are most likely to end up behind a desk in the Ministry of Agriculture or touring in a jeep telling others how to run *their* farms.

But life can be exceedingly harsh for the sizable pockets of seriously deprived rural families who still live in poverty in various OECD countries, and also in the Eastern socialist countries. And to meet their needs, a great deal of pertinent education will be required by all those concerned, not through the schools alone but through a wide range of nonformal educational activities.

IMPACT OF DEVELOPMENT ON LEARNING NEEDS

By all odds the most prolific breeder of new human learning needs throughout the world since World War II has been development itself. By development is meant all kinds of technological, economic, social, and cultural changes and advances, many of which are stimulated by new national and international development policies and programs. Although the aggregate increase in the number of learners has clearly had a sizable impact on world educational requirements, it seems evident that the increase in the lifetime learning needs of the average learner resulting from these dynamic development factors has been an even greater cause of the explosive growth of overall learning needs.

If this were not the case, learning needs in industrialized countries would by now be relatively stable, which clearly they are not. To cite just a few familiar examples, consider the vast number of workers, consumers, and students who have had to come to terms with computers and pocket calculators over the past ten years. Consider the learning implications for medical doctors, nurses, and pharmacists of the existence today of drugs, the great majority of which could not even have been prescribed 20 years ago. Consider also the many learning adjustments that must be made by the numerous workers who change jobs, or whose jobs change, every year. Or consider the impact that the unprecedented explosion of knowledge has each year on the learning tasks of conscientious teachers in a wide variety of fields, at every level of the education system. A steady flow of new technologies in agricultural production, processing, and marketing is constantly creating new learning needs on the part of farmers and others involved in agroindustries.

The learning needs of people all over the developing world are likewise being affected by new technologies—both home grown and imported. The impact is by no means limited to the relatively small fraction of the labor force employed in the modern sector of cities. Affected also are millions of large and small farmers, craftsmen, repair shop operators, and people in trades of every stripe who must constantly learn how to deal with new and unfamiliar products and methods. For example, any visitors from industrialized countries who are accustomed to taking the family car to a modern garage for repairs (which generally involves replacing the malfunctioning component with a brand-new spare part at considerable expense) are usually astonished to discover how repair problems are handled in countries such as Bangladesh, India, and Indonesia. In these countries most motor-driven vehicles—cars, buses, trucks, or tractors—are kept in running condition by small, often illiterate entrepreneurs in backstreet shops with a few apprentices who have primary-school educations at best. More often than not they lack new spare parts and are obliged to improvise. Yet the life span of vehicles in these countries is often three to four times that in industrialized countries. The mechanical ingenuity and versatility of these indigenous mechanics, acquired on the job, are often impressively greater than those of technical school graduates in richer countries. Although an improvised homemade part is not likely to last as long as a new factory-made part, a repair based on improvisation is usually far cheaper and gets the vehicle back on the road. In any event, these indigenous improvisors constantly need to learn new things as unfamiliar new models and products appear. What applies to vehicles applies to other modern products that usually turn up initially in these countries as imports, such as radios, electric irons and washing machines, outboard motors, and diesel pumps.

Although many technological changes that generate new learning needs arise spontaneously from commercial trade, national and international development policies and programs, both economic and social, are also creating broad new learning needs that affect vast numbers of people. A good example, discussed earlier, is the new emphasis being given by national governments and external assistance agencies to meeting the basic needs of the rural and urban poor. It is worth repeating that the people themselves must ultimately be their own change agents, with learning as the catalyst.

Economic Changes

Changes in domestic economic structures and in international trade patterns are also among the important generators of new learning needs for millions of workers, management personnel, engineers, and industrial and agricultural researchers. Over the past 30 years, as such changes have taken place at an unprecedented pace in virtually all countries, millions of people have had to adapt to new types of jobs, usually requiring learning new skills. If and when the lumbering North/South negotiations over a New International Economic Order succeed in opening wider markets in the industrialized world for semiprocessed and manufactured goods from developing countries, this action will create a host of new types of jobs for workers in those countries, accompanied by a plethora of new occupational learning needs.

On another front, major recent political and economic changes in China have generated a vast range of new learning needs for farmers, industrial workers, and managers. The opening of international trade with Western nations, for example, carries with it a broad need for knowledge about new domestic and imported technologies, quality control of mass-produced items, competitive conditions in overseas markets, differentials in foreign exchange rates, and their implications for price structures of goods.

Yet the internal situation in China amounts to little more than an air bubble on the surface of the Pacific ocean in relation to the worldwide repercussions on learning needs that ensued in the 1970s when major political changes in the Middle East ushered in mammoth increases in world oil prices. The drive to develop alternative sources of energy in all oil-importing countries, to conserve on oil consumption, and to shift to new forms of energy, defined new learning needs that continue to branch and flare on all sides. "Energy learners" around the world range from ordinary household consumers of energy to research scientists, from geologists and oceanographers to architects of skyscrapers, from farmers to military strategists, from managers of industries and transportation networks to the heads of governments.

A more subtle creator of learning needs for ordinary householders in industrial countries, in all but the very highest income brackets, has been the steady increases over the years in labor productivity and wages, which have forced householders to install all sorts of labor-saving home devices (washing machines and driers, vacuum cleaners, power lawnmowers, and the like) and to become fix-it-yourself experts in order to avoid large billings from highly paid professional plumbers, electricians, carpenters, and auto mechanics. Anyone who does not know how to repair these gadgets, and to fix leaky faucets and broken electric plugs, is in real trouble. And this takes a lot of learning (usually the hard way).

Social Changes

Social changes, often tied to political and economic changes, are yet another major creator of new learning needs. One such social change in industrialized countries, which gathered additional force in the 1970s, was the sharp increases in the proportion of women entering the labor market, and the opening up to women of types of employment from which they had been previously excluded because of sex. This trend was especially marked in the eight OECD countries shown on Appendix Table 2.5. True, the great majority of women continued to enter traditional female types of employment such as schoolteaching, nursing, secretarial work, retailing, and assembly-line work in light industries. A significant number, however, who met and mastered the prerequisite educational requirements began to break into what had previously been male-dominated fields such as construction, fire and police services, law, engineering, and corporate management.

Along with this change went a corollary educational need that confronted the husbands of career women. Beyond comparison with the sporadic conditions that prevailed earlier, they had to learn how to take care of children and do the housekeeping when the mother was not at home, with all that this entails ranging from providing medical attention to shopping, cooking, and laundering. At the same time, higher divorce rates and more liberal custody laws, in addition to the changing role of women, have made it likely that more men may either need or want to assume the sole responsibility for maintaining the household and rearing children.

Along with the new educational needs posed by changes in the status of women, still other learning needs spring from the progressive aging of the world's population. In Europe, for example, 17.4 percent of the population was over age 60 in 1975, whereas an estimated 24.7 percent will be over 60 in 2025. In the same period, those over 60 in North America will rise from 14.6 to 22.3 percent.[13] This trend is already raising hob with the financial reserves of governmental and private pension and social security programs that were founded before this aging trend had become apparent. It will also create problems for school systems as the public costs of supporting the elderly conflict increasingly with the costs of educating the young. This trend is also pregnant with new demands for educational services, since many of these senior citizens are displaying a hunger for more learning. To satisfy this hunger, the French, for example, have created a new type of nongovernmental institution for the elderly called the "université du troisième age."[14] The first one was established in Toulouse in 1973, and since then more than 50 others have come into being. Other institutions to meet the educational demands of the elderly are taking shape in such countries as Poland and Italy. In the United States "the graying of the nation" has gone hand-in-hand with the onset of "the graying of the campus." One of the main indicated paths for future growth in American higher education lies in providing for the learning needs and interests of older, part-time students.

At the other end of the age spectrum—especially among infants and pre-school-age children of working mothers, but also of nonworking mothers—there is another rapidly growing and increasingly recognized array of needs, in both developed and developing countries. These needs run the gamut from health and nutritional care and socialization to various kinds of cognitive and affective learning, including language and communication skills. If these needs are not met at an early age, the rest of an individual's life can be blighted. Psychologists and other child development experts now widely agree that, by the age of six, the personality, attitudes, and values that a child will carry through life are largely formed. There is also considerable research evidence showing that performance in school is strongly influenced by the child's preschool experiences—physical, emotional, and intellectual.

Over the past decade or more there has been significant worldwide growth of various public and private programs designed not only for the custodial care of infants and young children but for their broader, rounded development. Some of the most effective of these also deal with the education of parents. All told, however, these programs in the aggregate are still only scratching the surface of a mammoth need, which will grow step by step with urbanization and with the increase in numbers of working mothers and divided families.

Another large group whose learning needs have been seriously neglected is the physically and mentally handicapped. In recent years, especially in the more developed countries, increased attention has been paid to the needs of this group, but there is still a very long way to go. The problem is of staggering dimensions in the developing world. In some of these countries voluntary groups have addressed the problem to the best of their ability and created a greater public awareness. But the need is of such enormous magnitude that these private efforts can make only a small dent in it.

ADDING IT ALL UP

We have sought in this chapter to provide an overview of the explosive growth of human learning needs and educational demands since World War II among various subgroups in different parts of the world and to examine the principal forces behind these proliferating needs and demands. Because of this great concatenation of forces—continuing rapid population growth and urbanization in developing countries; high rates of migration in virtually all countries; the vast acceleration and spread of new knowledge and technologies; and all of the far-reaching economic, social, political, and cultural changes everywhere—the whole world wakes up each day faced with a new and larger variety of learning needs.

There is no reason to suppose that this explosive growth of learning needs will subside in the near future. On the contrary, the signs all point to its continuing acceleration for as far into the future as can be foreseen.

This brings us to some pointed questions about the supply side of the educational equation. How well have nations kept pace in meeting these growing and changing learning needs of their respective populations? What major gaps presently exist between the two sides of the equation, and who is being most seriously penalized? And what is the present outlook? What will be required to close these gaps and to prevent new and larger ones from evolving? The next chapter takes a first look at these crucial questions.

NOTES

1. Jean van der Tak, Carl Haub, and Elaine Murphy, "Our Population Predicament: A New Look," *Population Bulletin,* Vol. 34, No. 5 December 1979, pp. 3–4 (Washington, D.C., Population Reference Bureau, Inc.).
2. Ibid., p. 15.
3. Leon Tabah, "World Population Trends: A Stocktaking," *Population and Development Review,* September 1980, p. 363. (New York, Population Council). See also the comprehensive review of population trends and their implications in World Bank, *World Development Report 1984* (New York: Oxford University Press, 1984).
4. United Nations, *Selected Demographic Indicators by Country, 1950–2000* (New York: United Nations, 1980), p. 19.
5. Tabah, "World Population Trends," p. 364.
6. The most recently revised projections are given in *Trends and Projections of Enrolment by Level of Education and by Age, 1960–2000 (as assessed in 1982)* (Paris: UNESCO, Division of Statistics on Education, Office of Statistics, March 1983). A technical explanation of the projection model is provided in the earlier provisional edition of this document (September 1977).
7. U.S. Committee on Refugees, *World Refugee Survey, 1982* (New York: American Council for Nationalities Service, 1982).
8. George Beier, Anthony Churchill, and Michael Cohen, "The Task Ahead for the Cities of the Developing Countries," *World Development,* Vol. 4, No. 5, May 1976 (reprint ser., no. 97; Washington, D.C.: The World Bank, 1976).
9. Ibid.
10. *Educating for the Year 2000—Agricultural Education and Training in the European Community* (Enstone, Oxford: Arkleton Trust, 1978), pp. 4, 29.
11. World Bank, *World Development Report 1982* (New York: Oxford University Press, 1982).

12. Philip H. Coombs, Roy C. Prosser, and Manzoor Ahmed, *New Paths to Learning: For Rural Children and Youth* (Essex, Conn.: International Council for Educational Development, 1973), pp. 13–15.
13. *International Health News,* Vol. 3, No. 4, August 1982, Washington, D. C.: National Council for International Health.
14. *UNESCO Adult Education: Information Notes,* No. 1, 1980 (Paris, UNESCO).

Appendix Table 2.1 The Expanding World of Learners, 1950–2000 (in millions)

	1950		1975		2000	
	No.	Percent	No.	Percent	No.	Percent
World total	2513	100.0	4033	100.0	6199	100.0
More developed regions	832	33.1	1093	27.1	1272	20.5
Less developed regions	1681	66.9	2940	72.9	4927	79.5
Africa	219	8.7	406	10.1	828	13.4
East Asia	673	26.8	1063	26.3	1406	22.7
South Asia	706	28.1	1255	31.1	2206	35.5
Latin America	164	6.5	323	8.0	608	9.8
Oceania	13	.5	22	.5	30	.5
Europe and U.S.S.R.	572	22.8	728	18.1	832	13.4
North America	166	6.6	236	5.9	289	4.7

Source: United Nations, *Selected Demographic Indicators by Country, 1950–2000* (New York: United Nations, 1980).

Appendix Table 2.2 Trends in School Age Populations, 1960–2000

	Numbers (in millions)		
Ages (in years)	1960	1980	2000
More developed regions			
6–11	108	105	109
12–17	91	111	109
18–23	88	116	104
Total	287	332	322
Less developed regions			
6–11	317	495	664
12–17	249	445	616
18–23	217	389	550
Total	783	1329	1830

Source: UNESCO, *Trends and Projections of Enrolment, 1960–2000 (as assessed in 1982)* (Paris: UNESCO, Division of Statistics on Education, Office of Statistics, March 1983).

Appendix Table 2.3 Projected Adjusted Gross Enrollment Ratios by Regions and Levels[a] 1980–2000[b]

		Ratios		
Region	Year	First Level	Second Level	Third Level
Developed countries	1980	107	78	30
	2000	105	87	38
Developing countries	1980	86	31	7
	2000	96	49	12
Africa	1980	78	21	3
	2000	93	43	6
Latin America	1980	104	44	14
	2000	109	67	26
South Asia[c]	1980	83	31	7
	2000	93	47	10

[a]Adjusted for differences between countries in number of grades at each level.

[b]First level is primary, second level is secondary, and third level is postsecondary education.

[c]Not included are the People's Republic of China and the Democratic People's Republic of Korea.

Source: UNESCO, *Trends and Projections of Enrolment, 1960–2000 (as assessed in 1982)* (Paris: UNESCO, Division of Statistics on Education, Office of Statistics, March 1983).

Appendix Table 2.4 Basic Health Indicators[a]

	Year	Low-Income Economies	Middle-Income Economies	Industrial Market Economies	Eastern Europe and U.S.S.R.
Life expectancy at birth (in years)	1981	50	60	75	72
Infant mortality (0–1), per 1000	1981	124	81	11	25
Child death rate (1–4), per 1000	1981	21	11	(.)	1
Population per physician	1980	15,846	5,332	554	356
Population with access to safe water (percent)[b]	1975	29	50	—	—
Daily per capita calorie supply	1980	2,050	2,579	3,433	3,412

[a]Not including China and India.

[b]Data from *World Development Report* 1982.

Source: World Bank, *World Development Report 1983* (New York: Oxford University Press, 1983).

Appendix Table 2.5 Increasing Female Participation in the Labor
Force in Eight OECD Countries

Country	Percentage of Working Age Females in Labor Force	
	1975	1982
Canada	50.0	59.0
Denmark	63.5	72.7 (1981)
Italy	34.6	40.7
Japan	51.7	55.0
Norway	53.3	65.4
Portugal	51.8	57.4 (1981)
Sweden	67.6	74.6
United States	53.2	61.5

Source: OECD, *Employment Outlook,* mimeographed (Paris: OECD, Manpower and
Social Affairs Committee, June 1983).

CHAPTER 3

QUANTITATIVE GROWTH ON THE SUPPLY SIDE

CHAPTER 2, which sketched the swift growth of learning needs on the demand side of the world's educational equation, leads logically to a matching sketch of the shape of things on the supply side, including both major changes since the late 1960s, when a world educational crisis came into view, and further changes in the offing.

Before anything further is said, however, a problem of exposition must be touched on. Even if it were possible to encompass in a sweeping stroke everything that belongs on the supply side of the educational picture, the text would buckle under the weight of more data than it can coherently carry. Hence, it seems best to divide this material into two parts. The first part will include the quantitative expansion of educational services, not only in the realm of formal education but in the equally vital realms of nonformal and informal education. The part reserved for treatment in the next chapter will assess the qualitative dimensions of the supply picture. At the end of that chapter, we will identify the major gaps between the demand and supply sides of the educational equation around the world.

NATIONAL AGENDAS, PRIORITIES, AND STRATEGIES

The aims of formal education were dramatically enlarged in the 1950s and 1960s by the thrust of two convictions—a political one and an economic one—shared by virtually all nations. The political conviction, simply stated, was this: the best available way a democratically inclined state could overcome gross disparities rooted in past prejudices and socioeconomic injustices was by a massive expansion in education. In programmatic terms, this meant universal primary education for children, increased access for all young people to secondary and higher education, remedial literacy instruction for adults, equal educational opportunities for women, and broader adult education options.

The economic conviction lent strong support to the first conviction and was itself reinforced by studies in the relatively new field of educational economics. These gave a scientific gloss to the view that national growth flowed from technological progress and increasing labor productivity, which in turn flowed from progress in formal education. The studies also laid the basis for a theory of human capital, which treated formal education as an investment whose economic returns could be statistically measured by means of a cost-benefit analysis applied to wage structures. Political and educational leaders could thus draw on economic arguments to brace the case for allocating large portions of a national budget to educational spending.

Among national agendas for educational expansion, the priorities set reflected domestic conditions that framed the stage for action. Not surprisingly, therefore, developed and developing countries struck out in different directions, reflecting the major differences in their starting points.

Developed Countries

In the developed countries, where universal primary education had long since been achieved, the swift expansion of formal secondary and higher education was set as the immediate and main goal. Its attainment, so it was hoped, would do two things. First, it would create the preconditions for the upward mobility of all young people. No longer would so many be stopped in their ascent by educational barriers—the congealed deprivations of their family and class origins. The right of access to expanded secondary and higher education would enhance the opportunities for personal fulfillment among all young people, depending on their native talents, interests, and ambitions. Second, educational expansion at these levels would provide the requisite brainpower and prime motive power for technological advancement, for larger and more efficient production, and for rising incomes and living standards.

Among the developed countries, however, there were important differences in how the common aim was approached, reflecting differences in their history and culture and educational styles and structures. The expansion efforts in most Western European countries centered on their inherited academic secondary schools and on universities. Here and there, however, some new types of secondary schools were introduced (for example, the "modern school" in the United Kingdom in the mid-1940s and the "comprehensive school" in Sweden in the early 1960s). In higher education a few new experimental universities were introduced and various nonuniversity institutions were either expanded or created anew, such as Sussex University and the polytechnics in the United Kingdom, the Instituts Universitaires de Technologie (IUTs) in France, the University of Constance and the Fachhochschule in West Germany, and the regional universities in Norway.

Still, where academic secondary schools and universities were concerned, the takeoff point for their expanison in Western Europe was not something new for a new age. It was for the most part the preexisting elitist system of secondary and higher education, with its uniform curriculum and national standards and its extremely competitive and selective criteria for admission.

This system was originally designed to serve only a small and largely privileged fraction of the age group. The chosen few constituted the circle of "winners" destined for high places in government, education, the sciences and humanities, and the professions. The bulk of the population, not having access to higher education, were consigned to the circle of "losers" destined only for workhorse careers in commerce, industry, and agriculture or as government clerks. After World War II, however, Western European nations, propelled by a powerful public zeal to democratize education and all other institutions, embarked on a linear expansion of the existing elitist structure of secondary and higher education so as to accommodate a democratic mass of students. In other words, with some notable exceptions, the preexisting system was not fundamentally altered but simply made bigger. Students in the mass were subject to the same regimen of instruction and standards of performance, without regard to their varying interests and aptitudes. This, as we shall see, led to some serious problems of maladjustment.

The secondary and higher education systems in the United States—more by accident than by design—had always been far more diverse and served a far larger proportion and wider range of young people than the old elitist systems of Western Europe. As a result, even before World War II the American educational pyramid already looked like an actual pyramid, whereas the European ones resembled a spear standing on a broad box. Still, as the war ended, the United States was only partway along its ascent to full mass education. In the postwar years, many domestic impulses converged to make access to higher education the emblem of a fairness revolution. The visible signs came in many forms—special education benefits for veterans of the armed services, subsidized professional education in fields such as medicine, an expanded system of federal and state guaranteed educational loans, or outright grants to individuals. At the same time, civil rights legislation and antidiscrimination rulings by courts opened institutional doors to higher learning and to professional schools within them, to applicants previously denied entry because of race, sex, or ethnic origin. Also, at the same time, the public demand for institutions of higher learning located physically closer to potential pools of students led to the creation of new branch campuses of state universities and to a distinctive feature of the postwar expansionist drive— namely, the proliferation of locally based two-year community colleges with widely varying programs and standards.

By thus becoming increasingly diversified in the postwar years, the U.S. higher education system activated and catered to a tremendous latent market of interested learners who would not have been served by a less diversified and geographically dispersed system. (A prominent European university rector who toured American higher education instituions for the first time in 1960 exclaimed with astonishment, "America has a college for everyone—whatever his or her background or academic ability!") An increasing proportion of these learners proved to be nontraditional students, that is, adults seeking to continue their formal education, usually on a part-time basis, either to improve their occupational status or out of sheer interest in learning.

Eastern European socialist countries and the U.S.S.R. also featured a growing variety of secondary schools and specialized postsecondary institutions apart from the universities. In the U.S.S.R., for example, of the 861 higher education institutions in existence in 1977–78, only 63 were universities, whereas the rest were specialized institutions in technical, pedagogical, and other applied fields.[1] Also in the U.S.S.R., as much as half the total enrollments in postsecondary institutions consisted of nontraditional students, mostly workers on study leave or taking part-time evening and correspondence courses who could earn a regular degree from one or another of the established institutions. A similar pattern tended to be followed by the various new socialist regimes established in Eastern Europe after World War II.[2] Various means were devised to democratize access to universities. In Poland and Czechoslovakia, for example, children of workers and peasants were granted preferential points at the preentry stage for qualifying examinations. In East Germany, where no such qualifying examinations were given, a secondary-school certificate was the only entrance requirement.[3]

Developing Countries

In the developing nations, many of which consisted of a sea of mass illiteracy, priority was given to universal primary education, following the historical model of the developed countries whose educational pyramids had been built from the ground up. Thus, the uniform goal adopted by education ministers of Asia, Africa, and Latin America at UNESCO's landmark regional conferences in the early 1960s was to complete universal primary education within 20 years (only 10 years in the case of Latin America), while at the same time setting up a modest core of secondary and higher education structures, all to be fleshed out at a later time.* With universal primary education, at least children would no longer be afflicted for life with the inability to read, write, or compute. With a common primary schooling, so the theory went, all would have an equal start in life regardless of sex, family background, or geographical location.

The foregoing objective was linked to another objective espoused by education ministers and by UNESCO in the early 1960s. Specifically, they set themselves the task of eradicating illiteracy among unschooled adults within the same 20-year period set for the attainment of universal primary education. In this way, it was hoped, each country within a single generation would achieve complete literacy at all age levels of the population. Moreover, these humanistic aims were linked to the immediate need to create an abundant supply of educated manpower, thought necessary to fuel sustained national economic growth. This need in particular attracted the politically strategic support of economists.

Most of the developing countries started in the 1950s or early 1960s with only a "pocket edition" of an imported colonial education system that was never designed to fit their particular needs and circumstances. Thus, they faced a hard choice (though this was much less clear at the time than later). Should they adhere to and expand the imported model, or should they develop a home-grown model that might adopt selected elements from those of other countries? The pressure toward rapid educational expansion determined their choice. There were no better time-tested alternatives available and no time, it was felt, to design and experiment with new, untried models. Moreover, the imported colonial models carried prestige and had served well historically in their countries of origin; therefore, why should they not serve the newly independent countries just as well? To ask that question was to answer it in the affirmative. In any event, the developing countries, virtually without exception, clung to their respective imported systems, hoping in due course to make necessary adaptations to the local conditions.

The colonial educational legacies were in fact gradually modified in many countries, though rarely in any drastic way. Local history, for example, took the place of French or British history, whereas in second-

*A similar conference for the Arab states was held in Tripoli in 1966.

ary and higher education new emphasis was given to courses in mathematics and modern science. But there was another aspect to the modifications that occurred. In many countries, the inherited colonial systems were overprinted by unfamiliar educational institutions and practices imported, by way of foreign aid programs, from an odd-lot assortment of other industrialized countries. When put to the test of actual practice, some of the imports worked reasonably well, but others wandered aimlessly, like displaced persons looking for a place to rest.

As a consequence of the foregoing, the developing world by 1980 resembled a great international exhibition hall displaying assorted educational models and philosophies from all over the industrial world. These ranged from agricultural high schools and colleges to teacher training institutions; from different national species of secondary-level vocational-training schools to assorted postsecondary technical institutes; and from classroom radio and TV instructional systems to diverse brands of out-of-school "distance learning." Though much was new and different, and one could make a case that this diversity was all to the good, still the developing countries had not succeeded in fashioning their own unique and coherent formal education systems, adapted to their own particular needs, circumstances and objectives.

EDUCATION'S NEW LOOK BY 1980

By the close of the 1970s, every country's formal education pyramid looked very different from its picture 20 years earlier. In the case of the more developed countries, for example, those in Western Europe had fleshed out the second and third tiers of their educational structures and had taken giant steps toward opening them up to mass education. The U.S.S.R. and the Eastern European socialist states had made their own impressive movements in the same direction. The United States, with Canada close behind, had graduated from the stage of mass education to what the Carnegie Commission on Higher Education aptly called the stage of universal access to secondary and higher education. At the same time, developed countries outside of Europe and North America, such as Japan, Australia, and new Zealand, had greatly expanded the second and third tiers of their formal education structures.

And the developing countries? By prodigious efforts, they too had negotiated giant movements in the direction of broadened educational opportunities. Still, in reality their educational pyramids as of 1980 bore little resemblance to what their ministers had envisaged at the regional educational conferences held in the early 1960s in Karachi, Addis Ababa, and Santiago-de-Chile, and in Tripoli in 1966. In retrospect of 20 years, it turned out that priority had gone less to the achievement of universal primary education, as their ministers initially affirmed it would, than to the expansion of secondary and especially higher education. Thus, in the two decades between 1960 and 1980, the annual percentage rates of expansion of enrollments at the secondary and, especially, at the higher education level had consistently outstripped the growth in primary education by a wide margin. The statistics alone showed that virtually all developing countries, in constructing their educational systems, had veered away from their original model reflecting the historical pattern of growth of the industrialized countries. They had not built their educational structures from the ground up, so much as from the top down.

The apparent reasons for this deviation will be discussed later. Meanwhile, two qualifications to the previous paragraph should be inserted here. The first concerns the relative growth rates of different education levels. It was inevitable, and therefore expected, that the enrollment growth rates would be greater in secondary and higher education than in primary education, simply because they started from a numerical base that was so much smaller. What was *not* expected was that the spread between the rates of expansion at the different levels would be as great as it turned out to be. Evidence of this wide spread will be discussed later. The second qualification relates to the wide differences in educational growth rates in different geographic areas within countries that are masked by aggregate nationwide statistics. For example, by the late 1970s a substantial number of developing countries had all but achieved universal primary education in the more affluent neighborhoods of their major cities, while at the same time, universal primary education in the urban slum areas and surrounding shantytowns was still a distant dream. Much more striking, by the end of the 1970s a good number of developing countries had achieved statistical enrollment ratios in secondary and higher education equal to or even higher than those prevailing in the early 1950s in France, England, and Germany.

This was indeed progress of sorts, yet all the details making up the bright side of the educational picture were darkly overcast from another side by a reality common to the developing countries. Specifically, education in their rural areas stood in bleak contrast to the picture in their urban areas. Yet it was in the rural areas that most of the children of most developing countries were growing up—and these very areas continuously amounted to semiarid educational deserts.

By 1980, the projected target year for completing universal primary education, not only was every developing region still a long way from the goal, but it was doubtful if many countries would reach it even by the year 2000. On the other hand, ironically, a considerable number of developing countries had substantially overshot their original expansion targets for secondary and higher education well before 1980.

Statistical Indicators of Formal Education's Growth

These broadly outlined education trends can be seen more clearly under the focusing lens of four commonly used quantitative indicators of growth. It will be seen below that each tells a somewhat different story and has its own peculiar limitations. Nonetheless, despite some serious shortcomings, these quantitative indicators, based mainly on data gathered annually by UNESCO from its individual member states, are the best (and only) means available of obtaining a broad worldwide picture of growth trends in formal education. At the same time, an observer of the picture should bear in mind the paradox that the data often do not really mean what they seem to mean.

Enrollment Totals. Numerical enrollment figures, the first and most basic of the four growth indicators, are generally expressed in national aggregates, with each of the main educational levels shown separately. Enrollment data are not entirely comparable from one country to another, and this fact can deceive unwary users of such statistics. If too fine precision is not sought, however, composites of enrollment figures from different countries can show the general trends in any of three contexts: within each region, between more developed and less developed countries, or among low-, medium-, and high-income countries.

So used, these enrollment figures illuminate two striking phenomena, depicted in Figure 3.1. First, in a single generation, from 1960 to 1980, the world's total enrollments doubled. According to UNESCO's count, the total for all educational levels combined rose from 327 million in 1960 to an estimated 641 million in 1980, meaning that educational systems within this 20-year period expanded by as much as they had in the whole of previous history.*

*The UNESCO data used in this report do not include the People's Republic of China, the Democratic People's Republic of Korea, and Namibia. However, in March 1983 UNESCO for the first time published separate enrollment statistics on China, which substantially alter the picture given in Figure 3.1. Estimated enrollment (all levels) in China in 1980 totaled 204 million, equal to one quarter of the world total (including China) and one third of the developing world total. [*Trends and Projections of Enrolment by Level and by Age, 1960–2000 (as assessed in 1982). (Paris: UNESCO, Division of Statistics on Education, Office of Statistics, March 1983), Table 1, p. 11*].

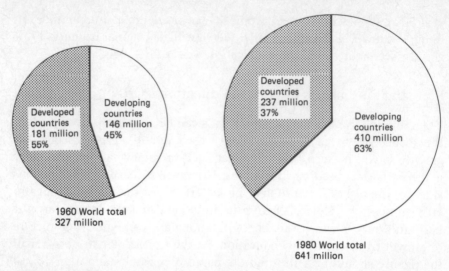

Figure 3.1. Distribution of world enrollment growth between developed and developing countries (not including China) at all levels, 1960–80. [Source: UNESCO, *Trends and Projections of Enrolment by Level of Education and by Age, 1960–2000 (as assessed in 1982),* (Paris: UNESCO, Division of Statistics on Education, Office of Statistics, March 1983), Table 1, p. 11.]

An even more striking phenomenon is that the developing countries, despite their great economic handicaps, account for the major share of this great increase. Their aggregate enrollments (at all levels) skyrocketed from 146 million in 1960 to 410 million in 1980, nearly a threefold increase. The developed countries, for their part, increased their total enrollments from 181 million in 1960 to 237 million in 1980, or by less than one third. The net effect of these differential rates of increase was to boost the developing countries' share of total world enrollments from 45 percent in 1960 to 63 percent by 1980.

Appendix Table 3.1 provides a more detailed picture of this growth, broken down by developing regions and by education levels. What stands out is the much greater percentage increase in *all* regions in second- and especially third-level enrollments than in primary-level enrollments between 1960 and 1980. In Latin America, for example, during the 20 year period primary enrollments rose by 134 percent, secondary enrollments by 493 percent, and higher education enrollments by 831 percent.

These raw enrollment figures convey a much rosier picture than actual conditions in developing countries warrant. For one thing, they are heavily padded with students repeating a grade and many others who will either drop out or be pushed out before completing the cycle they are in.

A recent UNESCO study of wastage in primary schools in Asia, Africa, and Latin America showed that repeaters account for 10 to 30 percent of primary school enrollments in the majority of countries studied. It also revealed shockingly high primary-school dropout rates (that is, low retention rates). In more than half of the 36 countries studied, from 20 to 75 percent of all children enrolled in the first grade in the mid-1970s failed to reach even the fourth grade, and far fewer reached the final grade of the primary cycle.[4]

Besides high dropout rates there is also the widespread phenomenon of low attendance; many pupils counted as enrolled are often absent at least one third of the official school year, which is already short. Beyond this, local schools in many developing countries substantially overreport enrollment figures by local schools in order to obtain larger subsidies or simply to look good to higher authorities. According to a 1977 report to the Indian government, "There is evidence to show that this over-reporting is large (it varies from 8 to 47 percent) and that it is larger in those States which are backward in education."[5] Finally, it is not unusual for national ministries of education to submit inflated annual estimates to UNESCO when they do not have the actual figures. All this is not to say that these reported enrollment statistics have no real meaning, but simply to emphasize that they must be interpreted with great caution. The same applies to the statistics examined in the following section.

Gross Enrollment Ratios by Levels. This second indicator of the gross enrollment ratio (often referred to as the GER) is the one most commonly used by UNESCO, the World Bank, UNICEF, and others as a gauge of educational progress. It shows the percentage relationship in a given year between (a) total enrollments at each education level and (b) the total estimated population in the age bracket officially corresponding to each level. Thus, for example, if in 1980 country X had a total primary school enrollment of 800,000 and a total estimated population of 1 million children in the officially designated primary-school-age bracket of 6 to 11, its primary level GER would be 80 percent.

Judged by this indicator, the developing countries as a group made impressive progress at all levels of education during each of the past two decades, as will be seen from Table 3.1. To be sure, they did not reach their goal of universal primary education on schedule, but they did, according to these figures, increase their GER at the primary level from 60 percent in 1960 to 74 percent in 1970 and 86 percent by 1980. Proportionately, they made substantially greater gains in secondary and especially higher education—as did the developed countries. These compos-

Table 3.1 Trends in Gross Enrollment Ratios, 1960–80

Region	Year	Adjusted Gross Enrollment Ratios (%)[a]		
		First Level	Second Level	Third Level
Developed countries	1960	106	55	12.8
	1970	106	70	23.4
	1980	107	78	30.0
Developing countries	1960	60	13	2.0
	1970	74	22	4.3
	1980	86	31	7.4
Africa	1960	44	5	0.7
	1970	57	11	1.6
	1980	78	21	3.2
Latin America	1960	73	14	3.0
	1970	92	25	6.3
	1980	104	44	14.3
South Asia	1960	62	15	2.2
	1970	74	24	4.6
	1980	83	31	6.7

[a]Adjusted, that is, for country differences in the length and official age span of elementary schooling.
Source: UNESCO, *Statistical Yearbook 1983* (Paris: UNESCO, Office of Statistics, 1983).

ite averages for large numbers of countries, however, conceal wide differences among the various regions (as shown on Table 3.1), and among individual countries within each region.

Here again, however, we must insert another warning about educational statistics. The gross enrollment ratio is not only the most commonly used indicator of educational progress but also the most misleading one, especially as applied to developing countries, where it often overstates the reality by 20 percentage points or more. This is why countries or regions that have not in fact achieved universal primary education may nevertheless show a GER in excess of 100 percent.

In the simple example given above, the reader unfamiliar with the pitfalls of educational statistics is likely to conclude that country X, with a primary level GER of 80 percent in 1980, was within 20 percentage points of achieving its goal of providing all of its 6-to-11-year-olds with a full primary schooling. But this turns out to be a statistical illusion when we examine the actual situation more closely (which, though hypothetical, is fairly typical of many real developing countries.) The illusion has three faces.

First, for reasons noted earlier, the reported total enrollment figure on which the GER is based probably overstates the reality by a substantial margin. The accurate figure, let us say, is 720,000 enrolled, not 800,000 as stated in the example; hence the corrected GER is 72 percent, not 80 percent.

Second, of the 720,000 pupils enrolled, only 600,000 are of the correct official age (6–11) to be in primary school; the other 120,000 are either underage or, more likely, overage. In other words, the numerator and denominator of the ratio are incompatible. This further correction reduces the real ratio to 60 percent of the total 6-to-11 age group of 1 million actually enrolled.*

Third, let us suppose that a study of primary school wastage in country X has shown that only three out of five children enrolled in primary school in 1980 are likely to complete the full cycle; the rest will drop out or be pushed out along the way. Thus, all things considered, the reality is that country X in 1980 was only 36 percent, not 80 percent, of the way toward its goal of universal primary education—if by this we mean a situation in which virtually all children in a country are receiving a full primary education.**

In this connection there is one crucial indicator missing in the wealth of published school statistics. Few ministries of education in developing countries collect, or at least publish, statistics on the number of pupils who actually complete primary school each year. No such figures appear in UNESCO's *Statistical Yearbook*. Yet this is the only statistic that can

---

*The point should not be misunderstood. It is obviously good that children get to school whatever their age, even if it does not fit the official age bracket. However, treating them as if they were all within the "correct" age bracket inflates the GER. This means that 72 percent of all 6- to 11-year-olds are not enrolled (in this example), but something less than that. UNESCO statisticians point out that what the GER actually measures is the *capacity* of the primary school system, that is, the number of pupils it can accommodate, regardless of their age. They also point out that the enrollment totals for many developing countries, especially those that do not practice "automatic promotion," are heavily laden with repeaters who place an extra burden on available elementary school capacity.

**There is a widespread tendency to equate universal primary education with a GER of 100 percent. By this definition, one would have to conclude that Latin America had achieved universal primary education in 1980, when its regional GER stood at 104 percent (see Table 3.1). But this conclusion flies in the face of well-known realities. Recent UNESCO and other studies have shown that Latin American primary schools have the highest noncompletion rates of all the developing regions—in part because a high proportion of Latin American primary schools, especially in rural areas, are incomplete, having only one, two, or three grades, and nowhere for the pupils to go from there. There is also clear evidence that many Latin American children never enter school.

show conclusively how far a given country has actually progressed toward universal primary education, in the full meaning of that term. It is also an indispensable item of information for assessing the real performance and progress of any primary school system with a view to planning and managing it more effectively and improving its performance.

A frequently given reason for this omission is that many countries have no examination to mark the completion of primary school. Rather, they have an entry examination to junior secondary school, with a cutoff point geared to the capacity of the next level to accept students. One effect of this procedure is that a full primary schooling is not viewed as a terminal point and an important educational achievement in its own right. Another effect is to mark as failures all primary school completers who do not go on to secondary school. This is a vestigial remnant of the old elitist system, which produced far more failures than successes.

Shown in the accompanying box, with Brazil as an example, is a method for estimating the approximate primary school completion rate in a country.

The Example of Brazil

Brazil's eight-grade primary school system (nominally fitting the 7-to-14 age group) had a reported total enrollment in 1975 of nearly 20 million pupils. The total estimated population of this age group in 1975 was 22 million, giving an official GER ratio of 89 in UNESCO's *Statistical Yearbook* (1981). However, if the overage pupils (based on World Bank estimates) are subtracted, the net enrollment ratio is 71 percent.

This 71 percent figure, however, still does not tell us what proportion of Brazil's children were actually completing the eight grades of primary school in the 1970s. A rough answer to this question starts with the plausible (and perhaps generous) assumption that no more than 90 percent of all Brazilian children entered the first grade in the first place. A recent UNESCO study of primary school wastage concluded that only 39 percent of the total cohort that entered primary school in Brazil in 1973 would reach the fourth grade, and only 28 percent would reach (not necessarily complete) the eighth grade. Allowing for the 10 percent that never entered school, we arrive at the conclusion that only one out of four Brazilian children of age 7 in 1973 was likely to reach the eighth grade.

This is admittedly a "ball park" estimate, but it undoubtedly comes closer to the truth than the impression conveyed by the 89 percent gross enrollment ratio shown in UNESCO's 1981 *Statistical Yearbook*.

Enrollment Ratios by Age Groups. This third indicator is quite different from the GER. It shows what percentage of each school age group in a country's population (for example, ages 6–11, 12–18, 19–24) is actually enrolled *somewhere* in the formal education system, and indirectly, what percentage is out of school. The figures shown in Appendix Table 3.2 confirm the steady progress made over the past two decades in all major regions of the world in raising the education participation of each school-age group. In South Asia, for example, between 1960 and 1980 the proportion of the 6-to-11 age group enrolled climbed from 48 to 66 percent. The corresponding figures for the 12-to-17 age group rose from 19 to 32 percent, and for the 18-to-23 age group from 3.4 to 9 percent. Similar significant increases are shown in Appendix Table 3.2 for Africa, Latin America, and the Caribbean.

The main limitation of this particular indicator is that it does not show *where* in the educational system the members of each age group are enrolled or how they are distributed by levels. Its compensating virtue, however, is that it gives a considerably more accurate picture than the GER of where things actually stand in terms of the proportion of each age group that is—and is not—enrolled somewhere in the system.

The contrast between the two indicators is brought out by the comparative figures shown in Table 3.2. To take the example of Latin America, the gross enrollment ratio of 104 percent could mislead the unwary reader into believing that all primary-school-age children were attending school in 1980. But the corresponding age enrollment ratio corrects this false impression by revealing that only 81 percent of all 6- to 11-year-olds were enrolled that year, meaning that Latin America still had some distance to go before it achieved universal primary education.

Another completely different type of false impression is corrected at the secondary level. Here, the GER figure for Latin America implies that only 44 percent of those corresponding to the official secondary-school-age group are enrolled in school, whereas the age enrollment ratio reveals that actually 64 percent of the 12-to-17 age group is enrolled somewhere in the system. The explanation, of course, is that many are not in secondary school but are overage pupils in primary school. The same reasoning applies at the third level. The age enrollment ratio reveals that 22.2 per-

Table 3.2 Comparison of Different Enrollment Ratios, 1980

	Adjusted Gross Enrollment Ratios			Enrollment Ratios by Age Groups		
	First	Second	Third	6–11 Years	12–17 Years	18–23 Years
Africa	78	21	3.2	63	37	7.9
Latin America and Caribbean	104	44	14.3	81	64	22.2
South Asia	83	31	6.7	66	32	9.1

Source: UNESCO, *Trends and Projections of Enrolment by Level and by Age, 1960–2000 (as assessed in 1982)* (Paris: UNESCO, Division of Statistics on Education, Office of Statistics, March 1983).

cent of the 18-to-23 age group in Latin America is enrolled somewhere in the system, but many are obviously overage students in secondary schools and not enrolled in higher education, since the third level GER is only 14.3 percent.

Public Expenditures on Education. A quite different indicator of educational growth is the trend in public expenditures on education. Since the matter of educational costs and finances will be discussed at length in Chapter 5, it will suffice to say here that this indicator reflects a substantially greater increase since 1960, in monetary terms, than the previous three enrollment indicators. In other words, the average cost per student in the system as a whole rose substantially over the two decades.

THE SLOWDOWN IN THE 1970s

A vital question is particularly pertinent to a reassessment of the crisis: Did the rapid expansion of formal education systems in the 1960s slow down appreciably in the 1970s, as anticipated by the 1968 report on the world educational crisis?

Two sets of evidence throw light on this question: first, the trends in *percentage rates* of enrollment increases, shown in Appendix Table 3.3, and second, the trends in *absolute* enrollment increments over five-year periods shown in Appendix Table 3.4.

Developed Countries

This evidence provides a clear-cut answer to the question in the case of the developed country group. As will be seen from Appendix Tables 3.3 and 3.4, after the end of the 1960s both the enrollment growth rates and the numerical enrollment increments fell steadily in the developed countries, bringing their overall educational expansion to a virtual halt by the end of the 1970s. During the last half of the decade their secondary and postsecondary enrollments still grew moderately, but this growth was offset by an absolute drop in primary level enrollments, bringing systemwide enrollment growth to zero by 1980.

This stagnation of formal education in the developed countries resulted mainly from the demographic reversal in their school-age population during the 1970s and the high level their educational participation rates had reached by then. Growing education budget stringencies, though very real, were not the decisive factor.

Developing Countries

Changes in educational growth trends in developing countries during the 1970s, compared to the 1960s, were not as clear-cut, and the picture differed greatly from region to region and country to country. There seems little doubt, however, that the earlier strong momentum of educational growth was rapidly losing its force in the great majority of these countries, especially in the late 1970s, and that this deceleration was likely to continue far into the 1980s. The main reason was financial shortages. Unlike the situation in developed countries, the continuing rapid growth of the school-age population, plus the still relatively low enrollment ratios in most developing countries, would undoubtedly have resulted in considerably greater educational growth in these regions during the 1970s in the absence of serious financial constraints. The surprising thing is that so many developing countries, especially in Africa, did as well as they did in adding to their enrollments during the 1970s, given their formidable financial obstacles.

However, the impressive primary level enrollment increments in Africa, shown in Appendix Table 3.4, are heavily weighted by the spurt toward universal primary education during the 1970s by just a few countries—particularly Kenya, Tanzania, and Nigeria. Many other countries in the region lagged well behind.

Paradoxically, although the African region as a whole fell substantially short of achieving the Addis Ababa target of universal primary education by 1980 (defined at the time as a gross enrollment ratio for the region of 100 percent), the *numerical* enrollment level implied by this target was actually reached (at least statistically) by 1977 and substantially exceeded by 1980. The main explanation of this apparent paradox is that the growth of the school-age population was grossly underestimated when the targets were set in 1961. The actual estimated size of the population in the 6-to-11 age group in 1980 turned out to be more than 60 percent larger than originally envisaged (53.5 million as compared to 32.8 million).[6] This once again highlights the enormous impact of high population growth rates on the ability of poor countries to meet the education needs of their children and youth.

Conclusions

Weighing all of the foregoing evidence, we conclude at this point that during the 1970s, throughout the developed world and in most of the developing world, the unprecedented educational expansion of the two previous decades had reached a major turning point and began decelerating, in many instances virtually stagnating. In general, this slowdown began somewhat later and more gradually in the developing world than in the developed world. There were also wide differences among individual countries. The oil-rich countries, for example, and a few others in relatively favorable economic positions, were able to sustain their expansion better than those whose economic growth rates were low and whose international financial position was crippled.

The preceding pages have drawn attention to the serious inadequacies of educational statistics, especially in developing countries, and to the exaggerated impression of progress often conveyed by the published growth indicators (above all, the GERs). Our purpose in doing so has not been to belittle the actual progress but rather to keep the true situation in as clear and accurate perspective as possible. For to overestimate what has already been accomplished is to underestimate the magnitude of the unfinished tasks. Moreover, the illusions fostered by inflated claims of progress can lead only to the inevitable shock of disillusionment.

As things stand, even after due allowances are made for concealed exaggerations, the weight of the evidence shows that, in purely quantitative terms, educational systems the world over, and especially in the developing countries, have expanded dramatically in the past two decades. At the same time, however, we must postpone judgment on what has certainly been impressive numerical progress until we consider, in the next chapter, the qualitative aspects of this progress.

But there is one conclusion that can be firmly stated here. This is that educational systems everywhere are severely handicapped by lack of sufficient up-to-date knowledge above themselves—about their changing internal dimensions and performance and about the adequacy of their responses to important changes taking place in their environment. As mentioned earlier in this chapter, their present information systems, from bottom to top, and their analytical capacity for making good use of vital information flows are grossly inadequate to meet the needs of intelligent self-evaluation, planning, and management and for designing and implementing essential educational changes and innovations.

This does not imply criticism of UNESCO's statistical staff, which, in fact, should be commended for the steady improvements it has made over the past decade in its analytical and reporting services. The root of the problem lies in the individual countries on whose statistical reports UNESCO statisticians must depend. At relatively small cost, compared to the vast outlays being made on education, their inadequate internal reporting and analytical services could be vastly improved. It is hard to conceive of any comparable educational investment at this stage that would pay more substantial dividends. One hopes that external assistance agencies—such as The World Bank, various bilateral agencies, and UNESCO itself—will recognize this as a particularly good opportunity to be helpful.

THE OUTLOOK FOR FORMAL EDUCATION

The future direction of formal education enrollments in developed countries can be foreseen fairly clearly, at least in general terms if not in detail. Elementary enrollments, now well below their earlier peaks, will experience a temporary upturn starting in the second half of the 1980s as the children of the post-World War II baby boom send their own children to school in increasing numbers. This second baby boom will subsequently reach the secondary- and higher-education levels in the 1990s. But because of the present, record-low level of birth rates in the developed world, this secondary boom will be much smaller than its predecessor. It will, however, have an important impact on costs and expenditures and could cause some troublesome shortages of teachers and classrooms if not adequately planned for.

Another proviso should be added concerning the outlook for higher education in developed countries. Enrollments of regular full-time students coming directly from secondary schools were already flattening out or declining in the early 1980s. At the same time, however, enrollments of nontraditional older students, mostly studying part time and often in noncredit courses, were on the rise in many countries and are likely to continue growing. Thus, the anticipated stagnation of overall enrollments in the 1980s may be far less than many people in higher education have feared. Of course, much will depend on the degree of encouragement given to such nontraditional students in each country and each institution. This is already very strong in such countries as Sweden and the United States and the Eastern socialist countries but still relatively weak in some other developed countries.

The developing countries face a very different outlook, mainly for three reasons previously discussed: first, their child and youth population is still growing rapidly; second, their enrollment ratios at all levels are still relatively low (especially among rural children and youth); and third, their resource constraints are far greater.

It will be helpful at this point to refer back to Chapter 2 to the UNESCO projections of the enormous enrollment increases (shown in Figure 2.3), which would be required in each developing region to follow the general trend of enrollment growth that prevailed during the height of the expansion. A different way of viewing this same scenario is presented in Figure 3.2, which shows (in the unshaded portion of each panel) the actual observed increases in enrollment ratios by different age groups from 1960 to 1980, and (in the shaded sections) the projected increases from 1980 to 2000. In examining these upward-trending lines in all of the developing regions, one should bear in mind that the size of the population of each of the indicated age groups is steadily expanding, thus requiring a greater and greater educational effort to gain each successive percentage point of the ratio.

Let us suppose for the moment that, by some great good fortune, all developing countries succeeded in achieving these enormous projected increases. Where would matters stand by the end of this century? Where would universal primary education stand? How many children and teenagers would still be out of school? What would be the state of adult literacy and illiteracy in the Third World by then?

The answers are jolting. First, according to UNESCO's projections, by the end of the century no developing region as a whole would yet have achieved universal primary education (though some individual countries probably would have come close). Latin America would have come nearest, with 89 percent of its 6- to 11-year-olds enrolled—compared to 80 percent in Africa and 77 percent in South Asia. But enrollment, as was pointed out earlier, does not necessarily mean completion of primary school or gaining of permanent literacy.[7]

Second, despite these rising enrollment ratios the developing world would still have, according to these optimistic UNESCO projections, 103 million out-of-school children in the 6-to-11 age group by 2000—compared to 114 million in 1980—and the number of out-of-schoolers in the 12-to-17 age group would have increased from 136 million in 1980 to 222 million in 2000.[8] This is because the gap between the rising enrollment curve and the rising school-age population curve, representing the out-of-school children and youth, narrows very little up to the year 2000 in the case of the 6-to-11 age group and continues to widen for the 12-to-17 age group. To be sure, the *percentage* of out-of-schoolers would have declined

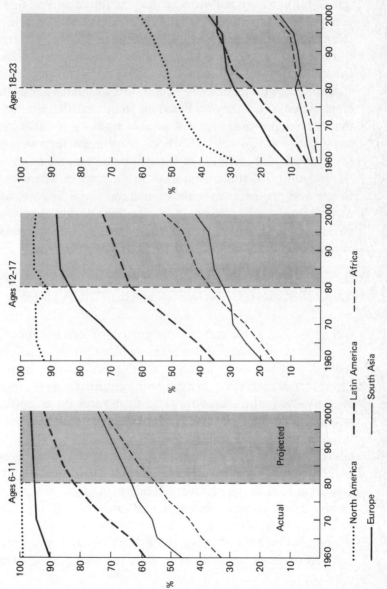

Figure 3.2. Past and projected enrollment ratios by age groups, 1960–2000. [Source: UNESCO, *Trends and Projections of Enrolment by Level and Age, 1960–2000 (as assessed in 1982)* (Paris: UNESCO, Division of Statistics on Education, Office of Statistics, March 1983).]

by then, but this would be little comfort for the many millions still on the outside looking in.

And third, what about adult literacy? Another set of UNESCO projections indicates that, assuming all the children who attended primary school for at least a few years actually acquired and retained literacy, the percentage of literate adults in the developing world would have increased from an estimated 43 percent in 1970 to 61 percent in 1990. But the *absolute number* of illiterate adults would also have increased, from an estimated 544 million in 1970 to 659 million in 1990.[9]

All of these projections, of course, are speculative. But the point to be emphasized is that they are based on an optimistic assumption—namely, that developing countries will be able right up to 2000 to continue the same kind of high rates of school enrollment increases they achieved in the 1960s and early 1970s. We will be better able to pass judgment on the feasibility of this assumption in Chapter 5 when we examine the trends and prospects for educational costs and finance. Meanwhile, let us shift our attention to another important part of the overall education picture that has been too long neglected by educational analysts and policymakers.

THE UPSURGE IN NONFORMAL EDUCATION

Ironically, just as the earlier rapid growth of formal education was losing its momentum in the 1970s, a much older mode of education, bearing the new name of *nonformal education,* got a vigorous boost. Some of the forms it took, especially in developing countries, were home-grown varieties, whereas others were imported from more developed countries. The latter included, for example, various occupational and professional skill training programs, agricultural and other types of extension services, adult literacy classes, and continuation studies at various education levels. They also included diverse learning activities fostered by a wide assortment of nongovernmental organizations such as youth groups, women's associations, business and professional organizations, labor unions, peasant societies, and farmer cooperatives. The great majority of the nonformal education activities, both old and new, were outside the purview of ministries of education and the managers of formal education.

Reactions of Adult Educators

Most members of the long underappreciated and undersupported adult education fraternity greeted the new upsurge of interest in nonformal education enthusiastically, and they did more in its cause than any other professional group. To their eyes, this new interest promised greater recognition and support and broadened opportunities for their endeavors. This enthusiasm, however, led adult educators into a thicket of problems, once it became clear that the new concept of nonformal education embraced a far wider range of learning objectives and clienteles than even the most liberal definition of adult education had ever contemplated. Part of the trouble revolved around the questions: Who is an "adult"? Should out-of-school teenagers be included in adult programs? If not, then who should and would take responsibility for serving the imperative learning needs of this very large and important group en route to adulthood? If, on the other hand, out-of-school teenagers were to be included, then adult education could be a confusing misnomer. (The Adult Education Division of Thailand's Ministry of Education solved this problem by officially defining an adult as "any person 12 years of age or more, not enrolled in school.")

Another part of the trouble centered on an even thornier question. What subjects and learning objectives should adult education include, and what should it *not* attempt to cover? If it stuck to subjects schools and colleges taught it would be on safe and familiar turf, for adult education had always operated as a stepchild in the shadow of the formal education system. By stopping there, however, it would fail to address a high proportion of the most urgent learning needs of adults, especially the poorest ones in greatest need of help. But suppose that adult educators branched out into such areas as primary health care, family planning, agricultural extension for small farmers, and occupational training for out-of-school youth? They would then be invading the well-established bureaucratic turf of an array of specialized ministries that were already far more extensively engaged in nonformal education than the ministry of education itself, even if they did not call it by this name.

Adult educators are still uncertain about the proper limits of their role, but they are nevertheless infused with more enthusiasm and energy than ever before and marching with proud banners flying high. Ironically, though, within the different specialized ministries such as agriculture, health, and labor, people engaged in various types of practical training and extension work had not generally thought of themselves as adult educators, so they were as surprised to learn that they were practicing nonformal education as was the old gentleman who discovered he had been talking "prose" all his life.

The Growth of Nonformal Education

As noted earlier, there is no reliable way to measure quantitatively the growth of nonformal education in any country, much less to compare trends in different countries as we did earlier for formal education. Because such activities are extremely heterogeneous, they simply do not lend themselves to any common statistical indicators such as enrollments, enrollment ratios, or total expenditures. Nevertheless, an abundance of scattered evidence the world over enables one to form reasonable judgments about the pace and main directions of nonformal education's growth in the past decade. Our review of a wealth of such evidence, drawn from many sources and from direct observations, supports two important conclusions.

First, even before the upsurge of interest in the 1970s, far more nonformal education activities already existed in virtually every country than anyone, including the national education authorities, realized. This conclusion is supported in part by informal sample inventories conducted in the early 1970s by ICED in partnership with local researchers in several countries, such as India, Kenya, the Philippines, Sri Lanka, and Tanzania.[10] It is borne out by additional inventories made in other countries. A sample survey of Colombia, for example, yielded an estimate of 10,000 or more identifiable nonformal education projects and programs in the whole country (not counting the myriad of nonformal learning provisions buried in various types of specific development projects).[11] The Colombia survey revealed that a substantial majority of these programs had been established in the 1960s and early 1970s and that they existed in both rural and urban areas, though more so in the latter than in the former. It also showed, surprisingly, that most operators of such programs were unaware of the existence of more than two or three other nonformal education programs, which suggests the need for a better exchange of information and ideas among the members of this poorly organized community. Useful steps are now being taken in a number of countries to promote such exchanges. India's Ministry of Education and Culture, for example, recently published a directory of some 150 major organizations in India engaged in nonformal education. Libya and Sudan are reported to have developed a "map" of adult education opportunities for the guidance of potential users.

The second conclusion is that the 1970s saw a widespread growth of nonformal education. This again is supported in part by ICED's case studies in more than two dozen widely scattered developing countries and by numerous other studies and published reports in the 1970s. The ICED cases illustrate the great diversity of such programs and their close links with specific development objectives and local needs, which cut across such fields as agriculture, water supply, health, family planning, rural industry, and occupational training for women and out-of-school youth. The case studies also illustrate the various ways in which local people and communities are playing a key role in providing and utilizing such education in conjunction with local development activities. A few brief examples illustrate the variety of different types of nonformal education activities uncovered by these case studies:

- In East Java, the *Jombang Youth Program,* a locally initiated program (unknown to the authorities in Jakarta at the time ICED examined it), was providing remedial schooling and do-it-yourself training, combined with earning cash for out-of-school teenagers in a wide assortment of occupations, such as rearing fish in ponds made by the teenagers themselves, rice hulling, producing eggs for sale, and making dresses and other items sold through a youth-run cooperative.
- In Thailand, four relatively large-scale programs were examined. They included a "second chance" school equivalency program for out-of-school youth; Mobile Trade Training Schools serving youth in smaller towns and surrounding rural areas; the Community-Based Family Planning Service, a lively nongovernmental grass-roots program, also concerned with primary health care; and the government-managed Lampang Rural Health Development Project that covered most of an entire province and used local volunteer health workers.
- In Bangladesh, two dynamic nongovernmental rural programs, the Savar People's Health Program and the Bangladesh Rural Advancement Committee (BRAC), both multipurpose rural self-help programs that span a wide variety of activities.
- In Sri Lanka, the well-known and rapidly expanding Sarvodaya Movement makes extensive use of educated urban volunteers and specially trained local young people to serve the needs of the poorest of the rural poor.
- In Colombia, the National Apprenticeship Service (SENA) rural outreach occupational training program serves youths and adults, males and females; and the Accion Cultural Popular (ACPO) program with its own nationwide radio network, weekly newspaper, and tailor-made self-instructional materials, works with organized local learning groups. All are aimed at uplifting poor *campesino* families in the remotest rural areas.
- In India, the Social Work and Research Center in Rajasthan is a unique voluntary organization, created by young urban university graduates, that encourages community self-help efforts in such matters as farming and irrigation; health, nutrition, and family planning; and small-scale rural industry involving both men and women.
- In the Republic of Korea, the Community-Based Integrated Rural Development (C-BIRD) program, under which clusters of villages do

their own development planning and implementation, draws on selected types of governmental and other outside assistance as necessary to break the local development bottlenecks.

These are but a small sample of the programs throughout the developing world today in which effective use is being made of many different forms of nonformal education. New initiatives are springing up all the time.

More and more governments of developing countries have taken steps to stimulate, assist, and harmonize nonformal education activities by both governmental and voluntary organizations. Indonesia, for example, in the mid-1970s created a new Directorate of Nonformal Education within the National Ministry of Education and Culture to serve as a clearinghouse and support center for other ministries and nongovernmental organizations involved in nonformal education, as well as to oversee all such programs for which the education ministry itself is directly responsible. Also in the mid-1970s, India's Ministry of Education and Culture transformed its relatively weak Department of Adult Education into a strong Department of Nonformal Education, which has since made extensive efforts to mobilize and provide material and professional aid to various voluntary organizations operating at the local level in a nationwide drive to expand nonformal education. In 1978 a new National Institute of Education was established in Turkey, under the Ministry of Education, to provide training and research services in nonformal education. More recently, the Ministry of Education in Botswana established a new Department of Nonformal Education that absorbed the Botswana Extension College and its innovative "distance learning" programs.

Strong support for nonformal education was provided to developing countries during the 1970s, and is still being provided, by bilateral and international agencies and by a host of nongovernmental organizations to strengthen and broaden nonformal education in various fields through different national ministries and voluntary organizations.

Shortcomings and Practical Problems

Here again, however, as with formal education, it is important to guard against an exaggerated impression of progress. Compared to the situation before 1970, significant progress has been made in nonformal education. Yet most programs are small; they operate in a limited geographic area, serve a limited clientele, and have at best taken only a small step toward meeting the total needs. Well over half the rural families in the developing world, for example, still lack the most rudimentary educational and related services for primary health care, safe and convenient water supply, family planning, agricultural improvement, locally relevant occupational training, and effective programs for improving the status of women and the welfare of young children. All these require, among other things, large doses of nonformal education. A study in Ethiopia in the 1970s, for example, showed that agricultural extension services were confined to farmers living within 10 kilometers of all-weather roads, thus leaving out 80 to 85 percent of the total rural population. The situation is typical of that in many other developing countries and applies not only to agricultural extension but to all types of rural improvement services.

Some complex and difficult organizational problems must also be overcome if progress in this field is to proceed more rapidly. The problems stem in part from the fact that nonformal education enters into practically every kind of development activity and involves nearly every governmental agency and innumerable voluntary organizations. Most of them, however, have a compulsion to "go it alone" and to avoid meshing their efforts with those of sister agencies operating in the same geographic areas and serving the same basic clientele. An additional complication, though on the whole perhaps a fortunate one, is that (unlike formal education) nonformal education depends on no single national budget. Its resources come in many forms from many sources, most of which are inaccessible to formal education. However, just as adult education was in the past the half-starved orphan of ministries of education, nonformal training and extension programs in specialized agencies dealing with agriculture, social welfare, health, public works, and so forth, also tend to get a low budgetary priority.

A further handicap in virtually all countries is the lack of any efficient system for providing competent professional support services, such as program design and evaluation, staff training, preparation of training materials and various types of technical assistance, to the different ministries and other organizations involved in nonformal education. Because of the previously mentioned compulsion of each organization to be self-contained and independent of other organizations, the quality, coverage, and effectiveness of their respective nonformal education activities often fall far short of what they could be if the same resources were used in concert with those of other agencies.

Finally, many types of nonformal education programs, particularly those with no ensured source of continuing annual income, often have limited survival power. They start with enthusiasm, run for a while, and then disappear. This is not always bad, though. Not infrequently a nonformal education program, based on voluntary learner participation, has gone out of business because its intended clients voted against it with their feet. After sampling it, they stayed away because, by their reckoning, they did not derive enough benefit to justify their investment of time and effort, a common occurrence among adult literacy classes. This continuous consumer evaluation and "voting" helps to keep nonformal education programs on their toes, except in cases such as malfunctioning agricultural extension services whose survival is virtually guaranteed by an annual allocation from the public budget. What a difference it could make if there were an equivalent kind of effective consumer evaluation to keep formal schools on their toes!

THE ENRICHMENT OF INFORMAL EDUCATION

As noted earlier the most ubiquitous and, in the long haul, most important type of education on the supply side of any nation's education equation is informal learning—the spontaneous, unstructured learning that goes on daily in the home and neighborhood, behind the school and on the playing field, in the workplace, marketplace, library and museum, and through the various mass media, all of which constitute a person's informal learning environment. What an individual can learn from his or her particular environment, however, is confined to what that environment has to offer. Thus, the pertinent question to be asked here is: What progress has been made over the past 10 to 20 years toward enriching the educative potentialities of informal learning environments around the world?

Obviously no one can answer this question with any degree of precision, but is is nevertheless important to ask and to think about seriously. One reason the question is seldom the object of serious thought is that most people automatically assume governments can do nothing about informal learning, that they can only run such organized activities as schools and agricultural or health services. But a moment's reflection shows that a government's cultural, information, and broadcasting policies and programs can have a sizable impact—for better or worse—on the learning environments of the young and old alike. Government policies that, through tax incentives or public subsidies and freedom of the press, for example, encourage private organizations engaged in useful educational, cultural, and similar activities can have a profound long-run influence on the quality of any nation's informal learning environment. Seldom are such matters considered and weighed with an eye to the contribution each can make to enriching and broadening a nation's entire learning network, beyond what organized formal and nonformal education can do.

Significant Changes in Learning Environments

It is especially difficult to trace what has been happening in recent years to these informal educational environments of people in different parts of the world. Some useful clues, however, about certain important aspects of the matter can be obtained by examining available evidence on changes in the education level of parents and in the availability of various types of information and cultural materials and media.

The Rise in Parental Education. If we accept a view widely held today among behavioral scientists, namely, that the education level of a child's parents is likely to have a profound and lasting influence on the child's lifelong values and behavior, including his or her appetite for learning, we can conclude that an increasing proportion of all babies born each year throughout the world are coming into a somewhat richer home-learning environment than their predecessors. This is certainly one of the important benefits of the great worldwide growth of enrollments and participation rates since the early 1950s. It has meant that a higher proportion of today's young parents 20 to 40 years old have had more years of formal education than their parents or grandparents had. Moreover, this trend is likely to continue for many years. There are, of course, a great many exceptions, especially among children of the poorest rural and urban families in developing countries where universal primary schooling has not yet been established. But it is to be hoped that their children and grandchildren will fare better.

Having more years of formal schooling than one's parents, of course, does not necessarily make one "better educated" in the larger sense, nor a better parent. We all know of examples to the contrary. But we are speaking here of the average, not the exceptions that prove the rule. In all events, the belief that education produces better parents has been an article of faith in all societies the world over for many years, and practical experience on the whole appears to validate that faith.

Publication of Books. Another widely shared view among child development experts is that the availability of books, magazines, and newspapers, in and around the home, significantly strengthens a young child's informal learning environment and later performance in school. This, of course, is another of those generalizations that is broadly valid but not an ironclad rule. The figures shown in Appendix Table 3.5 on world trends in book production reveal two important trends: (1) a significant rise in the number of book titles produced per million inhabitants between 1960 and 1980 in all regions and (2) enormous disparities in this respect between the developed and developing regions.

To cite the extremes: in 1980, 542 book titles per million inhabitants were published in Europe (including the U.S.S.R.) against 28 per million population in all of Africa. Looked at from a different angle, Africa, Asia, and Latin America, with some 70 percent of the world's entire population, produced only 27 percent of the world's book titles in 1980. By contrast, Europe, the U.S.S.R., and North America, with only 20 percent of the world's population, published nearly three quarters of all the books. These regional totals, of course, mask great differences among individual countries. Within Asia and the Middle East, for example, the number of titles published in 1980 was about 46,000 in Japan, 13,000 in India, 1300 each in Pakistan and Bangladesh, and only 200 in Saudi Arabia. In Africa in the same year, Egypt published about 1700 titles; Nigeria, 2300; Tunisia, 100; Mali, only 6; and several of the smaller and lower income countries, none at all. In Latin America annual book production in the late 1970s ranged from about 18,000 titles in Brazil to less than 400 in Chile, and apparently none at all in several countries. By contrast, the United States and the U.S.S.R. both published an average of about 85,000 titles in 1978; West Germany, more than 50,000; the United Kingdom, more than 38,000; France, about 25,000; and the Netherlands more than 13,000. In relation to their smaller populations, the Scandinavian countries were among the largest publishers of all. These intercountry differences, within and among regions, are partly explained by differences in size and income levels, but undoubtedly another major part of the explanation lies in significant educational and cultural differences.

Circulation of Newspapers. The circulation of daily newspapers is another significant indicator of what has been happening to the informal learning environments in various regions and also of the prevalence of literacy. The average circulation per thousand inhabitants, as shown in Appendix Table 3.6, rose substantially between 1965 and 1979 throughout the developing world: in Africa from 11 to 20, in Asia from 41 to 70; and in Latin America from 76 (1972) to 95 in 1979. Newspaper circulation also rose, though less sharply, in Europe, the U.S.S.R, and North America. Again, however, we find enormous regional disparities. Compare, for example, the circulation of 394 per thousand population in the U.S.S.R. and 265 per thousand in Europe with Africa's 20 per thousand, Asia's 70 per thousand and Latin America's 95 per thousand.

Radio, Television, and Film. Since 1965 more and more of the world's information, education, news, and entertainment has been provided by the electronic media of radio and television, with films lagging well behind.

Seating capacity of movie houses per thousand inhabitants, shown on

Appendix Table 3.7, leveled off or declined during the 1970s in all regions (except for a small increase in North America). This decline probably resulted largely from depressed economic conditions, especially in the developing regions and, in the case of Europe and North America, from the growing competition of television.

The number of radio and TV transmitters and receiving sets, on the other hand, increased sharply throughout the world between 1965 and 1979 (see Appendix Tables 3.8 and 3.9). The boom in radio and television in North America was so great during this period that by 1980 there were more than 600 TV sets per thousand inhabitants and an average of almost 2 radio sets per individual. By contrast, Africa had only 87 radio receivers per thousand inhabitants in 1980 (up from 33 in 1965) and only 15.3 TV sets per thousand (up from 1.9 in 1965). The number of radio receivers totaled 110 per thousand people in Asia in 1980 (up from 39 in 1965), and more than doubled in Latin America to 302 per thousand. The number of television receivers also expanded rapidly in these two regions but were still far scarcer than radio sets. In Europe and the U.S.S.R., television was rapidly catching up with radio.

The most striking international communications breakthrough in this period was the introduction of intercontinental communication satellites, capable of bringing major news events—an Olympic meet, a coronation, a war, even close-ups of men landing on the moon—instantaneously into homes in the far corners of the earth. This incredible technological development has enormous implications for the informal learning environment of hundreds of millions of people throughout the world.

Although the content and quality of the "messages" conveyed by these electronic learning media often leave much to be desired, many highly informative and instructive broadcasts enable vast numbers of children and adults to learn important and interesting things about the world that they could never learn in school.

Apart from the great increases in reading materials and the electronic media over the past 20 years, the substantial increase in the number of and attendance at public libraries, museums, theaters, exhibitions, and other important vehicles of knowledge, ideas, and culture has further enriched the informal learning environments and the lives of great numbers of people.

SOME PRELIMINARY CONCLUSIONS

We pause here to see where our unfolding analysis has taken us thus far and where it will move in the pages ahead.

We set out in this chapter to draw a picture of the supply side of the world's educational equation, which could then be compared with the sketch of learning needs on the demand side of the equation developed in the previous chapter. Because the supply side is too large a subject to be dealt with in a single chapter of reasonable length, we decided for convenience to divide it into two parts, focusing on the quantitative dimensions in the present chapter and on the qualitative dimensions in Chapter 4. After examining these dimensions, we should be in a position to compare the two sides of the world's educational equation and identify major gaps requiring special attention.

Even at this stage, however, some preliminary conclusions can be drawn. First, any adequate assessment of a nation's, or the world's, educational supply provisions requires an examination not only of its formal education system but also of its nonformal and informal learning provisions and resources. Together these constitute a complex lifelong learning network that serves a great variety of people's changing learning needs from infancy and youth to old age.

The second conclusion concerns the monumental quantitative expansion of formal education systems throughout the world since the early 1950s. In the course of this massive growth, which has been mainly a linear expansion of inherited prewar educational models, the structural profile of educational systems has been greatly altered. This alteration is mainly the result of differential rates of expansion at different education levels, and between urban and rural areas in the case of developing countries. This particular pattern of expansion has created (or exacerbated) some important problems of maladjustment that will be examined in later chapters.

The third conclusion concerns the prospects for future quantitative growth of formal education. The outlook for industrial countries is already fairly clear, at least in general terms. Their great educational expansion that began in the 1950s reached its greatest momentum in the 1960s, then slowed down sharply in the 1970s and came to a virtual halt by 1980. There is little reason to expect any major revival in the developed world during the next two decades of the earlier large expansion to meet the needs of more school-age children and youth, although an increased number of them will have to be accommodated, starting in the mid-1980s, as a result of the second-generation baby boom which has grown out of the larger, earlier one. There is a strong likelihood, however, of a steady increase of enrollments (mainly part time) on the part of older youth and adults (nontraditional students) seeking to update and continue their education for occupational and other reasons, especially at the postsecondary level. Most of these, however, can be accommodated in existing facilities and, to a substantial degree, by existing staff.

The pace of educational growth had also slowed substantially in most developing countries by the late 1970s, though generally not as soon or as drastically as in the developed countries. Because of their continuing population growth, however, and their still relatively low educational participation rates (especially in rural areas), these countries will be under strong pressure to continue their educational expansion for many years. But their practical ability to do so is in serious doubt, except for the relatively few in an unusually favorable economic position and a number of others with an especially strong political commitment to educational expansion at the sacrifice of other public services. In short, the future educational picture in the developing world promises to be mixed—ranging, at one extreme, from a few countries that will continue to expand substantially (though at a slower rate than previously) to a much larger number at the other extreme that will find it difficult to expand at all.

The fourth conclusion is that nonformal education, contrary to the slowing growth trend in formal education in the 1970s, experienced a strong surge of growth, especially in developing countries. Much of this increase was associated with the new policy emphasis on rural development and on meeting the basic needs of both the rural and urban poor. The extent to which this growth will continue hinges heavily on the degree to which this new emphasis is sustained in coming years and implemented on a much broader scale.

The final conclusion pertains to the growth of informal education or, more precisely, to the strengthening of informal learning environments around the world over the past two decades. Here the most difficult measurement problems of all are encountered. Nevertheless, strong indirect and measurable evidence, relating particularly to the increasing average educational attainment of young parents and to substantial growth in the print and electronic communications media, shows that informal learning environments in most of the world have been substantially enriched. As with other educational modes and resources, however, there are severe disparities between the developing and developed world. This important area of informal human learning, which has been neglected by educational analysis in the past, merits much more attention in the future by educational analysts, planners, and policymakers.

NOTES

1. U.S. Office of Education, *Education in the U.S.S.R.: Current Status of Higher Education* (Washington, D.C.: U.S. Department of Health, Education, and Welfare, Office of Education, U.S. Government Printing Office, 1980), p. 33.

2. Franciszek Januszkiewicz, Jan Kluczynski, and Stefan Kwiatkowski, "Higher Education in European Socialist Countries: Current Conditions—Developing Trends—Perspective," paper prepared for International Council for Educational Development (Warsaw, Poland: Research Institute for Science Policy, Technological Progress and Higher Education, 1979).
3. U.S. Office of Education, *Education in the USSR.*
4. UNESCO, *Wastage in Primary and General Secondary Education: A Statistical Study of Trends and Patterns in Repetition and Drop-out* (Paris: UNESCO, Office of Statistics, November 1980).
5. Government of India, "Interim Report from Working Group on Universalization of Elementary Education" (New Delhi, Ministry of Education and Social Welfare, 1977).
6. Birger Fredriksen, "Progress Towards Regional Targets for Universal Primary Education: A Statistical Review," paper presented at a conference of the United Kingdom Development Studies Association at the University of London Institute of Education, June 20, 1980.
7. UNESCO, *Trends and Projections of Enrolment, 1960–2000 (as assessed in 1982) (Paris: UNESCO, Division of Statistics on Education, Office of Statistics, March 1983).*
8. Ibid., Table 12, p. 42.
9. UNESCO, *Estimates and Projections of Illiteracy* (Paris: UNESCO, Division of Education Statistics, Office of Education, September 1978), p. 111.
10. Manzoor Ahmed and Philip H. Coombs, eds. *Education for Rural Development: Case Studies for Planners* (New York: Praeger Publishers, 1975); Philip H. Coombs, ed., *Meeting the Basic Needs of the Rural Poor: The Integrated, Community-Based Approach* (New York: Pergamon Press, 1980).
11. William J. Platt, "Toward Initial Learning Systems," in *Convergence* Vol. IX, No. 1 (Canada: International Council for Adult Education, 1976).
12. Ahmed and Coombs, *Education for Rural Development;* and Coombs, *Meeting the Basic Needs of the Rural Poor.*

Appendix Table 3.1 Growth of Enrollments by Levels and Regions, 1960–80[a]

Region	Level of Education	Number Enrolled			Percentage Increase 1960–1980
		1960	1970	1980[b]	
Developed countries	Primary	124,077	137,711	125,454	1
	Secondary	46,429	70,519	80,574	72
	Higher	9,599	21,105	29,719	214
	Total	180,105	229,335	235,747	31
Developing countries	Primary	121,982	204,343	291,968	142
	Secondary	21,788	51,034	96,611	358
	Higher	2,625	7,037	16,763	523
	Total	146,395	263,483	405,342	181
Africa	Primary	19,312	33,372	61,284	218
	Secondary	1,885	5,353	13,798	636
	Higher	185	479	1,366	709
	Total	21,382	39,204	76,448	259
Latin America	Primary	27,601	47,062	64,549	134
	Secondary	3,039	7,428	17,655	493
	Higher	573	1,640	5,156	831
	Total	31,212	56,229	87,361	182
South Asia	Primary	73,595	121,296	168,854	128
	Secondary	16,196	37,439	61,561	298
	Higher	1,818	4,821	9,819	411
	Total	91,602	163,556	236,234	163

[a]Does not include the People's Republic of China, the Democratic People's Republic of Korea, and Namibia.

[b]Adjusted for country differences in the length and official age span of elementary schooling.

Source: UNESCO, *Trends and Projections of Enrolment, 1960–2000 (as assessed in 1982)* (Paris: UNESCO, Division of Statistics on Education, Office of Statistics, March 1983), pp. 60–62.

Appendix Table 3.2   Growth of Enrollment Ratios by Age Groups, 1960, 1970, and 1980

Region	Age Groups	Percentage of Age Group Enrolled at Any Level		
		1960	1970	1980
North America	6–11	100	100	100
	12–17	92	95	96
	18–23	29	46	51
Europe	6–11	89	93	94
	12–17	59	70	79
	18–23	12	21	29
Africa	6–11	34	43	63
	12–17	16	26	37
	18–23	2	4	8
South Asia	6–11	48	58	66
	12–17	19	28	32
	18–23	3.4	7	9
Latin America and Caribbean	6–11	58	72	81
	12–17	37	51	64
	18–23	6	11	22

Source: UNESCO, *Trends and Projections of Enrolment by Level and by Age, 1960–2000 (as assessed in 1982)* (Paris: UNESCO, Division of Statistics on Education, Office of Statistics, March 1983).

Appendix Table 3.3 Annual Percentage Rates of Enrollment Growth by
Levels and Regions, 1960–80

Region	Level of Education	1960–65	1965–70	1970–75	1975–80[a]
Developed countries	Primary	1.5	0.6	−1.0	−0.9
	Secondary	6.3	2.3	2.4	0.3
	Higher	9.2	7.2	5.2	1.8
	Total	3.3	1.6	0.7	−0.2
Developing countries	Primary	6.4	4.2	3.9	3.4
	Secondary	10.6	7.6	6.7	6.0
	Higher	11.9	8.9	10.9	7.2
	Total	7.2	4.9	4.7	4.
Africa	Primary	6.4	4.9	6.3	6.2
	Secondary	11.6	10.4	10.4	9.5
	Higher	10.9	9.0	13.5	8.7
	Total	6.9	5.6	7.1	6.8
Latin America and Caribbean	Primary	5.6	5.4	3.6	2.8
	Secondary	10.4	8.6	10.5	7.3
	Higher	9.8	12.4	17.4	7.1
	Total	6.2	6.0	5.2	3.9
South Asia	Primary	6.7	3.6	3.4	2.8
	Secondary	10.6	7.0	5.2	5.0
	Higher	12.8	7.8	8.0	6.7
	Total	7.5	4.4	4.0	3.5

[a]UNESCO provisional estimates.

Source: UNESCO, *Trends and Projections of Enrolment (as assessed in 1982)* (Paris: UNESCO, Division of Statistics on Education, Office of Statistics, March, 1983), Table 1, p. 11.

Appendix Table 3.4   Enrollment Increments by Five-Year Periods, by Regions and Education Levels, 1960–80 (in thousands)

Region	Level of Education	Number Enrolled			
		1960–65	1965–70	1970–75	1975–80
Developed countries	Primary	9,652	3,982	−6,491	−5,765
	Secondary	16,622	7,468	8,984	1,071
	Higher	5,317	6,189	6,049	2,565
	Total	31,591	17,639	8,542	−2,129
Developing countries	Primary	44,669	37,692	42,523	45,103
	Secondary	14,287	16,029	20,124	24,383
	Higher	1,971	2,441	4,779	4,948
	Total	60,927	56,162	67,426	74,434
Africa	Primary	6,992	7,068	11,973	15,939
	Secondary	1,384	2,084	3,428	5,017
	Higher	126	168	423	465
	Total	8,502	9,320	15,824	21,421
Latin America and Caribbean	Primary	8,609	10,853	9,190	8,297
	Secondary	1,939	2,550	4,863	5,263
	Higher	341	725	2,015	1,503
	Total	10,889	14,129	16,068	15,063
South Asia	Primary	28,036	19,665	22,296	21,261
	Secondary	10,550	10,693	10,749	13,373
	Higher	1,494	1,516	2,265	2,733
	Total	40,080	31,874	35,310	37,367

Source: UNESCO, *Trends and Projections of Enrolment, 1960–2000 (as assessed in 1982)* (Paris: UNESCO, Division of Statistics on Education, Office of Statistics, March 1983).

Appendix Table 3.5   World Book Production by Regions, 1960–80

Region	Number of Titles (in hundreds)			Titles per Million Inhabitants		
	1960	1970	1980	1960	1970	1980
Europe and U.S.S.R.	239	317	406	374	464	542
North America	18	83	116	91	367	468
Africa	5	8	13	19	23	28
Asia	51	75	145	53	62	56
Latin America	17	22	34	79	78	93

Source: UNESCO, *Statistical Yearbook, 1982* (Paris: UNESCO, Office of Statistics, 1982).

Appendix Table 3.6   Daily Newspapers by Region, 1965 and 1979

Region	Number of Newspapers		Circulation per Thousand Inhabitants	
	1965	1979	1965	1979
Europe	2200	1740 (1977)	256	265 (1977)
U.S.S.R.	640	690 (1977)	264	394 (1977)
North America	2200	1910	247	258
Africa	200	170	11	20
Asia	640	2420	41	70
Latin America	1211 (1972)	1210	76 (1972)	95

Source: UNESCO, *Statistical Yearbooks* (Paris: UNESCO, Office of Statistics, 1966, 1974, 1980, and 1981).

Appendix Table 3.7 Movie Theaters and Seating Capacity by Region, 1965, 1970, and 1978

Region	Number of Movie Theaters (in hundreds)			Seating Capacity per Thousand Inhabitants		
	1965	1970	1978	1965	1970	1978
Europe and U.S.S.R.	193.6	213	207	120	135	112 (1977)
North America	18.5	16	18	35	50	53
Africa	2.6	3	3	5	6	5
Asia	16.4	15	18	6	8	8
Latin America	—	12	10	—	25	19

Source: UNESCO, *Statistical Yearbooks* (Paris: UNESCO, Office of Statistics, 1980, 1981, 1982).

Appendix Table 3.8   Radio Broadcasting Transmitters and Receivers by Region, 1965, 1979, and 1980

Region	Number of Transmitters		Receivers per Thousand Inhabitants	
	1965	1979	1965	1980
Europe	4170	6190 (1977)	249	381 (1977)
U.S.S.R.	410	3500 (1977)	319	515 (1977)
North America	6170	9800	1173	1970
Africa	500	850	33	87
Asia	1390	2900	39	110
Latin America	3470	4350	138	302

Source: UNESCO, *Statistical Yearbooks* (Paris: UNESCO, Office of Statistics, 1980, 1981, 1982).

Appendix Table 3.9 Television Transmitters and Receivers by Region, 1965, 1979, 1980

Regions	Regular TV Transmitters		TV Receivers per Thousand Inhabitants	
	1965	1979	1965	1980
Europe	3,550	16,300 (1977)	132	264 (1977)
U.S.S.R.	650	1,840 (1977)	69	238 (1977)
North America	2,820	4,450	355	619
Africa	100	260	1.9	15.3
Asia	1,100	10,400	18	54
Latin America	250	700	32	107

Source: UNESCO, *Statistical Yearbook* (Paris: UNESCO, Office of Statistics, 1980, 1982).

CHAPTER 4

THE CHANGING QUALITATIVE DIMENSIONS

THE PICTURE sketched above of the supply side of the world's educational equation is incomplete, for it does not include its qualitative dimensions. In other words, it reveals nothing about the critical issue that is central to the educational process—the nature and worth of what is actually taught to and learned by real people in a real world by means of formal educational systems and nonformal education programs. To complete this picture, the present chapter focuses on questions bearing on these qualitative dimensions.

Two preliminary points should be emphasized at the outset. First, *qualitative dimensions* means much more than the quality of education as customarily defined and judged by student learning achievements, in terms of the traditional curriculum and standards. Quality, as viewed here, also pertains to the *relevance* of what is taught and learned—to how well it fits the present and future learning needs of the particular learners in question, given their particular circumstances and prospects. It also refers to significant changes in the educational system or subsystem itself, in the nature of its inputs (students, teachers, facilities, equipment, and supplies); its objectives, curriculum, and educational technologies; and its socioeconomic, cultural, and political environment.

Second, the questions to be considered are, as the 1968 report acknowledged, shot through with imponderables. "In grappling with them," and here we repeat the language of that report, "we can go astray if we oversimplify, overgeneralize, overreact—or if we seek only what we want to find, and find only what we seek." As it happened, however, few educational policymakers and planners did in fact grapple seriously with these questions during the hectic years when boosting enrollment statistics through linear expansion of inherited educational systems took precedence over all else. The consequences, underlined in the 1968 report, were as follows:

- Not only was the quality of education (in the narrower conventional sense) deteriorating in many places, but educational systems were becoming increasingly maladjusted in relation to the real learning needs of students and the development needs of their changing societies.
- The maladjustments already visible constituted the essence of the world educational crisis.
- The crisis would steadily worsen unless educational systems made drastic qualitative changes from within so as to adapt themselves to the rapidly changing world of which they were a part.

The key question from the vantage point of the 1980s is this: To what extent, and in what ways, has this crucial qualitative side of the educational crisis seen in the late 1960s changed in recent years, and how is it likely to change in the future?

Answers to this and related questions cannot be reduced to precise statistical measurements as could those related to enrollments and educational expenditures. What is said about them tends to be rooted in individual judgments, which in turn take their bent from each observer's particular background and experience, social philosophy, values, and pedagogical biases. In fact, even the same words, such as quality, standards, relevance, and effectiveness, used by observers can mean very different things to different people, resulting in a great confusion of tongues when they venture to talk to each other. Precisely because of this, we must extend these introductory remarks a little further to explain how the basic concepts used in this chapter differ from the meanings commonly ascribed to them.

GETTING THE SUBJECT IN FOCUS

Criticisms of educational quality have a venerable pedigree. Recall the dialogues of Plato, in which Socrates "went after" the Sophist teachers of Athens. Yet, although criticism of educational quality has been heard over the milennia, the case today differs from that in times past. First, the difference entails a sharp rise in the decibel level; and second, what is heard comes from a broad spectrum of societies.

Two Views of "Standards"

Contemporary critics who bemoan "the disastrous decline of educational quality" include those who cite "the good old days" when they went to school. Their remembrance of what those days were like adds up to the following scenario: the curriculum stuck to the basics, with no frills and soft options; teachers were dedicated and conscientious, maintained strict discipline, and insisted on high standards; students took their studies more seriously, worked harder, and learned more than they do today. Ergo: "Turn back the clock to the good old days and back to the basics."

This is not the place to ask whether schooling ever really worked in the way claimed in an imagined Golden Age or whether schools have since "gone to pot" almost beyond redemption. This is the place, however, to ask a fundamental question about the critics. Are they animated by a realistic and valid concept of quality and standards, congruous with the nature of a swift-changing and greatly diversified world?

Their criticism appears to rest on an essentially static concept of quality. That is, it is tied on the one side to an earlier era's conventional school objectives, content, methods, and clientele and on the other side to a set of standards often viewed as immutable truths whose absolutes are good for all times and all places. Hence, any deviations from the time-honored curriculum and educational ground rules constitutes, prima facie, a dangerous heresy and a threat to quality and standards. So it was, for example, in Western Europe in the 1950s when great academic battles raged over proposals to eliminate Latin and Greek as compulsory requirements for university admission, so that students would have the option of substituting science and mathematics to prepare themselves for life in an increasingly technological world. The opponents insisted that this would undermine traditional standards and quality.

The fundamental issue is not whether all proposed educational changes are good, or conversely, whether all resistance to such proposals is wrongheaded. The issue is whether in the world of today it makes sense to perceive educational quality and standards in terms of fixed and universal absolutes.

Quality and standards are in fact *relative* matters—relative to the particular time and place and to particular learners and their circumstances. What constituted a good education for secondary students growing up in France or England or the United States in the nineteenth century is surely inadequate for their counterparts today and still more so for those who will be born in the twenty-first century. Thus, the challenge to educational planners and teachers today is not how to get back to the standards, curricula, and methods of the "good old days." It is how to formulate standards and programs that will prepare young people to function effectively on the rapidly moving and changing frontiers of the future. The criteria for judging any educational proposal must therefore be: education for whom, for what purpose, and under what conditions.

When put to such a test, an educational diet suitable for teenagers growing up in the milieu of today's postindustrial societies will not prove equally suitable to their counterparts growing up in the milieus of Afghanistan, Upper Volta, or Paraguay. Does this mean that young people in developing countries should be given a second-class education? It does not. Many young people in developing countries, however, are getting only a second-class version of some developed country's education, one that would not fit them even if the import was first class. They are getting the second-class version, with its gross misfit, in the dubious name of international standards—for the most part a misnomer referring to the prevailing educational orthodoxies of one or another metropolitan country.

False Comparisons

Many vociferous critics have committed the error of making invidious comparisons between the quality and effectiveness of educational systems in dissimilar countries, or between the past and present record of educational performance in the same country, ignoring the very different contexts. No less a distinguished person than Admiral Hyman Rickover, the "father" of the nuclear submarine, fell into this trap when he blamed the "intellectual softness" of American high schools for having allowed the Soviet Union to race ahead of the United States in the 1950s to launch the first sputnik into outer space. The criterion of excellence he is reported to have had in mind in making this sweeping indictment was the clearly superior academic achievement record of the gymnasium students in Holland, compared to that of the general run of American high school students. The error lay in the fact that American high schools served the entire age group, an extremely heterogeneous student body only some of whom were college-bound. By contrast, the Dutch gymnasiums at the time were catering to a small, rigorously selected, and homogeneous fraction of the whole age group, all of whom were preparing for entry into the university. If Rickover had compared the top-scoring 5 or 10 percent of Dutch and American students, the spread between their respective academic achievement levels would have been far smaller and less misleading, although improvements were unquestionably in order for American high schools and perhaps for the Dutch gymnasiums as well.

This same statistical rule was similarly overlooked by a recent Presidential Commission on Education in the United States, which cited with alarm the downward drift ever since 1950 of average student scores on the College Entrance Examination Board's Scholastic Aptitude Tests (SATs). In 1950, only a relative handful of all American high school students—those aspiring to gain admission to the most selective and prestigious colleges and universities—took the College Board tests. Since then, the proportion and diversity of students taking these tests have increased greatly to include practically all students with any thought of going on to any kind of postsecondary education. Inevitably the *average* scores have declined, but this in itself does not prove that the top-ranking students aspiring to enter the top-ranking higher institutions in the early 1980s—or, for that matter, the lower ranking students hoping to enter less selective institutions—have received a poorer quality secondary education than their respective counterparts in the early 1950s. The basic point is that over the past 30 years, in practically all countries, the rise in educational participation rates at each level has resulted in much larger student bodies and in greater diversity of their characteristics.

This does not deny the possibility that genuine erosion of quality has indeed occurred in many school systems. This possibility can never be ignored or glossed over. But it is also possible that the critics, like Don Quixote, are tilting at statistical windmills.

Democratic mass education does not automatically preclude the level of educational excellence achieved under the old elitist models. More education does not have to mean worse education. But we must recognize that this can happen, particularly because the task of a democratically oriented mass education system is inherently much more difficult than that of an elitist system. The mandate of the elitist system is to select "the best" through a series of increasingly fine-meshed academic screens; it is to groom them for top positions in the society, discarding all the rest as failures, as if on a social trash pile. The mandate of a democratic mass educational system, by contrast, is to develop not only the potentialities of the most talented but the potential of *every* member of each new generation, whatever that potential might be. To put it differently, the elitist system is expected to produce far more failures than successes, whereas the democratic mass system, despite its far larger and more diversified student clientele, is expected to produce *only* successes.

Here, then, is the key to why the newly "massified" education systems in the more developed world have encountered and continue to encounter pedagogical and social problems far more painful than those that beset their elitist predecessors. As for the developing countries, their pedagogical and social problems are doubly painful because their imported educational systems never fit them too well in the first place.

With these concepts and cautions, we can now return to the key question posed at the start of this chapter: What has been happening around the world to the qualitative dimensions of education?

IMPACT OF ENVIRONMENTAL CHANGES

In assessing and explaining the performance of the schools, most people, and even many professional educators, tend to focus almost exclusively on the internal "school factors," as if schools existed in a social vacuum. Clearly these internal school factors are crucially important, including such things as the objectives and curricula of the school, the competence and attitudes of the teachers, the materials and equipment they have to work with, and the educational technologies in use. But so also are the environmental factors, many of which have undergone great change in recent times. Some examples are cited briefly here and will be elaborated in later chapters.

Impact of the World Recession

The prolonged world recession and inflation that began in the early 1970s had multiple and mostly adverse repercussions on educational systems everywhere. The recession subverted educational budgets and teachers' salaries. It also wrought major changes on other fronts: in employment prospects that dashed the hopes and plans of students; in the curriculum and student academic choices; in the career expectations and morale of teachers and administrators; and in the public's attitude toward and support of schools and colleges. The recession also exacerbated the already serious educational malady that Ronald Dore aptly christened "The Diploma Disease," the frantic chasing after paper credentials, not for any intrinsic educational worth they presumably represented, but for their expected market and social-prestige value.[1]

Still, in the same way that some things appear more clearly against a dark background, the deeply troubled economic conditions, and especially the sharp rise in youth unemployment, helped clarify the thoughts of educators, government officials, employers, and other concerned parties. They began to reexamine the validity of their conventional assumptions about the relationship between education and work and to search for ways to smooth the rocky transition of young people from the world of schooling to the world of work. Concurrently, nonformal education was invested with a greater measure of legitimacy, and more attention was paid to what it might contribute to the solution of the complex problems bearing on the relationship between education and employment.

Sociocultural Upheavals

Since the end of World War II, basic social institutions, belief and value systems, and codes of behavior—the cement that holds societies together and gives them their special identity—underwent substantial changes in all societies. But the pace of change accelerated considerably in the 1970s, with serious side effects for the schools. The precise causes and manifestations differed in kind and intensity from one country to the next, but all were part of a worldwide pattern of fundamental cultural transformation.

In the postindustrial Western societies, for example, sociological observers called attention to the breakdown of the family as the most basic guardian and educator of children and youth. They cited sharp increases in divorce rates and single-parent families, the rise in the proportion of working mothers whose "latchkey kids" returned from school each day to an empty home, the growing generation gap, the breakdown of communication between parents and children, and the frightening increase in runaway adolescents. Nor was this all. They noted the declining influence of religious institutions on both the young and the old and the lessened role of agencies such as youth organizations, social groups, and small employers that had long made their important respective contributions to the education, socialization, and upbringing of young people. The clergy, politicians, journalists, and worried parents decried the decline of moral standards—whether the index was the rise in teenage pregnancies, the spread of alcohol and drug abuse, the appalling increase in automobile and motorcycle accidents involving young people, or the upsurge of youth crimes.

We will look more closely at these cultural, social, and political changes in a later chapter, and at the impact they have had and are continuing to have on education. The pertinent point here is that the situation was ready-made for seeking scapegoats, and the schools turned up number one, with television a close second and overblown government bureaucracies right behind. School authorities, for their part, noted that the root of the disturbing problems was in the home itself. Too many parents were sloughing off onto the schools their own responsibilities, which the schools were neither designed nor equipped to handle. If, as surveys showed, the average child was spending more hours a week before a television tube than in the classroom and not doing homework or reading good books, or if the child was allowed to run loose on the town with an unwholesome peer group, free of parental supervision or constraint, there was little the school and teachers could do to control the situation.

Nevertheless, the schools more and more, both by public pressure and by choice, attempted to move into the vacuum by adding new objectives, activities, and personnel. Many, for example, introduced courses in driver training, sex education, drug abuse, and various practical training courses aimed at making teenagers more employable. They also introduced various "fun courses" with little intellectual content or rigor, designed to keep nonacademically inclined potential dropouts in school until graduation. Many schools also installed psychological counselors, family guidance workers, and, in the worst situations, security officers to police corridors. In most schools, especially secondary schools, it was at best an uphill fight, but for those in the decaying central cities it often seemed a losing battle.

It would be wrong, however, to overdraw the negative aspects of the picture—dead wrong to assume that all young people in the industrialized countries of the West were drawn into the dark side of this so-called youth counterculture. Besides, as will be noted later, there were some bright and promising educational and cultural developments in the 1970s, both within and outside the schools, affecting infants, children, youth, and adults.

These negative tendencies, including disenchantment of youth with established authority and the overthrowing of old codes of taste and behavior were not confined to the West. They showed up in Eastern socialist countries as well, though they were generally more constrained and less publicized.

Still, taking the world as a whole, the greatest social, political, and cultural turbulence during the 1970s was experienced in many of the developing nations, although, again, there were wide variations in both form and intensity. The Western-model schools and especially the universities, as carriers of foreign cultural and intellectual ideas and forms of behavior, were generally riven by such turmoil. Students typically were in the vanguard of political protest movements, often aimed at dethroning domestic rulers or discrediting particular foreign powers. Not all student demonstrations, however, were animated by idealistic and selfless objectives. In India, for example, universities have been continuously hit by self-serving and frequently violent protests in which students have demanded their "rights." Some of the rights demanded have been in reaction to official crackdowns on widespread cheating on examinations, or in protest against examination questions allegedly "off the syllabus" and, therefore, "unfair." Many others, which have often led to extensive property destruction and bloody police confrontations, involved demands for reduced student rates on buses or in restaurants and theaters. Whatever the purpose of particular strikes and demonstrations, be it political, cultural, or self-serving, the effects have seriously disrupted educational processes in many developing countries in all regions.

The examples cited of the impact of sociocultural forces on education in developed and developing countries barely scratch the surface of such a complex subject. But perhaps they suffice to make the main point. In an evaluation of the qualitative dimensions and trends in any educational system, program, or institution, whatever its level, nature, or form of organization, it is not enough to focus only on its internal affairs. Assessing the factors in its external environment that greatly influence its character and performance is equally important.

CHANGES IN THE SCHOOLS AND COLLEGES

The 1970s witnessed substantial changes and innovations in formal education systems all around the world, in their structures, objectives, curricula, teachers and teaching methods, and relations with their environment. Nonetheless, if one were to take a global photograph of all the world's schools and colleges and universities on a given day in the early 1980s, most would look almost exactly as they did in a picture taken 10, 20, or 30 years ago. As the French say, *"plus ça change, plus c'est la même chose"*—the more things change the more they stay the same.

Why the seeming paradox? True, as the record shows, a vast range of salutary changes were introduced in the majority of national education systems in the 1970s. For the most part, however, they were small, piecemeal changes and did not alter the basic framework, character, or direction of the system. What was, and still is needed, is much more fundamental change. Not that top educational administrators were blind to the need for far-reaching changes. Most of them by the early 1970s, caught by a rising crisis around them, were acutely aware of the urgent need for major changes, and many made valiant efforts to bring them about. But to institute even small changes in an educational system is hard. The surprising thing perhaps is that so many useful improvements were made in the 1970s, no doubt because, in contrast to earlier decades, the need for change had become far clearer, and the climate both inside and outside educational systems was generally much more conducive to change. Not that all the changes constituted a step forward; some clearly moved in the opposite direction.

Five internal school factors in particular strongly influence the quality, relevance, and effectiveness of education: objectives, curricula, teachers, teaching materials, and educational technologies. We will look at these, bearing in mind that, as in other matters, the picture with respect to these factors is very mixed, showing different degrees of improvement (or retrogression) in different places.

CHANGES IN OBJECTIVES AND CURRICULUM

The ambitious and lofty official statements of objectives of school systems and what is actually done are rarely congruous. It is far better, therefore, to judge school systems more by their deeds than by their verbal vaunts. Viewed from that perspective, most educational systems in both developed and developing countries have broadened their objectives since the 1960s in an attempt to serve more effectively certain important needs of national development as well as particular segments of their broadened student clienteles. Almost invariably, they added these new objectives without subtracting any of the old ones, thus enlarging their overall workload.

In the case of the developed countries, as already mentioned, the secondary schools increasingly assumed functions and tasks related to the care, behavior, guidance, occupational training, and general upbringing of children and teenagers—tasks that had previously been viewed as the prime responsibility of the family and other institutions. In doing so, however, the schools often had less time and energy left for more traditional education functions, starting with the three Rs, which everyone still expected them to perform better than ever.

At the university level in some developed countries, higher institutions did trim some objectives during the 1970s, often for the first time in memory. Prodded from one side by tightening budget constraints and from another by the shrinking employment market for certain types of graduates who were costly to produce and drained scarce resources away from other academic sectors, the higher institutions in question began to retrench. They cut various services, and in the extreme lopped off whole specialized departments and schools—always a painful process for all affected parties.

Many higher institutions in developing countries in the 1970s moved in the opposite direction. Despite their increasingly tight financial position, they added new objectives, including research and service functions as well as new courses. The added activities were often designed to plug gaps in programs relating to important national development needs—for example, effective managers of development projects and programs, competent top-level specialists for rural health programs, and a wider spectrum of agricultural research specialists. These countries, understandably and correctly, endeavored to free themselves from perpetual dependence on the universities of more developed countries to meet their high-level manpower needs. Even more than was true of the universities, nonuniversity postsecondary institutions in many developing countries tended to broaden and strengthen their programs, including their service activities, to accommodate pressing development needs in their particular area of specialization.

As for the secondary schools, in many developing countries their common condition in the 1970s was one of uncertainty about their objectives and programs. Well before the 1970s, many academic secondary schools that had long concentrated on preparing students for university entry tried to become multipurpose institutions serving a broader spectrum of students and needs, including specific types of occupational training, through "terminal" programs. In addition, various types and models of specialized secondary-training institutions, mostly imported, had been created earlier to meet different middle-level manpower needs. By 1970, however, the performance record of these modified academic schools and of the new occupationally oriented secondary-level training schools was burdened by disappointments and by shortfalls in earlier expectations. Among other things, their cost-effectiveness was often strikingly low when gauged by the meager success of their students in obtaining (or accepting) the kinds of jobs they were ostensibly trained for. Thus, by the 1970s, school authorities were caught in the cross-tensions between conflicting realities. They were more acutely aware than ever of the importance of preparing employable young men and women and of broadening the excessively narrow academic focus of the traditional secondary schools. Yet their earlier experiences with disappointments and failures made them hesitate to strike out in new directions.

It is impossible to estimate with any precision the extent and importance of curricular changes in education systems around the world since the late 1960s, though from the standpoint of volume, they undoubtedly exceeded those of comparable earlier periods. Merely to leaf through the mass of worldwide published reports on educational changes and innovations is enough to see that the overwhelming majority involved the curriculum—usually only one particular piece of it.

In developing countries, efforts to strengthen science and mathematics courses, notoriously weak areas in their old curricula, generally led the list of changes. Most of the countries that had inherited their curricula from colonial powers made strides in adapting the content of subjects such as history and geography to their own purposes. With the encouragement of international organizations, especially UNESCO, new subjects were injected into the school curriculum, either as distinct new courses or as new content infused into existing ones. Among the leading subjects on this list were development, environment, population, and, as a late starter, drug abuse. Many multilingual developing countries also tried, heroically, to come to grips with their acute and exceedingly difficult "language of instruction" problem, particularly at the primary level—a problem looked at more closely in a later chapter.

Education systems in the more developed countries tended to be preoccupied with two types of curriculum-related problems. The first involved updating, strengthening, and increasing teaching effectiveness in many of the old standby subjects, especially reading, mathematics, and science. The second, and much more difficult problem is inherent in any democratic mass educational system: the need to adapt the curriculum and methods to a more diversified student body—to faster and slower learners, to more and less academically motivated, to the wide spectrum of interests and career aspirations of students, and to the college-bound and the terminal students as well as the "undecideds."

Making fundamental curricular changes and improvements is not something that can be achieved merely by a manifesto and a flick of the wrist. (It is not too difficult for outside advisers to say what is wrong with the existing curriculum and how it should be altered and enriched. But *doing* it is a different matter.) To have any real chance of success, the first requirement is to achieve a wide understanding of what is proposed. The second is to generate a broad-based supportive consensus among those who will have to carry it out, the teachers and their supervisors who are scattered all across the country. This requires a major teacher-training effort and the careful preparation of teacher manuals, textbooks, and other appropriate teaching materials and aids. Merely to distribute these items physically is itself a major undertaking in countries with no warehouse facilities and poor postal services. All this, if well done, can easily take three or four years. Then comes the follow-up: checking on how things are going, answering queries from teachers, finding out how the students are taking it and how well they are learning, and perhaps making necessary adjustments in the light of feedback. And just about then, in the best of all worlds, it would be time to start updating and revising the curriculum again.

Even allowing for delays and misfires, however, available but fragmentary evidence suggests that curricular changes and improvements have been making greater headway in the educational systems of most countries over the past ten years than perhaps ever before.

THE CHANGING SUPPLY AND ROLES OF TEACHERS

The quality of education and the learning achievement of students depend heavily on the competence, personality, and dedication of the teacher. But this is not the whole story. They also depend on the conditions under which the teacher and students are working—for example, on whether the size of the class is manageable and its atmosphere conducive to learning, and whether there is an ample supply of equipment, textbooks, and other learning materials. Not least of all, they depend on the characteristics of the students themselves—on whether they are well nourished, physically and mentally healthy, strongly motivated to learn, and enjoy strong family support.

By 1980, the number of employed teachers had increased dramatically throughout the world over the levels of the 1960s, reflecting the steady expansion of teacher supply. As shown in Table 4.1, the increase during these 15 years for all levels combined was 33 percent in developed countries and 125 percent in developing countries. By far the greatest percentage increases were in higher education, where teacher costs per student are greatest, and the lowest percentage increases were in primary education. The latter fact ties in with the great lag referred to earlier in the quest of developing countries for universal primary education.

Table 4.1 Worldwide Growth of Teaching Staff, 1965–80 (Index: 1965 = 100)

	Year	First Level	Second Level	Third Level	Total
Developed Countries	1965	100	100	100	100
	1980	111	139	212	133
Europe (including U.S.S.R.)	1965	100	100	100	100
	1980	104	140	218	128
Northern America[a]	1965	100	100	100	100
	1980	117	139	203	139
Developing Countries	1965	100	100	100	100
	1980	196	261	432	225
Africa	1965	100	100	100	100
	1980	259	424	495	296
Asia	1965	100	100	100	100
	1980	170	222	290	194
Latin America[a]	1965	100	100	100	100
	1980	208	205	547	229

[a]As defined by UNESCO, Northern America includes Bermuda, Canada, Greenland, St. Pierre and Miquelon, and the United States of America. Latin America includes the rest of America.

Source: UNESCO, *Statistical Yearbook, 1982* (Paris: UNESCO, Office of Statistics, 1982).

The Teacher Situation in Industrialized Countries

In many industrial countries, the teacher supply pendulum swung so far in the 1970s, in combination with a shrinkage of demand, that the earlier shortages turned into troublesome surpluses, prompting education authorities to cut back teacher training programs. In England and Wales, for example, steps were taken to reduce the number of openings in teacher training colleges from 114,000 in 1971 to 45,000 by 1981 (painful news for many professors in these colleges and for teenagers aspiring to become teachers). However, these apparent teacher surpluses did not bring as much relief to harried school administrators as was at first expected. In many instances they proved to be a mirage.

The main factors that caused the shrinkage of teacher demand were, first, the relatively high participation rates that had by then been attained at all levels, and second, the decline in enrollments because of the sharp drop of birth rates in the 1960s. Interestingly enough, despite tightening budgetary constraints and shrinking primary and secondary school enrollments, most school systems in developed countries managed to maintain the size of their teaching staff fairly intact. The effect was a reduction in pupil/teacher ratios. In the United States, for example, the sum total of primary and secondary school enrollments fell from 51.4 million in 1969 to 47 million in 1979, whereas the average number of pupils per teacher declined from 22.3 to 18.8.[2] An OECD survey in the late 1970s showed similar reductions in the pupil/teacher ratio in other member states, and a number of them anticipated still further reductions in the 1980s.[3]

Many OECD countries took advantage of the improved teacher supply situation to provide special services to physically, mentally, and socially handicapped children and to enrich educational services for all students in such subjects as art and music. In Sweden and the United States, among others, schools in "problem neighborhoods" serving low-income pupils, often including numerous immigrant children, were given additional resources to recruit teachers with foreign language abilities and other special qualifications and to experiment with various types of alternative schools for students (mainly at the secondary level) who were misfits in the regular schools.

Developed countries also seized this opportunity to upgrade their teaching staffs by replacing unqualified with qualified teachers and by strengthening in-service training provisions for existing teachers. In France, large numbers of temporary auxiliary teachers who had been hired earlier to fill the gap were now replaced by fully certified tenure teachers. In Denmark the number of graduate-level replacement teachers available for primary and lower secondary schools rose from a mere 50 in 1974 to nearly 2000 in 1980; the proportion of university graduate teachers in the Norwegian schools was expected to grow from 83 percent in 1975 to 95 percent by 1990.

A study in the United States showed that public school teachers in the 1980s would be better prepared than their predecessors; by 1981 an all-time high of 99 percent of them possessed a four-year bachelor's degree, and about 50 percent had a master's or higher graduate degree, in contrast to less than 24 percent 20 years earlier.[4] At the postsecondary level in the United States the proportion of college and university teachers possessing a PhD degree had also moved up sharply; those without one were a rapidly vanishing species. By the early 1980s the American academic market for new PhDs had become so glutted that in most disciplines there were often several dozen eager applicants for any reasonably attractive college or university opening.

The much-heralded teacher surplus in developed countries soon changed its spots in several ways, and for several reasons. First, teacher-training enrollments decreased as students learned of the declining job prospects in teaching and shifted their aspirations to more promising fields. As a consequence, the output of newly trained teachers shrank and school officials had fewer candidates to choose from. Second, and especially worrisome from a longer range point of view, the average intellectual caliber of students who did opt for teacher training declined from previous levels. The dean of Stanford University's School of Education in an address to the National Academy of Education in 1981 reported with some alarm that in a recent study comparing the aptitude scores of college entrants preparing for different professions, those enrolled in teacher training came next to the bottom of the list.[5]

Third, despite the general softness of the market for teachers, acute shortages of well-qualified ones developed in certain fields, especially the sciences, mathematics, and technical subjects. To start with, fewer able secondary students were electing science and mathematics courses in the 1970s, in part because of the growing disenchantment among young people with a world that seemed dominated and threatened by science and technology, but also because of the growing shortage of able and stimulating secondary teachers who could attract students into these courses. Thus, the colleges and universities began receiving fewer able and well-prepared students desiring to major in science, mathematics, and technology—and to become teachers. Meanwhile, despite the recession, the competition of the industrial, commercial, and government market for science and technology graduates grew briskly during the 1970s, especially because of the rapid growth of the new computer, silicon chip, and other high technologies. As a result of this competition, new science and mathematics graduates could get in industry double the starting salary that the schools were able to offer, plus prospects of much faster advancement.

This shortage of science and mathematics teachers illustrates vividly the dilemma that education systems face when they get out of kilter with the changing needs and demands of the surrounding economy and society. What can such a system do, given its financial and other constraints, to put things right? One solution being attempted in some systems is to conduct crash courses to convert teachers in surplus fields, such as language and literature, into teachers of science, mathematics, and computer programming. No doubt this will succeed in some cases, when the individuals concerned happen to have an aptitude and fairly good grounding in science and mathematics waiting to be tapped. But it seems highly unlikely that there are enough such cases to meet the need, or that this is a satisfactory long-term solution. Obviously, the only real solution is to improve science and mathematics teaching and to encourage science and mathematics as an essential part of everybody's general education, starting with the elementary and secondary school and continuing through the college and university. But even this will not solve the problem as long as schools and colleges cannot compete successfully with other bidders for an adequate share of their own best science and mathematics graduates. A major fundamental stumbling block here is the uniform teacher salary schedules based on credential levels and years of service, irrespective of the subject taught or teaching ability.

If school systems scrapped this salary uniformity and paid what was required to compete with other bidders, they could, presumably, attract able people into science and mathematics teaching. However, it is hard to imagine any educational policy change that would anger teachers' unions more or create more divisiveness within teaching staffs. Understandably, therefore, policymakers shy away from the challenge to take this wild bull by the horns. They resort instead to such palliatives as special fellowships for college students willing to commit themselves to teacher training in scarcity fields.

The subject of teacher salaries, working conditions, and job security became a matter of increasing contention in the 1970s in more and more developed countries—and a spur to strengthened teacher union activities. The contributing factors, mentioned earlier, are worth restating. The combination of rapid inflation and tightening education budgets was causing a serious erosion of the real incomes of teachers, while falling enrollments and growing teacher surpluses were creating deep anxieties among teachers over job security—all coincident with a mounting criticism of schools and teachers for the alleged decline of quality and standards. A subtler but no less important contributor was the withering away of the high respect and status teachers had traditionally enjoyed in the community, which had inspired many able teachers to stick with their profession even though its financial rewards were lower than they could have received in other fields.

The natural response to these changed conditions on the part of many teacher organizations, which had long been sedate professional societies dedicated to promoting educational improvements, was to take on the characteristics and militant tactics of hard-bargaining trade unions. Countries and communities that had never known teacher strikes were soon besieged by them. All across the United States, for example, the social science curriculum took to the streets as children watched their teachers picketing the schools and chanting slogans, and as bewildered volunteer school board members found themselves sitting across the table from teachers at tense collective-bargaining sessions far into the night.

The bargaining often extended well beyond salary and fringe-benefit issues to such matters as imposing limits on working hours, class size, and pupil/teacher ratios; eliminating lunch-room and playground duties for teachers; paying extra for additional hours spent on after-school extra-curricular activities; and providing teacher aides to assist teachers and, in some cases, even security guards to protect them and the students against violent acts.

All this, combined with the increasing bureaucratization and sociological diversity of the greatly enlarged education systems, not only altered the atmosphere and human relations within the schools but also eroded their relations with parents and the community. The bargaining process also had a rigidifying effect that inhibited needed changes and innovations in the schools essential to improving their quality, efficiency, and effectiveness.

Another factor added to the inventory of teaching problems in developed countries. Teachers, including very able and motivated ones, in many schools lacked the supplies and equipment they needed for their work, especially in scientific and technical studies. Such items are usually the first to be cut when school budgets are under pressure. Ironically, a major reason for these shortages was the pressure of rising teacher costs and lower student/teacher ratios against tighter budget ceilings.

A related problem concerned the great difficulty teachers have trying to keep abreast of new knowledge in their particular subject, as well as new pedagogical developments. Teachers generally are given little time, incentive, or practical support for self-improvement. In-service training programs can help, but many of them that involve a scatter pattern of summer or weekend courses at a nearby college or university are hardly the answer. They are primarily designed as a means for teachers to accumulate credits toward a higher salary bracket rather than a means of enriching, updating, and upgrading the teachers' knowledge and competence.

Still, these problems and difficulties should neither be overdrawn nor allowed to obscure the brighter spots in the recent teaching picture in developed countries. An objective on-site examination of what is actually going on in many schools, and in many colleges and universities, belies the impression of apocalyptic disaster critics often convey. No doubt, all schools could stand improvement; they always could, and some are in far worse shape than others. In almost any country one can come upon horror stories about children who have completed primary and even lower secondary school and still cannot read a newspaper, much less a serious book; who cannot add, subtract, multiply, or divide a simple set of numbers; who cannot analyze a slightly complex problem or express themselves clearly either in writing or orally. Such conditions, wherever they exist, are certainly a proper cause for serious concern and corrective action. But they should not be blown all out of proportion to the rest of the picture. They are the dramatic stuff of which headlines are made and about which college professors write scathingly critical books attacking the schools. But just as lawbreakers get far more headlines than lawabiders, so also these dramatic cases of educational failure obscure the much larger number of cases of able and hardworking teachers helping students to learn better, and much more, than their parents and grandparents did a generation or two ago.

The Teacher Situation in Developing Countries

The problems of teachers and teaching conditions that troubled developed countries in the 1970s were mild compared with those that besieged developing countries. Here again, generalizations can be very misleading because the differences between individual schools, communities, and countries are just as great in the developing world as they are in the developed world.

Despite severe obstacles and handicaps, most developing countries managed somehow to enlarge their teaching staffs dramatically. In Africa, for example, as the figures in Table 4.1 show, the total number of teachers at the primary level grew between 1965 and 1980 by 159 percent, at the secondary level by 324 percent, and in higher education by 395 percent. Questions of quality aside, this was a tremendous accomplishment, unparalled in all history. But inevitably this growth slowed down in the latter half of the 1970s as the demand for new teachers declined. The demand declined not because the need for more teachers had diminished, but because the money to hire them was simply not available.

Countries unable to expand their teaching force further were faced with the ugly choice of either freezing enrollments, in the interest of preserving quality, at a time when the majority of their children were not even getting a full primary education, or spreading their teachers thinner and thinner over more and more students at the expense of quality. Largely under political necessity, they usually chose to sacrifice quality for quantity. Thus, in many places class sizes grew to grotesque proportions, often with a poorly trained and distraught teacher trying to keep order, and with few if any textbooks or other essential supplies and equipment to boost the teacher's productivity.

Some countries—Ethiopia is an example—adopted double and triple shifts in their primary schools, and sometimes even four daily shifts in secondary schools. These were straightforward measures to increase enrollment numbers, but how much learning the children acquired is problematic. This is not to say that double shifts per se inevitably lead to poorer learning results; there are cases that disprove this. But if the overriding objective is simply to produce higher enrollment statistics, whatever the cost in learning results, this is one obvious way to do it.

Paradoxically, despite severe budgetary constaints and makeshift efforts, the qualifications profile of the teaching staffs in many developing countries increased significantly between 1965 and 1980—that is to say, the proportion of "qualified" teachers with officially recognized credentials increased. It did not necessarily follow, however, that the quality of education increased correspondingly, for the quality of teacher training behind these credentials often left much to be desired. Moreover, because of the wide salary spread between unqualified and qualified teachers, the replacement of the former by the latter greatly boosted the teacher salary bill. In typical situations in which administrative and teacher salaries already accounted for well over 90 percent of total recurrent costs, this left little or no money in overstrained school budgets for the things teachers need to be productive—books, supplies, equipment, and in-service refresher training. These critical items, as well as the repair and maintenance of facilities, were usually the first to suffer when things had to be cut from the budget.

Thus, a great many teachers, both qualified and unqualified, were forced to teach with one arm tied behind them, like a farmer without a hoe or a plow. This often meant that everyone was going through the motions of schooling, but with little being learned. The travesty was compounded in many developing countries by a policy of automatic promotion of pupils, designed to open up space for oncoming students and to reduce dropouts. In its actual operation it often meant that pupils who automatically moved up to the next rung of the academic ladder without having gotten their feet firmly planted on the previous one would slip further and further behind.

Again, this picture, though very real and pervasive, should not be over-drawn, for a random sampling will reveal many encouraging exceptions of cases in which good teachers, reasonably supplied and equipped, have produced praiseworthy learning results. Unfortunately, these cases are largely found in the urban areas and typically involve middle- and upper-class neighborhoods and children with strong parental support. The rural areas, as mentioned earlier, often resemble semiarid education deserts devoid of quality education. Not only do rural areas usually get the poorest teachers but they also have a high proportion of poor children with the weakest family support. These are the children who really need the best teachers but they are the last to get them. To make matters worse, rural children in tribal and ethnic areas are often obliged to cope with an utterly unfamiliar foreign medium of instruction, which even the teacher may not know well.

The picture at the university level in developing countries is relatively bright even if far from ideal, as a result of the substantial progress made since the 1950s in strengthening the supply of high-level manpower in most developing countries (though here again there are wide variations). A decade or two ago, hundreds of professors from Europe and North America were standing in as teachers in the new colleges and universities of developing countries, until such time as enough of their own bright young people had been trained abroad and could take over. By the end of the 1970s this picture had changed dramatically. Even in Africa, which was most dependent on foreign secondary and higher education teachers, the visitor today finds an impressive number of first-rate local faculty members in these relatively new universities. Many are doing fine teaching and, in some cases, good research as well—when they get the chance. But they are usually quick to point out some problems. A frequent one is that they are often grossly overloaded with students. Though this condition exists in most countries in developing regions, it is perhaps most dramatically manifest in India because of its extraordinary size and number of colleges and universities, and because any serious effort at selective admission has long since been abandoned there. As a result, even in the most prestigious institutions, the classrooms and lecture halls are often so overcrowded that students line the floors and window sills and can scarcely hear the professors' voice, much less have a dialogue with them. Able Indian commentators regard this as a caricature of a university education. A similar condition can be found in a number of Latin American countries. Thus far, at least, some African countries have managed to hold on to relatively strict admission standards and to avoid such a destructive tidal wave.

Another problem frequently mentioned by faculty members, particularly those with higher degrees earned in major research universities abroad, is their feeling of intellectual isolation and stagnation. They are cut off from the flow of new developments and professional literature in their particular field and from the stimulating discussions with their professors and intellectual peers they had come to value so highly overseas. Often adding to this frustration is the lack of opportunities to do research, which played such a central role in their foreign training and which they had come to view as a necessary foundation for good university teaching. But many also confess that the research methodologies they learned in an industrialized country and the research problems on which they cut their teeth were often not relevant to their own country's problems. To that extent they felt somewhat miseducated.

EDUCATIONAL TECHNOLOGIES

Any review of trends in the qualitative aspects of education around the world would be incomplete without an examination of recent developments in educational technology and the important lessons in this area brought to light by extensive research and evaluation studies in the 1970s.

People tend to equate the term educational technology with the new media and electronic devices that have grown out of the postwar communications revolution—television and miniaturized radios, audio and videocassettes, "teaching machines," language laboratories, computers, and communication satellites. It is as if education never had any technologies until these appeared on the scene—a narrow view, which is also one of the major reasons the hopes that rode on so many new media experiments have ended in disappointment. The devices in question certainly have a high *potential* for assisting learning; properly used, they can help increase the quality and availability of education at affordable costs. But all too often in the past, enthusiastic advocates of one or another particular new technology have mistakenly regarded it as a complete and self-contained teaching/learning system in itself instead of seeing it as only one component of such a system. Such one-eyed promoters in the 1950s and 1960s often viewed their favorite technology—be it educational films, radio, teaching machines, or open- or closed-circuit television—as a cure for whatever ailed the schools. With their favorite technology in hand they went scouting for an educational problem to solve, which usually meant superimposing the new technology on the malfunctioning existing teaching/learning process like an added geologic layer.

The add-on inevitably increased the cost of the system, but it seldom achieved a commensurate improvement in the system's efficiency and quality. The initial illusions that eventually ended in the shock of disillusionment made the new media suspect among many educators, students, and the general public.

The 1968 crisis report adopted a much broader view of educational technologies and, rejecting this add-on approach, advocated a comprehensive reexamination and overhauling of teaching/learning systems as a whole. Educational technologies, the report observed,

> range from the lecture method to the Socratic dialogue, from the seminar to the drill session. They include the blackboard, desk, and textbook; the pupil-teacher ratio and the layout of classrooms and corridors; the chronological grade system, the academic calendar, and the school bell that punctuates time into modular units; the examinations and grades that influence the students' futures. Each of these is an integral part of a "system" and a "process" whose ultimate objective is to induce learning.

It continued, developing a point that has been repeatedly confirmed by more recent evaluation studies of new media projects:

> [It should be] apparent that a dispute about the technology of education which is confined to the question of whether or not to use the "machines" comprising the "new media," poses the wrong question. The real issue is whether all the ways of doing things carried over from the past are still relevant and sufficient to education's needs, or whether certain subtractions and additions would improve the situation. In short, the issue is whether it is necessary, desirable, and possible to recast fundamentally the whole of education's technology, combining the best of the old and the modern in ways that will form an essentially new, integrated "system" of teaching and learning, capable of yielding better results for any given level of effort.

The Rise and Fall of Instructional Television

In the euphoric education atmosphere that prevailed in the 1950s and much of the 1960s, unbounded enthusiasm and high hopes in many quarters greeted television, whose glamour and extraordinary capacity to combine sight and sound and deliver them instantaneously to classrooms over large areas overshadowed the earlier new media of films and radio. With the push of a button or flip of a switch—so it was claimed at one extreme—the best teachers in the nation could enter every classroom bringing with them a foreign language, vivid laboratory experiments, and a host of other things of great educational value that were well beyond the reach of the ordinary classroom. As a counterpoint to this claim, critics presented an apocalyptic vision of these new machines. In their outlook, these devices would dehumanize the classroom, snuff out the possibility for dialogue, stuff students only with facts to be memorized, thwart the development of their analytical abilities and value judgments, and worse yet, put teachers out of work.

Still, despite the apocalyptic forecast, the classroom instructional television movement gathered rapid momentum, first in several industrialized countries of Western Europe and North America, where the main objective was to update and enrich the curriculum and improve quality. Subsequently, with the help of foreign aid, the movement spread to a variety of developing countries in Africa, Asia, and Latin America, where the aim was not only to improve quality but, more important, to expand access to formal schooling quickly and at an affordable cost.

The movement reached its high point of sophistication in the United States when the Midwest Program of Airborne Television Instruction (MPATI) literally took off on the wings of an elaborately equipped four-engine aircraft on the opening day of school in the fall of 1961, circling all day long over a designated spot in the state of Indiana. The aircraft was the equivalent of an 11,000-foot-high broadcasting tower whose simultaneous messages over two separate channels could reach classrooms within a 600-mile radius—a vast area covering both the cities and rural areas in large portions of six states in the American midwest. The carefully prepared videotaped programs, produced by some of the nation's finest teachers, encompassed key subjects in the curriculum from grades 1 through 12. These videotaped programs, many of which set a new standard for quality, were also made widely available in other sections of the country through ground-based educational TV stations. Its projected cost per student per year, even if no more than half the public schools in the receiving area made regular use of its services, was estimated to be about equal to the cost of a single textbook. The project was widely acclaimed by teachers, students, and parents and operated with considerable success for a few years. But when the time came to shift the operating cost burden from the Ford Foundation to the budgets of state and local school systems that were benefiting from the service, they were unable to get together on paying their modest shares. It was primarily on this bureaucratic rock that MPATI foundered, though other factors also played a role.

By the end of the 1960s, the great boom in classroom instructional television that had begun with such promise in the developed countries in the 1950s had lost its momentum and leveled off far short of earlier expectations. Though it did not die altogether, it came to be viewed as a fringe benefit that teachers could take or leave as they saw fit.

In the developing countries as well, the high hopes held for instructional television had waned by the end of the mid-1970s, primarily because many practical difficulties had been encountered in applying it effectively and because costs proved to be higher, and results lower, than had initially been projected. The details of these practical difficulties were brought into jolting focus by the first wide-ranging evaluation of many specific projects in many countries, conducted by the International Institute for Educational Planning (IIEP) in Paris in the mid-1960s. The findings of this landmark study, since verified by many other evaluations, were sobering to all true believers in instructional television, including the authors of the final report.[6]

In essence, the report said that few of the projects examined were living up to expectations; most were malfunctioning, some badly so—but not because television's high potentiality as an educational tool was a myth. The basic problem was the way this new technology was being used and misused. Typically, projects had been poorly planned and rushed into operation without adequate preparation. The lion's share of the budget and attention had gone to the hardware, to the serious detriment of producing good and appropriate software. Typically also, the broadcast programs were simply add-ons to what had already been going on in the schools; few serious attempts had been made to overhaul the basic curriculum, to revise the entire process of teaching and learning, and to integrate the television technology and programs into the whole process. Teachers who were expected to use the broadcasts were rarely consulted during their preparation, were not given sufficient training to use them effectively, and were not provided with a feedback system to inform those on the production and sending end about what was going well or poorly, or not going at all, in the classroom. In Nigeria, a field check by an IIEP evaluator revealed that in a majority of the pilot TV schools the sets were not even turned on because no one had trained the teachers how to retune them when the sound and image went awry. Then there were the now-familiar mechanical and logistical problems that were often overlooked by project designers in those early years—breakdowns and voltage fluctuations in the electricity supply, sketchy postal systems that failed to deliver program schedules and teacher manuals on time, and the almost total lack of a repair and maintenance infrastructure to keep the sets in operation. In more than a few instances, it was obvious that the project never should have been started, that in the particular circumstances television was simply an inappropriate technology ahead of its time, and that some simpler and less costly, even if less glamorous, technology such as radio could have been more effective and far less costly and difficult to manage.

This IIEP report, however, did not stop with pointing out what went wrong and why. It extracted from these past experiences, good and bad, a variety of positive lessons and practical guidelines and soon came to be regarded as the bible by media project planners in many countries (including the United Kingdom, for example). Guideline No. 1 was: Don't start with a piece of technology and go looking for a problem to solve; start with the problem and then look around for some appropriate technologies to solve it. Second, the report pointed to inadequate investment in good quality software (program content) as the Achilles' heel of most instructional TV and radio programs; the hardware usually gobbled up most of the available budget, and it was erroneously taken for granted that the educators could produce adequate programming "on the cheap." A third important conclusion of the IIEP report was that the supplementary use of television simply to enrich the same old curriculum was its least cost-effective use. Its cost-effectiveness would be far greater if the introduction of instructional TV was seized as the occasion for sweeping improvements in the old curriculum and a fundamental reordering of the whole teaching/learning system and process, as distinct from merely superimposing TV instruction on the old curriculum.

This more radical strategy was followed to a degree by two later ambitious instructional TV experiments in the Ivory Coast and El Salvador.[7] Subsequent evaluation studies of these projects credited them with significant improvements in learning, yet both eventually encountered their own substantial obstacles, primarily related to costs and finance and the perennial difficulties of gaining acceptance of radical innovations in formal education systems.

The Burgeoning of "Little Media"

In 1973, when E. F. Schumacher's *Small Is Beautiful* appeared, advocating the use of "appropriate technologies" for economic purposes in developing countries, Wilbur Schramm's *Big Media, Little Media* also appeared with a similar message for education.[8] It distinguished between big media (complex, sophisticated and expensive technologies such as television, sound films, and computers), and little media (simpler tools such as radio, slides, audio tapes, and projected transparencies). Its thesis was that too much emphasis had been given to the glamorous big media, especially in the context of developing countries, and too little to the more feasible and affordable little media as educational tools.

Also in the early 1970s, development communication experts increasingly were rediscovering traditional forms of local communication—puppet shows, folk drama, ballads, and the like. These, used in conjunction with other activities, offered several advantages. They were inexpensive; they were familiar and credible to local people; and they could convey information and ideas tailored to the support of local development objectives such as improved primary health care, growing nutritious family foods, family planning, and self-reliant community development.

This discovery of traditional local communication media was paralleled by a shift on the part of the media experts from their earlier single-medium fixation to a multimedia strategy. A major stimulant to this shift was the heightened interest of policymakers in the 1970s in promoting comprehensive rural development and spreading nonformal education to serve the basic needs of many thousands of out-of-school youth and adults. A further stimulant was that communications experts had come to realize by now that it is generally much easier and more effective to introduce innovative combinations of educational technology and relevant learning content into an out-of-school learning milieu because, in contrast to formal schooling, there are few hallowed pedagogical dogmas to overcome and less "unlearning" is required.

The New Interest in "Distance Learning"

These basic changes in the thinking of educational communications specialists created a strong fillip in the 1970s in what came to be called "distance learning"—a broad rubric which, like nonformal education, covers a great variety of ways of providing the stuff of learning far beyond the walls of schools and colleges to widely scattered learners of different ages and types who have a strong motivation to acquire new knowledge and skills. Typically, these distance learning programs employ a multimedia approach, including radio (much less costly and more flexible than TV), print materials, and correspondence—often tied in with local discussion groups and audiovisual aids.

Some distance learning programs provide types of learning equivalent to that provided by formal schools and colleges, to audiences beyond their practical reach. One example is the radio-cum-correspondence program in Kenya, which has provided many schoolteachers and other interested learners, mainly in rural areas, with an opportunity to pursue various secondary-school subjects. By far the best known and most influential example, however, is the Open University in the United Kingdom. It shattered precedent and more than a century of tradition by proving that, through a combination of well-prepared TV and radio programs and integrated self-study booklets, supplemented by learner/tutor correspondence and occasional weekend group meetings on a campus, a first-class university education could be provided in a wide range of subjects to thousands of mature and hungry learners studying on their own at home. Moreover, it proved that this could be done at significantly less cost per learner than in the regular university. The Open University is perhaps the most outstanding example in recent times of a truly radical and fundamental educational innovation—not just a piecemeal innovation at the edges of the established system, but one that created a whole new teaching/learning system. Its results have been so convincing that it has already been emulated in various forms in numerous other countries. There are now between 20 and 30 open universities and open colleges of different varieties scattered across both the developed and developing world.

These two examples represent creative hybrids of formal and nonformal education. Another example of a school-oriented distance learning program is the radiophonic schools in several Central American countries. The majority of distance learning programs, it should be noted, are directed primarily at out-of-school audiences whose learning needs lie beyond the scope of the schools and relate to their everyday living needs. One of the oldest and most noteworthy of these is the Acción Cultural Popular (ACPO) program in Colombia, whose multimedia approach, including a nationwide radio network, Sunday educational newspaper, study booklets, recordings, and local self-formed village study groups, has brightened the lives of many thousands of poor rural *campesinos*.[9] Another noteworthy example is the imaginative and professionally crafted distance learning program in Botswana, which benefited from technical assistance by the International Extension College in Cambridge, England.[10]

THE BALANCE SHEET AND OUTLOOK

At this point we can draw together the foregoing findings on both the demand and the supply sides of the world educational equation and identify, at least in a preliminary way, major gaps and disparities between the two. Critical issues associated with these gaps and disparities will be examined more closely in later chapters. This much, however, is already abundantly clear: All over the world the supply side of the equation, despite its dramatic quantitative growth (especially in formal education), is seriously out of balance with the dynamically growing and changing demand side. The growing maladjustments observed in the 1968 report between education systems and the changing world around them have not diminished in the intervening years; they have increased. There is every reason to expect them to keep increasing in the absence of strong corrective measures.

These maladjustments, disparities, and deficits are obviously much greater in developing countries, but they are also sizable and serious throughout the industrialized world. In either world they cannot be remedied simply by doing more and more of the same, for this would only make the problem worse. Nor can they be remedied merely by tinkering with the existing objectives, curricula, teacher training, salary provisions, and educational technologies of formal education systems, if for no other reason (though there are others) than because some of the most massive and important unmet learning needs belong to people outside and beyond the present reach of schools and colleges. These needs belong to many millions of preschool-age children, out-of-school youth, and adults in all walks of life. They belong especially to the masses of illiterate poor and politically voiceless who inhabit stagnant rural areas and urban slums; to disadvantaged minorities and girls and women who have long been discriminated against. They belong to the long-neglected physically and mentally handicapped; to the unemployed skilled and unskilled workers in industrial countries whose jobs have disappeared into obsolescence and who must now acquire different skills to fit new kinds of jobs. These unmet learning needs belong not least of all to the overburdened teachers and administrators on whom each society depends to prepare the new generation to cope effectively with the undefinable but surely quite different circumstances, problems, and opportunities of the twenty-first century.

It would be naive to suppose that this great backlog of educational deficits and maladjustments can somehow be disposed of by the year 2000, and it would be grossly misleading to encourage people to believe this. But it would be neither naive nor misleading to assert that a large dent could be made in these problems and that their growth could at least be halted over the next two decades, *provided* there is a broad understanding of the nature of the problems and a strong determination to make the necessary investment of resources and to undertake the radical educational changes essential to overcoming them.

We will discuss the nature of some of these required educational changes in future chapters. It is appropriate, however, to comment here on the potentialities of alternative educational technologies and strategies previously discussed. In so doing we must suppress the temptation to look for miracle cures or succumb to peddlers of patent medicines who claim to possess such cures. As one thoughtful observer recently wrote:

> The 1980s present difficult challenges to the shapers of the generation who will be living in the twenty-first century. We no longer have the right to be naive about vague promises. We no longer have the right to believe that technologies per se—as sophisticated as they might be—will be able to straighten out complex and difficult situations. We are not entitled to simplify complex problems merely by using sophisticated technologies.[11]

True enough. But neither can we afford to turn a blind eye to the stock-pile of potentially useful educational technologies already at hand. The 1970s witnessed a revolution in the hardware of communications, including the silicon chip and the minicomputer, and within close reach is the technology to create a two-way system of instantaneous communication between teachers and distant students. Such innovations have a history of rapidly declining costs. Though the cost of some of them may remain beyond the financial reach of many developing countries for quite some time, they are already within reach in many developed countries. The central problem, as in the past with films, radio, and TV, is how to furnish such hardware with appropriate software and to integrate it with all of the other essential components of well-balanced and well-functioning teaching/learning systems designed to serve various educational objectives and clienteles.

Traditionally, and up to the present, education has been the last in line to adopt promising new technologies—including even the book (which even the great Socrates disdained on the grounds that a student could not talk back to a book, ask it questions, and have an enlightening dialogue). Yet the book finally made it. Perhaps in the foreseeable future many of the newer technologies will make it. At least there are some encouraging signs that times are changing.

Within the past several years, for example, millions of children in the developed world have learned to use the electronic hand computer. Most of them learned at home, to be sure, but they are now bringing them to school in sizable numbers. More and more schools in these countries, just within the past few years, have been acquiring microcomputers that are helping children to learn to read and write, to calculate, and to think analytically.[12] Numerous secondary schools and colleges are now offering courses in computer programming, and even learned professors are now writing their books with the help of electronic word processors. Even before these electronic devices had found their way into academic classrooms, many school systems, especially the colleges and universities, had harnessed the computer for management purposes.

None of these new gadgets, or all of them together, should be expected to perform educational miracles. They will not lessen the need for good teachers or for talented creators of good learning materials. But they have a high potential, if well used, for enhancing the productivity of teachers and the motivation and learning achievements of students, and not least of all for greatly widening the access to learning for motivated learners outside of the schools.

Obviously, for cost and other reasons, advances in harnessing these high tech devices to educational purposes will come more slowly in developing countries. But these countries need not sit idly by in the meantime, clinging to the old and outmoded technologies. A sizable inventory of much lower cost technologies, such as audiocassettes, miniaturized battery radios, slide films, and even self-produced movie films, not to mention various homemade technologies, are already available to them. All of these technologies are already being put to use, here and there, in many developing countries, but still in far too few places and, for the most part, outside the schools. It will take further research and evaluation to learn how best to use these new educational technologies; to blend them in with the best of the old technologies; and most important of all, to treat each one not as a self-contained teaching/learning system but rather as one useful element in a more complex teaching/learning system—a system that can be more flexible for meeting the different learning needs, styles, and tempo of various groups in each society.

Where, then, does all this leave us? What are the realistic prospects for narrowing the great existing educational gaps and at the same time improving the quality and relevance of education and keeping pace with the growth of knowledge and the constantly changing learning needs of the people? What are the prospects for overhauling the technologies of education and for boosting the productivity of teachers and the learning achievements of students, both young and old?

These things take time; there is almost always strong human resistance to educational change and innovation, and even if there were not such resistance many other practical obstacles must be overcome. One of the first of these to come to the mind of any educational administrator is *money,* and as shown in the next chapter, there is ample reason to be concerned about this formidable obstacle.

But what if money were no problem? Would all countries move speedily and creatively toward overhauling their educational systems and services, toward expanding and improving both their quantitative and qualitative dimensions and reaching out to the educationally unserved? The answer is no. Changes in education simply do not happen that easily.

But is this any reason to despair? Again the answer is no. And it is an answer based not simply on dreams and wishful thinking but on hard realities. One of the realities is that, despite all the shortcomings, misfires, and maladjustments discussed in this report, education has made tremendous headway in most of the world over the past three decades. The second reality is that education today has at its disposal a far broader and stronger set of tools to work with than ever before; the problem is to learn how to put these tools to work in a more effective and affordable manner. It also has at its disposal a stockpile of valuable lessons based on three decades of hard-won experience. Again the problem is to dig out these lessons and put them to good use.

The third reality is that the urgent need for radical educational change—change that moves forward, not back to the "good old days"—has come to be more clearly and widely recognized. Hence the climate today is much more conducive to change than ever before. Finally, the most important reality of all is that people the world over, in defiance of the crisis of confidence in education that has gained currency in some circles, have great faith in education. They want more and more of it, and they will not be denied. The proof of this, shown by the evidence in the next chapter, is that the people and leaders of all nations have demonstrated a remarkable willingness to make great financial sacrifices for education. There is no reason to suppose that they will now suddenly change their minds, even though the financial going gets even rougher.

NOTES

1. Ronald Dore, *The Diploma Disease: Education, Qualification and Development* (London: George Allen & Unwin, 1976).
2. *Digest of Education Statistics, 1982* (Washington, D.C.: National Center for Education Statistics, 1982).
3. *Teacher Policies in a New Context* (Paris: Organisation for Economic Co-operation and Development, 1979).
4. *Digest of Education Statistics, 1982.*
5. *Academy Notes* (Pittsburgh: National Academy of Education), Vol. 12, No. 1 (Summer 1981).
6. Wilbur Schramm, P. Coombs, F. Kahnert, and J. Lyle, *The New Media: A Memo to Educational Planners* (Paris: International Institute for Educational Planning/UNESCO, 1967).
7. J. K. Mayo, R. C. Hornik, and E. G. McAnany, *Educational Reform with Television: The El Salvador Experience* (Stanford, Calif.: Stanford University Press, 1976).
8. Wilbur Schramm, *Big Media, Little Media* (Stanford, Calif.: Stanford University, Institute of Communication Research, 1973).
9. Stephan F. Brumberg, "Columbia: A Multimedia Rural Education Program," Ch. 1 in: Manzoor Ahmed and Philip H. Coombs, ed. *Education for Rural Development: Case Studies for Planners* (New York: Praeger, 1975).
10. For references to numerous educational radio programs, see Dean T. Jamison and Emile McAnany, *Radio for Education and Development* (Beverly Hills, Calif.: Sage Publications, 1978).
11. Joao Batista Araujo e Oliveira, "Making Good Use of Educational Technology," *Prospects,* Vol. XII, No. 3 (Paris: UNESCO, 1982), pp. 345–46.
12. Ladislaw Cenych, "Computer Education," in *Newsletter* (Paris: European Institute of Education and Social Policy, No. 14, October 1983).

CHAPTER 5

THE GROWING FINANCIAL SQUEEZE

PREDICTION

Managers of educational systems, reading the 1968 report on the world educational crisis, were riveted by its analysis—based on rough-hewn data—of the financial aspects of the crisis. No doubt some believed that other aspects of the crisis were not applicable to their own cases. None, however, could confidently assume that their particular educational systems were beyond the reach of what the report had to say about the financial prospects education faced. The prospects presented in the report were as follows.

The halcyon days were over for virtually all educational systems in both the industrially advanced and the developing nations. In contrast to their relatively favorable ability to levy claims on public resources in the 1950s and 1960s, education managers and their systems would soon be caught in a squeeze between rising unit costs and resisting budget ceilings. When a ceiling would be reached, as well as its particular height, would differ from one country to the next, depending on domestic conditions. But no educational system anywhere, the report observed, could continue to command a rapidly increasing share of available resources without producing serious stresses and distortions in the whole society and economy. This was not a matter of philosophy but of elementary arithmetic. Any nation's economy at a given time had a limited income to deploy, and what went to education was taken from other uses. Thus, it could be expected that the claims of education on national resources would encounter increasing competition from the claims of other important needs and areas such as agriculture and industry, roads and housing, and important social needs, such as health, old age security, and unemployment relief. In more than a few countries, unfortunately, education's toughest adversary would be the military budget.

It followed, then, that sooner or later in every country education's share of national economic resources would stop growing; in some countries, it might even be forced to shrink. To compound the problem, the report noted, educational costs per student had a tendency to keep rising, especially because of built-in cost escalators in teacher salary structures with no offsetting improvements in productivity. In other words, each year educational systems would need more money simply to accomplish the same results as in the previous year. To do more, and to do it better, would require still larger budgetary increments—all this apart from the need to keep up with inflation.

Most developing countries faced especially grim educational financial prospects, given prevailing trends in their general budgetary situation and their accumulated financial commitments. The current operating cost portion of their public budgets had proliferated rapidly, leaving little room for development investment. Civil service establishments had expanded and become very expensive. The debt service obligation on foreign loans had steadily increased and in many cases had already reached ominous proportions. A growing number of countries had become saddled with large military and police costs. Critical food problems had pushed dramatically into the foreground, demanding urgent attention. For all these reasons, most developing countries would find it increasingly difficult to enlarge the share of their total resources going to education, or, in some cases, even to maintain the current share.

What seemed true in 1968 is no less valid today. Organized educational systems do not run on slogans and good intentions. They run on money. Not that all the problems of education can be solved by throwing money at them. But without the money to secure the essential physical resources of education (buildings, equipment, materials, supplies) and the human resources (teachers, administrators, custodians), organized educational systems would collapse onto an empty center. With money, the nonfinancial problems of education become more tractable.

Because the vast educational gaps and expanding needs examined in earlier chapters have staggering financial implications for all nations, particularly for the developing nations, which have the largest burden to bear, this chapter reexamines from a current perspective the 1968 predictions of an encroaching financial squeeze. Two questions are central to the inquiry. First, did educational systems in fact encounter an implacable financial squeeze in the 1970s? Second, looking to the future, how much more education will various countries, and low-income ones in particular, be able and willing to pay for in the 1980s and 1990s?

The first question, since it refers to what has already happened, can be answered with available evidence. The second question cannot be answered with assurance; the most one can do is track recent trends and shifts already shaping the future and assess the key factors likely to influence each country's ability to increase its future investment in education.

Evidence and Caveats

The core data about educational expenditures come from the *Statistical Yearbooks* and various special reports prepared by UNESCO's Division of Statistics on Education. These, augmented by a number of individual country and regional studies prepared by other organizations, especially the World Bank, provide a more substantial body of evidence on the financial aspects of education than was available in 1968. In the language of the law courts, however, the net effect amounts not to a proof "beyond a reasonable doubt," but only to a "preponderance of the evidence."

UNESCO's statistics on educational expenditures, as in the case of enrollments, are only as good as the raw data each country supplies. There are three particular pitfalls to be wary of in the case of educational expenditure data. First, expenditures are usually reported in current prices, which in times of high inflation (as in the 1970s) give a distorted picture of the actual increase in real expenditures, measured in constant prices. Moreover, the reported figures often refer to "budget allocations," not to actual expenditures. Many countries, for logistic, bureaucratic, and other reasons, often do not spend all the money allocated to education. Second, only public expenditures on formal education are reported to UNESCO by most individual countries, resulting in a substantial understatement of overall educational expenditures in these countries, especially where private educational institutions are important and where considerable resources go into nonformal education. Even in public formal education, families often spend substantial amounts on fees, uniforms, books, and supplies—all of which are omitted from the reported expenditures. Moreover, one can never be sure whether even all the public expenditures are included, particularly those at the state, district, and local levels. Reported enrollments, on the other hand, include both public and private education; thus, when UNESCO calculates "expenditure per student" by dividing public expenditures by total public and private enrollments, the resulting amount per student can be a sizable understatement. Third, the conversion of educational expenditures from local currencies into corresponding U.S. dollars to facilitate intercountry comparisons and the calculation of regional totals involves a number of technical complexities that can also result in substantial distortions.

Still, once all these grounds for caution are candidly stated and carefully weighed in the balance, we can proceed in the spirit of Plato's remark: "What I am about to tell you may not be precisely true, but something very much like it is."

TRENDS IN PUBLIC EDUCATIONAL EXPENDITURES: 1960–79

The world total of public expenditures on education, in current prices converted to U.S. dollars, soared from $158 billion in 1970 (up from $51 billion in 1960) to $530 billion in 1979, as shown in Figure 5.1. Although a large portion of this nominal growth was eaten up by inflation, the remaining *real* increase was still substantial. In all regions, the increase in expenditures far outstripped the growth in enrollments. As Figure 5.1 shows, however, the distribution of educational expenditures has been very lopsided between the developed and developing countries. (A further breakdown by developing regions is given in Appendix Table 5.1.) The growth in the developing countries was from just over $12 billion in 1970 to $66 billion in 1979, whereas the growth in the developed countries in the same period was from $146 billion to $464 billion. Expressed in percentages, the developed countries' share of total world expenditures was 88 percent in 1979 against their share of total world enrollments (all levels) that year of about 37 percent. Conversely, the developing countries, with 88 percent of total enrollments, accounted for only 12 percent of total expenditures.

Four factors account for most of this great disparity: (1) the real costs of educational inputs, particularly teacher and administrative salaries, are considerably higher in developed countries; (2) the real inputs per student (for example, in facilities, equipment, teaching materials, and teacher hours per year) are also generally much greater in developed countries; (3) the enrollment figures for developing countries, as noted in Chapter 3, tend to be substantially inflated; and (4) much higher proportions of developed country enrollments are at the secondary and higher education levels, where per-student costs are considerably higher.

Meanwhile, one other quick notation may help fix the magnitude of the real differences in expenditures between developed and developing countries. In 1979, Europe and the U.S.S.R. (with less than 18 percent of the world's population and 23 percent of total world enrollments) and the United States and Canada (with less than 6 percent of the world's population and 10 percent of total enrollments) each spent about three times as much on education as all of the developing countries combined.

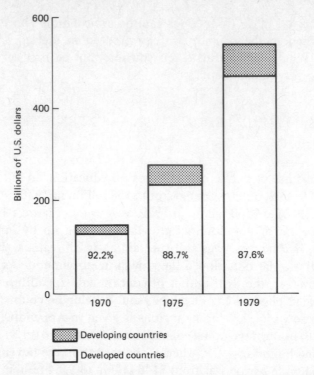

Figure 5.1. Public expenditure on education in the world, 1970, 1975, 1979 (in current prices and U.S. dollars). (Note: The People's Republic of China, Democratic Kampuchea, Democratic People's Republic of Korea, Lao People's Democratic Republic, Lebanon, Mongolia, and Vietnam are not included.) [Source: UNESCO, *Public Expenditure on Education in the World, Regional and Country Trends, 1970–1979* (Paris: UNESCO, Division of Statistics on Education, Office of Statistics, October 1982), p. 3 (mimeo).]

Three Indicators of National Effort

The significance of educational expenditure figures becomes clearer when the data to be examined are viewed through the lens of three national indicators of educational efforts. The first of these is the ratio of Public Expenditure on Education to the Gross National Product (the PEE/GNP ratio). This ratio, as indicated in Figure 5.2, rose steadily in all regions of the world from 1960 to 1975, meaning that national public educational expenditures increased annually at a faster rate than the GNP, thereby giving education an increasing share of the national economic pie.

What happened after 1975 is a different story, which we will come to shortly. Meanwhile, it is worth noting that the developing countries as a group, starting from a lower level, increased their educational effort proportionately more than the developed countries, from an average of 2.3 percent of GNP in 1960 to 4.0 percent by 1979, or by three quarters. In

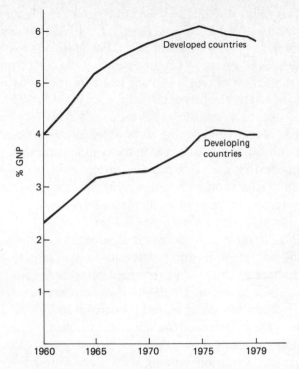

Figure 5.2. Public expenditure on education as a percentage of the GNP. [Source: UNESCO, *Public Expenditure on Education in the World, Regional, and Country Trends, 1970–79* (Paris: UNESCO, Division of Statistics on Education, Office of Statistics, October 1982), mimeo.]

the same period, the developed countries as a group increased their PEE/ GNP ratio from 4.0 percent to 5.9 percent, or by less than half.

Once more a special caution is in order here, because this PEE/GNP ratio plays tricks at times, particularly in periods of economic slowdown, such as the 1970s and early 1980s. The point is that education budgets are "sticky." They can move up substantially from one year to the next but they cannot easily move down. This is so because in the short run they are composed largely of fixed commitments and costs: the pupils, teachers, and buildings are already there, and the teacher salary bill (which often accounts for 90 percent or more of the total) cannot be easily reduced because of contract and other commitments. The GNP, on the other hand, can move up and down more quickly from year to year, especially when heading into or out of a serious recession. Thus, if the GNP of a country happens to decline sharply in a particular year, the "sticky" education budget—adopted well ahead of the new fiscal year—suddenly constitutes a higher percentage of the reduced GNP, even if the education budget has simply stood still. The PEE/GNP indicator signals an increased educational effort by this country, but in fact the country is simply maintaining its previous level of effort. For these reasons, year to year trends in PEE/GNP ratios of countries during the 1970s may not be a very reliable indicator of trends in their real educational financial effort.

A second indicator, the percentage of a country's Total Public Budget allocated to education (the PEE/TPB ratio) is a relatively more reliable gauge of what is really happening. It is especially significant because it reveals how education did each year in the competition with other public agencies and services and thus provides direct evidence of the relative priority given to education. In addition, it is expressed in terms of a country's own currency and price movements and avoids the distortions that often result from conversion into U.S. dollars.

This PEE/TPB ratio also increased significantly almost everywhere between 1960 and 1974, meaning that education was progressively getting a larger share of the total government budget. According to World Bank calculations, based on UNESCO data, the average for the developed country group moved up from 11.3 percent in 1960 to 15.6 percent in 1974, while the average for the developing country group rose from 11.7 percent to 15.1 percent over the same period.[1] Again, the group averages conceal wide variations among individual countries. World Bank estimates for the 1973–75 period showed a range from 3.8 to 36 percent in developing countries.

A third indicator is the amount of public funds spent on education per inhabitant of a country. It is a measure of the general public's sacrifices in behalf of education. This indicator also moved up steadily throughout the world between 1970 and 1979, as shown in Appendix Table 5.2. A substantial portion of these increases, especially in the 1970s, was offset by inflation, but much of it was real. This is clearly demonstrated by estimates made for 24 European and North American countries. Without exception, each one substantially increased its real per capita expenditure on education, and over half of them more than doubled the amount between 1965 and 1976–77.[2] No similar analyses are available for developing countries, but scattered evidence points in the same direction.

Reversal in the 1970s

These three indicators show that the 1960s were favorable years for education budgets throughout the world. But for the reasons indicated earlier, education systems could not continue indefinitely to get an increasing share of national economic resources without seriously crippling other public services and perhaps the whole economy. Eventually, in every country, education's percentage share of the GNP and national budget would inevitably level off and, in some cases, even decline. This would not mean, however, a sudden freezing of all education budgets and an end to all annual increments. Rather, it would mean that in the future such increments would have to keep in line with (or fall below) the current rate of increase in the GNP and total public expenditures.

The prediction of the 1968 report on the world educational crisis began to materialize sooner than expected. The actual turning point for the majority of countries had arrived by the mid-1970s, earlier for some and later for others, depending on local circumstances. This inevitable deceleration in the growth of educational expenditures was accentuated by the sharp rise in oil prices in 1973 and the world economic downturn and associated disorders that followed. For the first time since the educational boom got under way in the early 1950s, several countries in each region actually experienced a negative rate of growth of their public education expenditures, measured in constant prices.[3]

This slowdown during the 1970s is confirmed by two of the previously discussed indicators. First, a glance at Figure 5.2 reveals that for the developed country group as a whole, the ratio of public education expenditures to the GNP peaked in 1975 and thereafter declined. Similarly, but with a two- or three-year lag, the same ratio for the three major developing regions also stagnated. And since the GNP itself declined in a number of these countries, the growth of their real educational expenditures slackened even more than the percentages in Figure 5.1 suggest.

Second, to test what happened to education's share of total public budgets, the figures for a sample of 40 developed and developing countries with available UNESCO data were examined for the period 1970–79. These countries were classified regionally according to whether public expenditures on education as a percentage of the total government budget (the PEE/TPB ratio) increased, decreased, or showed no significant change (either up or down by less than 1 percentage point) between 1970–73 and 1978–79, the latest period for which these data were available. The results, shown in Table 5.1 are revealing. Among the 12 developed countries in the sample, 10 either reduced their ratio or recorded no significant change, whereas only 2 increased their PEE/TPB ratio in this period. Out of the sample of 28 developing countries, 22 either decreased their PEE/TPB ratio or recorded no significant change, whereas 6 increased their ratio.

THE IMPACT OF INFLATION

The slowdown in the growth of real educational expenditures in the 1970s, and in some cases the absolute decline, was concealed by raging

Table 5.1 Trends in Ratio of Public Expenditures on Education to Total
Government Expenditures, 1970–79[a]

	Number of Countries	Direction of Change		
Region		Decreased	No Significant Change	Increased
Developed	12	6	4	2
Developing				
Africa	8	3	3	2
Asia	9	2	4	3
Latin America and Caribbean	11	6	4	1
Subtotal	28	11	11	6
Total	40	17	15	8

[a]Less than 1 percentage point change (±).
Source: Calculated from data in UNESCO, *Statistical Yearbook, 1982* (Paris: UNESCO, Office of Statistics, 1982).

inflation, which played havoc with education systems. Education budgets everywhere, with the partial exception of some Eastern European centrally planned economies, were sharply eroded by rising prices, though again there were wide variations among countries.

The figures in Appendix Table 5.3 show the much increased rate of inflation during the 1970–81 period compared to the 1960s for different groups of countries classified by per capita income levels. These are average annual rates of inflation that compound the total inflation each year. For 34 low-income countries the average annual rate between 1970 and 1981 was 11.2 percent (compared to only 3.5 percent for the decade of the 1960s). But for the upper-middle-income developing countries it was even worse—an annual average of 18.6 percent from 1970 to 1981, in contrast to only 3 percent in the 1960s. The rate for the industrial market countries was much lower (9.9 percent), but lower in this case meant far higher than they were accustomed to. Thus, wherever one looked, what appeared on the surface to be briskly rising educational expenditures (in current prices) actually proved to be a far more modest increase in real terms, if not an actual decline.

The most agonizing educational dilemma posed by inflation in both developing and developed countries concerned the salaries and wages of teachers, administrators, and service personnel, which, as mentioned previously, often account for up to 90 percent or more of the current educational budget (depending on the country and the particular level of education). On the one hand, if teachers' salaries and wages fail to keep pace with the cost of living, they undergo a reduction in real income, their morale suffers, and some of the ablest shift to better paying jobs, thus pulling down the quality of instruction. On the other hand, to keep raising teachers' salaries in line with rising prices adds a further burden to already hard-pressed school budgets, often at the expense of other items such as books and supplies that are needed to sustain teacher productivity. In developing countries it could also mean depriving disadvantaged children and youth of a much needed chance for an education. In short, inflation, piled on top of an already serious budgetary squeeze simply compounded the financial crisis of education systems.

One of the results in many countries was the strengthening of teachers' organizations and their transformation from professional societies into hard-bargaining trade unions. In the United States, for example, where teacher strikes had been almost unthinkable a generation earlier, they became common in many cities and towns; through their aggressive unions, teachers acquired, and applied, powerful political clout on the national as well as local scene. This was even more the case in many developing countries, where teachers were a large proportion of the nation's relatively small educated elite and their leaders knew how to work the levers of power.

RISING REAL EDUCATIONAL COSTS

The tightening financial constraints on education systems, as was said earlier, comes from increasingly resistant budget ceilings on the one side and from relentlessly rising costs per student on the other. These two factors, compounded by inflation, can force the vitality out of an educational enterprise.

The astonishing thing, considering that education has been the world's largest growth industry over the past 30 years and, in most countries, the largest devourer of taxpayers' money, is that so little is known about the behavior of educational costs by educational administrators or anyone else. The conventional line-item budget is designed to satisfy the needs of auditors, not the needs of cost-conscious educational managers seeking ways to improve the efficiency and effectiveness of their school system or higher educational institution. Such budgets usually differentiate between capital and recurrent expenditures and break down recurrent costs between such items as teacher salaries and benefits, supplies, repairs and maintenance, and so forth. But they fail to reveal the connection between these line-item expenditure categories and the various objectives and components of the educational program, or how efficiently the available physical, human, and financial resources are being used in terms of the learning results achieved. Few school administrators, for example, have any real idea of what it is costing to bring their pupils up to a prescribed level of literacy or numeracy, or how the classroom time of teachers is divided between different functions and learning objectives. Few college and university administrators have solid information on the extent to which various facilities are underutilized or how the costs per student compare among different courses, subjects, or professional fields.

In the absence of such basic data, educational managers are severely handicapped in seeking to improve cost-effectiveness and to explore and assess alternative possible ways of getting more and better quality results within the limits of available resources. Yet practical cost-accounting and analytical methods for doing these things have been devised and tested over the past two decades. If put to work they could help fill this void and make a major contribution to better educational planning and management and greater efficiency in the use of limited resources—for both formal and nonformal education. The cost of instituting such information and analytical systems, and of training people to use them, would be minor compared to the sums spent on education and the high returns such an investment would bring. In the years immediately ahead, many educational systems and institutions will face the choice of instituting improved methods of cost analysis or undergoing progressive deterioration of efficiency and quality.

Rising Cost Per Student

The real cost per student, in virtually all educational systems, has a perverse tendency to keep rising from year to year, even if quality stands still or declines. Special studies in a number of developed countries (unfortunately, there have been few such studies in developing countries) all testify to this phenomenon.

A study in Sweden, for example, showed that the annual cost per student in the Stockholm comprehensive schools, measured in constant 1968 prices, rose steadily from 3793 Swedish kroners in 1963 to 5904 Skr in 1975, an increase of 57 percent in just over ten years. A somewhat less refined study in Canada found that the real cost per student (in 1960–61 constant Canadian dollars) at the primary and secondary level rose by 65 percent between 1960–61 and 1973–74 and at the university level by more than 40 percent. A longer time series in the United States, adjusted to 1979–80 prices, shows an almost uninterrupted increase in current annual expenditure per student in primary and secondary schools from $395 in 1929–30 to $2275 in 1979–80. (Supporting data for these three country examples are given in Appendix Tables 5.4 to 5.6.) An analysis of real expenditures per student year in higher education in 13 Western European and 6 Eastern European countries from 1965 to 1976, based on UNESCO and OECD data, showed a similar general upward trend, though with occasional deviations, especially in Eastern Europe.[4]

All the studies share important limitations. In particular, because they are based on the average cost per student from year to year, they ignore sizable variations in cost between different fields and institutions. They also ignore important programmatic changes over time that can substantially alter the average cost, such as trading quality for quantity, and sizable shifts in the proportion of total enrollments from high- to low-cost types of institutions or fields of study. Despite such limitations, however, these studies in developed countries all underscore the tendency of real costs per student to keep rising over time.

Whatever evidence is available on developing countries points to the same conclusion. There are cases, however, in which economies of scale, especially in higher education, appear on the surface to be holding down or even reducing the cost per student. But there is always a good possibility in such cases that the stable or declining average cost per student mainly reflects either a shift of the overall enrollment pattern toward lower cost types of education or a decline of quality resulting from overcrowding, or both.

The Illogic of Teacher Salary Structures

There is no mystery about the underlying causes of this phenomenon of rising unit costs in education—in contrast to declining unit costs in many other types of productive enterprises. Two of these causes in particular merit attention: first, the labor-intensive character and unchanging technologies of education; second, the uniform teacher salary structure, with its different levels and classifications and built-in escalator provisions, that treats all teachers in a given category as if they were alike.

Education is highly labor-intensive and has not substantially altered its technologies for many generations, which has inhibited increases in teacher productivity and prevented increases in student/teacher ratios consistent with maintaining or increasing learning achievements. Meanwhile, however, many other productive enterprises that employ comparable high-level educated people have steadily increased their productivity—and hence their real wages and income—by adopting a succession of new productive technologies and by becoming increasingly capital-intensive. In an effort to attract a sufficient share of their own ablest grad-

uates to teaching careers, education systems have been obliged to keep
raising teacher salaries and emoluments to remain competitive with
those offered by competing employers bidding for the same caliber of
manpower. The inevitable result has been to keep raising the teacher cost
per student without a commensurate improvement in what the students
learn. The alternative of allowing teacher salaries to lag behind other salaries is self-defeating, for it simply results in losing many of the best
teachers and recruiting a poorer caliber of new ones. This is precisely the
situation in which education systems in many countries have found
themselves in recent years.

The problem is compounded by the uniform salary structure, which is
based on the premise that all teachers perform essentially the same functions, have equivalent responsibilities, achieve much the same learning
results, and, therefore, should all receive the same pay. The only salary
differentials provided for are tied to differences in the formal academic
qualifications and cumulative years of service of each teacher. (Though
in theory all are equal, some are obviously more equal than others.)

Most other professions (for example, medicine, law, engineering) are
organized on the basis of a division and hierarchy of functions, with corresponding financial rewards based on each individual's demonstrated
level of professional competence and designated functional responsibilities. The teaching profession, by contrast, has no such hierarchy of functions and responsibilities. In theory, teachers all have the same job—to
preside over a conventional classroom of students, to teach them whatever they are supposed to learn, and to perform such other ancillary tasks
as presumably only a professionally trained adult can perform (though
actually many of these time-consuming tasks could be done by untrained
aides and are a waste of the teacher's professional talents). Thus, all teachers step onto the escalator at the bottom of the salary structure and ride
up together over the years. The only way an able teacher can get off that
escalator and step onto a higher-level one is to stop teaching and become
an administrator, which means losing a good teacher without necessarily
getting a good administrator.

The Need to Reorganize the Teaching Profession

Under this uniform salary schedule, the present educational systems fail
to attract the ablest young people to teaching and to hold them in the
profession, particularly in national economies where attractive alternatives are readily available to them. Further, the systems fail to make the
best use of the particular talents and strengths of individuals who enter
teaching.

Various patchwork proposals crop up from time to time designed to overcome what is plainly irrational and counterproductive in a uniform salary structure and monolithic job description where all teachers are treated alike. One of these proposals, a favorite in the United States, is the "merit pay" idea, whereby outstandingly able teachers would get a substantial salary bonus, while still performing the same role as all other teachers. In times past, however, the teachers themselves and their unions have shot down the merit pay proposal. They asserted that no one—least of all school administrators—could be trusted to be a competent and impartial judge of the best teachers. Nor did they themselves want the responsibility of being the judges of their peers. In addition, they feared, not without reason, that the invidious distinction made between merit and nonmerit teachers, all presumably doing the same job, would create divisiveness and hard feelings within the teaching staff. Moreover, what parents would be content to have their child taught by a nonmerit teacher when there was a merit teacher in the classroom down the corridor?

Such patchwork devices as merit pay would at best be only mild and temporary palliatives. The only satisfactory solution lies in a fundamental restructuring of the teaching profession, based on a clear division of functions and responsibilities that candidly recognizes the differing abilities among individual teachers and enables school systems to make the best use of each one's particular abilities and potential. The team teaching concept, one of the most promising alternative possibilities, has already enjoyed a fair amount of encouraging experience.

This concept is based on the division of labor idea that underlies most modern progress. It makes a break from the traditional practice of a single teacher working in isolation with a fixed group of learners, doing whatever needs to be done by an adult in the situation. In its simplest form, a team made up of an experienced teacher and a less trained, lower paid teacher's aide work together with a larger than normal group of learners. The aide performs various tasks that must be done but that do not require extensive professional training—handing out books and supplies, cleaning the blackboard, correcting multiple-choice tests, and helping the chronic absentee in the back row to catch up, tasks that ordinarily divert much of a well-trained teacher's time and energy from actually teaching. With an aide, the teacher is free to concentrate on those tasks that require professional skill and, even with more learners in the group, can achieve better learning results. With this division of labor, the teacher's professional skills are more fully utilized, the teacher's productivity is increased, and the students learn more. This can happen at no greater cost per student, *provided* the class size is sufficiently enlarged and there is an appropriate spread between the teacher's salary and the pay of the teacher's aide.

In a more elaborate version, the teaching team might be composed of (a) a master teacher who coaches, leads, and orchestrates the team, (b) two or more regular teachers, each with certain particular teaching strengths and preferences (for example, one in teaching language and communication skills, another in teaching science and mathematics), (c) one or two novice teachers undergoing training, and in some cases (d) one or more highly competent radio or TV teachers who, operating from a distance, serve, in effect, as members of a substantial number of such local teaching teams.

A team of this sort, of course, can effectively serve a large group of students—not all in the same room all the time but divided into different-sized subgroups in the course of the school day for different purposes and activities. While some students are receiving special tutorial assistance, others will be participating in various instructional groups, and still others working on their own for a period reading a book, writing a paper, or doing a special project. Under this more flexible and diversified system, members of the team—collectively having different types and levels of experience, skill, and ability—can make the optimum use of their respective capabilities, thereby enhancing the effectiveness and productivity of each individual member of the team. At the same time, they can cater far more effectively to the differing needs, abilities, and problems of the individual learners in the large group being served.

Under team teaching, it is both logical and tolerable to pay different members of the team differently in accordance with their various abilities and the functions they perform. This is in sharp contrast to the simplistic merit pay approach, which makes invidious distinctions between neighboring teachers in the same school who, in principle, all have the same job and are supposed to perform the same functions.

To appreciate the difference between the team teaching concept and the way things now operate in the schools, one only has to imagine what would happen to the productivity (and earnings) of a skilled surgeon who had to do everything for each patient that needed doing, from administering the anesthetic, fumbling around for the next tool needed in the midst of the operation, making the patient's bed, serving meals, and emptying bed pans. An absurd example? Certainly. Yet this is precisely what is expected of the skilled teacher in the conventionally organized teaching–learning process throughout the world. As long as the job description, functions, and pay of the teacher with rare ability are identical to that of the mediocre teacher who happens to have the same formal academic credentials and equal years of service, school systems will continue to suffer from a self-inflicted wound. As things stand, their own ablest students—who know much more about teaching as a career than any other, because of their long years of exposure to it—will hardly be tempted to make this their first career choice, or if they do, to stay with it very long.

Particularly Difficult Situations

This teacher salary structure and classification system have especially troublesome consequences in two quite different types of current situations, the first relating mainly to developing countries and the second to developed countries.

In the process of rapidly expanding their enrollments in the 1960s and early 1970s, many developing countries, especially in Africa, were forced to staff their primary schools with large numbers of so-called unqualified and underqualified teachers with insufficient formal training to meet official qualification standards. They also had to borrow many temporary secondary and university teachers from developed countries until they could expand their own supply. Most of these countries have since been making strong efforts both to upgrade their primary school teaching staff and to replace expatriate teachers with their own national teachers at the secondary and tertiary level. In the process, however, many have run into much greater increases in teacher costs than they had anticipated. In most African countries, for example, the spread between unqualified and qualified teachers in the official salary structure is very wide. Thus, a determined policy to eradicate the high proportion of unqualified teachers in primary schools, both by giving some further training and by replacing others with newly trained young qualified teachers, has resulted in an enormous increase in the overall teacher salary bill, *even for the same number of teachers teaching the same number of pupils.* And who can say for sure whether the pupils are then actually learning more? Who can be sure of this, especially if the increased teacher salary bill crowds out the budget item for textbooks and other supply and equipment items so essential to the productivity of the teachers (whether qualified or unqualified) and to the learning achievements of the pupils?

The replacement of foreign teachers in secondary schools and universities with indigenous teachers can have the same major budgetary impact. To the extent that the services of the former foreign teachers were contributed, more or less free-of-charge to the recipient country, that country must now pay the local rate for their replacements. And in Africa, the rate for secondary and college level teachers, carried over from the colonial period, is high in relation to the general average of wages and the average per capita income. Thus, "Africanizing" the teaching staff, which is unquestionably a desirable objective, can be expensive in terms of boosting per pupil costs. The reverse can also happen. To the extent that a particular country had been hiring foreign teachers on contract with its own funds, at a cost well above the local rate, their replacement with local teachers would help reduce costs.

The second situation, which is already gripping most developed countries and sooner or later will also grip developing countries, entails the impact on teacher costs per pupil when the rapid expansion of enrollments finally slows down substantially or comes to a halt, as it already has in Europe and North America. During the rapid expansion, many new teachers are hired yearly at the bottom of the salary scale, thus holding down the overall average of teacher costs. When the expansion slows down or stops, however, the hiring of new low-priced young teachers also falls off sharply, and the escalator provision of the salary structure, which awards automatic increases for years of service, takes hold. As the existing faculty ages, the teacher salary bill and cost per student steadily increases, with no assurance that the quality and effectiveness of the teaching will get any better with age.

Mention should also be made of another cost-increasing phenomenon that is likely to occur when enrollments flatten out or decline. When the pressure for further expansion ebbs and enrollments decline, education systems are not inclined to reduce their teaching staff proportionately; instead they may turn their attention to improving quality and adding services. They may reduce class size and the pupil/teacher ratio and provide increased services they could not afford during the period of rapid expansion, such as art and music courses and special programs for slow learners, handicapped children, and the gifted.

Rising Costs in Higher Education

Colleges and universities are especially likely to keep increasing their real cost per student. The reasons are lucidly set forth in a recent study for the Carnegie Commission on Higher Education in the United States by Howard R. Bowen, a veteran student of the economics of education who has held both professorial and administrative positions in a variety of U.S. public and private higher institutions.[5] Bowen's findings are expressed in his "five laws," summarized in the accompanying box. His thesis is that the quality and prestige of higher institutions are judged primarily by the richness of their inputs per student, not by any careful evaluation of their outputs. These institutions raise all the money they can and spend all they raise; yet they never feel they have enough.

Bowen's study focused on American higher education, but his findings have relevance for colleges and universities the world over. As a breed, they have often demonstrated their unique ability even in times of financial adversity to garner more funds than other schools, especially the primary schools. One reason is that most universities have considerably greater autonomy, public prestige, and access to the seats of power than

---

Five Laws on Higher Education Costs[6]

1. *The dominant goals of institutions are educational excellence, prestige, and influence.*

The "excellence" or "quality" of institutions is commonly judged by such criteria as faculty/student ratios, faculty salaries, number of PhDs on the faculty, number of books in the library, range of facilities and equipment, and academic qualifications of students.

These criteria are resource inputs, most of which cost money, not outcomes flowing from the educational process. The true outcomes in the form of learning and personal development of students are, on the whole, unexamined and only vaguely discerned.

2. *In quest of excellence, prestige, and influence, there is virtually no limit to the amount of money an institution could spend for seemingly fruitful educational ends.*

Whatever level of expenditure is attained is seldom considered enough. Institutions tend, therefore, to spend up to the very limit of their means.

As a result, the financial problems of rich institutions are about as severe as those of all but the most impoverished institutions. This is especially so because whatever expenditures are once admitted into the budget become long-term commitments from which it is difficult ever to withdraw.

3. *Each institution raises all the money it can.*

No college or university ever admits to having enough money and all try to increase their resources without limit.

4. *Each institution spends all it raises.*

Many institutions, however, accumulate reserves and endowments. These savings are derived primarily from gifts designated for endowment and not from voluntary allocations of current income.

In most institutions, the accumulations are of negligible amounts. The few institutions that become very affluent, however, are able to save substantial amounts and accumulate significant endowments.

5. *The cumulative effect of the preceding four laws is toward ever-increasing expenditure.*

The incentives inherent in the goals of excellence, prestige, and influence are not counteracted within the higher educational system by incentives leading to parsimony or efficiency.

The question of what *ought* higher education to cost—what is the minimal amount needed to provide services of acceptable quality—does not enter the process except as it is imposed from the outside.

The higher educational system itself provides no guidance of a kind that weighs costs and benefits in terms of the public interest. The duty of setting limits thus falls, by default, on those who provide the money, mostly legislators and students and their families.

individual schools, particularly those in centralized school systems that are held on a short leash by a ministry of education. A related reason is that occupants in seats of power are generally anxious for their own children to make it into the university; besides, many are also proud alumni of the public university and are anxious to see their alma mater do well. In countries such as Canada, the United States, and a number of Latin American countries that have a mixture of public and private institutions, only the most prestigious and best endowed of the private colleges and universities (generally those with affluent alumni) can cope with stormy financial weather as effectively as the publicly supported institutions.

RESPONSES OF EDUCATION SYSTEMS TO THE SQUEEZE

Despite their natural inclination to keep raising unit costs (usually in the name of "maintaining and improving quality," or at least to keep it from eroding), schools, colleges, and universities in most countries have been forced to trim their financial sails in recent years because of tightening budget ceilings. Such trimming, even in the relatively affluent industrialized countries, is always a painful process for administrators, teachers, students, and all others directly affected. Needless to say, it usually encounters stout resistance.

The recent educational trimming in the developed countries has taken a variety of forms. At the school level, declining enrollments have been accompanied by mounting pressure to close surplus schools, to reduce staff, to curtail teacher training, to defer repairs and maintenance, and to cut out what many critics consider frills in school programs. At the college and university level, the prospect of stagnating enrollments has led to sharp curtailment in hiring new faculty members, in adding new courses to the curriculum, and in capital improvements and expansion. In some instances, specific courses—even whole program segments of universities that were regarded as not pulling their financial weight—have been cut out. Western European countries have reimposed tight admission quotas *(numerus clausus)* in high-cost fields of study that were seen as oversubscribed in relation to the needs and demands of the employment markets. Most of these Western European countries, which formerly welcomed foreign students and generously subsidized their higher education with public funds, introduced various restrictive measures in the late 1970s to curtail the rising flood of foreign students and to reduce public subsidies to them.

The situation in developing countries is marked by more unpalatable choices. The most obvious choice for policymakers is either (1) to clamp the brakes on further expansion of enrollments, especially in higher education, in order to preserve some semblance of quality and at the same time to slow the growth of the educated unemployed, or alternatively, (2) to yield to the pressure of popular demand by spreading limited educational resources even thinner over more and more students at the expense of quality and effectiveness. For obvious pragmatic and political reasons that educational policymakers can ill afford to ignore, the latter choice has prevailed in most cases. The continued quantitative expansion has meant enlarging classes (often to monstrous sizes); doubling and sometimes even tripling school sessions per day; cutting expenditures on textbooks, library materials, and other essential supplies; and deferring necessary repairs and maintenance, thus "consuming" existing capital facilities and equipment rather than preserving and adding to them.

There is, however, a third option, albeit not an easy one. It is to reduce the cost per student, while at the same time preserving and enhancing quality (including relevance and effectiveness), by seeking out various ways to improve the internal efficiency of schools and especially universities and other postsecondary institutions. In the years immediately ahead, this approach will not be simply an available option but an absolute necessity for all educational systems if they are to remain viable.

Illusory Cost Reductions

There is an important difference between *real* cost reductions per student, and *apparent* reductions that prove to be illusory. Two examples will help make the point. First, in many developing (and developed) countries the rapid expansion of higher education enrollments has involved shifting an increasing proportion of students to the lower cost types of institutions (e.g., two-year nonresidential colleges) and lower cost fields of study (e.g., humanities, law, commercial studies). This can have the effect of reducing the overall average cost per student in higher education as a whole, but not the real cost per student in each institution and field of study that make up the overall average. In other words, the declining overall average cost per student does not reflect a genuine "economy of scale" since the product mix is not the same as earlier. It may be a good thing to do in some circumstances, but it avoids the real issue of achieving greater internal efficiency.

The second example is one in which the average cost per student declines simply because the same resources are spread thinner over more and more students, resulting in an erosion of quality and effectiveness. Such apparent savings are a pure illusion and can lead to educational bankruptcy.

The extent of such erosion has varied widely from country to country and from institution to institution within the same country. Latin America, for example, presents a picture of contrasts. In some Latin American countries many of the public universities are awash with students, taught largely by part-time professors; the curriculum is often archaic, and the quality of education is generally considered to be abysmally low. Typically, in these same countries, the most prestigious universities are the few existing private ones (often church-connected); these maintain high admission requirements and performance standards and have a larger proportion of full-time faculty, many with postgraduate degrees. Interestingly, however, the pattern in Brazil is quite the opposite. The highest quality institutions in Brazil and the most difficult to enter are the strongly supported federal universities, along with a handful of top-flight private universities. In 1979, the ratio of applicants to vacancies in these strongest universities was over 10 to 1.[7]

Why this striking difference in Brazil? It has to do with farsighted planning and determined implementation. The national government has been spending sizable amounts each year on a carefully tailored program designed to strengthen the faculties of the federal universities, especially at the postgraduate level, by sending able young faculty members for advanced study to leading overseas research universities and to Brazilian institutions already strong in selected fields. Generally speaking, the state universities (supported by individual state governments) are the next highest ranking institutions. They, too, have a surfeit of applications over vacancies. The third tier of postsecondary institutions catches the spill-over from the more prestigious public and private universities. It consists of an assortment of some 800 private "isolated schools" and "federated" institutions, most of which provide instruction in one or two particular specialties (such as accounting, business administration, law, or health) and charge substantial tuition fees. Contrary to the experience of most Latin American countries, this private sector absorbed a disproportionate share of the astonishing tenfold increase in Brazil's higher education enrollments between 1965 and 1982. It buffered the public sector insti-tutions against the full force of the social demand for higher education. In the period from 1970 to 1980, for example, when total enrollments trebled (from 456,000 to 1,380,000), the private sector enrollments increased by 350 percent whereas public sector enrollments increased by only 250 percent. Because of their faster growth, private institutions in 1980 accounted for over 60 percent of total higher education enrollments in Brazil.[8]

Cost Differentials by Level

The wide differences in cost per student at different levels of formal edu-cation are also important. Table 5.2, based on calculations by the World Bank, compares (necessarily roughly) the average spread between public expenditures per student year in primary education and higher education in different regions in 1976. In the industrialized countries, on the one extreme, public expenditures per student in higher education averaged only about twice the expenditure per pupil at the primary level. (The costs would be much higher, however, for the strongest four-year colleges and universities, especially at the postgraduate level in fields such as sci-ence, engineering, and medicine.) At the opposite extreme, in sub-Saharan Africa, public expenditures per student year in higher education averages as much as 100 times that in elementary education. In other words, one student in higher education can cost the equivalent of 100 students in primary schools. The ratio is less extreme in the other devel-oping regions but much higher than in the industrialized countries. As noted in Chapter 3, enrollment at the third level, in all developing regions, has been expanding far more rapidly than at the first level. This helps to explain why primary education, especially in rural areas, has

Table 5.2 Comparison of Public Expenditures on Elementary and Higher Education per Student, 1976 (in U.S. dollars)[a]

Region	Higher (Postsecondary) Education	Elementary Education	Ratio of Higher to Elementary Education
Sub-Saharan Africa	3819	38	100.5
South Asia	117	13	9.0
East Asia	471	54	8.7
Middle East and North Africa	3106	181	17.2
Latin America and Caribbean	733	91	8.1
Industrialized	2278	1157	2.0
U.S.S.R. and Eastern Europe	957	539	1.8

[a]The figures shown are averages (weighted by enrollment) of costs (in 1976 dollars) in the countries in each region for which data are available.

Source: World Bank, *World Development Report, 1980* (Washington, D.C.: The World Bank, 1980).

been so starved for funds and why these countries have fallen so far short of their goal of universal primary education.

Another way of viewing these cost differentials is in terms of each nation's average per capita income, as shown in Figure 5.3. In these terms, according to World Bank calculations, primary education is relatively cheap in all regions, with expenditures ranging from a low of about 12 percent of per capita income in Asia and Latin America to a high of 25 percent in Western Africa, with the OECD countries falling in between. Expenditures per secondary student are also relatively modest, except in sub-Saharan Africa, where it averages between 125 and 145 percent of per capita income. But again, the dramatic contrast is in higher education. At this level, public expenditures per student in the OECD countries average less than 60 percent of per capita income, compared to 120 percent in Latin America, over 200 percent in Asia, and from 900 to 1400 percent in Africa.

To keep things in perspective, however, it should be pointed out that per capita income in the OECD countries is far higher than in most developing countries. Although public expenditures per student at each level of education in the OECD countries are lower as a percentage of per capita income, they are much higher in actual dollar terms than in most developing countries. This is true even in higher education (except for Africa, including North Africa). Figure 5.4, also based on World Bank estimates, compares these actual dollar expenditures by level between 36 low-income developing countries and the OECD countries. The absolute

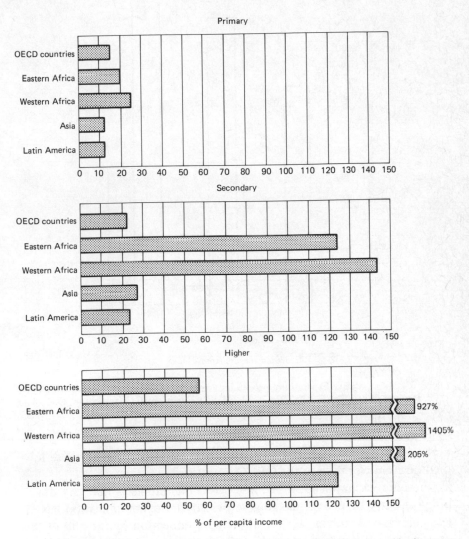

Figure 5.3. Public expenditures per student as a percentage of national per capita income, circa 1975. [Source: Based on World Bank Staff Working Paper No. 246, *Patterns of Educational Expenditures,* (Washington, D.C.: The World Bank, November 1976).]

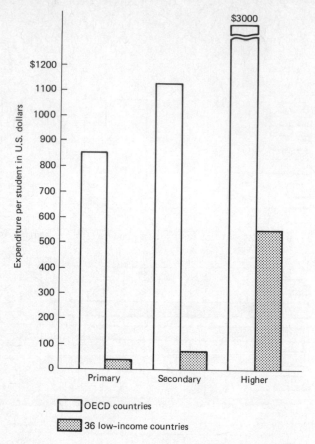

Figure 5.4. Comparative expenditure per student in high- and low-income countries, circa 1975. [Source: World Bank, *Education Sector Policy Paper, 1980* (Washington, D.C.: The World Bank, 1980).]

money cost per student, at every level, is drastically lower in these low-income countries than in the OECD countries.

One obvious implication of these cost differentials is that any developing country that continues to give priority to higher education has far less chance of achieving universal primary education by the end of this century than if it puts a cap on higher education expenditures.

THE FUTURE?

What then is likely to happen to the financial crunch that gripped education systems throughout the world with increasing intensity during the 1970s and early 1980s? Will it relax its grip, or tighten it still further? Will education budget ceilings become even more resistant to annual increases, and will the real cost per student continue to rise? Or will these previous trends be reversed?

Prospects for the World Economy

Answers to these questions will depend in part on future world economic conditions, including such factors as international trade, capital flows, energy and commodity prices, interest rates, debt burdens, and rates of inflation and economic growth. No one can predict these matters with certainty, but two things at least are clear. First, the economies of individual countries have become more interdependent than ever before; prosperity in the developed world and that in the developing world are intimately linked and they will generally move up or down together. Second, because of these close linkages, whatever happens to general world economic conditions will have a profound impact, for better or worse, on all national budgets and, thus, on all education budgets.

By 1984 most but not all international forecasters were cautiously optimistic that a recovery was under way from the paralyzing worldwide recession of 1980–81—the worst since the Great Depression of the early 1930s. Looking to the next ten years, however, they did not expect economic growth rates in most countries to regain the high levels of the 1960s and early 1970s, and they were particularly pessimistic about the prospects for the low-income group of developing countries, especially in Africa.

Revised World Bank economic growth projections up to 1995 for various income groups of countries, shown in Appendix Table 5.7, portray three possible scenarios—low, central, and high. These projections represent *group* averages; some members of each group may fall well below the average and others well above. The text of the *World Development Report, 1983,* in which these projections appear, observes somberly that "even with a GDP growth rate of 5 to 6 percent between 1975 and 2000, more than 600 million people will remain below the poverty line in developing countries in the year 2000, unless the pattern of growth is modified to put more emphasis on poverty alleviation." The text goes on to point out that "the current projections clearly suggest more moderate growth prospects and thus reinforce the need for policies not only for stimulating growth but for curbing population growth and meeting basic needs."[9]

These economic growth projections are hardly inspiring news for the managers of education systems. Taken in combination with other recent economic trends and forecasts—as they relate, for example, to depressed commodity prices, high interest rates, slackened capital flows, enormous debt burdens facing developing countries, the likelihood of continuing high unemployment rates, trade deficits, and protectionist maneuvers on the part of some of the strongest industrial countries—the general outlook for most national education systems would appear to be one of continuing financial belt tightening. In short, the golden years of the 1950s and 1960s are clearly over—the years when the growth of education budgets in most countries steadily outpaced the growth of the GNP and overall public budgets. From here on, the general financial weather outlook is likely to be cloudy and stormy.

Variations by Countries

The foregoing prognosis is not intended to suggest, however, that the future educational financial squeeze will be the same in all countries. Several key factors will strongly influence the level of each individual country's future expenditures on education. These factors include (1) the country's future rate of economic growth, (2) the share of its total income and resources already devoted to education, (3) the behavior of educational costs per student, (4) the amount of educational assistance received from external sources (in the case of developing countries), and (5) especially crucial but most difficult to anticipate, the relative priority given to education by the country's people and leaders.

Because these factors vary from country to country, only as each country is separately diagnosed can one arrive at a reasonable judgment about the severity of its future educational cost and financial squeeze. Drawing on what is already known from past and present experience, however, it is possible to venture the following general comments about the above key factors likely to influence the level of a country's expenditures on education.

1. As already emphasized, each country's future rate of economic growth will inevitably be conditioned by broader world economic conditions and events. But it will also be strongly influenced by the country's own economic policies, by changes (or the lack of changes) in its economic structure, and by how well it develops and utilizes its available resources, including especially its human resources. History plainly teaches that no nation can remain half educated, or waste half its human potential, and expect to prosper economically.
2. Almost all countries, rich or poor, will find it more difficult in the future to increase the percentage share of their national income going to education, partly because education's share has now reached a substantially higher level than it was 20 years ago, but also

because other pressing national needs and accumulated commitments are competing more strongly with education than in earlier years. The venerable "law of increasingly difficult increments," a distant cousin of the law of diminishing returns, says that each percentage point increment in education's share of the public budget is much harder to come by than the previous increment. This law will be hard at work as educational administrators struggle for a budget increase each year. Many will find that their most immediate problem is simply to hold on to the percentage share of the budget that education had the previous year.

3. The stiffest challenge facing education managers in the years ahead is to stop the persistent rise in real cost per student, the other arm of the financial pincer, while at the same time improving the quality and relevance of education. The implications of this challenge permeate virtually every aspect of educational systems. Only major changes in educational structures, logistics, technologies, and programs will be able to cope with them—and such changes, history shows, do not come easily or quickly.

4. The outlook is that many (not all) developing countries will require much more rather than less external assistance for educational development over the next decade, although often not of the kind they have been getting. The need will be particularly great in sub-Saharan Africa and in particular countries in other regions that got a late start on educational development. Unfortunately, however, from the present vantage point, the realistic prospects for their actually getting substantially more educational assistance from the outside are not bright, for reasons we will consider later in Chapter 10.

5. Almost all countries, both developing and developed, accorded education a very favorable priority in the 1950s and 1960s, at the expense of various other budgetary claimants. Contrary to popular impression, education still enjoys a fairly high budgetary priority and strong public and political support in most countries, notwithstanding the mounting criticisms that have been leveled at it in recent years. Relatively few of the critics and grumblers have been advocating major slashes in the education budget; what they want is to see the money used more equitably, efficiently, and effectively. The big difference today is that the education budget has now grown to immense proportions rivaled only, in some countries, by the military budget. The situation has drastically changed over the past 20 years, not because the people and leaders have changed their minds about the value of education, but because there are other important

values and needs that must also be attended to. This new condition is likely to endure as far into the future as anyone can now see. For as overall public budgets become increasingly strained and as other large world and domestic problems and needs move to the fore, such as rural development, urban blight, food, energy, environment, health, housing, population, unemployment, and security, education, though strongly desired and supported, will do well simply to maintain its present share of the budget.

6. Education's strongest competitor for resources over the next 20 years in developed countries may prove to be the senior citizen group (aged 60 and above) whose percentage of the total population will be increasing steadily, placing a growing burden on the working-age population. Because of increasing life expectancy, a similar trend is at work in developing countries, but its full impact will take longer to be felt.

In the final analysis, however, the priority a particular society attaches to education in comparison to other public goods and services is most strongly influenced by that society's cultural background and traditions, its present goals and aspirations, and, not least of all, the nature of its political system and climate. With other things being equal, some societies, including some of the poorest, will undoubtedly invest considerably more of their scarce resources in education than other societies.

Are the UNESCO Projections Feasible?

To conclude this sobering prognosis of educational financial prospects around the world, we must refer back to UNESCO's worldwide enrollment projections to the year 2000 presented in Chapter 2 (see Appendix Table 2.3 and Figure 2.3) and ask a blunt question: What are the realistic chances of countries, especially developing countries, actually realizing these projected increases? UNESCO's statisticians, for their part, did not try to answer the question; their main purpose was to show what would happen *if* the observed rates of enrollment increases prior to 1980 in various countries and regions were to continue on the same general path to 2000. The question of financial feasibility, however, must be squarely faced.

The UNESCO projections, as we saw in Chapter 3, would require the developing countries of South Asia and Latin America to increase their overall enrollments between 1980 and 2000 by as much as their total increment between 1960 and 1980 and, in the case of Africa, by twice as much. By contrast, in order to match the UNESCO projections, the developed countries of North America would have to enlarge their enrollments between 1980 and 2000 by only two thirds of what they added from 1960 to 1980, whereas the countries of Europe would not have to increase their enrollments at all over their 1980 total.

If our foregoing prognosis is anywhere near correct, it will plainly be impossible, barring some miracle, for the majority of developing nations—at least if they adhere to their present types of education systems and practices—to come close to achieving UNESCO's projected increases. These projections, as ambitious as they may seem, do not anticipate the attainment of universal primary education in either Africa or South Asia by the end of this century and are ambiguous about Latin America. On the other hand, the developed countries, given fair economic weather and the will to do so, could readily attain the modest projections laid out for them, although not without a serious effort.

One encouraging note should be added to this otherwise bleak assessment: a sizable expansion of nonformal educational activities for youth and adults could be achieved over the next two decades without critically impairing the budgets of formal education systems. This is so because the great bulk of these nonformal activities could find support from both public and private sources not generally accessible to formal education—including ministries other than the ministry of education, private organizations and individuals, and local communities.

WAYS TO COMBAT THE SQUEEZE

The foregoing conclusion suggests the need for a different approach to that customarily followed by national educational planners and managers. The customary approach entails two steps. The first is to project, on the basis of available demographic data, the increased number of potential enrollees at each level over the next five years or so. The second, using the present estimated cost per student at each level or possibly allowing for some increase, is to calculate the budget increment that would be required to absorb them. This increment is invariably much larger than education is likely to get, thus requiring a budget-cutting exercise once the appropriation is made in order to bring the budget into balance with what education actually gets.

Our suggestion, therefore, is that planners start from the other end, by making some high, medium, and low projections of how much money is realistically likely to be available for education over the next five to ten years. With these financial projections (which will usually be considerably lower than the budgetary requirement figure arrived at in the customary way), the planners and managers could then ask some very practical questions about how this money could most fruitfully be deployed. For example, what trade-offs might be possible between quantity and quality and between different levels of the system? How might the internal efficiency of schools, colleges, and universities be enhanced so as to reduce the cost per student, consistent with preserving or enhancing the learning results? How might the productivity of teachers—by far the most costly of all the educational inputs—be progressively increased over the next ten years? How might facilities and equipment—the second most expensive set of inputs—be more fully and productively used? What basic changes would be required in the present structure, logistics, educational technologies, and academic time schedules to effect these improvements in efficiency and learning effectiveness?

Similar questions could be asked about potential additional sources of educational revenues. In many countries, for example, the children of affluent families could be required to pay a reasonable share of the costs of their university education, now largely subsidized by public funds, with appropriate provisions for scholarship grants and loans for able but less affluent students. Consideration might also be given to transferring more of the burden of primary education to local communities, with special help for those who could least afford it.

These are the serious issues that need to be explored creatively and boldly—by planners and administrators in consultation with teachers, students and parents, local authorities, and the general public—if any real progress is to be made toward easing the growing cost-finance squeeze. Some education systems and individual institutions have already been probing some of these questions, with encouraging consequences. In many places, however, these are the issues that get swept under the rug, partly because everyone is so busy just maintaining the status quo, but also because simply asking the questions conjures up disturbing visions of radical changes. But this is precisely the point. Radical educational changes, at least in terms of conventional educational practices, are imperative if educational systems in the future are to perform effectively the tasks expected of them. The sooner educational planners and managers, and all other interested parties, recognize this need and act in concert to move the change process forward, the greater chance the younger generation will have of receiving an authentic, relevant, and equitable education. There should be no illusions about how quickly these things can happen, the process of social change being what it is. But without a concerted effort, and soon, the situation is almost bound to grow worse rather than better.

NOTES

1. World Bank, *Education Sector Paper* (Washington, D.C.: The World Bank, 1980), p. 67.
2. UNESCO and United Nations Economic Commission for Europe, *Development of Education in Europe: A Statistical Review* (Paris: UNESCO, April 1980).
3. See J. C. Eicher and F. Orivel, *The Allocation of Resources to Education Throughout the World* (Paris: UNESCO, 1980).
4. Jean-Pierre Jallade, "Expenditure on Higher Education in Europe: Past Trends and Future Prospects," *European Journal of Education,* Vol. 15, No. 1 (March 1980), pp. 35–48.
5. Howard R. Bowen, *The Cost of Higher Education: How Much Do Colleges and Universities Spend per Student and How Much Should They Spend?* (San Francisco: Jossey-Bass Publishers, 1980). Report prepared for Carnegie Commission on Higher Education.
6. Adapted from the *Chronicle on Higher Education* report on Howard Bowen's findings, December 1978.
7. Heitor Gurgulino de Souza and Gladstone Rodrigues da Cunha Filho, "Higher Education in Brazil: Basic Facts and Figures," an unpublished paper presented to an International Council for Educational Development seminar, Rio de Janeiro, April 1983.
8. Ibid.
9. World Bank, *World Development Report 1983* (New York: Oxford University Press, 1983), p. 39.

Appendix Table 5.1 Worldwide Trends in Public Expenditure on Education, 1970–79 (in current prices)[a]

Regions	Billions of U.S. Dollars		
	1970	1975	1979
World total	158	330	530
Developed countries	146	293	464
Developing countries	12.4	37.2	65.6
In Africa	2.4	7.0	12.8
In Asia and Oceania	4.5	16	27
In Latin America and Caribbean	5.5	14.2	25.8

[a]Not including the People's Republic of China, Democratic Kampuchea, Democratic People's Republic of Korea, Lao People's Democratic Republic, Lebanon, Mongolia, and Vietnam.

Source: UNESCO, *Public Expenditures on Education in the World, Regional and Country Trends, 1970–1979,* mimeographed (Paris: UNESCO, Division of Statistics on Education, Office of Statistics, October 1982).

Appendix Table 5.2 Public Expenditure on Education per Inhabitant, 1970–79 (current prices)[a]

Regions	U.S. Dollars					
	1970	1975	1976	1977	1978	1979
World	57	108	115	122	157	162
Developed countries	136	262	280	307	366	403
Developing countries	7	19	22	24	27	31
In Africa	8	18	21	24	27	30
In Asia and Oceania	13	26	42	17	18	20
In Latin America and Caribbean	20	45	50	53	60	73

[a]Not including the People's Republic of China, Democratic Kampuchea, Democratic People's Republic of Korea, Lao People's Democratic Republic, Lebanon, Mongolia, and Vietnam.

Source: UNESCO, *Public Expenditure on Education in the World, Regional and Country Trends, 1970–1979,* mimeographed (Paris: UNESCO, Division of Statistics on Education, Office of Statistics, October 1982).

Appendix Table 5.3 Inflation in 117 Countries, 1960–81[a]

Region	Number of Countries	Average Annual Rate of Inflation (%)	
		1960–70	1970–81
Developing			
Low income	34	3.5	11.2
Lower middle income	39	2.8	11.1
Upper middle income	21	3.0	18.6
High income oil exporters	4	—	18.2
Developed			
Industrial: market economies	19	4.3	9.9
Total	117		

[a]Not including People's Republic of China, Democratic Kampuchea, Democratic People's Republic of Korea, Lao People's Democratic Republic, Lebanon, Mongolia, and Vietnam.

Source: World Bank, *World Development Report 1982* (New York: Oxford University Press, 1982).

Appendix Table 5.4 Sweden: Increasing Cost per
Student in Stockholm Comprehensive Schools,
1963–75 (in Swedish kroner)

Year	Per Student Expenditure at Current Prices	Per Student Expenditure in Constant 1968 Prices
1963	2,472	3,793
1964	2,711	3,874
1965	3,091	3,981
1966	3,456	4,034
1967	4,083	4,278
1968	4,447	4,447
1969	5,123	4,902
1970	5,855	5,195
1971	6,469	5,117
1972	7,538	5,539
1973	8,374	5,678
1974	9.665	5,813
1975	11,439	5,904

Source: A. Harry Passow, Harold J. Noah, Max A. Eckstein, and John R. Mallea, *The National Case Study: An Empirical Comparative Study of Twenty-One Educational Systems* cited in Torsten Husén, *The School in Question* (New York: Oxford University Press, 1979).

Appendix Table 5.5 Canada: Trends in Real Cost per Student, 1960–74
(constant 1960–61 Canadian dollars)

Year	Elementary and Secondary	Index	Postsecondary Nonuniversity	Index	University	Index
1960–61	$305	100	$ 915	100	$1603	100
1965–66	387	127	884	97	1787	111
1970–71	522	171	1218	133	2539	158
1971–72	531	174	1296	142	2494	156
1972–73	509	167	1147	125	2375	148
1973–74	504	165	1162	127	2264	141

Source: Compiled from Canadian Country Paper, Commonwealth Education Conference, Accra, Ghana, March 1977.

Appendix Table 5.6 United States: Total and Current Expenditures
per Pupil in Average Daily Attendance, 1929–30 to 1979–80

School Year	Unadjusted Dollars		Adjusted Dollars (1979–80 purchasing power)	
	Total	Current	Total	Current
1929–30	108	87	490	395
1939–40	106	88	589	489
1949–50	259	209	849	685
1959–60	472	375	1247	991
1969–70	955	816	1963	1677
1979–80	2494	2275	2494	2275

Source: Digest of Education Statistics, 1982 (Washington, D.C.: National Center for Education Statistics, U.S. Government Printing Office, 1982).

Appendix Table 5.7 Past and Projected Growth of Gross Domestic Product,
1960–95 (average annual percentage change)

Country Group	1960–73	1973–80	1980–82	1982–85	1985–95 Low	Central	High
All developing countries	6.0	4.7	1.9	4.4	4.7	5.5	6.2
Low-income							
Asia	4.6	5.4	4.1	4.5	4.5	4.9	5.3
Africa	3.5	1.4	0.5	2.9	2.7	3.3	3.9
Middle-income							
Oil importers	6.3	5.2	1.2	4.5	4.4	5.7	6.9
Oil exporters	7.0	3.7	1.7	4.0	5.3	5.7	5.8
Industrial countries	5.1	2.5	0.4	3.0	2.5	3.7	5.0

Source: World Bank, *World Development Report 1983* (New York: Oxford University Press, 1983).

CHAPTER 6

EDUCATION AND EMPLOYMENT

In its approach to the troubled partnership between education and employment, the 1968 report on the world educational crisis observed straight off that "the point at issue has a potential political hurricane wrapped inside it." The same point at issue is all the more volatile and complex today, as we will show after we dispose of the preliminary task of tracing the genealogy of today's troubled and troublesome incongruities between the world of education and the world of work.

BACKGROUND

Technical education is not an invention of modern industrialized societies. Throughout human history, a generally recognized cardinal aim of education in any organized society has been to prepare each new generation for a productive working life. One of the main functions of traditional puberty rites in African tribal societies, for example, was to train the young in the inherited, time-tested technologies of hunting, fishing, cropping, and other essential survival skills. In biblical times, the Talmud in its discussions of law and ethics, enjoined every father to teach his children a trade—an injunction that was reflected in the range of trades represented by the Apostles of the New Testament. And again, in ancient China and India, as well as in medieval Europe, gifted artisans, craftsmen, and other specialists passed on their unique skills and lore to the next generation by the meticulous training of young apprentices through what we today would call nonformal education.

As long as the economies of the simpler societies were slow to change, the modes and content of their technical education tended to remain quite similar from one generation to the next. This ceased to be the case when societies began to grow and change rapidly and to become increasingly interdependent. With that, the organization and technologies of their economies became more complex and sophisticated. Their products, once destined only for a local market, became more diversified as markets themselves became more integrated with the larger world economy. All this has had a far-reaching impact on both general and technical education.

For one thing, today's economies require a wider range of specialized human skills and technical knowledge in order to function effectively and to keep moving ahead. In response to these needs, technical education, in the broadest sense, has become increasingly diversified and formalized (though a high proportion of it is still acquired through apprenticeships and on-the-job training). Moreover, because of rapid technological and economic changes it is not enough merely to provide preemployment education to the young; whatever specific occupational skills they may be taught in their teenage years are likely to become obsolete, or at least to require substantial supplementing, when the young learners enter the world of work. Not only do specific jobs and the nature of work itself keep changing, but, more than ever before, people keep changing jobs. This is especially true in the more mobile and dynamic industrialized countries, but it is increasingly true also in less developed countries. Today in the United States, for example, one worker in every seven changes occupation or employer every 12 months. This does not include the unrecorded changes in job functions and technologies for those who stay put, as in the case of bank clerks, travel agents, and many other workers who lately have had to learn how to do business with computers. In short, technical education has become a lifelong process and necessity for an increasing proportion of each nation's labor force.

Before World War II there was scarcely a book with the word *development* in its title, nor were there university courses in development, or development experts, or development institutes. Following the war, however, for the first time in history, national development suddenly became the transcendent goal and guide to both national and international policies and programs throughout the world, especially in the newly independent nations. This was the context in which the extraordinary worldwide educational expansion took off.

To be more explicit, the time-honored symbiotic relationship between education and work became the basic rationale for the great postwar educational expansion in the 1950s and 1960s. The particular strategy of linear expansion that was adopted almost universally rested on three assumptions unique to the period: (1) that a steadily increasing supply of educated manpower (usually meaning secondary and higher education graduates) was essential to national economic growth; (2) that the existing formal education systems, inherited from the past, were reasonably well-adapted to producing the kinds of manpower needed; and (3) that the growing economies of nations would continue to have an insatiable appetite for all the educated manpower their educational systems could provide.

These three assumptions had a decisive influence on the direction that educational development took in both developed and developing countries. Leading economists sanctified them by proclaiming that increased expenditures on education were a good investment in economic growth. But as helpful as this slogan was in winning ever larger education budgets, it failed to answer three important questions: Education for what purpose and for whom? What different kinds of education and how much of each? What are the most efficient and effective ways of providing this needed education?

Simply expanding the existing educational system indiscriminately without reasonably clear answers to these basic questions would inevitably lead to gross imbalances and waste. This indeed was already happening. By the 1960s some developing countries were finding themselves with more graduate engineers than middle-level technicians to support them, or more doctors than nurses, so that high-level professionals frequently ended up doing the work of middle-level personnel. In other cases—for example, in Ethiopia in 1961—ambitious plans were launched for a new or enlarged university, followed by the belated discovery that the expected flow of qualified secondary-school graduates would be insufficient to fill the new places.

The New Focus on Educational and Manpower Planning

By the early 1960s, such conspicuous miscarriages inspired a broad-based demand for a new kind of educational planning that would ensure the balanced internal growth of education systems to keep them in harmony with the needs of the economy. UNESCO's new IIEP, established in 1963, took the lead in responding to that demand. It devised new research-based planning concepts and methodologies and began training a new breed of educational planners, especially for developing countries. The OECD, for its part, launched a series of educational-cum-manpower planning projects in several southern European countries. These efforts were soon reinforced by other international, regional, and national research and training programs and by numerous academic economists and other social scientists.

But planning a nation's educational development in conjunction with its economic and social development proved to be considerably more complicated than it had first appeared. Plotting a time path toward the widely adopted goal of universal primary education was a fairly straight-forward statistical exercise, based on demographic projections. As long as the inherited model of primary schools was adhered to, it simply involved calculating how many more children were in the age group each year, how many more teachers and classrooms would be needed, and how much more money would be required to secure them. (It was not until some years later that the problem of where to place the new schools was seriously addressed.) Planning the growth of secondary and higher education, however, was another story. At these levels, the matter of matching educational output with future national manpower requirements became an important and very complicating factor. Many different kinds of educational preparation were needed for many different kinds of manpower—ranging from clerks and technicians to high-level experts in agriculture, industry, health, and administration, not to mention the wide variety of teachers needed to staff the expanding educational system itself.

Because it required many years to educate such specialists, and additional years to "tool up" the educational system for the purpose, it was necessary to visualize the economy's needs no less than five to ten years ahead. But to do this with reasonable accuracy and sufficient specificity, including the qualitative as well as quantitative dimensions of the manpower needed, proved virtually impossible. The difficulty stemmed in part from the lack of reliable basic data to go on, but even more from the unpredictable changes underway in the economy, the widely divergent views among different sectoral ministries and specialists as to what the priorities should be, and above all from the absence of any realistic, comprehensive, and well-integrated overall national development plan. Even the Soviet Union with its elaborate and highly centralized system of economic and educational planning and manpower allocation found it increasingly difficult to make things happen and fit neatly together as planned.

Competing Schools of Thought

The new breed of "manpower planners" that emerged in this context in the 1960s tried to help educational planners take dead aim at critical manpower bottlenecks to economic growth, themselves assuming the difficult task of projecting the economy's future middle and higher level manpower requirements. They did their best in the circumstances and succeeded to a limited extent in spotting some serious gaps and imbalances. Their projection models, however, were necessarily programmed with arbitrary "guesstimates" that frequently bore little resemblance to what the reality turned out to be beyond the next two or three years. Moreover, they were using employment categories and ratios drawn out of the experience of Western industrial societies that often did not fit the conditions and needs in newly developing countries.

A different school of economists, of the neoclassical stripe, were strongly critical of the manpower approach to educational planning, on various theoretical grounds, so it developed a basically different approach. This so-called cost-benefit approach used an intricate quantitative methodology (irreverently described by some opposing economists as a statistical house of cards) to calculate for any given country separate rates of return on past educational investments in primary, secondary, and higher education. This was done essentially by comparing the previous average cost per student at each educational level with the subsequent average earnings of workers emerging from the different levels. The idea was that by comparing these rates of return with each other and with the yields on investments elsewhere in the economy, national decision makers could determine how best to allocate future resources, both within education and between education and alternative types of investment, in order to reap the highest marginal yield in all directions.

Interestingly enough, such cost-benefit exercises in the various developing countries in which they were conducted almost invariably showed the following patterns. First, the overall yield from education was generally higher than from most other investments in the economy. Second, there was a substantially higher "social" rate of return on public investments in primary education than in higher education, which suggested that, from a public point of view, primary schooling had been underinvested and higher education relatively overinvested. The pattern also showed a significantly higher rate for the private than for the social return on investments in higher education—an indication that individuals profited more from heavily subsidized university education than the society at large.

This cost-benefit approach, however, was subject to as many theoretical objections and practical shortcomings as the manpower approach. The basic data underlying the calculations were wobbly at best. Moreover, the resulting rates of return, even if they could be assumed to be accurate, applied only to the past and might well change considerably in the future as a result of educational expansion and changes in the economy and wage structures. These differing rates of return by education levels could at best only tell educational planners and decision makers in what *direction* to increase or slow down investment, but not by *how much.* In addition, most of the cost-benefit exercises implicitly treated each education level as though it were homogeneous. They usually failed to differentiate, for example, between the yield on secondary general education and vocational or technical education, and at the postsecondary level between liberal arts and various professional fields. These distinctions, however, were at the heart of the difficult choices that planners and decision makers were obliged to make.

The fundamental shortcoming of both the manpower approach and the cost-benefit approach was that each was essentially a "numbers game"—one that ignored vitally important qualitative deficiencies and maladjustments in existing educational systems and specific programs. They tacitly assumed that what was being taught and learned in the present system was generally satisfactory in terms of what was actually needed. They thus served to reinforce the inappropriate strategy of linear expansion, which itself was essentially a numbers game.

All this is not to suggest that the efforts invested in the manpower and the cost-benefit approaches to educational planning went for naught. On the contrary, despite their practical limitations, both approaches at least had the merit of encouraging planners and decision makers to think in clearer, more rigorous, and comprehensive terms about how best to allocate limited resources among different parts of the educational system and how to match the system's performance and products with realistic national development needs. By and large, however, neither of these competing concepts and methodologies appears to have had any decisive impact on the actual policies and patterns of educational development in most countries, whether developing or industrial. The notable exceptions were the Soviet Union and some of the socialist countries of Eastern Europe, where manpower planning was taken very seriously and strongly influenced the evolution of secondary and especially postsecondary education.

In actual practice, educational plans in most countries and especially the *real decisions* (which often deviated widely from the plan) were shaped by a third and much more pragmatic approach that came to be called the social demand approach. This label, however, is deceptively simple. The approach is in fact a highly complex amalgam of technocratic statistical calculations and projections, strongly leavened by diverse and competing professional biases, philosophical convictions, and political interests and pressures. The final product—the pattern of education development that actually unfolded—might best be compared to an elaborate stew concocted by numerous cooks, each with his or her own favorite recipe and condiments. Still, it would perhaps be fair to say that, much more than the other two approaches, the social demand approach reflected the voice of the people. The fact that some people had stronger voices than others helps explain why the development of rural education lagged seriously behind urban education in virtually all developing countries and why the rate of growth of secondary and especially university education greatly outpaced that of primary education. It also explains why educational planning is and always must be more an art than a science (particularly a quantitative science), and why, whatever its ideology, educational decision making in any country is, in the final analysis and inescapably, a political process of give and take.

Needed Changes in Educational Planning

The preceding in no way denigrates the substantial progress made during the 1960s in improving educational planning concepts and techniques, for without a reasonably well thought out and balanced plan to start with, the subsequent political decisions on actual budget allocations could be disastrously ill informed.

By the end of the decade, sufficient experience had been attained with educational planning to reveal some of its key strengths and weaknesses and the main directions in which it now needed to be broadened and improved. Specifically, there was growing agreement that it needed (1) to be extended downward from the purely national aggregate level closer to the local realities, (2) to give greater attention to much needed structural and qualitative changes and innovations in the formal education system, (3) to be extended in appropriate fashion to the broad and diversified terrain of nonformal education, (4) to address and remedy serious geographic and social disparities and inequalities, (5) to place greater emphasis on reducing educational costs, consistent with preserving and enhancing quality, and (6) to integrate educational development more harmoniously with the broader process of social and economic development. In short, educational planning itself needed to be more than yet another numbers game. Instead of reinforcing the educational status quo by concentrating on simply making the present system bigger, it needed to become an effective instrument of educational change and innovation. And rather than confining itself exclusively to the formal education system, it needed to take broad account also of various important types of nonformal education. This would call for a quite different kind of planning.

Prospects as Viewed from the Late 1960s

In examining the subject of education's relations with employment and development needs, the 1968 report on the world educational crisis first took up the question of how well educational systems could meet, and were actually meeting, the important human resource requirements for national development. Based on scattered evidence drawn from a wide variety of countries, it concluded that there were numerous gross disparities—qualitative and quantitative—between the kinds of manpower most needed and the kinds, quality, and proportions actually being turned out by educational systems. These disparities were seen to be most egregious in developing countries, which could least afford the luxury of ill-fitting educational systems. "A developing country," the report observed, "can land in deep trouble by slavishly adhering to the educational forms of industrialized countries, in a context where they simply do not fit."

Another large part of the problem was the inappropriate choices made by students, or their counselors, in selecting a major field of study, particularly at the university level. The typical picture in most developing countries showed a highly distorted pattern of graduates in relation to urgent national development needs: a heavy preponderance, for example, of graduates in humanistic studies and law (over 90 percent in some cases), less than 10 percent in natural sciences and engineering, and often fewer than 3 percent in agriculture, the area of greatest development need at that stage in almost all developing countries. Student choices, however, were generally more rational than they might appear. In the first place, they were strongly conditioned by what the university actually had to offer, and most universities in the developing world were conspicuously weak in all the mathematical- and science-based fields, and many had no agricultural faculty at all. Second, student choices were also influenced by the structure of salary incentives in the economy, which were often grotesquely at odds with national development priorities and the corresponding pattern of human resource needs. Manpower planners were either oblivious to these distorted and counterproductive incentive structures or felt powerless to change them.

Another and related incongruity was noted in the report. Entire education systems, from primary school through the university level, were tightly geared to producing workers for the modern sector of the economy, largely in the cities, whereas the great majority of workers for years to come would live out their working lives in the traditional rural areas or in the informal sector of urban economies. Unfortunately, the imported educational systems were ill designed to prepare young people who would constitute this great majority of workers with the appropriate attitudes, knowledge, skills, and motivation to take the lead in modernizing their own rural communities and urban slum areas.

The report's discussion then shifted abruptly from the question of meeting manpower shortages to what it asserted "is fast becoming a more serious manpower question—whether enough new jobs of the right sort can be found for the newly educated." It flatly predicted that in the not too distant future virtually every country, including the industrialized ones, would encounter a serious problem of educated unemployed. Its reasoning was simple and straightforward.

The output of graduates from secondary schools and higher institutions in practically all countries was growing more rapidly than the economy's capacity to create new jobs of the kinds and levels customarily associated with various academic credentials. Thus, once the supply of these credentials had caught up with the backlog of manpower deficits, employment markets would become saturated and turn from sellers' to buyers' markets.

This was not just a theoretical speculation. The report demonstrated that the phenomenon of educated unemployed had already appeared on a disturbing scale in such countries as India, Egypt, the Philippines, and several Latin American countries. The industrialized nations, the report warned, were not immune to this contagious disease; it was bound to strike them eventually, although how soon and in what exact form was not yet clear.

Unemployed graduates, the report hastened to point out, would not be condemned to permanent unemployment. Rather, they would continue to search for a preferred job as long as they could hold out, but failing to find one, they would eventually settle for something less, beneath what they considered to be their qualification. In so doing, they would take jobs previously occupied by people with lower educational credentials, who in turn would now be forced to move downward on the job scale. As this bumping process proceeded, the ultimate burden of real unemployment would be borne mainly by those at the bottom with the least educational qualifications.

THE TURN OF EVENTS IN THE 1970s

The report's gloomy prophecy soon started to be realized. An abrupt turn of events in the early 1970s rudely shattered the earlier optimistic assumption that the growing economies of both developed and developing countries could indefinitely absorb all of the middle- and high-level manpower their expanding educational systems could provide. The phenomenon of educated unemployed—a term first coined in India some years earlier—now began to spread across both the developing and the industrialized worlds. Paradoxically, in the midst of this growing abundance of educated manpower, selective shortages of particular types of manpower still persisted (the very thing the manpower planners had sought to avoid).

In these changed circumstances, the old euphoria that had infused the great educational expansion of the 1950s and 1960s soon gave way to a darkened mood of skepticism, anxiety, and in some quarters downright cynicism. National educational authorities, economic experts, and political leaders were besieged by insistent questions: What had gone wrong? What had caused this reversal, and who was to blame? What did it mean for the future? What could be done to remedy the problem?

In a happier historical view of the case, continued increases in labor productivity, which supported increases in real wages and living standards, had tended to go hand-in-hand with increases in the educational prerequisites for employment. Over the last 75 years, for example, in both Europe and North America there had been a dramatic rise in the educational qualifications necessary for employment as a schoolteacher or college professor, a physician or lawyer, a licensed plumber or toolmaker. In the 1970s, however, what had once been the normal gradual adjustment process no longer held sway. The sudden acceleration in the upward scaling of credentials in relation to jobs, caused by the greatly increased influx of educated young people into saturated employment markets, which were further weakened by a sharp recession, was in turn the cause of widespread personal pain and ominous political rumblings.

Meanwhile, various diagnoses and prescriptions were offered from various quarters. Frustrated students pointed an accusing finger at the Establishment, which had let them down, and they called vaguely for radical changes in the political and economic status quo. The political storm that shook France to its foundations in the spring of 1968, for example, was precipitated mainly by university students in the social sciences and the humanities who began to realize that the kinds of jobs they had been counting on were far scarcer than expected. Their slogan, "All power to the Imagination!" was a linguistic invention representing their reaction to the lack of employment opportunities in prospect for themselves in the cherished public sector.

Elsewhere in the Western world, beginning in the late 1960s and extending into the 1970s, student unrest in the universities over new grievances merged with the unrest springing from unredressed old grievances. The growing spectre of unemployment among secondary-school and postsecondary graduates, plus the tightening of budgets for educational spending, fueled criticism of the general lengthening of studies—the process that was once viewed as holding the key to economic and social progress. In addition, the growing stagnation of higher education coincident with reduced economic growth and employment opportunities led to curbing of those liberalizing trends that had been reducing inequalities in higher education. In the absence of strong antidiscrimination legislation and major changes in government and private recruiting practices, the reinstitution of *numerus clausus* restrictions in more and more Western European universities appeared to be signaling a reversal of the strong democratization movement of the previous 20 years.

Business leaders meanwhile tended to place the blame for rising youth unemployment squarely on the educational system for turning out "bookishly trained students lacking employable skills." Their implicit assumption was that if students had been taught practical things they could find jobs. Other critics, however, took a jaundiced view of this sort of practical training. One of them, Professor Philip Foster, blasted the whole concept in his famous piece, "The Vocational School Fallacy," based on his evaluation of such schools in Ghana.[1] Similar critics dwelt on the fact that despite the heavy investments in technical education and vocational training, the results from the standpoint of efficiency and economic growth were not encouraging. For one thing, the youths for whom these programs were meant either were not drawn to them or rated them a second choice far behind their preference for the prestigious long cycle of regular educational courses. Moreover, students emerging from vocational schools often ended up in jobs that made little or no use of their specialized training. For another thing, employers themselves complained that the costly technical and vocational schools offered obsolete regimens of instruction not suited to the current needs of business.

In addition to these inefficiencies, critics in the developing world pointed to the adverse connection between the spread of even limited modern primary and secondary schooling in the countryside and an unchecked rural exodus of its product to the teeming cities with their scanty employment opportunities. Although embittering disappointments were commonplace in the cities, few youths of rural background would listen to the kind of advice a Zambian farmer gave his son who failed to find employment in the city:

I tell my son [so the farmer was quoted as saying] that if you can't get employment, you get your hoe and try to grow something to eat. You take your axe and you build your house. You can take something else, if you have the strength, like to put a bee-hive on the branch of a tree and you will get some honey and it will help you. That is how we old people survive. But if you stay like that [hoping for a job] then how are you going to live?[2]

Many economists, meanwhile, attributed the growing educated youth unemployment problem mainly to the economic slowdown caused by skyrocketing oil prices and the sharp world recession in the mid-1970s.

The more optimistic ones predicted that the problem would subside as soon as national economic growth rates recovered. The less optimistic, however, expressed fears that this was more than a conventional cyclical downturn—that the underlying causes were more fundamental and enduring and could be corrected only by major structural reforms in the economy. Still another diagnosis—a favorite among manpower experts who had earlier been strong advocates of rapid educational expansion— was that education systems had now reached excess production and were exceeding the capacity of economic systems to create new jobs; the obvious solution was to cut back on educational output.

Meanwhile, educators themselves, unable to believe that any nation could suddenly find itself overeducated or that landing a first job was the cardinal purpose of an education, were caught in the middle, trying to keep their creaking institutions together amid a mounting storm of criticism, declining public confidence, and tightening budgets.

The Great Transition

There was undoubtedly some element of truth to most of these conflicting diagnoses. But the more basic explanation is the one noted in the first chapter: between the late 1960s and early 1970s, practically all national economies throughout the world were making the wrenching transition from an era of ubiquitous educated manpower shortages to a new era of growing surpluses. To the surprise of many educational and manpower planners, whose attention had previously been fixed on averting manpower bottlenecks to economic growth, the rapidly increasing output from secondary and higher education had finally caught up with the backlog of deficits and begun to exceed the effective demands of employment markets. This fundamental historic shift in the relation of educational supply to employment demands exposed a variety of imbalances and maladjustments that could not be eliminated simply by an improved rate of economic growth. Although the most visible evidence was the alarming rise in youth unemployment, many other maladjustments of a more qualitative nature were hidden beneath the surface.

This basic shift from a seller's to a buyer's market for educated personnel was exacerbated by the world recession of the 1970s, but it was bound to happen in any case. Its impact varied in form and severity from country to country and region to region, but scarcely any country escaped unscathed. And contrary to the optimistic notion that it was simply a temporary cyclical problem that would soon subside, the rate of youth employment, including educated youth, continued to mount to all-time high levels throughout the 1970s and well into the 1980s.

CAVEATS ABOUT EMPLOYMENT STATISTICS

Before we examine more closely the contrasting experiences of developed and developing countries, it is important to insert three cautionary notes about unemployment statistics.

First, the concept of unemployment originated in industrial societies, where the great majority of the labor force is employed for wages and salaries by various public and private organizations and only a relatively small minority is self-employed. In these economies, the measure of unemployment is essentially the difference between the total number of workers and would-be workers in the national labor force and the number actually employed full time. In this context, persons working only part time are considered underemployed.

This concept of unemployment in the industrial countries, however, does not fit the economies of most developing countries, where only a relatively small proportion of the national labor force—often no more than 10 percent—is employed for regular salaries and wages in the modern sector, whereas the great bulk of the labor force is self-employed in agriculture and other small-scale enterprises, or doing irregular odd jobs for others. This point will be elaborated later; it is enough for the moment to say that published unemployment figures on developing countries should be viewed with extreme reservations.

Second, statistical services of individual countries, including industrialized countries, use different concepts and ways of measuring employment and unemployment in their labor force. Intercountry comparisons, therefore, can be misleading; the most trustworthy comparisons are between successive years in the same country.

Third, the common notion that an increase in unemployment in any country means a simultaneous decrease in the number employed is often mistaken. This would be true if the size of the total labor force remained constant from one period to the next, which is seldom the case. In most countries during the 1960s and 1970s, the labor force increased steadily. So, in many cases, did their total employment. But if these increases were not fast enough to keep pace with the influx of new entrants to the labor market, unemployment also grew. The United States and Canada, as will be seen in a moment, are particularly striking examples of the latter phenomenon.

With these important caveats in mind, we turn now to a closer examination of what actually happened during the 1970s to youth unemployment, and especially of educated youth, in the developed and developing countries.

GROWTH OF YOUTH UNEMPLOYMENT IN OECD COUNTRIES

For two decades following World War II, with occasional ups and downs, the various OECD countries had experienced highly favorable economic weather—vigorous economic growth, rising productivity and per capita real incomes, and expanding employment. During the 1960s, they had kept inflation down to an average of 3 to 4 percent and the unemployment rate close to the "frictional" level of only 2 to 3 percent, despite the increasing surge of young people and women entering the labor market.

The climate changed dramatically during the 1970s, a period marked by dark clouds and a succession of increasingly heavy storms. Economic growth slackened and in some countries dipped at times into the negative column. Inflation acquired so much momentum that by 1980 the seven major OECD countries experienced an annual average inflation rate of over 12 percent. Unemployment rates also moved into the double-digit bracket in several countries. By 1982 the total number of unemployed in the OECD area stood at 30 million—three times more than in 1970.

To keep things in perspective, however, two related phenomena underlying this rise in unemployment figures should be noted. First, the size of the overall labor force of the OECD countries expanded substantially (by 14 percent) during the 1970s, primarily because of the torrent of young people from the earlier baby boom coming onto the labor market and the sharp rise in the proportion of women (especially married women) seeking employment.* Second, despite the inclement economic weather, total employment in the OECD countries also grew substantially during most years of the decade—from 298 million in 1970 to 330 million in 1980 (then slacking off in the next three years). But since the growth of the labor force outstripped the increase in employment, the gap between the two, namely, unemployment, grew steadily after 1975. The relative movements of these three key variables from 1960 to 1982 are shown graphically in Figure 6.1. It should be added that these trends and levels varied in the different OECD countries although all were affected in some degree. Most of the growth of both the labor force and employment was concentrated in the United States, Canada, and Japan.[3]

---

*In the seven major OECD countries, the average participation rate in the labor force for women aged 15 to 64 years rose from 50.5 percent in 1975 to nearly 60 percent in 1982. In the United States it rose from 53.2 percent to 61.5 percent, and in Canada from 50 percent to 59 percent.

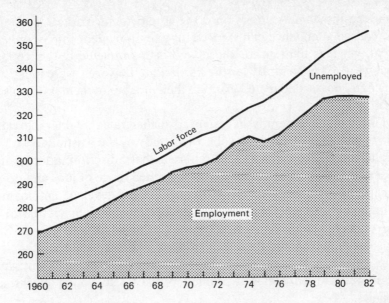

Figure 6.1. The growing employment gap in OECD countries, 1960–82. [Source: Redrawn from *The OECD Observer* (Paris: Organization for Economic Cooperation and Development, March 1982).]

The impact of the sharp increases in unemployment in the OECD countries during the 1970s fell with three- and fourfold force on the younger members of the labor force (age 15–24) compared to older and more experienced workers. The figures in Appendix Table 6.1 show the ratio of youth unemployment rates to adult unemployment rates for selected OECD countries and how this rate grew during the 1970s. In 1980, the youth unemployment rate in the United States, Canada, and Japan, for example, was double or more the rate for adult workers; in Australia, France, Spain, and the United Kingdom it was more than triple; and in Italy it was seven times as great. Between 1980 and 1982 the youth-to-adult unemployment ratio declined slightly in most of these countries, not because youth employment increased but because adult employment decreased.

Within this broad and heterogeneous youth population, unemployment hit certain subgroups much harder than others. Unemployment rates varied inversely with the level of education attained. The rates for those with college and university degrees were lower than for those with only secondary school diplomas, whereas those with incomplete secondary schooling were hardest hit. In the United States in 1975, for example, among the recent newcomers onto the employment market, those with some college attendance experienced an unemployment rate of only 6.5 percent, whereas the rate for those who had completed only secondary school was 16.5 percent. By far the hardest hit, however, were those with an incomplete secondary education; their unemployment rate was 37 percent.[4]

Young women generally experienced higher rates of unemployment than young men. A UNESCO-sponsored study by the Australian Council for Educational Research (1979) reported that "discrimination against girls seems to be pervasive: they enter a limited range of jobs and do not attain parity with boys in terms of hierarchical level of employment within the various employment fields."[5] The most serious victims of all, however, were young members of ethnic and racial minority groups who were socially and culturally disadvantaged and had minimal schooling. In Europe this applied especially to the children of foreign "guest workers"; in the United States it applied primarily to young blacks and Hispanics.

The deep concern of policymakers in the OECD countries over the high and rising level of youth unemployment prompted the OECD Secretariat to concentrate attention on the problem throughout the 1970s, with particular emphasis on the connection between education and work. The various OECD papers and publications on this subject, based on special studies and numerous meetings of experts and policymakers, would fill a fair-sized bookshelf. The OECD Secretariat conducted a wide-ranging review of youth unemployment in 1980 and its report concluded that there had been little improvement since the previous review in 1977:

> With very few exceptions, Denmark, Germany, the United Kingdom, and the United States being the most noteworthy, youth unemployment rates have continued to rise, increasing from 10.4 percent in 1976 to 11.3 percent in 1979 for the OECD area as a whole (excluding Turkey) and this over a period when the overall rate of unemployment declined slightly (from 5.4 to 5.1 percent). As a result the proportion of young people in total unemployment has risen from 44 to 47 percent. The average period of unemployment for 16–25 year olds has also increased in virtually every country for which data are available. . . .[6]

To attempt to diagnose the complex causes of this phenomenon would carry us beyond the scope of this report. However, it will be useful to look briefly at three sets of basic forces that converged in the 1970s and seriously upset the supply/demand balance of the employment equation.

Demographic Factors. The 1970s saw a flood of aspiring young job-seekers, products of the postwar baby boom, pouring out of schools and colleges and into the labor market. In the special case of the United States and Canada, the flood had actually set in strongly during the 1960s, ahead of Europe, because their baby boom had peaked somewhat earlier. This helps explain why youth unemployment rates in North America had already reached 10 percent when the 1970s began and were much lower at the time in most Western European countries.* A further factor that differentiated North America from Europe was the more rapid increase there in the number and proportion of women (of all ages) entering the labor force during the 1960s and 1970s.

What it all added up to was that an abnormally large increase on the labor supply side of the employment equation in the OECD countries just before and during the 1970s, resulting primarily from the youth bulge and the increased proportion of women entering the labor force, presented their economies (some more than others) with the enormous challenge of creating enough additional jobs to absorb all these newcomers. Clearly, their economies were not up to the challenge, as we shall see presently.

Economic Growth and Structural Factors. The persistent rise in unemployment during the 1970s, especially youth unemployment, is only partly attributable to the sluggish overall economic growth rates in the OECD countries. It was also a result of technological and structural maladjustments in these economies and changes in their international markets. Agricultural employment, because of technological innovations, continued its long downward slide, side by side with increasing physical production. Manufacturing employment, for its part, virtually stagnated, while tighter public budgets slowed the further growth of civil service employment. Thus, nearly all of the absolute increase in employment was in the service sector, which provided over 30 million new jobs in the OECD area between 1970 and 1979.[7] In the United States in particular, where total employment rose from 81.8 million in 1970 to 101.4 million by 1980, practically all of the new jobs were created not by giant corporations but by small businesses, which typically were more labor-intensive and more dynamic, but not enough so to absorb all the unemployed.

---

*Youth unemployment in the OECD countries would have been even higher had it not been for the fact that a growing proportion of young people were extending their years of education beyond the compulsory level. Often their chief motivation was to improve their educational credentials so as to compete more effectively for the available scarce jobs.

Employment Market Structural Factors. Compared to more experienced adult workers, especially males, young job-seekers entering most labor markets found (and still find) the cards stacked against them, placing them at a competitive disadvantage in bidding for available jobs. Their increasing number was in itself a handicap, but there were also a variety of built-in institutional obstacles in the employment market, including the general preference of employers for mature and experienced job applicants. From the employer's point of view, inexperienced young recruits often translated into higher costs and risks for the work they performed, taking into account the extra training costs involved, the legal minimum wages they must be paid, and the substantial added costs of mandatory social security payments and other fringe benefits.

Another set of obstacles is the seniority and other job protection provisions for existing workers, established by legislation and by collective bargaining agreements, which become especially important in a period of soft employment markets. Their net effect is to shunt many young people into the least secure and least rewarding segments of the overall employment market. As a recent OECD report observed:

> The labour market has become increasingly segmented between the economically strong and protected who have good jobs and the economically weak and disadvantaged who move between "bad" jobs. Those who are forced into involuntary mobility carry a disproportionate share of the costs of structural change. [Put differently] if many workers are secure in their jobs, the working lives of others are far more unstable.[8]

Supporting evidence for these observations turned up in several studies in Europe in the 1970s. They revealed that high job turnover rates are a key characteristic of young people's, especially teenagers', work experience; they shuttle more frequently than adults between employment, unemployment, and nonparticipation in the labor force. A study in France revealed that young workers register five to six times with the employment service before finally finding a stable job.[9]

Another OECD report (July 1980) observed that although unemployment rates among young people are typically lowest for those with the highest level of education, "more and more young people with above average educational qualifications are experiencing spells of unemployment. . . . Indeed, some Member Countries (for example, Italy and Spain) have very high rates of unemployment among young people holding higher education degrees."[10]

Youth Attidudes and Morale

To these three sets of causal factors a more nebulous fourth may be added, namely, the negative and defeatist attitudes and values of many young people, especially underprivileged ones, toward work. A recent OECD/CERI survey had delved into this question in several countries and came up with some sobering conclusions:

> ... the problem of unemployment among the least privileged youngsters stems from a lack of self-confidence and entrepreneurial spirit as well as a lack of basic skills. ...
>
> Far from being consistently restless and angry [as commonly believed] these youngsters can best be characterized as increasingly apathetic and detached from their social environment, showing little interest in improving their life prospects or in actively escaping the dead-end jobs their lack of qualifications open to them. ...
>
> ... [they] approach the labour market having already conditioned themselves to take as little advantage of existing opportunities as possible. In other words, these youth are often "realistic" about job prospects to the point of creating a self-fulfilling prophecy about their employment opportunities.[11]

The same study found that the deterioration of job opportunities was producing a different and even more worrisome reaction among better educated young people with more privileged backgrounds.

> For the first time in several decades, youths—especially from the middle classes—are faced with the feelings of powerlessness and lack of control over their lives which have long been the lot of the lower socio-economic classes. Faced with this unfamiliar and stress-provoking situation (and coupled with the perception that nothing is being done to alleviate their problems), these youngsters may increasingly resort to socially deviant behavior. ...
>
> There are warning signals, that, of all youth, this group is the one most likely to react "badly" to difficult employment conditions and, perhaps, to resort more to anti-social behavior, e.g., crime and drug abuse.[12]

These, of course, are the kinds of problems that give educators sleepless nights—the kinds that schools and teachers find it most difficult to cope with. But society tends to look to the schools to resolve these excruciating human problems that other social institutions, including the family, so often feel unable or unwilling to deal with.

As the decade of the 1980s dawned in the industrialized countries of the West, the problem of youth unemployment, with all its bewildering side effects, seemed no closer to solution than ever, nor did the underlying economic problems. The question on everybody's mind was: What does the future hold? What can economic policy, educational policy, and social policy do to eradicate these grave maladjustments? We will return to these questions; in the meantime we must take a look at some parallel problems in another group of developed countries.

THE CASE OF THE EUROPEAN SOCIALIST COUNTRIES

Although their political ideology and their manner of running their economic systems are different from those of the Western capitalist countries, the U.S.S.R. and the Eastern European socialist countries felt the impact of the same powerful demographic, educational, and economic forces that converged on the Western industrialized countries in the 1970s.

Similarities with the West

Demographically, as in the West, the now mature children of the postwar baby boom came flooding into the labor force in the second half of the 1960s and throughout the 1970s. The effect of this sharp upswing in the number of young workers was to transform the overall manpower situation from one of sizable shortages in the 1950s and 1960s (in part because of the low birth rates during World War II) to one of relative abundance in the 1970s.

This new situation, as in the West, was further complicated by the much higher proportion of young people who had completed secondary or postsecondary education and joined the labor force than in previous decades. In the U.S.S.R. and the other Eastern European socialist countries, total higher education enrollments and the number of annual graduates more than doubled between 1960 and 1977 (see Appendix Tables 6.2 and 6.3). Meanwhile the number of higher education graduates employed in the national economies of most of these countries had also more than doubled or trebled by the mid-1970s (see Appendix Table 6.4). These included a mixture of regular day students and a substantial proportion of workers who had earned degrees through correspondence or evening programs.

As in the West, these educated young people who flooded the labor market in the 1970s taxed the capacity of the socialist economies to absorb them and the ability of the centralized system of manpower allocation to place them all in appropriate jobs that matched their new educational qualifications. Even if this system had been working with high efficiency (which the evidence suggests it was not), it would have been mathematically impossible to place all of these people in the kinds of jobs their credentials would have commanded ten years earlier. The only way to make the adjustment was by downgrading educational credentials, and this is evidently what happened in many cases.

Differences Between East and West

One big difference between East and West was that in the centrally planned socialist countries, in line with their strong commitment to a policy of full employment, there was virtually no open youth unemployment in the 1970s—at least as officially reported. Actually, however, there was a sizable (but unmeasured) amount of hidden unemployment in the form of young people who were dissatisfied with their assigned jobs and drifted around looking for something better, often moving from one region to a more promising one. This problem was sufficiently serious to prompt the Soviet government to condemn the drifters as social misfits and to mount a strong campaign to turn public opinion against such deviant behavior. It seems unlikely, however, that this hidden youth unemployment in the Eastern socialist countries ever reached the proportions of officially admitted open youth unemployment in the West. As near as can be judged, the manpower allocation systems in the centrally planned economies, for all their admitted shortcomings and miscarriages, did apparently manage to locate or to create some sort of job assignment for most young people—even if it meant, for example, assigning some university graduates with poorer academic records as clerks in Moscow's GUM Department store. This downgrading of their aspirations and credentials was undoubtedly disappointing to the graduates involved, but it was far better than being unemployed. Moreover, they could perhaps take some comfort from the fact that many of their counterparts in the West were experiencing similar demotions.

Another notable difference between East and West was that the centrally planned socialist countries, according to their official statistics and claims, managed to maintain relatively higher and steadier economic growth rates during the 1970s and more stable price levels. These broad statistical indicators, however, cannot be taken at full face value for they mask some serious and well-documented economic problems and imbalances encountered by various Eastern socialist countries during the 1970s and early 1980s, such as those in agriculture and consumer goods and in hard currency reserves essential for technological and other essential imports from the West. They also mask widespread consumer complaints that the apparent price stability was often achieved by extremely tight rationing and by downgrading the quality of consumer goods and services.

Internal Criticisms

The 1970s also witnessed in the Eastern socialist countries a rash of sharp internal criticisms against the cumbersome bureaucracy and inefficient operation of the educational planning and manpower mechanisms for matching educational programs and outputs to the priority needs of the economy and society and to actual job openings. University administrators complained of the lack of flexibility to adapt their institution's program to changing conditions to make the optimal use of the resources available to them. They bristled especially at the standardized and inflexible directives they often received from the center concerning such matters as admission quotas and procedures, staff allocations, equipment, and curriculum changes—only to be countermanded by a new and contradictory directive when they were in the midst of implementing the first one.

Graduates themselves were among the strongest critics, not so much of the central planning system in principle, but of the inefficient way it was being run. Surveys conducted in Poland in the early 1970s, for example, of recent higher education graduates and others who had graduated five or six years earlier, revealed that 25 percent were employed in jobs they considered incompatible with their field of study; however, they were given no opportunity to change to more appropriate jobs.[13] Nearly half of them also complained that their abilities and knowledge in professional work were not being sufficiently utilized. Some 40 percent reported that the transition from school to work had been a traumatic experience, mainly because they had imagined their future job to be much better than it actually was, especially in terms of wages, organization of work, and human relations. The educational system itself did not escape their criticism; 44 percent of the graduates complained that they had not been given sufficient expert knowledge and information about the principles of work organization. This survey, it should be noted, was made in 1971, before the full brunt of the postwar baby boom had yet reached higher education and hit the employment market. It seems reasonable to suppose that the complicated manpower allocation system encountered even greater difficulties when this occurred later in the 1970s and as more and more specific manpower requirements became saturated by the flood of educated youth.

An opinion survey conducted in the Soviet Union among graduate engineers working in various industries and research recorded that 42 percent were "satisfied" and 21 percent "very satisfied" with their work, whereas 27 percent were "dissatisfied," and another 10 percent were either "indifferent" or expressed no opinion.[14] Presumably their respective attitudes reflected in part their assessment of the education they had received and its relevance to their present job, but this element was apparently not factored out in the survey.

Putting on the Brakes

To their credit, the planners in most Eastern socialist countries, unlike many Western educational and manpower planners, apparently foresaw as early as the mid-1960s an impending surplus of graduates and began to slow the rapid expansion of higher education. In the case of the U.S.S.R., total higher education enrollments had increased by an astonishing 1,465,000 in the five years from 1960 to 1965, bringing the total to 3,861,000. The increment for the period 1965–70, however, was cut by half, to 720,000. It was cut further still to 273,000 in the 1970–75 period, and then rose to 381,000 between 1975 and 1980 (see Appendix Table 6.3).

Significantly, the major part of these cutbacks in the U.S.S.R. was not in regular day students but in the nonconventional students who earned equivalent higher degrees through evening and correspondence courses. During the earlier acute manpower shortage period, these nonconventional students had risen sharply and by 1965 accounted for over 55 percent of total annual admissions to higher institutions. After 1965, however, their proportion declined steadily, reaching 39 percent in 1980, with a corresponding increase in the proportion of regular day students from 44 percent in 1965 to 61 percent in 1980. It seems evident from the figures shown in Appendix Table 6.5 that a basic decision was made in the mid-1960s to freeze or reduce the number of evening and correspondence students and to confine all further growth of enrollments to regular day students. This was a convenient way to hold down the prospective surplus of graduates without upsetting the higher education institutions and to quiet the growing complaints over the inadequate quality of the nonconventional graduates. Most Eastern socialist countries began their slowdown after 1970, although there were variations between them, as shown in Appendix Table 6.6. Between 1975 and 1977, the total enrollment of regular day students leveled off or declined in all six countries—Bulgaria, Czechoslovakia, Hungary, the German Democratic Republic, Poland, and Romania.

THE CASE OF DEVELOPING COUNTRIES

Although the youth employment problem in industrialized countries was more severe in the late 1970s and early 1980s than at any time since the Great Depression of the 1930s, it paled by comparison with the employment problem confronting educated youth in most developing countries. The situation varied considerably, of course, from place to place, but practically all developing countries experienced an increasingly serious quantitative and qualitative imbalance between the output of their education system and corresponding job opportunities in the marketplace. In general, although there were still selective shortages, the kinds of modern sector jobs previously associated with various educational credentials became increasingly scarce in relation to the number of credentials chasing after them. In many countries the mismatch became so severe as to challenge the basic integrity of their education system and the efficacy of their whole educational development strategy.

Causes and Effects

Two sets of factors, discussed in earlier chapters, sharply differentiate the education/employment situation in developing countries from that in industrialized countries: the structure of their economy and labor force, and the large-scale demographic growth and geographic redeployment taking place.

With respect to the first of these, the urban modern sector of these less developed economies—the capital-intensive sector that uses more sophisticated technologies, places a premium on educational credentials, and provides more secure and much better paying jobs—is limited in size and employs a relatively smaller proportion of the national labor force (often only 10 to 15 percent). Yet the prime purpose of the formal education system, as viewed by parents, students, and teachers is to prepare young people to work and live effectively in this circumscribed modern sector. The effect of this striking incongruity between the purposes of education and the realities of the economy has been that schools have stimulated the aspirations of many young people for a kind of life and work they will never actually achieve. The resulting large and growing gap between aspirations and opportunities has engendered great strains within these societies and in the lives of millions of young people and their families.

To complicate matters further, in many developing countries the government and the education system are still the dominant employers of graduates. In the early stages after national independence there were many more jobs available than qualified persons to fill them. But later as the personnel slots in government bureaus and available teaching posts became filled (often with underqualified people), and as the national budget became too strained to permit continued personnel expansion, the demand for new graduates slumped sharply. This happened first in those newly independent countries, especially in Asia, that had made an early start on rapid educational expansion, but during the 1970s the same kind of imbalance spread rapidly across other developing countries. Skyrocketing oil prices and a severe world recession and inflation came along just in time to make matters worse.

Demographic factors operated independently of the economic factors. The continuing rapid expansion of the child and youth population in these countries exerted heavy pressure on their educational system to keep expanding, especially at the secondary and tertiary levels, and overwhelmed their economy's capacity to absorb additional educated manpower in the same types of jobs as earlier. At the same time, education tended to accelerate the large migration of rural young people to the cities in search of a better life. The rural youngster who completed primary school was eager to go to the city, either to climb further up the education ladder or to pick up a wage-paying job in the modern sector. But the capacity of the already bloated cities to house and employ all these young migrants became increasingly saturated. The chances of the partially educated rural teenager to find a modern job in the city, or any paying job at all, kept diminishing to the point where many were forced to return to their rural home and try to pick up the pieces of their broken lives. This was usually a psychologically traumatic experience, for in everyone's eyes including their own, they had failed. Worse, they were now ill equipped to live in either the urban or the rural world, for while they were in school and in the city looking for a job, their peers were learning farming and local crafts and getting adjusted to the reality that they would probably have to live out their lives in the countryside.

The size of the gap between employment aspirations and actual opportunities in each country is mainly a function of four dynamic variables: (1) the number and proportion of its young people entering the employment market each year with various formal education credentials, (2) the size of its modern sector and the proportion of the total national labor force it employs, (3) the annual rate of growth of new jobs in the modern sector, and (4) the proportion of nonmanual (white collar) jobs offered by the modern sector (which are of prime interest to secondary school and college graduates).

We can illustrate how these variables work by two cases drawn from a study for the International Labor Office in the mid-1970s, covering a wide range of developing countries.[15] The study showed that by 1973, Kenya and Ghana were both already experiencing a sizable "aspiration/opportunity" gap, because their small modern sector accommodated fewer than 10 percent of the working-age population, whereas half of their school-age children were now completing primary school and greatly increased numbers were obtaining secondary and higher education credentials. If these trends continued, the study concluded, the number of young people with educational credentials for "white collar" jobs would exceed the number of such jobs available by an increasingly wide margin.

The unbalanced forces in Kenya and Ghana not only generated rising unemployment among educated youth but had three other important effects. First, they fueled a "qualification spiral" that forced up the level of credentials required for various jobs. Clerical jobs, for example, that formerly required only a primary-school certificate, now required a secondary-school certificate. Bachelor degree holders who used to count on getting top-level positions now found themselves scrambling for jobs that used to require only a secondary-school certificate. Second, this qualification spiral in turn increased the pressure for greater educational expansion, for the higher the credential a young person possessed, the better shot he or she would get at one of the scarce good job openings in a labor market surfeited with credentials. Third, as enrollments in secondary and higher education continued their rapid expansion, under conditions of increasingly stringent education budgets, quality was traded for quantity, thereby reducing the educational value of credentials along with their market value.

The Ambiguous Meaning of Unemployment

National employment and unemployment statistics, as noted earlier, can be very misleading in developing countries, not only because their reporting services are generally weak but even more because these concepts and ways of measuring them that apply to industrialized countries simply do not fit the conditions of less developed economies where self-employment and unsteady odd jobs play such dominant roles. In low-income countries small farmers, craftsmen, and tradesmen and their families typically account for the bulk of the national labor force.* Even in the best of times many of them see little in the way of hard cash; they are busy just trying to feed and clothe their family and keep alive, and any surplus they are lucky enough to produce is likely to be bartered rather than sold

---

*Paradoxically, rural women work just as hard as and often harder than men, yet official national labor force statistics of rural workers invariably show far more men than women.

for cash. Even in the worst of times they are not idle, in the sense that an unemployed auto worker in Detroit or Stuttgart is idle. On the contrary, they are likely to be working longer hours than ever just to survive. Moreover, the length of their work week fluctuates sharply with the rhythm of the crop cycle: they work long hours during the planting and harvesting seasons and are substantially underemployed in between, especially those with few if any productive resources of their own. Thus, high underemployment rather than unemployment characterizes most rural areas.

Given these ambiguities, it is far more realistic in the case of workers outside the modern sector to equate unemployment with the degree of poverty rather than the number of hours worked, or not worked, per week. Theoretically, if these people had access to adequate resources—to ample land, water, agricultural inputs, and improved technologies—and if the market incentives were favorable, they could be much more productive. And if they could work a "normal" full workweek year-round, combining farming with other economic activities, their productivity and income would be far higher. Then rural economies could be transformed and massive rural poverty steadily reduced. But unless and until this happens, the concepts of full employment and unemployment as used in the West have little relevance to major portions of the national economies of developing countries. The breadth and depth of poverty is a far more meaningful measure of the waste of potentially productive human resources, whether educated or uneducated.

Western employment concepts have considerably more meaning, however, for the secondary-school or university graduates in developing countries who are actively looking for a salaried job in the modern urban sector. These are the people most likely to turn up on the "live registers" of government employment exchanges, until they finally find a job or, becoming discouraged, drop off the register and join the hidden unemployed.

Although nobody knows exactly how many unemployed secondary and higher education graduates there are in these countries, virtually all observers, including government experts, agree that the number in most cases has grown to shockingly high levels and is continuing to grow. Observers also agree that a large proportion of recent secondary and higher education graduates who are employed have accepted jobs that, by previous standards, are well below their educational qualifications.

Educated Unemployed in Asia

The situation, as near as one can tell, is grimmest in several Asian countries. Cited here are some sample figures from several studies made over the past decade. They should be seen only as clues, not as complete and accurate accounts of the reality, because they were necessarily based on tenuous evidence.

- In India the number of college and university graduate job-seekers registered on the government's employment exchange more than doubled between 1961 and 1967, from 56,000 to 121,000. In the next four years the number more than doubled again, reaching 288,000 in 1971. In the early 1960s the problem centered on graduates with an arts degree; the market was still relatively strong for science and engineering degree-holders. But by 1971 job-seekers with science degrees had risen to 25 percent of the total graduate unemployment and those with engineering degrees to 10 percent. To be sure, they tended to be the lower ranking graduates from weaker institutions, but nevertheless, they held recognized degrees.* Several years later, in 1978, according to press reports, the government estimated that 700,000 graduates were by then looking for work, and their number was increasing by 150,000 each year.[16]
- Pakistan was evidently no better off. A survey of a sample of Punjab University graduates in 1972, for example, showed that three or four years after completing their studies, 47 percent remained unemployed.[17] A national survey in 1972 concluded that 16.8 percent of matriculates or higher (those completing ten or more years of formal education) were unemployed, compared to 15.5 percent of primary school leavers (some with partial secondary education).[18]
- In Sri Lanka, of the total estimated unemployed population in the early 1970s, nearly half (45 percent) had received some secondary education and over half of these had passed the GEC (0) level.[19]
- In Thailand, an official survey revealed that the unemployment rate among higher education graduates, which stood at 25 percent in 1973, had shot up to nearly 46 percent in 1975.[20]
- In the Philippines, nearly one third of secondary school and college graduates were reported to be unemployed in the late 1970s.[21]

There is a tragic irony about this high unemployment among the educated youth of Asia; the rate of unemployment tends to be highest for

---

*The Indian government now regards the live register as too unreliable to be used as an indicator of unemployment trends. For one thing, the register fails to reveal hidden unemployment of graduates who have not registered or have dropped off the registry, either because they have lost faith in the employment exchange as a means of finding a job, or because they have given up the search in despair.

those with the most years of education. A perceptive study of graduate unemployment in India in the late 1960s explained this upside-down phenomenon mainly in terms of the lengthening of the job search by new graduates.[22] In countries where job mobility is very low and a degree is a badge of both social and economic status, new graduates have a powerful incentive to hold out for a preferred job as long as they possibly can (and as long as their family's resources permit), lest they be tagged and disadvantaged for life by settling for an inferior job at the start of their career. This explanation clearly had much merit in the 1960s, and no doubt still does, but in the intervening years the employment market for graduates has deteriorated much further, to the point where many are now having great difficulty finding even an inferior job. In the spring of 1978 a respected journalist with long experience in India made the following report:

> In Calcutta these days, any Western businessman is likely to be accosted on the street by well-spoken young men who fall in step with him and ask if perhaps he might be looking for a clerk or an assistant. And on a busy intersection in Madras stands a college graduate in a threadbare gray suit, holding a toy boat he has made out of matchsticks, offering it for sale day by day.
>
> These are India's educated unemployed—millions of literate, presentable, often Westernized young men and women for whom there is no work. They constitute a special aspect of this country's poverty, and a growing problem that has made the Government planners take a second look at the goal of giving everyone as much education as possible.
>
> And so the Government has decided to slow down on university education and "discourage the indiscriminate opening of many new secondary schools," emphasizing instead adult literacy programs, vocational education and primary schools.[23]

Educated Unemployed in Africa and Latin America

What about the sub-Saharan African countries that got a later start on independence and on economic and educational development than most Asian countries? Almost without exception these countries gave a high priority to education in the 1960s and early 1970s, rapidly boosting their output of students at all levels, as well as sending many abroad for higher education. At the same time, they concentrated on building up the tiny modern urban sector of their economy, which by the early 1970s had grown significantly, but far less than their enlarged supply of educated young people. Consequently, they soon began to feel the sharp pangs of educated youth unemployment, already so familiar in Asia. By 1980 the problem had reached disturbing proportions in practically all of these new African nations. In the International Labour Office (ILO) study referred to earlier, it was calculated in the case of Kenya, for example, that in 1973 total new jobs in the modern sector could accomodate less than 22 percent of the education system's overall output that year, though nonmanual (white collar) jobs were equivalent to about half of the secondary and higher education output. The study's projections for 1980, however, suggested that, even assuming an optimistic 5 percent growth of modern sector jobs every year, the supply of new nonmanual jobs would then be equivalent to only 28 percent of secondary and higher education output (assuming enrollments at these levels continued to expand at the pre-1973 rate). The projected 1980 situation for other African countries in the ILO study's sample was generally similar to Kenya's. In retrospect, judging by the low economic growth rates in African countries during the 1970s, these projections for 1980 were perhaps on the optimistic side.

Latin America, for which fewer specific estimates of unemployment are available than for Asia, presents a more mixed picture because of the great diversity of educational and economic conditions in different countries. Those with relatively large and rapidly expanding modern sectors—in particular Brazil, Mexico, and Venezuela—were able to provide proportionately more modern sector jobs for the newly educated than more agrarian countries such as Ecuador, Bolivia, Honduras, and Peru. Both sets of countries, however, underwent explosive increases in the output of secondary schools and university graduates during the 1960s and 1970s. Hence they were all experiencing in varying degrees painful problems of educated youth unemployment and inflation of educational qualifications by the late 1970s and early 1980s, though perhaps not quite as painful as those of India and some other Asian countries.

LOOKING TO THE FUTURE

If, as historians tell us, "the past is prologue," then the foregoing analysis of the deterioration of youth employment opportunities during the turbulent 1970s should shed instructive light on some nagging questions about the future. Are employment prospects for the newly educated likely to improve or to worsen in coming years? What principal factors will determine the answer, and how are these factors likely to behave? In what ways and to what extent does the outlook for developed and developing countries differ? Most important, what can be done to improve the prospects?

Nobody's crystal ball can provide immutable answers to these questions, but this does not mean that we must move blindly into each new day and year with no notion of what it may hold. For, despite its inevitable surprises, the shape of the future is already being molded by the visible trends of living forces all around us today. Some of these forces are shaping the future supply side of the employment equation, others the demand side.

We will explore these two sides separately. First, however, in order to avoid a distorted and unduly pessimistic view of the matter, we should recall what has already been accomplished over the past three decades to improve the educated manpower supply of nations. Notwithstanding the criticisms within this report of past educational assumptions, policies, and practices, we should recognize the positive consequences of the extraordinary efforts made by virtually all countries, rich and poor alike, to educate their young people and develop their human potential. The positive consequences, on balance, constitute a high yield on these past investments in future social and economic development.

The point is vividly illustrated by the late Professor Fred Harbison's observations to an IIEP seminar in Paris in the early 1960s en route home from one of his many missions to help introduce manpower planning in Africa (in this instance, Kenya and Tanzania). "It is easy to take a census of the high level manpower [university graduates] in these countries," Harbison explained, "you can practically count them on the fingers of two hands and in less than a week know them all by their first names." That was in the early 1960s. In the two succeeding decades the high-level manpower stock in these countries has grown almost unbelievably, through a combination of overseas study and the greatly enlarged output of their own new universities. The number of graduates from the Universities of Nairobi and Dar-es-Salaam in 1980 alone far exceeded the total stock of graduates in these countries 20 years earlier. Similar impressive gains were achieved by many other developing countries.

The same sort of educational upgrading of the population and labor force has taken place in the developed world since World War II. As noted previously, the number of higher education graduates actively working in the U.S.S.R. economy grew from 3.2 million in 1959 to nearly 9.5 million in 1975, and the proportion of young workers with a secondary education also increased dramatically. Similar educational upgrading of the population and labor force occurred in the OECD countries. In the United States, for example, the proportion of young adults (age 25–29) with four years of high school or more increased from 52 percent in 1950 to 86 percent in 1980, and those with four or more years of college increased from 8 to 23 percent.[24]

To be sure, such increases in the educational profile of any nation's labor force, measured solely by years of schooling and the increased quantity of various academic credentials, is no conclusive proof of a corresponding qualitative improvement. But there can be no reasonable doubt that, as unmeasurable as it may be, there has been a sizable overall qualitative improvement in most national manpower pools as a result of these massive educational efforts. How effectively this educated manpower is actually being used is another matter, to which we will return shortly.

Future Manpower Supply. Meanwhile let us look more closely at the supply side of the employment equation—the quantity and quality of human resources likely to be available to serve future social and economic development needs in various countries. Four things can be said with reasonable certainty.

First, the overall size of the labor force will continue to grow between now and the year 2000 in virtually all countries. However, the growth in the industrial countries will be minor compared to the enormous growth in the developing world. This means that the economies of the developing countries will have to work far harder than those of developed countries to absorb the new entrants to their labor force.

Second, as a result of the divergent demographic trends reviewed earlier, the young adult component of the labor force (age 18–23) in the more developed regions, according to medium projections, will shrink by more than 10 percent between 1980 and 2000, while the same group in less developed regions will increase by more than 40 percent. Thus, the problem of providing new jobs for young entrants to the labor force will ease somewhat in the North, but greatly intensify in the South.

The third safe prediction is that the educational profile of the labor force will continue to move up in both the developed and developing worlds. How rapidly it does so in any particular country will depend on further increases in the country's education participation rates. But even if present rates remained static, the education profile of the overall labor force would automatically increase as better educated younger workers replace less educated older workers leaving the labor force. Thus, the sizable increases in education participation rates achieved in virtually all countries over the past 20 years will continue to have a large payoff for many years to come.

Future Manpower Demands. On the demand side of the employment market, the question for both developed and developing countries is whether their respective economies will be able to provide enough jobs for all these newcomers. In particular, will the modern sector of the economy provide enough openings of the right kind to match the qualifications and expectations of those emerging from the middle and upper levels of the formal education system? How will future job opportunities be distributed among different occupations and parts of the economy, and how will the newly available manpower be channeled into or away from these occupations?

The answer to these questions will depend in each case on several variables. Among the most important are (1) the rate of growth of the overall economy and of its modern sector; (2) changes in the structure, technologies, and product mix of the economy; (3) changes in the larger world economy beyond the control of any individual nation; (4) the academic choices of students and the quality and relevance of the education they bring to the marketplace; and (5) the structure of incentives and disincentives that influence the allocation of available specialized manpower.

Conjectures. No one can predict with certainty the precise behavior of these key variables 10 or 20 years ahead, even for a single country, much less large groups of them. However, on the basis of facts and forecasts discussed previously we can venture the following conjectures:

1. Economic growth rates in the foreseeable future, in the majority of developing and developed countries, will probably rise above the most depressed levels of the 1970s and early 1980s, but they are unlikely to regain, much less exceed, the peak levels achieved in the 1960s. The prospects are particularly bleak, however, for low-income nations of Africa, several of which actually suffered negative per capita income growth rates in the past decade.

2. Although the modern sector of many developing economies has grown substantially over the past 20 years, it is still but a small fraction of the total economy in most cases and, even under favorable conditions, will grow only slowly in the future. Moreover, any given percentage of growth of output in this capital-intensive and higher-wage-paying sector of the economy will create a substantially smaller corresponding increase in new jobs. The labor-intensive informal and rural sectors of the economy are by far the most promising creators of more new jobs, but most of these jobs will pay much less than most of those in the modern sector and will not require high educational qualifications.

3. Unless recent world tendencies toward intensifying protectionist

trade barriers are reversed, employment prospects for educated youth (and for workers generally) tied to international trade will be seriously impaired in practically all countries—particulary in developing countries.

4. Student academic choices, as well as the allocation of educated manpower to different occupations and segments of the economy, will continue to be strongly influenced by the structure of incentives and disincentives associated with various types of occupations, and also by rigid hiring practices in various employment markets. Unless the present incentive structures are substantially overhauled and made more compatible with priority national needs, especially in developing countries, student academic choices and the actual allocation of educated manpower will continue to run seriously counter to each country's social and economic development objectives.

5. Likewise, unless the increasingly strong linkages in all countries between various educational credentials and specific types of jobs are severed—which seems highly unlikely—the qualifications escalation will further intensify, with more and more jobs being filled by overqualified people. At the same time, the bumping process will go on, progressively passing the ultimate burdens of unemployment down to those with the least educational qualifications or none at all.

When we examine these conjectures collectively and realistically, in the light of things said elsewhere in this report, there is no escaping two disturbing conclusions. First, in the absence of sweeping readjustments and innovations in both educational and economic systems, the world of education and the world of work will become increasingly unbalanced and maladjusted in most it not all countries over the next 20 years. Second, the major cause for concern lies in the developing world, especially in the low-income countries, for even with a steady annual rate of economic growth of 5 or 6 percent it would be exceedingly difficult for them to educate effectively and create adequate employment for their rapidly expanding youth population. The more developed countries, with their stronger and more flexible economies, larger and more diversified educational provisions, and declining youth population, can undoubtedly make the necessary adjustments more readily, though not without wise and determined economic and educational policies, and, even then, not without considerable pain and difficulty.

NOTES

1. Philip Foster, "The Vocational School Fallacy in Development Planning," in *Education and Economic Development,* eds. Arnold Anderson and Mary Jean Bowman (Chicago: Aldine, 1965), pp. 142–66.
2. Trevor Coombe, *Basic Education and Educational Reform in Zambia* (The Hague: NUFFIC/CESO, 5–8 June 1978), pp. 15–16.
3. The various data in this paragraph were drawn from the December 1980 edition of the *OECD Economic Outlook,* No. 28, December 1980; and the *OECD Labour Force Statistics* (Paris: Organisation for Economic Co-operation and Development, 1983).
4. Ladislav Cerych, "Youth Employment: The Potential and Limitations of the Education System," in *Youth-Education-Employment,* Proceedings of an ICED International Symposium, held at Fere-en-Tardenois, France, 27–30 April 1977 (Paris: Institute of Education of the European Cultural Foundation, January 1978), Table 2, p. 27, based on U.S. Department of Labor Statistics.
5. Millicent Poole, "Analysis of Educational Wastage in Australia," in *Education in Asia and Oceania: Reviews, Reports, and Notes,* No. 17, September 1980 (Bangkok: UNESCO Regional Office for Education in Asia and Oceania), p. 40.
6. Reprinted from *The OECD Observer,* No. 105, July 1980.
7. Ibid., No. 115, March 1982.
8. Ibid.
9. M. Prieur, "Les Jeunes, l'emploi et la Formation" (Paris: Centre d'Information, 1978).
10. Reprinted from *The OECD Observer,* No. 105, July 1980.
11. "The Aspirations of Young People," reprinted from *The OECD Observer,* No. 105, July 1980, p. 18, based on a survey by OECD's Center for Educational Research and Innovation (CERI).
12. Ibid.
13. Barbara Liberska, *Education and Youth Employment in Poland* (Berkeley, Calif.: Carnegie Foundation for the Advancement of Teaching, 1979) (a study prepared for the Carnegie Council on Policy Studies in Higher Education).
14. D. Chuprunov, R. Avakov, and E. Jiltsov, *Enseignement supérieur, emploi et progrès technique en URSS* (Paris: UNESCO, International Institute for Educational Planning, 1982), Table 31, p. 112.
15. Ronald Dore, John Humphreys, and Peter West, *The Basic Arithmetic of Youth Unemployment* (Geneva: Institute of Development Studies, University of Sussex, March 1976). Prepared for and published by the International Labour Office.
16. *The New York Times,* 28 May 1978.
17. A. A. Anwar, *Problems of Unemployed of the Educated Manpower* (Punjab, Pakistan: Board of Economic Inquiry, 1973), p. 9.

18. Pakistan Government, *1972 Housing, Education and Demographic Survey,* Table 23; cited in *Educational Issues in Pakistan: A Sector Memorandum* (Washington, D.C.: The World Bank, August 1977), p. 50.
19. Marga Institute, "The Employment Situation in India, Bangladesh and Sri Lanka," an analysis prepared for the Commonwealth South Asia Symposium on Employment Strategies and Programmes held at Chandigarh, India, February 1976.
20. *Survey of Educated Unemployed* (Bangkok: National Social and Economic Development Board, 1975).
21. Malcolm Adiseshiah, "Future Asian Education," a paper presented to an International Institute for Educational Planning seminar in Paris on Long-Term Prospects for the Development of Education, October 1978.
22. Mark Blaug, P. R. G. Layard, and Maureen Woodhall, *The Causes of Graduate Unemployment in India* (London: Penguin Press, 1969).
23. William Borders, *The New York Times,* 28 May 1978.
24. *Digest of Education Statistics, 1981* (Washington, D.C.: National Center for Education Statistics, February 1981).

Appendix Table 6.1 Ratio of Youth to Adult Unemployment Rates in Selected OECD Countries, 1970–82

Country	1970	1976	1980	1982
Australia	2.1	3.3	3.8	2.9
Canada	2.4	2.5	2.4	2.2
Finland	1.8	2.7	2.8	2.9
France	2.2	3.2	3.6	3.7
Germany	1.0	1.7	1.5	1.8[a]
Italy	6.5	8.7	7.2	7.0[a]
Japan	2.2	1.7	2.0	2.1
Spain	3.0	3.6	3.8	3.9 (1981)
Sweden	2.4	3.1	3.6	3.3
United Kingdom	1.5	3.1	3.1	2.4
United States	3.1	2.6	2.6	2.3

[a]OECD Secretariat estimates.

Source: OECD, *Employment Outlook* (Paris: OECD, Manpower and Social Affairs Committee, 8 June 1983).

Appendix Table 6.2 European Socialist Countries: Higher Education Enrollments and Graduates, 1960–77[a]

Countries	1960	1965	1970	1975	1977	Percent Increase	
						1960–70	1970–77
Total Enrollments							
Bulgaria	48,880	84,467	85,675	106,055	103,662	75	21
Czechoslovakia	79,332	144,990	133,524	156,645	168,310	68	26
Hungary	37,996	93,957	78,889	107,555	110,528	108	40
Poland	161,008	251,864	322,464	468,129	491,030	100	52
Romania	61,980	130,614	151,705	164,567	174,888	145	15
U.S.S.R.	2,396,000	3,860,600	4,549,600	4,854,000	4,950,200	58	9
German Democratic Republic	88,545	111,591	127,585	137,854	130,201	44	2
Annual Graduates							
Bulgaria	5,789	7,781	12,409	14,661	16,556	114	33
Czechoslovakia	12,427	17,758	18,700	22,208	22,063	50	18
Hungary	5,628	13,938	18,220	24,275	25,996	224	43
German Democratic Republic	15,005	20,878	22,312	36,521	32,629	49	46
Poland	20,535	25,218	47,117	63,236	62,917	129	34
Romania	10,896	19,503	24,471	28,889	30,839	125	26
U.S.S.R.	343,800	403,900	630,800	713,400	734,600	83	16

[a]Includes evening and correspondence students as well as regular day students.

Source: F. Januszkiewicz, J. Kluczynski, and S. Kwiatkowski, "Higher Education in European Socialist Countries" (Unpublished paper prepared for the International Council for Educational Development, by the Research Institute for Science Policy, Technological Progress and Higher Education, Warsaw, Poland, 1979).

Appendix Table 6.3 Higher Education Enrollments in the Union of Soviet Socialist Republics by Type of Students, 1950–80 (beginning of academic year)

Year	Total No. of Students (in thousands)	Day Students		Evening Students		Correspondence Students	
		No. (in thousands)	Percent	No. (in thousands)	Percent	No. (in Thousands)	Percent
1950–51	1247	818	65.60	27	2.16	402	32.24
1955–56	1867	1147	61.43	81	4.34	639	34.23
1960–61	2396	1156	48.25	245	10.22	995	41.53
1965–66	3861	1584	41.03	569	14.74	1708	44.23
1970–71	4581	2241	48.92	658	14.36	1582	36.72
1975–76	4854	2628	54.10	644	13.30	1582	32.60
1980–81	5235	2978	56.87	649	12.40	1608	30.73

Source: D. Chuprunov, R. Avakov, and E. Jiltsov, *Enseignement supérieur, emploi et progrès technique en URSS* (Paris: UNESCO, International Institute for Educational Development, 1982).

Appendix Table 6.4 Trends in Higher Education Graduates Employed in Six Socialist Economies, 1960–75

Country	Year	Graduates Employed in National Economy	
		No. Employed	Index (1960 = 100)
Bulgaria	1960	92,638	100.0
	1966	129,469	139.8
	1970	163,218	176.2
	1974	199,839	215.7
Czechoslovakia	1960	158,000	100.0
	1966	227,400	143.9
	1970	277,100	175.4
	1973	334,900	212.0
German Democratic Republic	1960	108,100	100.0
	1965	186,139	172.2
	1970	261,500	241.9
	1975	398,900	369.0
Hungary[a]	1964	146,000	100.0
	1971	238,510	163.4
	1975	310,000[b]	212.3
Romania	1961	179,718	100.0
	1964	210,230	117.0
	1968	274,541	152.8
U.S.S.R.	1959	3,235,700	100.0
	1967	5,565,000	172.0
	1970	6,852,600	211.8
	1975	9,477,000	292.9

[a]Data only on graduates employed in socialized sector.
[b]Estimated.
Source: Januszkiewicz et al., "Higher Education in European Socialist Countries."

Appendix Table 6.5 First-Year Enrollments in Higher Education in the Union of Soviet Socialist Republics, by Type of Students, 1950–80

Students	1950	1955	1960	1965	1970	1975	1980
	Number (in Thousands)						
Regular day	228.4	257.2	257.9	378.4	500.5	593.9	639.9
Evening	9.1	28.4	77.0	125.2	127.4	239.7	134.3
Correspondence	111.6	175.8	258.2	350.1	283.6	270.2	277.7
Total	349.1	461.4	593.1	853.7	911.5	993.8	1,051.9
	Percentage						
Regular day	65.42	55.74	43.48	44.32	54.91	59.8	60.8
Evening	2.61	6.15	12.98	14.66	13.98	13.0	12.8
Correspondence	31.98	38.10	43.53	41.01	31.11	27.2	26.4
Total	100	100	100	100	100	100	100

Source: Chuprunov, Avakov, and Jiltsov, *Enseignement supérieur, emploi et progrès technique en URSS.*

Appendix Table 6.6 First-Year Enrollments of Day Students Only, Eastern European Socialist Countries, 1960–77

Country	Total Enrollment					Five-Year Increments			
	1960	1965	1970	1975	1977	1960–65	1965–70	1970–75	1975–77
Bulgaria	9,013	10,966	13,892	16,931	15,428	1,953	2,926	3,039	(1,503)
Hungary	7,890	14,154	14,502	17,250	17,134	6,284	348	2,748	(116)
German Democratic Republic	—	16,360	26,734	27,782	26,043	—	10,374	1,049	(1,740)
Poland	26,560	38,312	53,783	76,318	72,511	11,752	15,471	22,535	(2,807)
Romania[a]	14,937	33,531	33,900	43,760	47,645	18,594	369	9,860	3,885
Czechoslovakia	17,008	24,050	25,865	30,139	30,714	7,042	1,815	4,274	575

[a]Total enrollment, including daytime, evening, and correspondence students.
Source: Januszkiewicz et., "Higher Education in European Socialist Countries".

CHAPTER 7

DISPARITIES AND INEQUALITIES

FOLLOWING World War II and the attainment of independence by many former colonial territories, the educational aspirations of common people the world over exploded like a genie from a bottle. The dramatic worldwide educational expansion that followed stemmed directly from these aspirations. In a larger sense, the expansion was also fueled by the widely held conviction among educators, social scientists, and national leaders that universal education was the instrument that would enable any nation to bring about fundamental social change, including the eradication of long-standing inequalities and injustices.

THE IDEAL VERSUS THE REAL

By the late 1960s, however, with the educational expansion now fully underway, it was becoming increasingly apparent that a great gap existed between the ideal that had animated the worldwide expansion and what had actually materialized. Evidently, the eradication or even the substantial reduction of inequalities in any society—including serious disparities within the educational system itself—was a far more complex and difficult affair than had initially been perceived. There was now growing evidence of obstacles and impediments. For example, educational leaders would lay out a new path toward equalizing educational opportunities for all children and youth only to be thrown off course by powerful interest groups or the wayward academic choices of students and their parents. A narrowly based elite governing a caste-bound society could honor in words the democratic aims of education, while at the same time showing by their actions a marked lack of enthusiasm for actually giving education to the masses, fearing that this would erode their own power. Even in

211

those cases when the ruling leaders were genuinely committed to spreading educational opportunities to all, their commitment did not guarantee success. The educational experts political leaders looked to to implement this democratic objective were themselves divided by arguments over how best to go about achieving mass education or even over whether it was a sound idea.

Yet another obstacle to achieving universal participation in education was that even when a local school was available, many parents and their children, particularly those handicapped by severe poverty, did not take advantage of it. Not least of the obstacles to achieving educational equality was the stubborn fact, often overlooked earlier, that all educational systems have a built-in bias favoring children whose parents attach high value to education and who instill in their offspring a strong motivation for education.

Typically, though not always, such parents are relatively well educated and well off economically; they enjoy reading books, magazines, and newspapers in the home; and they provide their children with a good middle-class vocabulary and syntax before they even enter school. Once the children enter school, this combination of motivation and good vocabulary and verbal skills becomes a crucial asset for winning good grades in any educational system. This advantage over their classmates with poorer motivation and inadequate verbal skills, and perhaps also with less self-confidence, tends to increase over the years, thus enabling those with a more favorable home background to proceed further.

It was not until the mid-1960s that behavioral science researchers began to look into the relative influence on student achievement of the school itself, on the one hand, and the individual student's home and cultural background on the other. Though the findings of this research were controversial and often misinterpreted, and clearly did not apply equally to different economic and social settings, the research had the beneficial effect of opening the eyes of many educational planners and the general public to important factors outside the school that strongly affect what happens inside.[1]

Despite this gap between the ideal and reality, countless individuals the world over, on gaining access to education that would have been beyond their reach but for concerted national efforts to provide it, moved on to rewarding careers. Yet insofar as societies as a whole were concerned, gross inequalities remained, throwing into bold relief a stark truth about the limits of education. Although education was an indispensable element of a multifaceted program for social change, it could not by itself eradicate all the inequalities imbedded in the texture of life for the inhabitants of a country.

Acknowledgment of this truth has increasingly reinforced the view that any attempts to transform a society by educational expansion must be preceded, or at least be accompanied, by far-reaching social, economic, and political reforms. Otherwise, exising disparities in the common life of a people will reassert themselves on the educational systems, making the top of the educational pyramid the citadels of special privilege. This line of argument was voiced, for example, in the opening of a 1976 draft document for educational reform in Zambia—an African country that had chosen the path of humanistic socialism.

> Society has not yet succeeded in creating a dynamic social structure and economic organization in rural and urban Zambia which would enable every school-leaver to be employed in socially constructive and productive work. Even when educational reform has been embarked upon, its goals will not be fully achieved until the socialist transformation of society has been accomplished. Before then, the contradictions between our Humanistic socialist convictions on the one hand and the actual injustices and disparities of wealth and status on the other will stand in the way of educational reforms. ... The longer education continues to be a passport to individual affluence and influence for the few, the longer it will be before education can be the well-spring of development for the nation as a whole.[2]

Living Examples

Education's inability, unaided, to remove existing disparities was not all that was plainly seen in the 1970s and 1980s. Another and even more disturbing aspect of the picture was that education itself merited the caustic biblical rebuke: "Physician, heal thyself!" For in many countries, and in varying degrees of seriousness, the very systems that were to help cure inequalities were themselves full of disparities. The most obvious of these took three forms: geographic disparities within the same country, disparities between the sexes, and disparities rooted in socioeconomic inequalities. Several quickly sketched evidentiary items will help introduce a broader and more detailed picture of these three categories.

- Although the ministers of education of Asia, Africa, and Latin America committed their nations in the early 1960s to a strategy of building educational systems from the ground up, starting with universal primary education, the strategy in action turned out to be the exact opposite. Almost without exception, as we saw in Chapter 3, the developing countries expanded enrollments at a much faster rate at the university and secondary levels than at the base of the system.

The result by the end of the 1970s was that a large majority of these countries were not even within striking distance of universal primary education, the target set for 1980 (1970 in the case of Latin America), but they had already substantially overshot their expansion targets for secondary and higher education. The following figures from a 1982 UNESCO assessment illustrate what had actually happened in the 20 years between 1960 and 1980: Africa increased primary school enrollments by 218 percent, while higher education increased by 709 percent. The corresponding figures for South Asia were 128 percent and 411 percent, and for Latin America, 135 percent and 831 percent.[3]

· In most developing countries, the disporportionate allocation of public funds to university education (which is the most expensive) had made such education, paradoxically, the least expensive, with costs largely covered by the national treasury. Those attending the universities were predominantly children of relatively affluent parents. But those at the base of the socioeconomic pyramid paid a sizable share of the taxes that, in effect, subsidized the education of the rich, who then got the best and highest paying jobs.

· Subordination of the interests of the many to the opportunities for the few is well illustrated in the countries of the former French Empire. Under the empire's highly centralized system of administration, every youth—whether in Mali, Upper Volta, Morocco, Vietnam, or Senegal—theoretically had a competitive chance to attend a university in France by scoring well on the baccalaureate entrance examination, given to all on the same day with the same questions asked. Local educational systems therefore were geared to preparing all young people for that chance, from the first grade onward, even though it meant preparing several hundred for every one who actually made it to France. The situation is still much the same today, except that some of these former French colonies can now also enter their own universities. The nagging question remains, however: How appropriate and useful to the vast majority of primary and secondary school pupils is an education designed primarily to get a tiny minority into the university?

· A further consequence of this rapid expansion of higher and secondary education compared to primary schooling, was that developing countries ended up with two distinct educational systems. The first is an urban system that has by now achieved close to universal primary schooling (except for slum children) and impressively high secondary and postsecondary enrollment ratios statistically comparable to, or even above, those in Western European countries in 1950. The second, referred to earlier, is a rural system, typically composed of thinly spread (often incomplete) primary schools, with few if any secondary schools above them or within easy reach. The practical effect of this dual system is that rural-born children, typically constituting 70 to 90 percent of all the nation's children, have a far smaller chance than their urban counterparts of entering and completing primary school, and still less of going on to secondary school or the university. It has been estimated, for example, that in the 1970s a youngster living in Bangkok had an 800-times better chance of being admitted to higher education than his or her counterpart living in the northeastern region of Thailand.[4] Surprisingly, these urban and rural education inequalities are greater in a number of Latin American countries, despite their higher per capita incomes and comparatively smaller rural populations, than appears to be the case in many lower income countries of Asia and Africa.

· Educational inequalities between urban and rural children, or between the sexes or different social classes, are not the monopoly of developing countries. As we shall see later, such disparities, though not as severe, also exist on a troublesome scale in OECD countries and in the Eastern European socialist countries.

VOICES OF CRITICISM

By the 1970s, newly emergent critics in both the South and the North assailed existing educational policies and practices from different perspectives and motives. Some among them dwelt on such negative aspects of the growth in schooling as the erosion of quality, the high wastage rates and other inefficiencies, the irrelevance of the curriculum, the preferential treatment accorded to universities, and the resulting neglect of primary schooling in the rural countryside. Other critics who focused on the persistence of social inequalities despite the large expansion of school systems seized on Emile Durkheim's theory of the "social reproduction" function performed by an education system and reshaped it to their own purpose. In their hands, the theory became a fundamental critique of how education, far from serving as an agent of social mobility and greater democracy, actually preserves and even aggravates social inequalities.

Meanwhile, leaders of opinion in Third World countries who gave priority to the quest for cultural identity condemned the alienation caused by educational models derived by inheritance or imitation from those of the dominant industrial countries. They accused universities in particular of creating new privileged minorities and an international elite, while the massive failure of schooling unsuited to national conditions fostered resignation in the face of social inequalities.[5]

Neo-Marxist critics, including a number of academics in North America and Western Europe, saw a pernicious conspiracy in the matter. In their view, the educational systems introduced in developing countries along the lines of capitalist models from the West were in no way meant to be vehicles of social change. They were meant to arm the ruling classes with a potent instrument for the perpetuation of their own power—by training the children of the exploited masses to be docile and obedient productive workers. Indeed, these critics asserted, this exploitive role of schools applied not only to the imported systems in developing countries but also to the education systems in the advanced capitalist nations from whence the imports came.[6]

Whether one accepts this conspiracy theory or not, certain facts are clear. In the capitalist world, children from middle- and upper-class homes have built-in advantages for securing access to the best of schools and colleges, and from there advancing to the places of command in the state and society. This is also true in developing countries, whatever their professed ideologies. And, significantly, a similar pattern has developed in the communist context of the Soviet Union and other Eastern socialist countries. In the Soviet Union, where the universities of Moscow and Leningrad hold the summit of prestige in the educational hierarchy, and are the takeoff points to major places of command, children of the Soviet equivalent of capitalism's comfortable middle- and upper-class homes are dominant in the profile of the student population. They are often the children of the academicians, the generals, commissars and party secretaries, and the noted performing artists. In other Eastern socialist countries, such as Hungary, although the percentage of third-level students who were children of workers or peasants had increased somewhat, they were still greatly underrepresented in relation to the large proportion of workers and peasants in the total population.[7]

The point to be stressed is simply this: educational inequalities are exceedingly difficult to root out in any society, whatever its official aims and ideology. History teaches that even violent revolutions do not guarantee their eradication, even 20, 40, or 60 years after the initial revolution. The old adage that knowledge is power has an important corollary: the children of those with power are blessed with the easiest access to knowledge, and thus to future power. Lenin's straightforward solution for ending this intergenerational perpetuation of power was to cut the Gordian knot by literally wiping out the power holders of the old regime and making a fresh start—rearing a new set of power holders imbued with a radically different ideology and set of goals. Ironically, the children of these new power holders are now disproportionately represented in the best schools and universities of revolutionary countries. Perhaps this says something about human nature, whose very existence Marx denied, arguing that people's views and values are shaped entirely by their environment. But what is absolutely clear is that no nation in the world today, whatever its ideology, has yet come close to eradicating serious socioeconomic inequalities that cast heavy shadows on its education system.

FOCUSING QUESTIONS

The extent to which one estimates these inequalities and injustices to have persisted, or even worsened, despite more than two decades of worldwide efforts to expand education at successive levels, depends on the view one takes toward the following questions: What do educational disparities mean? How can their presence be determined? Are statistical tables alone adequate for the purpose? What is meant by equal education? Should a country strive to equalize only initial access? Should it strive to ensure equal participation as well? Or, as some insist, should it even aim for equal learning achievements by all so that everyone emerges from the system "equally educated"?

Educational disparities are commonly taken to mean unequal access to formal education resulting from differences, for example, in rural or urban location, sex, socioeconomic, cultural, and ethnic origins and status. These types of disparities can be demonstrated statistically when it appears that a particular subgroup in a population as a whole is underrepresented in school enrollment figures. In aggregate form, however, statistical tables may conceal more than they reveal about disparities, the causes of which are far too complex to be explained by any single political or sociological theory. We will return to this point later.

What follows are five general propositions derived from the available evidence. First, widespread educational disparities—tied especially to geographical location, sex, and socioeconomic and ethnic status—still exist in virtually all countries and are most pronounced in the universities. Second, each kind of disparity may be treated separately for analytical purposes, but in reality they tend to be indivisible; wherever one kind of disparity appears in its most acute form, the others tend to also. Third, not surprisingly the disparities existing at this time are relatively greater in the developing than in the developing world. Fourth, contrary to the flat assertion that no progress has been made in the past 25 years in reducing educational disparities around the world, discernible progress has been made—though far less than would meet the high hopes and expectations of the 1950s and 1960s. Fifth, unless swifter and greater reductions occur, inequalities in education will prove an increasingly serious deterrent to overall social and economic advancement and an increasingly potent cause for political turmoil in many countries.

GEOGRAPHIC DISPARITIES

Throughout history, urban children have typically had better access to schooling than rural children of equivalent native intelligence and motivation. Within each of these two geographic categories, however, there have also been substantial differences. More prosperous villages, especially those "transitional" ones close to cities, have offered better educational opportunities than poorer villages in remote areas. Within urban areas, children from middle- and upper-class neighborhoods have generally had access to more and better education than the children in run-down slum areas and shantytowns.*

Developed Countries

In the highly industrialized Western nations, the former large rural/urban disparities in access to good primary and secondary schools, and especially to higher education, have diminished sharply over the past 30 years. Ironically, a reverse situation now exists in several countries: rural and suburban children and youth are often getting a better public education than the disadvantaged young people trapped in the decaying inner core of major cities. The reasons for this advancement in rural education include a dramatic shrinkage of rural populations, improved parental education, better transportation and communication, and strong public policies aimed at equalizing educational access, including the extension of higher education facilities to provincial towns and cities.

This is not to say, however, that the problem has disappeared. An

*The rural/urban distinction is used here for convenience, but any country seeking to assess its own situation will want to identify more refined types of spatial disparities, taking account, for example, of particular subareas occupied by certain ethnic or tribal minorities and linguistic groups. Such subareas often do not coincide with established political and administrative jurisdictions such as provinces, districts, and subdistricts, on the basis of which school systems are typically organized. An extensive research project of the International Institute for Educational Planning sheds valuable light on the complexities of these spatial disparities (see note 1).

OECD project in the late 1970s on Education and Local Development brought out three important facts that had been widely overlooked by urban-oriented experts.[8] First, there are approximately 220 million people still living in the rural areas of OECD member nations—a number comparable to the total population of France, Germany, Italy, and the United Kingdom combined. Among the less industrialized OECD countries that still have large rural populations, as in southern Europe, serious educational disparities persist between urban and rural areas despite improvements that have been made. Second, even in the more industrialized states of northern Europe and North America, as well as in Australia and New Zealand, there are still large pockets of educationally disadvantaged rural youth.* The problem in most cases is not that they lack schools to attend, but that the teachers are often less qualified, the curriculum is limited, and its standardized content is so urban-biased it discourages young people from pursuing productive rural careers and assuming leadership roles in developing their own rural environments.

In the Eastern European socialist countries, although geographical disparities are now considerably smaller than they were 30 years ago, they remain both quantitatively and qualitatively substantial for several reasons. The rural population is still sizable. Rural schools, despite strong efforts to expand and improve them, often lag behind urban schools, especially at the secondary level. Higher education institutions are not easily accessible to young people in remote areas. Perhaps most important, the average educational, cultural, and income level of rural parents is still low compared to that of many urban parents—a condition that tends to dampen the educational motivation and aspirations of the children.

In the U.S.S.R. the condition just described has significantly improved. Within the last ten years the U.S.S.R. has largely achieved its long-standing goal of extending compulsory schooling in rural areas through grade 10—a goal achieved much earlier in the cities. At the same time, in an effort to equalize access for different social groups, the U.S.S.R. in the 1970s also introduced new preparatory divisions in higher institutions. These are designed to give a year of special remedial work to inadequately

---

*Australia has at least partially solved this problem with an ingenious system of distance learning for widely dispersed children of farmers and ranchers in the outback. Classes are held by two-way radio supplemented by correspondence, all under the supervision of a parent (usually the mother). This system of distance learning has produced impressive results in many cases, comparable to and at times even superior to regular city schools. Once again, however, much depends on the level of the parent's education and the motivation of the children.

prepared bright children of both urban and rural workers before they enter the regular program. Virtually all Eastern European countries are making similar efforts to strengthen their rural schools. Hence in the next 10 to 20 years, the prospects for getting to upper secondary and higher education should steadily improve for able and motivated rural boys and girls.

Developing Countries

The situation in most of the developing world is dramatically different, and worse, although there are marked differences between individual countries, depending not only on their level of economic development and urbanization but also on the determination of their political leaders to erase the severe educational disadvantages of children and youth in especially deprived areas (both rural and urban).

Despite the generally drab picture of rural schooling, the rural education scene has not been entirely static. Over the years a trickle-down process in many developing countries has gradually improved the rural schooling situation, mainly at the elementary level. For when urban primary school participation rates began to approach 100 percent, available additional resources were directed toward the expansion of rural schools. The effects led to a slow increase in rural enrollments and a start on the task of reducing wide urban/rural gaps. In a few instances—Panama and Honduras are examples in Latin America, and Nigeria, Kenya, and Tanzania in Africa—governments assigned a priority claim on new budgetary resources for the most educationally deprived rural communities in order to quicken the pace at which disparities were reduced.

Yet this trickle-down process of narrowing spatial disparities works only if substantial budgetary increments continue to become available. Because the maintenance and operation of existing schools almost invariably have first claim on each annual budget allocation, and with costs continuing to climb, simply maintaining the status quo requires substantial annual budgetary increases. Here is the crux of the problem. For reasons given in our discussion of financial trends and prospects in Chapter 5, most school systems in developing countries are likely to find it increasingly difficult to secure large enough annual budget increments to expand and upgrade rural schools at more than a slow pace.

An Innovation Worth Watching

A few developing countries whose leaders are determined to achieve universal primary schooling in the near future have adopted more unconventional approaches. Tanzania is a case in point.[10] In 1974 a top-level decision was made to achieve universal primary education by the end of 1977. Such a goal plainly could not be attained by the conventional route for, apart from the large extra costs involved, it would require 45,000 additional trained teachers, and Tanzania's 35 Colleges of National Education had an output of only 5000 teachers per year. Thus, an interim shortcut was chosen that entailed what many regarded as a deliberate trade-off of quality for quantity. Sole reliance on qualified trained teachers for the expansion was replaced by the recruitment of trainee-teachers from among the large numbers of young people who had completed primary school. They were to divide their time equally between teaching, mainly in rural schools, and undergoing training by special tutors and experienced teachers. In addition, distance education (correspondence and radio programs) was to be used. After about two years of service, these new trainee-teachers (who received a very low salary) could be upgraded to Grade C teachers at more than three times their probationary salary if they passed a qualifying examination. By this means, some 45,000 new teachers were obtained by 1979 and, statistically, Tanzania achieved a gross enrollment ratio of 100 percent.[11] The problem of upgrading quality and financing a much-enlarged annual budget for teacher salaries still remained, of course. Nevertheless, a sizable dent had been made in providing access to primary schooling to great numbers of unserved rural children. The eventual evaluation of this unorthodox scheme should provide useful clues for other countries facing similar problems.

The Seamless Web of Poverty

Especially in the low-income countries, the prevailing dual urban/rural education system deprives a large majority of rural youngsters of even a full primary education, let alone a chance at a secondary or higher education. It is mainly the children of the poorest families in the rural areas and urban slums who account for the dramatically high figures of non-schoolgoers and early dropouts that show up in reports of governments and international agencies. These children are caught in a seamless web in which their bleak educational resources are connected with all the other afflictions of their existence—disease, contaminated drinking water, hunger, high mortality rates, and the need to work at an early age to support themselves and their families. It is enough to cite a few representative cases among the poorest African countries, drawn from three UNICEF field reports.[12]

Gambia. Gambia had a rural population in 1980 of over 80 percent with a life expectancy at birth for males of 39 years and for females of 43 years.

The national average of school enrollment in the 8-to-13 age group was only 36 percent. The percentage in rural areas was much lower. A UNICEF field report notes that rural children in particular "are subject to malnutrition, diarrhoea, and many parasitic infectious diseases, which combine to produce a very high mortality rate." Most of "the 132 health units are located in larger towns or villages; very few village health workers have been trained; and there are only 30 doctors and 174 registered nurses. The low level of education in the rural areas, coupled with poor hygienic conditions in the home, low family income, lack of safe drinking water or needed health services (including vaccination), all exacerbate the child's situation."[13]

Sudan. The infant mortality rate in southern Sudan—the poorest part of the country with few urban settlements—was 170 per thousand, compared to 110 per thousand in the north. A World Health Organization/World Bank study of the water supply and sanitation in 1978 stated that 46 percent of the overall Sudanese population had access to a safe water supply, but only 7 percent in the south had such access. In the school year 1978–79, for the country as a whole, a Sudanese child between the ages of 7 and 13 had only a 37 percent chance of being in school, and less than that among girls. The variations among provinces were striking. In the northern province 74 percent of the children (and a marginally smaller percentage of girls) had a chance of being in school, whereas in the Bahr-el-Gahzal southern province, children had only a 12 percent chance of being in school (girls had a 7 percent chance).[14]

Ethiopia. The Ethiopian population in 1980 was estimated to be 88 percent rural. Since 1950, striking progress has been made in increasing life expectancy at birth from 32 years to 39 years for males and from 35 to 43 years for females. Yet only 23 percent of all children were in schools nationally and, of these, only 14 percent of all girls. The rates in the rural areas were much lower. The level of illiteracy in Ethiopia is estimated to be in excess of 90 percent, and there is a general shortage of teachers, especially at the primary level. In the southern region, "some 50 percent of teachers are untrained. School facilities are frequently inadequate. In rural areas they are generally overcrowded, deprived of furniture, equipment and materials for learning and without access to medical care. Curriculae tend to be stereotypes, and their objectives are neither well defined nor related to the real development needs of rural areas."[15]

Kenya. Although this African country is much more advanced, both economically and educationally, than the preceding three, Kenya merits attention as an example of how an impressively high gross enrollment ratio often conceals large pockets of educational poverty in particular geographic areas. By 1976, as a result of tremendous sacrifice and effort, Kenya had reached a primary school GER of 93 percent. However, a breakdown of this aggregate statistic shows that, at one extreme, the three most economically advanced regions (central, eastern, and western) were already close to a 100 percent GER. But at the other extreme, in the poverty-stricken northeast region only 9 out of every 100 children between the ages of 6 and 13 were enrolled in school.[16]

Qualitative Disparities

Conditions that typify rural schools in many developing countries (and no few developed countries) are often even worse than the quantitative enrollment and noncompletion figures suggest, for such statistics conceal great qualitative shortcomings. Surveys and direct observation in many different developing countries have confirmed that schools in the hinterland generally have insufficient textbooks and other training materials and equipment and a disportionate share of untrained and unqualified primary teachers. They often have high pupil and teacher absentee rates and operate fewer days per year than many urban schools. Following are a few examples of the problems:

· A nine-country survey in Latin America in the mid-1970s revealed many such qualitative discrepancies.[17] In the specific instance of Bolivia, a substantial majority of the urban schools had maps for teaching geography, whereas only one quarter of the rural schools had any maps whatsoever.
· A different study in Jamaica in the 1970s showed that 58 percent of the teachers in rural Westmoreland were untrained, compared to only 17 percent in the capital city of Kingston.[18]
· The highest ambition of almost any well-qualified schoolteacher or university professor in Thailand is to teach in the magnet city of Bangkok. As a result, the qualifications of teachers in the north and northeast of the country are markedly lower than in Bangkok.[19]
· Fifteen countries replying to the United Nations Commission on the Status of Women attributed the lower quality of rural schools to lack of teacher preparation.[20]
· Even in Hungary, where quantitative disparities in urban/rural enrollments in primary education have all but disappeared, more than 11 percent of rural teachers in 1972 had no degree in education, compared to 7.5 percent in Budapest.[21]

Thus far we have spoken mainly about rural/urban disparities in primary education. The disparities at the secondary and postsecondary levels, however, are far greater. Rural secondary schools are few and far between in most developing countries. El Salvador, for one, had none at all in the mid-1970s, and there are many other such cases.[22] Universities and other higher institutions, even agricultural colleges in many cases, are concentrated in cities. With luck, a bright and motivated rural youngster who has completed primary school in his or her village may be able to stay with relatives in the city and gain admission to the next rung on the education ladder. But relatively few are that fortunate.

To sum up, the probability of a rural child of either sex getting an equivalent *quality* of education to that of an urban child is very low. The statistical probability of an urban boy climbing to the middle or the top of the education ladder is vastly greater than that of an equally bright and motivated rural boy. The prospects for a rural girl are even smaller in relation to an urban girl with the same endowments. This leads us to the matter of educational disparities based on sex.

SEX DISPARITIES

Sex disparities in education, like geographic disparities, have historically been prevalent in almost all societies, primarily for cultural reasons. This was true even in societies such as biblical Judea, classical Athens, and colonial New England, which otherwise placed a high value on learning. There were distinguished exceptions in which women attained educations equal to the very best offered men—as in the instance of England's preeminent novelists such as Jane Austin and Charlotte Bronte, or Abigail Smith Adams, the gifted wife of the second president of the United States. The exceptions, however, generally stemmed from the private instruction of girls and young women by learned fathers or private tutors. More recently there have also been outstanding exceptions in developing countries, for example, in India, Sri Lanka, and Dominica, where able and well-educated women were democratically elected to serve as prime ministers.

The relatively recent upsurge of concern over sex inequalities, not only in education but in employment and many other facets of life, has accelerated efforts to reduce discrimination against girls and women. In the developed world these efforts have focused especially on higher education and on opening up fields of study and employment previously reserved largely for males. Insofar as the developing world is concerned, it is now more widely recognized that the education of women holds the key to all other elements on which the transformation of societies depends—population control, family health, personal hygiene, nutrition, receptivity to innovations, and educational motivation of children.

Despite progress in eliminating sex disparities, however, many sizable inequalities clearly remain. On the brighter side of the picture, the proportion of girls enrolled at each educational level has risen perceptibly in all regions since 1965. These regional trends are portrayed by the UNESCO statistics in Table 7.1.

To take the case of higher education—the ultimate bastion of sex disparities in all educational systems—the proportion of females in total enrollments in developed countries as a group rose from 38 percent in 1965 to 47 percent in 1980. In the same 15 years the female proportion in higher education in the developing countries group rose from 27 percent to 34 percent. However, there are wide differences among individual countries in each of these groups. In the developed world, for example, women now constitute roughly half the university enrollments in such countries as Canada, Sweden, the U.S.S.R. and the United States, whereas in 1979–80 they still represented little more than one third in such countries as the Netherlands, the Federal Republic of Germany, and the United Kingdom, and only one tenth in Japan. Among developing countries, the differences are even greater, ranging from less than 20 percent of women in total higher education in such countries as Bangladesh, the Ivory Coast, Senegal, and the United Republic of Cameroon, to approximate parity between women and men, as of 1980, in such countries as Brazil, Burma, Panama, and the Philippines.

Table 7.1 Growth in Percentage of Females in Total Enrollments, 1965–80

	Primary Education (%)		Secondary Education (%)		Higher Education (%)	
	1965	1980	1965	1980	1965	1980
Developed countries	49	49	50	51	38	47
Developing countries	41	43	32	39	27	34
Africa (excluding Arab states)	40	42	35	38	26	32
Arab states	35	41	27	37	20	31
Latin America	49	49	48	51	33	42
Europe (including U.S.S.R.)	49	49	51	52	39	46
Northern America[a]	49	50	50	50	39	51

[a]In UNESCO terminology, Northern America includes Bermuda, Canada, Greenland, St. Pierre and Miquelon, and the United States.
Source: UNESCO, *Statistical Yearbook, 1982* (Paris: UNESCO, Office of Statistics, 1982).

Common Features of Sex Disparities

The evidence leads us to suggest five propositions concerning sex disparities in education that apply to most countries (and to a greater or lesser degree also to geographic and socioeconomic disparities).

The first proposition is that the lowest female ratios are generally found in countries in which overall participation rates (for both boys and girls) are still quite low (as in Africa, for example), or where deep-rooted religious and other cultural factors still strongly resist equality of education for girls and women (as in many, though not all, Islamic societies). Conversely, where rapid increases in educational enrollments have occurred, the percentage of women has generally increased more than proportionately. Brazil is a dramatic case in point. Between 1970 and 1980 total higher education enrollments in Brazil trebled, from 430,000 to more than 1,650,000; in the same period, female participation increased from 38 percent to approximately 50 percent.[23] In developing countries generally, rapid urbanization has also favored increased female enrollments, reflecting a faster breakdown of traditional cultural barriers in the cities than in the countryside.

To amplify the reference to Islamic societies, educational participation of females has improved dramatically since the early 1960s in a number of them. In Saudi Arabia, for one, girls accounted for only 9 percent of all primary enrollments, 1 percent of secondary, and zero percent of higher education in 1960. But by 1980, the female proportion had climbed to 39 percent in primary, 38 percent in secondary, and 29 percent in higher education. Even in much poorer Islamic countries, without benefit of large oil revenues, impressive gains have been made. In Bangladesh, with one of the lowest per capita incomes of all developing nations, the proportion of girls in total enrollments rose between 1960 and 1979 from 28 to 37 percent at the primary level, from 8 to 21 percent at the secondary level, and from 4 to 14 percent in higher education. Although Bangladesh and other predominantly Islamic countries are still far from achieving educational parity between the sexes, that they have moved this far in a single generation suggests that earlier cultural constraints against equal treatment for women have begun to erode significantly. Rapid urbanization has contributed importantly to this erosion, as witnessed by the generally much higher eduation participation rates for girls in the urban areas than in the countryside, where religious and other cultural inhibitions remain much stronger.

The second proposition is that wherever significant female disparities exist, they are always greatest in higher education. Disparities at the third level, however, are invariably rooted in inequalities at the secondary level, where the real sorting out of university-bound students takes place. By the same token, disparities at the primary level set the stage for those at the secondary level. It follows, therefore, that until sex disparities in primary and secondary education in developing countries are sharply reduced, those in higher education are bound to remain larger. That sex disparities have virtually disappeared (statistically) at the first two levels in most of Latin America and the Caribbean is the underlying reason that female representation in higher education for the region as a whole is now nearly as high as in Europe. Conversely, the persistence of sharp disparities in higher education in most Asian and African states goes back to preexisting disparities at the primary and secondary levels.

The third proposition is that the apparent overall statistical parity of male/female enrollments in higher education that has been achieved, or nearly achieved, in a few countries is a misleading indicator of educational equality. The overall enrollment ratio conceals sizable sex disparities in enrollments between different types of postsecondary institutions and different fields of study. In the Western nations, for example, it is common to find low female enrollments in traditional men's fields, such as the pure sciences, mathematics, engineering, medicine, law, and architecture, and disproportionately high female enrollments in the traditional women's fields, such as education, the arts and humanities, nursing, and home economics.

The fourth proposition, tied to the third, is that discrimination against women in higher education by fields of study is rooted in traditional sex biases and discriminatory hiring practices in different employment markets and professions, including the professoriate itself. It is reported, for example, that in a 1977 survey of 5000 Japanese business firms, 78 percent said they gave no opportunities to female graduates.[24] What incentive, therefore, does a bright young Japanese woman have to study business administration, engineering, or marketing at the university? Or even to aspire to becoming a university professor when over 90 percent of the university professors in Japan in 1979 were males?[25]

Such discriminatory hiring practices, however, have recently been breaking down in a number of developed countries (and to a degree also in some developing ones), in no small measure because of the international dynamism of the women's rights movement and, in certain countries, the adoption and more rigorous enforcement of antidiscrimination legislation.

These changes were especially dramatic in the United States during the 1970s, where they were reflected in large increases in female university enrollments in traditional men's fields. For example, the proportion of all professional law degrees earned by women in the United States shot up from 5 percent in 1970 to 30 percent in 1980 (in actual numbers, from 801 to 10,754). In the same period, medical degrees granted to women rose from 8 percent of the total to 23 percent (from 699 degrees in 1970 to 3486 in 1980). Dentistry degrees to women rose from almost nil in 1970 to 700 in 1980—a small percentage of the total of 5259, to be sure, but a breakthrough by women into a professional field long closed to them. American women have now even invaded the previously all-male sanctuaries of the national military academies and state and municipal academies for training firefighters and police. They are also becoming officers and directors of major corporations in previously undreamed-of numbers.

The fifth rule, and the most fundamental one for understanding the underlying causes of sex disparities in education, is that these disparities grow primarily out of the traditional culture, customs, and taboos of each particular society. Historically, in all societies living close to the survival level, male infants were valued more highly than female infants. This was basically for economic and security reasons, which then became sanctified by social and religious mores and expressed in different sex roles and dependency relationships, and in family and community power structures. Even after a given society had advanced well beyond the survival level, as in the case of today's industrialized nations, these ancient sex rites, attitudes, and behavior patterns lingered in modified form as "cultural survivals," eventually giving rise to women's rights movements.

But, in the poverty-blighted rural areas of many of today's developing areas, particularly in Asia, where literally millions of families are still living on the ragged edge of survival, the preference for boys over girls remains so strong that it is not unusual, for example, for the nutritional and health needs of young male children to be given priority over those of their female siblings. And in some areas, even the ancient practice of female infanticide still exists (as it did during the early years of the Industrial Revolution among poor working families in the factory cities of England and other European countries). Male babies in these situations are seen as future breadwinners and old-age insurance policies for their parents. In circumstances where there is not enough food to go around, female babies are often seen as just another mouth to feed. They will eventually get married, leave home, and raise their own children. Until then they will play a useful role in caring for their younger siblings and performing other household duties that will prepare them for their eventual role as wife, mother, and provider—but in their husband's home and family.

It is natural, indeed logical, in this context for these sex attitudes to carry over into education. If there is a local school to go to, boys will get first priority. For if education, as is generally believed, will enhance their earning power (best of all by getting them a wage-paying job in the city), they will be able to support the family more adequately and provide better for their parents in their old age. As perceived by many people living in more affluent circumstances, this treatment of girls is unfair and cruel. Nevertheless, it reflects the hard economic and cultural facts of life in poverty-stricken contexts. It is also one that, predictably, is bound to persist as long as extreme poverty continues to blight the lives of millions of families in the developing world. Even if more schools are established in these backward areas, the opportunity to take advantage of them will be rationed by poor families and communities in favor of male children.

Two factors reinforce the reluctance of parents in backward areas to send their daughters to school. First, sending children to primary school, not to mention secondary and higher education, is a costly undertaking from the family's point of view. Even if the school is tuition free (and often it is not), uniforms and school supplies must still be bought and fees paid, aside from which the child's labor at home and in the field must be forgone. Thus, again, if the family can afford to send only two or three of its six or eight children to school, the boys will usually come first. In many cases, even the boys will not remain in school for long; once they are strong enough to plow the field or tend the cattle, their time cannot be spared for "book learning."

The second factor is fear. A school may be available down the road that a daughter can attend and the parents can afford the sacrifices involved, but they may still balk at sending her to it. They fear the classroom give-and-take with boys or her exposure to a male teacher—all the more so once she has reached puberty. They may also fear the disapproval of their neighbors if sending a girl to school flies in the face of communal mores.

Looking to the future, it appears likely that in the 1980s and beyond, sex disparities in education will continue to narrow in most developed countries and also, though usually less rapidly, in most developing countries. In developed countries, the educational, economic, and social advancement of able women will be favored by the smaller age cohorts entering the professional and general employment market and (in many cases) the liberalized hiring practices of governments, private businesses, and universities. Similar forces of liberalization will no doubt be at work in varying degrees of intensity in many developing countries. In the latter countries, however, the continuing increase in the number of new entrants into the labor force each year, in the face of saturated employment markets, will tend to deter the expansion of women's opportunities.

SOCIOECONOMIC DISPARITIES

In both developing and developed countries, the most widespread and intractable disparities in all education, and particularly in higher education, are those rooted in socioeconomic, racial, and ethnic differences. These not only underlie the many geographical and sex disparities previously discussed but are also the most difficult to eradicate because they are often perpetuated in families from generation to generation.

It is worth repeating for emphasis that in virtually all nations today children of parents high on the educational, occupational, and social scale have a far better statistical chance of getting into a good secondary school, and from there into the best colleges and universities, than equally bright children of ordinary workers or farmers. This pattern shows up consistently in all of the studies of socioeconomic profiles of university students in both Western and Eastern Europe. If only because of arithmetic, the socioeconomic skewness of university student bodies has gradually diminished in most developed countries in response to increased enrollments and participation rates. Yet, to the surprise and often the consternation of many educators and political leaders, marked distortions in favor of well-born children persist. The evidence of bias also shows up at the secondary level. In France, Germany, Belgium, Italy, and Sweden, for example, the choice between short vocational secondary training and longer general studies is largely determined by social background.[26] The children of less-educated, lower income parents are heavily overrepresented in the vocational training schools and grossly underrepresented in the longer term general studies programs that prepare students for university entrance.

Though there have been relatively few systematic sociological studies of student backgrounds in developing countries—Latin America being a partial exception—there is no doubt that an even greater socioeconomic skewness exists in their universities. A study for the Inter-American Development Bank of prevailing conditions in a sample of 19 Latin American countries around 1970 compared the average number of years of schooling and the cumulative public educational expenditure per child for the children of families in different income brackets. The findings, summarized in Appendix Table 7.1, indicate that the average child in the low-income group (comprising about 85 percent of the total population of the group of countries studied) completed about 2½ years of formal schooling, at a total public cost of U.S. $113 per child. In contrast, the average child from the highest income group (about 5 percent of the total population) completed 17 years of schooling at a public expense of U.S.

$4753 per student.[27] Some observers have questioned the adequacy of the data on which these conclusions were based, and the possible margin of error in the resulting figures. Moreover, educational conditions in Latin America have improved considerably since 1970. Still, few informed observers of the Latin American educational scene, even now, would question the general thrust of the conclusions.

Paradoxically, as time goes on, the sociological imbalance in secondary and higher education is likely to become even more accentuated in countries (especially in Africa) that started off some 20 years ago with only a minieducation system and with very low parental literacy rates. In such situations, the first generation of secondary and university students inevitably includes a sizable percentage of bright children coming from poorly educated and illiterate parents. But with more and more young people joining the educated elite, their children will have a decided competitive edge in the future over the children of uneducated parents. A similar metamorphosis occurred in the U.S.S.R. Soon after its revolution, with the annihilation of the elite families under the Old Regime, the children of ordinary workers were more heavily represented in the then-available preparatory schools and universities than has since been the case.

The initial advantage enjoyed by children of more educated parents tends to broaden with each successive school year and level of schooling. In most of Latin America, for example, secondary schools are the main breeding grounds of the striking social inequalities that show up in the universities. Able and motivated children whose parents can afford to enter them into one of the best private secondary schools can almost be assured of admission to one of the stronger universities—or, better still, to a ranking American or European college or university. The less fortunate children must attend a less prestigious and often lower quality public secondary school, from which admission to one of the more reputable universities is far less likely. This Latin American pattern is duplicated in many parts of Asia and Africa.

None of this means that there is a strict correlation between intellectual ability and motivation for education on the one side and parental education and socioeconomic status on the other. Children born into very poor families have gravitated to schools from whence they rose to places of preeminence in their respective communities and nations. These successes, however, tend to be the exceptions to the rule. The findings of many empirical studies suggest that children whose parents are at the bottom of the socioeconomic hierarchy are not as inclined to seek or gain access to available educational facilities as are children from families located at the middle or top of the hierarchy. Psychologically, some are inhibited by a self-deprecating attitude and touch of fatalism that keeps them from going as far as they might. Still more, however, are turned away by economic barriers and by the need to work to help support their family.

Even if a bright and ambitious boy, born into humble circumstances, manages to make his way to the top of the education ladder and wins a degree, he may still find himself at a competitive disadvantage in relation to many of his classmates in landing a good job, for they are more likely to have "connections." And the more overcrowded the job market becomes, the more these connections count.

These long-standing socioeconomic inequalities, and the educational disparities arising from them, still exist in various forms and degrees in all nations today. Over the generations they have been gradually and substantially reduced—along with geographic and sex disparities—in today's industrialized countries that have enjoyed sizable economic growth accompanied by more equitable income distribution and, in some cases, by determined legal and other measures to eradicate blatant inequalities. On the whole, the prospects seem fairly good that these favorable trends will continue in such countries, although with periodic ups and downs tied to economic and political fluctuations, and not without continued determined efforts, frequently marked by controversy.

The long-term outlook for many of the developing countries in the middle-income bracket also seems reasonably favorable, provided that they manage their economies well and adopt and enforce strong and equitable income distribution policies and measures. Unfortunately, however, the outlook for the low-income developing countries in this respect—as in most others—is much more problematic. With their populations continuing to grow rapidly and their economies often lagging well behind, poverty—the prime breeding ground for educational and all other inequalities—may also continue to grow. This is not inevitable, for conceivably these gloomy trends, which have become so much more evident than they were 10 or 20 years ago, can be turned around. Turning them around, however, will require heroic efforts by the leaders of these countries and the people themselves, strongly reinforced by external assistance.

In the entire spectrum of countries, from the richest to the poorest, education will have a critical role to play in bringing about the social and economic changes essential to the reduction of gross inequalities. But, to repeat, education by itself cannot bring about these difficult socioeconomic changes. It can only perform its role well in conjunction with strong political, economic, legal, and other efforts pointed in the same direction.

POSSIBLE WAYS TO REDUCE INEQUALITIES

What can education systems do to help reduce the more glaring educational inequalities examined in this chapter—granted they cannot do it all by themselves? There are many options to choose from, some involving relatively minor changes in current practice. Some things can be done at little or no extra cost whereas others may be relatively expensive. Obviously each country will have to put together the combination of measures best suited to its own circumstances. The following suggestions are merely illustrative of the kinds of actions that merit consideration. Nor are they novel suggestions; they are drawn largely from what some countries are already doing.

Getting the Facts into the Open

The prime candidate in the developing world of those things that promise high returns at little extra cost is improvement in statistical reporting and analytical systems, so that the ministries of education and political leaders and the general public can actually know the nature and extent of existing inequalities and whether they are being ameliorated. This is also, as suggested in an earlier chapter, a feasible and productive matter in which external aid agencies can be of practical help.

Attacking Geographic Disparities. The first obvious requirement for reducing educational disparities within urban areas and between these and rural areas is to build up educational capacity and quality in the deficit areas. This means giving priority to these areas in the allocation of any new available resources or, if need be, transferring a portion of the resources now going to favored areas, preferably without reducing their educational quality, access, or effectiveness.

Rural educational growth in Panama was preceded by the Ministry of Planning's preparation of a "Poverty Map" of 100 communities requiring priority attention for integrated rural services.[28] A reallocation of resources must include not simply money but a redeployment of teaching and administrative talent as well. A policy of double shifts at the elementary level was initiated in rural areas of El Salvador in the 1970s, with teachers being paid a supplement (but not a double salary) for the double load. Evaluation of a preliminary pilot program indicated that achievement was unaffected by the shorter school day.[29]

To strengthen education in rural areas will require a substantial degree of decentralization of planning, curriculum development, teacher training, and financial discretion, all exercised within the broad framework of national policies but with sufficient flexibility to accommodate local diversities. Such controlled decentralization of highly centralized systems could lead to chaos, of course, in the absence of strong management teams in various regions and districts. But the development of such teams could greatly reduce the existing workload—including a vast amount of bureaucratic paper work—of the central ministry or department, freeing it to undertake certain essential planning, evaluation, and other management tasks that are now often neglected and also permitting some transfer of able personnel from the center to the field. To facilitate such personnel transfers, however, would necessitate an overhaul of the present hierarchical pattern of professional grades and salaries and a sizable strengthening of incentives and rewards for working outside the major cities.

Attacking Sex Disparities. The reduction of geographical disparities would not by itself overcome sex disparities. But it would at least be an improvement over the present situation in rural areas where often the majority of girls get no exposure whatever to schooling and no chance to improve their lives. In areas where parents are fearful of sending their daughters to schools with male teachers, a major effort could be made to train and hire more female teachers. Granted, there may be a shortage of educated girls for this purpose, but the shortage is never total. Some educated girls are available in most areas, or could be recruited from other areas, and if necessary as a transitional measure, teacher qualification standards could be relaxed somewhat. Wider employment opportunities would be created for able educated women while at the same time creating influential models for younger girls.

At the secondary and higher levels, where prospective employment opportunities strongly narrow the curriculum choices of female students, educators in both developed and developing countries might take the lead in getting the facts out into the open and initiating negotiations with government agencies and private employers to break custom by recruiting well-qualified girls and women for types of positions previously closed to them. Universities themselves, as employers, should be the first to set a good example. Women's organizations could also be encouraged to demand such changes in employment practices.

Attacking Socioeconomic Disparities. A first point of attack would be to reform the upside-down systems of educational financing prevailing in many developing countries, whereby low-income families who often cannot afford primary or secondary education for their own children are subsidizing high-cost free university education for the children of the affluent. The object of such a reform would be to make at least a full primary education fully free for all. Substantial tuition charges would be imposed in connection with postsecondary education for those able to pay them, but with loans and scholarships available for able and needy youth in order to break the economic barrier. It has been estimated that if upper income Latin American students were required to pay the actual costs of their schooling at the second and third level, the effect would cover over 14 percent of the entire public education budget of Latin America.[30]

An extensive reform would also contemplate two more lines of action. One would be to inaugurate remedial transitional programs from school to college for promising students with inadequate previous preparation, and who thus suffer in academic competition with better prepared students when they have to do their catching up after instead of before entering regular college programs. The other line of action would be to inaugurate work-study college programs, designed both to improve educational experiences through exposure to the world of work and to enable students to earn money for college costs.

Services for Preschool Children. At the tap roots of the educational system, in both developed and developing countries, the necessary changes would entail an enlarged and strengthened preschool education, especially for children of working mothers, and compensatory programs such as the Head Start Program in the United States for disadvantaged youngsters age four to eight.* Among other things, this would mean the spread of locally based day care centers for preschool children, particularly in urban slums and disadvantaged rural areas, with a combination of nutritional, health, recreational, and educational activities. With modest governmental and external assistance, this field is particularly promising for voluntary organizations.

There are those who question whether preschool programs or, alternatively, the expansion and improvement of primary schools should be the first priority of governments unable to provide adequately for both. As Gilbert de Landsheere, a long-time student of the subject, states the issue: "Is it worthwhile to invest heavily in primary teaching if, in the absence of pre-primary education, only superficial results can be expected

*Head Start was one of the Great Society programs initiated by President Lyndon Johnson in the late 1960s, with strong federal government support. The aim was to compensate for deficient home conditions of preschool-age children so that they would have a better start when they entered school. Although the jury is still out on the final evaluation of this program, and observers differ in their assessments, there is considerable evidence of positive results, some of which have shown up most clearly after several years.

for the majority of pupils?"[31] The actual choice until now has been consistently and almost universally in favor of the expansion of schooling for children over age six, with investment in secondary and higher education frequently supplanting the rhetorical commitment to primary education. According to a special UNESCO study, based on data for 1975, preschool enrollment constituted only 2.69 percent of the preschool-age population in selected European countries, 0.13 percent in Africa, 0.6 percent in Latin America, and 0.43 percent in Asia.[32]

The overall priority question can at least be confronted by examining those programs targeted to preschool children that focus on nutrition, health, the home, the preschool environment, or a combination of these factors. Although evaluative studies of the costs and educational benefits of these programs are few, our review of the evidence suggests that children with good preschool experiences are likely to do much better in primary school and less likely to drop out. It also suggests that it is possible that a major policy commitment to preschool children can be made without necessarily implying a costly across-the-board commitment to the full range of possible objectives and services. By this we mean that, unlike the more common priority commitment to secondary and higher education, a commitment to preschool learning can strengthen rather than erode a government's commitment to primary education. The low productivity of primary education in developing countries might be raised dramatically by substantial investments in the physical and mental development of preschool children. Even in a developed country such as the Netherlands, it is calculated that the cost of extending enriched learning experiences down to four- and five-year-olds would be partially offset by decreased later enrollments in costly special education and remedial courses because of early intervention against environmental retardation, including malnutrition.[33]

Alternative Approaches to Secondary Schooling. What is to be done to overcome the disparities rooted in the absence of secondary schools in the rural areas of the developing world, and the rejection of conventional secondary schooling by numerous teenagers in developed countries?

Here, as elsewhere, every ideal must express a realistic possibility of being fulfilled, or it is no more than a dream. It is scarcely realistic to expect every developing country to build a secondary school in every crossroads village. Even the developed countries lack the funds to do that, which is one reason for school-consolidation movements. Yet ministers of education in the developing countries might consider the cost-benefits of the establishment of centrally located magnet secondary schools designed to draw, on a competitive basis, the brightest students

Disparities and Inequalities | 237

from a large rural area of dispersed small settlements. In the absence of all-weather roads or adequate transportation that would permit the students in question to live at home, some might have to be housed and fed in dormitories at the magnet school—a practice not uncommon in a number of developing countries. None of this would come cheaply. But it would be for the ministers of education to decide whether the costs would be more than offset by what would be gained—the development of talent, the spur to ambition—as against the loss in dropouts and wastage in rural areas under conditions in which primary education seems to lead nowhere.

In the case of nonacademically motivated youth in the 12-to-16 age group in developed countries, who rebel against compulsory schooling, special work experience programs could be sandwiched in with the school experience, a practice that has worked well in the United Kingdom. Another possibility, tried out by a number of innercity school systems in the United States, is storefront schools that are more informal and flexible than massive formal high schools.

A variation on this objective, coupled with a school-financing objective, currently takes the form of so-called production schools in several Latin American countries such as Panama, Honduras, and Guatemala, and in Benin, Africa. (It is also reminiscent of the earlier Gandhian basic schools in India, which unfortunately did not survive the competition of conventional British-style elementary schools.) The institution at the elementary and intermediary level is both a school and a production unit, theoretically designed to strengthen and reinforce each other. Students in the school produce agricultural, wood, or other products either for the needs of the school itself, for sale on the market, or for their own home use. Academic subjects—reading, writing, and measurement skills, as well as natural sciences and technology—are integrated into and become the core of the productive process. At the same time, the integration of subject matter around a core agricultural or technical curriculum has major implications for the caliber and training of teachers, especially in fields such as agriculture, health, community development, and electricity, and can readily founder on this score. Carefully planned and nurtured, however, it offers important possibilities.

Reducing Dropouts

The need for measures designed to deal with the costly phenomenon of high absenteeism and dropouts, especially in the rural primary schools of developing countries, can hardly be exaggerated. One major reason for this phenomenon is that the environment within these schools and the education they provide is so poor, basically because, unlike the situation in many universities, too little is being spent per pupil. A possible cure for this malady that deserves consideration is to improve the internal efficiency of universities and to charge substantial tuition fees (as suggested earlier), thereby releasing funds that could be redeployed to strengthen primary education. But something more than spending more money per pupil is also required. The programs and schedules of the schools must be made more flexible and better attuned to the needs and conditions of each locality and to the outside obligations of the pupils. School schedules in agricultural areas need to be synchronized with the planting and harvesting peaks of the crop cycle. They must also provide opportunities for dropouts to "drop back in," and for "recurrent education" so that people can pick up the broken threads of their education and eventually achieve credentials comparable to those of regular students. The need for some such structure is common to both the developed and the developing countries.

Access to Rural Professional Careers

One of the greatest educational absurdities in many developing countries is that low-ranking urban secondary students who fail to gain admittance to the regular university nevertheless have a big advantage over brighter and highly motivated rural young people in gaining access to government and other professional careers in agriculture and other aspects of rural development. This is because the urban students, having gone through a stronger secondary school, have at least learned better than rural students how to pass the standard academic tests that determine admission to agricultural colleges (usually the last choice of the weaker urban students, but still a way into the civil service structure). One possible cure for this situation would be a major reform in the existing system for training and recruiting young people for government (or private) careers in rural services designed to enable bright and motivated rural youth to compete equitably with urban youth for such positions.

Educational Opportunities for Out-of-School Youth

Much could be done to reduce the huge waste of human resources represented by out-of-school youth in both developing and developed countries. Flexible and responsive nonformal education programs can provide important opportunities, both by making up for formal educational deficiencies and by providing usable occupational and other practical skills for these young people whose needs in most countries lie beyond the sphere of responsibility of any particular ministry. For one thing, well-tailored nonformal educational activities could do much to strengthen and broaden the various indigenous apprenticeship training provisions that already exist in developing countries and are the backbone of manpower development for much of the economy. Similarly, nonformal educational arrangements could lend important and continuing support to young people embarking on self-employment in their own small enterprise by filling significant gaps in their pattern of knowledge and skills requisite to success.

These suggestions on possible ways to alleviate educational disparities by no means exhaust the possibilities. Nor, as we said earlier, are they new ideas spun out of theory. They are already being tried out in a number of countries and seriously considered in others. Although we encourage still other countries to consider them, we would also stress the following caveats in order to keep things in perspective.

First, none of these is a miracle drug. All together they will not produce sweeping changes overnight. Even with a concerted effort and accelerated time schedule, and with all the best will in the world, the reduction of deep-seated educational inequalities is at best a gradual process. This is why we have repeatedly spoken in terms of the reduction, rather than the eradication of such disparities.

Second, the objective of improving quality is not inherently in conflict with the objective of improving equality of opportunity, but there will be occasions when the two clearly compete. When this is the case, alternative approaches and trade-offs must be carefully considered, with a view not to reaching the ideal but to reaching a reasonable and realistic compromise and balance.[34]

Third, reducing educational inequalities, even in tandem with major steps to improve educational efficiency, will generally require more, not less, educational resources. It would be a deception, for example, to suppose that reducing primary school dropout rates will save money—even though these high dropout rates now constitute a heavy waste of human and other resources. In most situations, to reduce dropouts will require investing more and better resources per pupil. Moreover, to the extent that the average pupil remains in school more years and completes the primary cycle, the total budgetary cost will increase, not decline. By the same token, success in increasing the participation of girls will almost inevitably require substantially increased overall educational expenditures.

Finally, attacking educational inequalities does not constitute a distinct objective and set of actions that can be separated from other critical educational issues and objectives. In the real world they are all of a piece.

240 | *The World Crisis in Education*

The critical need to improve educational efficiency, for example, cuts across a wide spectrum of issues, of which reducing inequalities is only one.

NOTES

1. Gabriel Carron and Ta Gnoc Chau, *Reducing Regional Disparities: The Role of Educational Planning* (Paris: International Institute for Educational Development/UNESCO, 1981), English and French editions. This report, and the series of country case studies that underlie it, are a rich source of useful ideas and specific examples concerning the various forms and causes of educational disparities. It also summarizes other pertinent research on the subject.
2. Cited by Trevor Coombe, "Basic Education and Educational Reform in Zambia," Paper presented at a symposium organized by the Netherlands Universities Foundation for International Cooperation/Centre for the Study of Education in Developing Countries, The Hague, 8 June 1978.
3. UNESCO, *Trends and Projections of Enrollment by Level of Education and by Age, 1960–2000 (as assessed in 1982)* (Paris; UNESCO, Division of Statistics on Education, Office of Statistics, 1983).
4. *Fourth Regional Conference of Educational Ministers, Country Reports,* Document ED/78-MNEDASO, Ref. 5 (Bangkok: UNESCO Regional Office, 1978), p. 2.
5. As an example, see Ali A. Mazrui, *Political Values and the Educated Class in Africa* (Berkeley: University of California Press, 1978).
6. See, for example, Martin Carnoy, *Education as Cultural Imperialism* (New York: David McKay, 1974); Samuel Bowles and Herbert Gintes, *Schooling in Capitalist America: Educational Reform and Contradictions of Economic Life* (London: Routledge & Kegan Paul, 1976).
7. Janos Timar, "L'Enseignement Superieur et le Developpement Economique et Technique et Hongrie" (Paris: International Institute for Educational Planning/UNESCO, 1981).
8. *Background Report: Final Conference: Education and Local Development,* Stornoway (Western Isles) Scotland, 1–5 June 1981 (Paris: Centre for Educational Research and Innovation/OECD). This report summarizes the findings of several country case studies and various seminars, and also presents the conclusions and recommendations of the final conference.
9. U.S. Office of Education, *Education in the USSR: Current Status of Higher Education* (Washington, D.C.: U.S. Government Printing Office, 1980).
10. Leo Dubbeldam, "Primary Education in the Third World: An Overview of Quantity and Quality," paper prepared for a seminar on Educational Planning in Developing Countries organized by the Nordic Association for the Study of Education in Developing Countries, University of Oslo, October 1982.

11. UNESCO, *Statistical Yearbook, 1982* (Paris: UNESCO, Office of Statistics, 1982), p. III.41.
12. UNICEF, *Country Programme Profiles* (Gambia, Sudan, and Ethiopia) (New York: UNICEF, Program Committee, 1980). It should be noted that the population and enrollment figures given in these UNICEF reports on Gambia, Sudan, and Ethiopia were the best available at the time but must be treated with caution. Ethiopia, for example, which had so far never had a population census, recently revised upward by a substantial number its estimates of the school-age population, which automatically had the effect of reducing its estimated GER at each level. Similarly, a recent study for UNICEF on the collection of educational statistics in Sudan found that, based on United Nations population estimates, the primary level GER was 51.4 percent, but using population data from local sources the GER was only 38.5 percent. See Birger Fredriksen, *A Review of the Collection of Education Statistics in Sudan,* consultant's report to UNICEF, Country Office, Khartoum, April 1982.
13. UNICEF, *Country Programme Profiles.*
14. Ibid.
15. Ibid.
16. David Court and Kabiru Kinyanjiu, "Development Policy and Educational Opportunity: The Experience of Kenya and Tanzania" (Paris: International Institute for Educational Planning/UNESCO, 1978).
17. Claudio de Mauro Castro, et al., "La Educacion en America Latina: Un Estudio Comparative de Costos y Eficiencia" (Rio de Janeiro: Programa de Estudos Conjuntos de Integracao Economica da America Latina, 1978).
18. Wills S. Jervier, *Educational Change in Post-Colonial Jamaica* (New York: Vantage Press, 1977).
19. Kamal Sudaprasert, Vichae Tunsiri, and Ta Gnoc Chau, "Regional Disparities in the Development of Education in Thailand" (Paris: IIEP/UNESCO, 1978).
20. United Nations Economic and Social Council, Commission on the Status of Women, 25th Session. "Study on the Equality of Access of Girls and Women to Education in the Context of Rural Development" (New York: United Nations, February 1973).
21. Zsuzsa Ferge, Evan Houvasi, and Julia Szalai, "Regional Disparities and Educational Development in Hungary" (Paris: International Institute for Educational Planning/UNESCO, 1978).
22. Brandon Robinson, *El Salvador Education Sector Analysis* (Washington, D.C.: U.S. Agency for International Development, July 1977), p. 8.
23. UNESCO, *Trends and Projections of Enrolment, 1983,* Table IX, p. 115.
24. United Nations Fund for Population Activities, "Malakas and Magandi," in *Populi,* Vol. 8, No. 3, (1981), p. 55.
25. UNESCO, *Statistical Yearbook, 1982,* Table 3.11, p. III-312.
26. Organisation for Economic Co-operation and Development, Meeting of the Education Committee at Ministerial Level, Item 5, "Educational Trends: Analytical Report" (Paris: OECD, 21 September 1978), p. 18.

27. Luis Ratinoff and Maximo Jeria, "Gasto Educativo, Financiamiento del Servicio y Democratizacion de la Ensenanza," paper prepared for seminar organized by the Inter-American Development Bank and the Government of Mexico on Financing of Education in Latin America, Mexico City, Mexico, November–December 1978.
28. UNICEF, *Country Programme Profile, Panama* (New York: UNICEF, Programme Committee, 1980).
29. Paulo Diebold de Cruz, *Executive Summary of El Salvador Education Sector Analysis* (Washington, D.C.: U.S. Agency for International Development, July 1978).
30. Ratinoff and Jeria, "Gasto Educativo."
31. Gilbert de Landsheere, "Pre-School Education in Developing Countries," Prospects, Vol. VII, No. 4 (Paris: UNESCO, 1977), p. 510.
32. UNESCO, *Pre-primary Education in the World: Regional Study 1960–1975* (Paris, UNESCO, May 1974).
33. "Nieuw onderwijs Kost in 1983" *Weekeditie Buitenland,* (Netherlands) No. 19 (August 8, 1979), p. 3.
34. Torsten Husén, "Problems of Securing Equal Access to Higher Education: The Dilemma Between Equality and Excellence," *Higher Education* (Amsterdam: Elsevier Scientific Publishing Company, 1976); Torsten Húsen, *The School in Question: A Comparative Study of the School and Its Future in Western Societies* (New York: Oxford University Press, 1979), especially Chap. 5 on "Education and Equality."

Appendix Table 7.1 Public Expenditures on Education per Child by Income Groups: A Composite Profile of 19 Latin American Countries (ca. 1970)

Population by Income Level	Percentage of Total Population	Average Years of Schooling	Cumulative Public Expenditure per Pupil (1970 U.S. dollars)
Low	65	2.47	113
Medium low	20	8.64	596
Medium high	10	14.25	2687
High	5	17.00	4753

Source: Luis Ratinoff and Maximo Jeria, "Gasto Educativo, Financiamiento del Servicio y Democratizacion de la Ensenanza," paper prepared for a seminar sponsored by the Inter-American Development Bank and the Government of Mexico on Financing of Education in Latin America, Mexico City, Mexico, November–December 1978.

CHAPTER 8

EDUCATION, CULTURE, SCIENCE, AND LANGUAGE

DIRECTIONAL SIGNAL

IN THE course of our earlier discussions, we noted that critical worldwide educational problems, such as quality and relevance, equality of access, education and employment, efficiency and finance, were not solely educational problems. This is because educational systems do not exist in a social vacuum. The tasks they are called on to perform, and their success in doing them are often strongly conditioned by environmental forces historically rooted in a local culture. These go far to determine, for example, whose children get to school and how long they stay there, the place of religion in the curriculum, the language of instruction, the extent of adult literacy, the share of the national income devoted to education, and who pays and who benefits.

How educational systems are constrained by forces rooted in a local culture, however, is only half the contemporary story. The other half is that in the last three decades forces external to the local culture have increasingly influenced local educational conditions and policies.

In Third World countries, in particular, local education has come under the powerful dominion of foreign educational models, languages, scientific thinking, and technologies, including modern mass communication media and the Western-inspired international ideology of "literacy." The consequences, however, have carried a double price tag. International and domestic educational circles alike have tended to gloss over local cultural complexities and to encourage the adoption of standardized international educational formulas that were wrongly assumed to fit all situations. They have also tended to overemphasize the economic aspects of education to the neglect of broader cultural values and political goals.

The aggregate effect of the two tendencies has been to reduce sharply the fitness and effectiveness of many educational systems.

Against the background of the foregoing comments, our aim in the present chapter is to examine some of the cultural complexities of which education is a part and thus to make the case for more realistic approaches to educational policies and programs. Two assumptions underlying what will be developed are best made explicit straight off. First, though currently debated educational issues such as science education, moral education, the language of instruction, and adult literacy are typically treated separately in international forums, they are in fact indivisible strands in a seamless web whose nature varies from one culture to the next. Second, domestic politics, contrary to the view long cherished by many Western educators that education is "above" politics, inevitably plays a major role in any national education system. Thus, unless the realities imbedded in these two assumptions are taken into account, educational planning and international cooperation in education can not only miscarry but on occasion, and despite the best of intentions, can do more harm than good.

EDUCATION AND CULTURAL UPHEAVALS

In a broad anthropological sense, the culture of any society includes the features that account for its distinctive identity, cohesiveness, and continuity. Culture includes the society's system of values, ideology, and social codes of behavior; its productive technologies and modes of consumption; its religious dogmas, myths, and taboos; its social structure, political system, and decision-making processes. A society's culture is expressed in many forms—in its literature, art, architecture, dress, food, and modes of entertainment—but its language and education are central to its identity and survival. Through its language, it conveys the ideas and the subtle nuances behind the words in common use. Historically, education's prime task in all societies has been to conserve and protect an inherited culture and transmit it intact to each new generation.

Few cultures, however, except those that have been totally isolated, remain static for any long period. Once a culture comes into contract with other cultures, through trade, military encounters, religious movements, voyages of discovery, and colonial ventures, its members borrow selected elements for assimilation into their own culture. The remarkable geographic spread of Buddhism, Christianity, and Islam; of Roman law, technologies of roadbuilding, and irrigation; of the Chinese compass and cuisine are among the well-known historical examples of cultural transfers and infusions.

All this has been true in the past and is true today as well, but with a major contemporary difference. Cultural infusions until the mid-twentieth century, were generally a drawn-out process, allowing time for each society slowly to absorb elements from other cultures without seriously disrupting or destroying its own culture. Since World War II, however, the process of cultural interbreeding and penetration has been vastly speeded up all over the world. Of equal importance, the dominant direction of these accelerated cultural infusions, including education, has run from west to east and from north to south (though a significant counterflow has been evident recently).

The varied range of cultural imports and influences has had equally varied effects. These influences have unhinged the traditional cultural patterns of many developing countries. They have fueled internal cultural collisions, civil wars, and revolutions. They have split newly independent nations into hostile tribal, religious, and linguistic subdivisions. In almost all developing countries they have engendered sharp divisions between the deep-rooted traditional culture that still dominates most rural areas and the heavily westernized modern cultural beachhead in the capital city—a beachhead symbolized by formal schools and universities, automobiles and jet airports, factories, Western dress, the use of a European language as the lingua franca, and, not least of all, capital cities bulging with central government bureaucracies.

Industrialized countries in the north, for their part, have not been immune to this great global tidal wave of external cultural influences and internal cultural upheavals. They are caught in wrenching transitions from the era of smokestack industrial economies to a new postindustrial era of high technology and expanding service industries and from elitist education systems to mass education. These transitions, in turn, have been paralleled by far-reaching changes in the nature of work and lifestyles, by the rapid erosion of old values and social codes of behavior, and by the deterioration of long-established political, judical, religious, and educational institutions, including the most basic of all educational institutions, the family. As in developing countries, a growing social and political fragmentation along ethnic, religious, racial, and linguistic lines has intensified political pluralism.

Among the main causes for the cultural upheavals visible throughout the world is the pell-mell spread of modern science with its irrepressible challenges to "things as they are." A related cause is the rapid growth of international trade and the spread of Western technologies and the mass media products, inevitably bringing with them built-in Western modes of thought and behavior that clash with the traditional values and mores of the importing countries. A third cause is education itself. The adoption in developing countries of Western educational models, including structures, curriculum patterns, textbooks, and teaching methods; the extensive use of foreign education advisors; the use of a European language as the medium of instruction; and, perhaps most important of all, the training of teachers and research scholars in advanced countries who become major "culture carriers" on returning home—all of these factors have combined to make education a major cultural change agent in developing countries. As such, education has had a far-reaching and often disruptive impact on traditional values, attitudes, and patterns of behavior. To an equal extent, but on the positive side, education has opened up broad new avenues of international exchange with a great potential for increasing mutual understanding and cooperation, which is beneficial to all humankind.

IMPACT OF SCIENCE ON EDUCATION

No subject in the curriculum has drawn greater worldwide attention over the past 20 years than science. The pressure for improving science education has come not only from scientists and mathematicians but from political and business leaders, farmers, military strategists, medical doctors, editors, parents, and, not least, the education systems themselves. The aim is not solely to produce more scientists and technologists; it is also to produce a new generation of citizens who are scientifically literate and thus better prepared to function in a world that is increasingly influenced by science and technology. UNESCO's efforts in this area have been outstanding and have won the support and participation of some of the world's ablest scientists and science teachers. Dozens of countries, especially in the Third World, have participated in UNESCO science education projects. The results have often been encouraging, but all such attempts to strengthen science education have also demonstrated the complexities of the task. Substantial time and resources are required to train and retrain competent teachers, to transform the old curriculum and methods, to create new teaching materials, and to buy proper supplies and equipment. Beyond the textbook and classroom, the task also entails the need to stimulate scientific curiosity through direct investigation of natural phenomena in the students' own environment.

Yet the logistical structures of conventional schools impose severe constraints on effective science education, as they do on other types of education that cannot be squeezed into the rigid framework of a fixed hourly schedule, along with a textbook, blackboard, and a teacher in a classroom. In this connection, Professor Peter J. Fensham, an experienced Australian expert on science education, observed, while making a case for more out-of-school science education, that although schools command about one third of a student's waking time,

> ... inside the school this time is almost always fragmented into small bits that give rise to limitations about what can be taught and learnt and how this can be done. Exploration and activity in a natural phenomenon or of a scientific instrument or a piece of technology take extended periods of time that are not available in the piecemeal timetables that schools create to meet the competing demands of different subjects and the requirements of the educational system—statutory breaks, compulsory occurrences, shared access to resources and traditional expectations.[1]

The most serious problem in almost all countries is finding and retaining science and mathematics teachers who are competent and inspiring. Even in the most scientifically advanced nations, as we noted earlier, far too few able secondary school graduates opt for teacher training in these fields. Of those who do, many are soon lured away into much higher paying jobs with better prospects for promotion in private industry or government.

Further difficulties arise from the popular confusion that lumps together science and technology as if they were the same thing. They definitely are not, although science is the mother of technology. Science and mathematics are the only subjects in the curriculum that can correctly be said to have international standards. One kind of physics, biology, or set of mathematical axioms is not valid in China or Nigeria and another in the United States or the Soviet Union. Aristotle put the point neatly more than two thousand years ago when he said, in his commonsense way, "Fire burns the same in Greece and in India." Technologies, on the other hand, do not have the same degree of universality as science. Technologies are parochial in the sense that they must be fitted to the particular local circumstances if they are to be cost-effective. This is what the recent talk about "appropriate technologies" for developing countries means. Moreover, technologies are in constant flux. In the developed countries, new technologies frequently replace old ones, as they do in developing countries, although generally on a lower level of sophistication and capital intensity.

The educational implications of this distinction between science and technology are of fundamental importance for developed and developing countries alike, especially with respect to vocational training. Vocational and technical schools can easily end up teaching their students narrow, specific job skills that may soon become obsolete—if indeed they are not obsolete already.

In a world in which technologies change swiftly, it is not enough and not of first importance to equip students with the skills essential to their *first* job. The real challenge is to equip them with more basic knowledge and skills that will enable them to adapt successfully in the future to a succession of *changing* jobs requiring different specific skills, many of which cannot now be foreseen. The question of whether learning specific contemporary occupational skills is or is not a good investment depends on circumstances; but learning certain elements of mathematics and science, along with the three Rs, is a young person's best insurance against becoming occupationally obsolete and technologically unemployable at a future date. Therefore, more and more schools in industrialized countries, and in some developing ones as well, are teaching primary and secondary students the language and basic principles of computers, which have an almost infinite variety of possible future applications.

In developing countries, the importance of achieving an elementary grasp of scientific principles and methods and of acquiring a scientific outlook is not limited to prospective employees in the modern sector of the economy. The small farmer and the small entrepreneur in a village or provincial town have an equal or perhaps even greater need for a rudimentary scientific education if they are to make the best of their situations. Unfortunately, however, they are far less likely than their urban cousins to get what they need. Besides, the importance of a scientific outlook and a familiarity with the role of technologies goes well beyond the objective of simply earning a living. It is important to other aspects of an individual's life, whether as a consumer, an informed citizen, a participant in public affairs, or just someone with a lively curiosity about the world.

The Special Needs of Developing Countries

Much has been said about the transfer of technology and know-how from more developed to less developed countries—the key concept underlying technical assistance in education, agriculture, health, and other fields. Many of the transferred technologies have proven inappropriate at the receiving end. It has become increasingly plain, moreover, that for purposes of long-term development, it is not enough simply to transfer existing technologies from an advanced country to a less advanced one. It is of the utmost importance that developing countries devise their own appropriate technologies. To achieve this, they need not only their own well-trained cadres of creative technologists but also a critical mass of basic scientists, with a support structure of research facilities, to spur and guide the development of locally relevant technologies.

Although this was less the case two or three decades ago, it is now especially important for industrialized countries and international agencies to help developing countries build their own scientific and technological capabilities rather than flooding them with short-term technical assistance experts. Visiting experts will still be needed for certain selected purposes, but the long-range need entails the building of indigenous scientific and technological capacity. In this connection, however, we must ask an important question.

Is Education Becoming a Dinosaur?

What impact has the recent proliferation of scientific and technological breakthroughs had on conventional educational systems, apart from obliging them to strengthen their science and mathematics offerings? The late Professor John Vaizey of England (Lord Vaizey of Greenwich) dealt with the question in an analysis prepared for this report, and his conclusion comes as a jolt.[2] He argued that modern science, with its experimental methods and fundamental principles that are universally applicable, has for the first time in human history created a truly universal ideology that transcends all other ideologies and great religions, and although "various religions and ideologies (like Christianity and Marxism) may endure, they only do so by coexistence with the principles of experimental science." At the same time, the extraordinary proliferation of technological breakthroughs that are creating abrupt discontinuities in the previously slow evolution of civilization has had great significance for education. The significance, Vaizey argues, is most profound:

All preexisting societies have lost their technological and ideological roots because the new [universal] scientific culture and its technical expression have created a literally new world, intellectual and physical. This means that educations's dual role—the handing-on of traditional techniques and (above all) traditional values—has been stood on its head. It becomes part of the process of adaptation to a kind of out-of-control change, progressing under its own momentum.

. . . The effect is to make all education in the traditional sense irrelevant. This is because each generation is faced with a completely new set of circumstances with respect of the basis of knowledge (apart from the key discipline of mathematics and the technique of scientific investigation); and a rapidly changing technology to set its hands on. Thus education, like other social structures concerned with handing on traditions and values, is inescapably dinosaur-like, in that it cannot change to a rapidly developing environment and thus becomes immediately out of date as a result of its very nature.

This inevitable lag of all social institutions in adapting to their rapidly changing environment, Vaizey goes on to say, lies at the heart of the modern dilemma:

> For by definition, it is impossible to establish institutions that are capable of infinitely elastic response to change, for the very purpose of institutions is to be established—that is to define that which is durable, so that it seems permanent, by making everything else transient. If there is nothing that is durable there can be no social institutions. Which is to say, that modern science and technology have created chaos.

Yet institutions such as education do continue to exist "since chaos is repugnant to the deep human need for permanence, that is, for security." Vaizey concludes his analysis with a paradox:

> [The very existence of educational institutions] is essential for the continuation of modern science and for the economic system which enables the technological artifacts which are its outcomes to be produced. But the institutions not only nurture the process of change that undermines them; they are perceived not as pillars that support but obstacles that obstruct.

Vaizey's hypothesis casts in bold relief the underlying dilemma of education systems today. Much of what is taught, as well as the methods and material, is subject to rapid obsolescence and inertia in the face of the need to change. Therefore, the central question to which we repeatedly return extends well beyond science education. It is whether schools and colleges and universities can learn to adapt themselves rapidly enough to the changing world around them to avoid becoming, like the dinosaur, museum pieces.

THE AMBIGUOUS ISSUE OF MORAL EDUCATION

The cultural eruptions sparked by recent scientific and technological revolutions have brought back into the spotlight the age-old question of moral education, with all its ambiguities and differing definitions.

In the nineteenth century, moral education was the staple of the curriculum in every common school throughout Europe and North America. It was taken as much for granted as the three Rs and the rising sun. What are now highly industrialized countries were then mostly rural; urbanization had not yet taken over. Most families were close-knit, religious loyalties and influences were stronger, and young people began work earlier. Indeed, the concept of adolescence—that troublesome stage between childhood and adulthood—had not yet gained currency. The family, the church, and the common school worked in tandem in the moral education of children. Primary school primers, such as McGuffey's *Reader* in the United States, were replete with moral lessons that reinforced what children were being taught at home and in Sunday School.

By the 1930s, however, the economic, political, and pedagogical climate had shifted drastically. Moral education (commonly confused with religious education) had come to be viewed by leading educational thinkers as anachronistic, especially in increasingly pluralistic societies in which public schools (unlike parochial schools) were now anxious to keep education strictly separate from religion. School administrators and teachers were more than willing to accept responsibility for teaching children the three Rs and for inculcating in them a "scientific spirit and outlook" (the new thing at the time), but they much preferred to leave moral upbringing in the sturdy hands of parents and the church or temple or mosque.

Schools continued to move further in this new direction until the late 1970s, when once again the climate shifted. By then the cultural upheavals referred to earlier had reached new heights, bringing with them a variety of disturbing behavioral problems that caused increasing anxiety among political leaders, law enforcement officers, school administrators, parents, and the public. The daily headlines trumpeted a host of worrisome social trends. Some alarmed observers foresaw another "decline of the Roman Empire"—a disintegration of the very fabric of established societies, with a consequent vacuum of values. To their way of thinking, the prime cause of this ominous social disintegration was the failure of schools to enforce high standards of behavior and to train young people to appreciate traditional moral values. The solution seemed obvious. It was to put moral education back into the schools along with the other basics.

All this, like an axiom in euclidean geometry, had the flavor of a self-evident truth. But was it true? Did the simplistic notion of a disastrous disintegration of traditional values that was largely the fault of the schools square with reality? It did not. What was really happening in North America and Western Europe, starting in the late 1960s, was that many young people, and adults as well, were vigorously challenging the cynicism of institutional leaders who piously preached the old values but whose conduct deviated sharply from them. The challengers were often those who stood by older values as applied to a new situation largely created by modern technologies. Often it was they who took seriously the ethical codes of the great religions, stripped of their accumulated theological and doctrinal dress, and tried to apply the principles of democracy—

hence the upsurge of the civil rights and women's liberation movements, the revival of attacks on big business and government corruption, and the environmental protection and antinuclear movements. The participants in these various movements were certainly not without firmly held values. On the contrary, to the discomfort of many politicians and members of the Establishment, they insisted on reviving the old moralities and on putting them into practice.

These vigorous new social movements bewildered many observers, including many who preached but did not live by the "old values," because they did not fit into any of the old familiar political categories, such as liberal and conservative. Moreover, they did not fit into any of the standard social, age, and geographical categories. The thousands of concerned people who turned out in the streets of Western European cities in the 1980s to protest nuclear missiles, or who voted in New England town meetings for a nuclear freeze, cut across all the familiar political, socioeconomic, and age categories. The same is true of the millions of people who joined protests against menacing air and water pollution by modern industry; against nuclear power plants of dubious safety; against the destructive exploitation of natural resources and endangering of wildlife species; and against the wanton sale to private interests of public lands and forests. Whether or not one agrees with their position or approves of their sometimes disruptive tactics, these people were clearly not simply promoting their immediate personal interests. Ironically, those who opposed them, usually in the name of the old values or of national security and economic progress, were often aligned with powerful vested interests primarily concerned with short-range profit-and-loss statements, all sharply at odds with the very values they preached.

This reincarnation of the old values in new forms and applications has not been confined to the Western industrial societies. It appeared with increasing frequency on the whole international stage from the 1960s onward—for example, in protests (often led by students) against tyrannical governments, in the demands of developing nations for a New International Economic Order, and in peasant movements demanding a political voice and a fair share of the benefits of national development. Education systems, caught in the middle of all this turmoil, have frequently been made a scapegoat. As noted, they have been charged not only with being lax about discipline and allowing academic standards to deteriorate, but also with putting wrong and dangerous ideas into the heads of their students.

The schools are imperfect, it is true. Of the things they do, they could certainly do many better. But on balance, their record of promoting respect for the old values and for democratic principles has probably been somewhat better than that of most other social institutions, including the family, that were traditionally the primary shapers of the values and behavioral standards of the young.

The growth in recent years of interest in moral education by thoughtful educators speaks for their serious concern about the matters just discussed. Nor is this concern limited to Western educators, for these problems now have counterparts in all countries. The theme of moral education (or values education) has therefore cropped up lately with increasing frequency in UNESCO and other international forums bringing together educational authorities from around the world. But difficult questions remain. Just what does "moral education" mean? Whatever it means, exactly what can and should schools do about it?

Moral education clearly means different things to different poeple, not only cross-culturally but within the same culture, especially in highly pluralistic societies. The late Professor Joseph Lauwerys of the University of London, an experienced international comparative educator, scientist, and philosopher, in a contribution for this report written in 1978, made the following observations:[3]

In some ways, these trends [of criticism of the schools and of demands on them] favour conservative, even reactionary, thinking and argumentation. Particularly in the advanced and wealthy countries there is a widespread feeling that what has gone wrong is the abandonment of the old, traditional virtues and beliefs. People, they say, are lazy and dissolute, encouraged by the pervasive T.V., the films, the colour magazines, pornographic books and so on. They have all learned to expect something for nothing and run away from hard work. The remedies proposed include religious revivals, yoga, mystical faiths, ecological appreciation, return to a life of nature and so on. They nearly always include the suggestion that more should be done in schools: stricter discipline should be imposed; attention paid to Moral Education (or "Values Education"); there should be a return to Basics (3Rs and some kind of vague religion); frills should be cut out. And so on.

Much of this, of course, is nonsense. We can move in many directions but certainly not straight back into our own past. But it is powerful nonsense— and dangerous. The task today is surely to turn the inchoate mass of doubt, uncertainty, puzzlement, anxiety into a constructive force: towards peace, security and the improvement of the human condition.

Viewing the matter of cultures and values historically and examining recent events, Lauwerys saw the present turmoil not as the destruction of old values but as a lively competition between old and new that is bringing inherent contradictions to the surface:

Long ago ... most of mankind tended to stay in one spot. ... Even as recently as 2,000 years ago it was only in a few world cities that cultures intermingled and reacted: Rome, Alexandria, Istanbul, Athens. Perhaps Peking. Over the rest of the planet, human beings met only those who accepted unthinkingly and uncritically the values and norms of their own culture and religion (*re-ligio:* that which binds together).

But now has come the time of the great wanderings. Everywhere cultures meet and clash; and so do their values and ideals. . . . Partly because of the widespread awareness that there are different and irreconcilable *Weltanschauung* but chiefly because people have become more aware of the nature of the beliefs they themselves accept or claim to accept, the internal contradictions of their own value systems have become obvious.

Thus what are we, in the West, to make of our own faith in the Christian-Democratic values of unselfishness, generosity, charity, love of neighbour, honesty, sincerity, etc. while we face the fact that the economic-social complex rewards and honours greed, self-seeking, dissimulation, cheating, corruption, envy, ambition, or power seeking?

Lauwerys argued that it would be a mistake to underrate the influence that schools and teachers have on the moral formation of their pupils, and he asserted that many teachers do in fact offer guidance and counsel—often counter to the temper of the times. But, he warned:

There is, everywhere, a tendency to load on to the school, tasks or responsibilities they are ill-fitted—indeed unable—to bear or to discharge by their very nature. So, at the moment, those in charge of States (the rulers) facing a situation where the old moralities seem to break down, call upon schools and colleges to handle the problems and to solve them.

What a load of nonsense! Simply think of schools as they are, of teachers as they are! Timid, tired, overdriven people of a modest, retiring, self-effacing, conformist, obedient type. Inside, of course, they seethe with indignation at the situations they face—but fear the confrontations that courage would demand. For they would not be supported by the authorities, whose deepest and most genuine interests lie in the perpetuation of their power rather than in the moral education of the people they rule.

Lauwerys recalled how his own views had changed since the 1930s when he and many of his contemporaries, under the influence of avant-garde mentors such as H. G. Wells and Herbert Spencer, were convinced that "mankind's ills would vanish if only everyone knew more science, understood its methods, and adopted in all areas a 'scientific outlook.'" Being himself a teacher of science and mathematics, he viewed religion ("however beautiful and attractive") as "opposed to progress of any kind . . . essentially backward-looking and reactionary. . . . Poetry and literature was 'lovely stuff' to be enjoyed [but] not in any way of genuine importance." In his retrospect on his early views, he drew the following conclusion:

It was a rationalist, secularized, empirical and pragmatic approach and somewhat narrow (tunnel vision) and one-sided. It assumed that the chief problems that faced mankind were simply material and only material: more food, more gadgetry, better transportation, more medical services. Given these, all would be well and both peace and plenty would reign. The educational concomitants (necessary) were clear. . . . More and more education (schooling) at all levels and especially in technology; more science, better taught.

By the late 1970s Lauwerys had adopted a broader and more critical outlook shared, he believed, by most of his generation of science teachers. Though science was still necessary, it was not sufficient:

The chief difficulties faced at this period of history lie not in the further development of technology but rather in the adaptation of the old morality to new conditions—and of then spreading the new morality around the world. . . . If this be true, then Moral Education has become strategic problem Number One in education and deserves attention and study.

But pending such further study, Lauwerys declined to offer any simple formula for the schools to adopt. He took heart, however, in the fact that over the past 20 years it has become possible in discussions everywhere to separate religious from moral education, thus greatly facilitating objective research and constructive discussion. "I cherish the hope that it may be possible, sometime, to draw up a list of Moral Principles accepted by all human beings everywhere. I believe this is now becoming possible."

One thing is certain about the issue of moral education. The debate over the issue will remain lively and important throughout the world as long as cultural upheavals continue, and as long as the morality taught by the schools and by the great religions (and preached if not always practiced by politicians) continues to clash with "the morality embodied and embedded in modern industry, commerce, and finance." The issue will be resolved in different ways in different societies—or left unresolved. But no society can remain indifferent to it. Nor is indifference possible for anyone involved in education, from top policymakers to classroom teachers. Sooner or later each must think the issue through, decide where he or she really stands on the matter, and act accordingly.

THE LANGUAGE DILEMMA

Moral principles are intimately tied to language—to the meaning of words and the concepts underlying them. Young German poets learned this lesson well when they discovered at the end of World War II how the Nazi regime had drained conventional words of their moral content.

Therefore, the first task of the young German poets was to restore the moral integrity of words before anything else could be written. In addition, only language can unlock thought and unleash the human brain's vast power. Language is also the principal vehicle for teaching and learning and a profoundly important element of any culture or subculture. Take away the culture's traditional language and its identity crumbles. Language differences are inextricably tied to ethnic, religious, tribal, and other differences and hence are freighted with potential political tensions and conflicts. Any nation that encompasses various ethnic linguistic groups, particularly if they overlap the borders of neighboring countries (which is the situation in most African nations as well as in a number in Asia and Latin America) inevitably faces serious difficulties in achieving a binding sense of nationhood among its different peoples. These internal language difficulties are compounded by each country's need for linguistic bridges to the rest of the world.

The issue of what language or languages to adopt as the medium of instruction at successive levels of education is one of the most pedagogically difficult and potentially explosive political issues faced by schools in a great many countries. The problem is particularly acute in developing countries, but it also exists on a serious scale today in many developed countries. Paradoxically, however, the choice of language of instruction is also one of the least appreciated of all the major educational problems that come before international forums. In the congenial atmosphere of a UNESCO conference in Paris, for example, it is easy to endorse the seemingly commonsense proposition that in the early primary grades young children should be initially instructed and made literate in their mother tongue before being introduced to a second and perhaps a third language later. This proposition, however, frequently turns out to be utterly impractical when pitted against the stubborn realities in multilingual countries when educational practitioners try to carry out such a policy. What is to be done, for example, if the child's mother tongue has not yet been reduced to written form—still often the case in Africa, in the indigenous Indian sections of Latin America, and in some parts of Asia? Even if the language is already written, what happens if the teacher, transferred from a different linguistic area 50 miles away, cannot converse with pupils, much less make them literate, in their local idiom? And what about textbooks? Is it feasible for a multilingual nation with a dozen or more different living languages to print schoolbooks and other educational materials in each language? Many are still having trouble providing sufficient textbooks in just one language.

Multilingualism, of course, is not only an educational problem. It hobbles national development efforts and inhibits the personal development and mobility of individuals. Not least of all, it breeds political problems by fostering misunderstanding and creating among different ethnic and tribal groups deep schisms and conflicts that undermine national cohesiveness and unity. Melvin J. Fox, a veteran Ford Foundation program officer concerned with problems of Africa, observes the following in a paper contributed to the present study:

> This is a period of pervasive sectarianism, when neither religions, ideologies, or nationalism can overcome the centrifugal force of tribalism. As exemplified by the 70 different Islamic communities, the many types of communist and socialist governments, the variety of one-party states, it is a period when ethnicity is stronger than nationalism, or the revealed directives of God. As the heart and soul of ethnicity, *language* is a factor that makes possible and reinforces such sectarianism, and in the process represents a powerful force against the nationalism that is essential for nation-building.[4]

Towers of Babel Everywhere

The Old Testament story in Genesis about the bewildering cacaphony of different tongues spoken in the crossroads trading town of Babel foreshadowed a multiplicity of such towns the world over thousands of years later. A sharp-eared linguistic expert today can easily identify a dozen or more languages being spoken during a 15-minute stroll down Fifth Avenue in New York, the Champs Elysée in Paris, through Trafalgar Square in London, or through the central market place in Lagos, New Delhi, or Cairo.

Just imagine having to formulate and implement a "pedagogically sound" language policy for the schools in Nigeria with its estimated 400 languages and dialects. Then imagine trying to sell an "educationally sound" solution to the national political leaders who are searching desperately for a common language that can overcome fractionalism and help unify the nation. We can get a somewhat closer look at this problem from the findings of two research studies in Nigeria in 1975.[5] The first, concerning language use in the mass media, revealed that only 27 of the 400-odd languages and dialects were used even slightly in radio broadcasts. "For people who do not understand either Hausa, Yoruba or English," the study concluded, "Nigerian radio broadcasts consist of little more than music." The second study dramatized the need to be multilingual in order to function successfully in the Nigerian economy. Out of a sample of nearly 200 traders and salaried workers in a suburb of Lagos, 17 percent spoke one language other than their own; 45 percent, two others; 29 percent, three others; and 4 percent, four others. Significantly, only

5 percent were monolingual in Yoruba, the main local language of that area.

Nigeria is admittedly an extreme case, but the same general pattern of linguistic fractionalism prevails throughout most of sub-Saharan Africa. Most indigenous African languages are tribal connected, but some of the most widely spoken ones are "pidgin" and Creole "contact" languages that evolved over the centuries from mixtures of base languages—including certain tribal languages plus elements of Arabic, Portuguese, French, English, or Dutch—to meet the compelling need of the people to break through these tribal linguistic barriers for trading and other purposes. Swahili is a classic example of such a contact language, especially in the coastal areas of Eastern Africa. Hausa is another, but it plays a dual role. It is the largest single mother tongue language in northern Nigeria and Niger, but it also serves as a contact language of trade known by millions of people along the old trade routes across Africa, from Ghana and Togo in the West to Sudan in the East.

These home-grown contact languages—made up of a blend of stripped-down vocabulary elements from various base languages fitted into a local grammar and syntax—have evolved over many generations and play major roles today in other areas of the world besides Africa. For example, Creole, the predominant mother tongue today among the ordinary people of Jamaica, is a descendant of pidgins that evolved centuries ago on the west coast of Africa as lingua francas. Other varieties of Creole still play a significant role among coastal peoples elsewhere in the Western Hemisphere—for example, in Brazil, Venezuela, and the states of Louisiana and Georgia in the United States. They have survived despite the now-dominant role of Portuguese, Spanish, and English, respectively, as the official national languages of these countries. Bahasa Indonesia, now the official national language of Indonesia, grew out of the ancient lingua franca widely used throughout the Malaysian region.

The colonial era further complicated the already complex linguistic situation in what we now call the developing world by superimposing one or another European language on all the existing languages and endowing it with special power and prestige. In the more than 30 years since the crumbling of the great colonial empires, their linguistic heritage has played an increasingly extensive role in the newly independent nations, no longer as a colonial language but as an indispensable vehicle for communication both internally and with the outside world. Without a knowledge of French, for example, citizens of any Francophone African country would find themselves linguistically isolated in their own area and at a severe disadvantage in trying to cope with the complexities of life if they get to the city. Without English, members of the Indian Parliament from different states would be unable to converse with each other or read official documents, and a student from Madras (where Tamil is used), studying at Nehru University in New Delhi (where Hindi is spoken) would be unable to comprehend many of the lectures or do the required reading. English has also become the de facto national language—or at least the closest thing to one—in many other newly independent member countries of the British Commonwealth, though for political reasons it has often not been so designated officially. In education, especially at the graduate level, English has become increasingly essential, even in some Francophone countries. Today it is the language of instruction in medicine at the University of Cairo, in law at the University of Khartoum, in agriculture in Tunis, in agricultural economics in Benin and the Ivory Coast, in political science at the University of Stellenbosch (the heartland of Afrikaanerdom), and in all graduate studies in Kenya, Nigeria, and Tanzania.

Ironically, in order to converse with each other about mutual African problems, officials and scholars from Francophone Africa must learn English, and those from Anglophone Africa must learn French.

Choosing a National Language

The choice of an appropriate national language has been one of the most anguished problems faced by the political leaders of newly independent multilingual countries of Africa and Asia. Their basic need was to build a cohesive sense of nationalism and overriding patriotism on the part of all ethnic and linguistic groups. To do this, a common language of communication was essential, and the schools were looked to as a crucial mechanism for spreading the national language. But what language should it be? To designate the former colonial tongue as the official national language, even though it might in fact be the principal lingua franca, would incite charges of neocolonialism. But it was just as risky politically to choose the indigenous tongue of any one internal ethnic group, for this was bound to stir resentment among the others. The best solution was to choose a neutral and widely known contact language, if one happened to be available, that was not identified with any one ethnic or tribal group. Thus, newly independent Indonesia, as noted above, chose Bahasa Indonesia, and Tanzania chose Kiswahili as their respective national tongues; each in its own context was made the compulsory language of instruction in the schools and the primary language of the mass media and government. To communicate with the outside world of business, diplomacy, and scholarship, however, English became a principal second language in the schools of these two countries. (In postwar

Indonesia English took precedence over Dutch, on the ground that the latter was not a widely used international language.)

India was not as fortunately situated for it had not inherited any widely used contact language other than English, but English smacked of colonialism and hence was not politically neutral. At the time of independence, the new ruling group of India designated Hindustani (Hindi), the predominant language of northern India, as the offical national tongue. Predictably, other regional language groups have continued to resent that decision and have engaged in repeated disturbances over it. The conflict has been most dramatically evidenced by university students in non-Hindi-speaking areas who feel at a serious disadvantage in taking competitive civil service examinations in Hindi for a prized post in the national government. The Hindi-speaking students of north India, on the other hand, have been vehemently, and sometimes violently, opposed to the use of English as an alternative language (even for streets signs in Delhi), for this would erode their linguistic advantage.

Linguistic Problems in the Developed World

Linguistic problems and their associated political problems also pose educational difficulties in many developed countries. From the beginning, the U.S.S.R. has had to do a delicate educational and political balancing act to maintain harmony and to achieve effective integration among its various cultural and linguistic groups. It has succeeded, on the whole (using Russian as the lingua franca), though not without occasional resentments and eruptions. Since World War II the U.S.S.R. has been performing an even more delicate balancing act with its Eastern European socialist neighbors, again using Russian as the lingua franca and Marxist-Leninist dogma as the binding cultural and political adhesive. This latest balancing act, however, has had some perilous moments when things threatened to come unstuck—as in Hungary, Czechoslovakia, and more recently, Poland.

Most Western nations have also confronted educational and political problems rooted in linguistic, religious, and related ethnic diversities, some going back in history and others of more recent vintage. The Scandinavian countries, Canada, the United States, and Australia, for example, have long had to cope with educational problems arising from distinctive languages and cultures of various Indian, Eskimo, and other indigenous groups. Belgium, the Netherlands, Scotland, and Wales continue to have tensions and flare-ups linked to internal linguistic schisms imbedded in long-standing religious and other cultural divisons. In Canada, the cultural and political conflict between French-speaking Quebec and the English-speaking provinces has led to a bilingual compromise whereby all Canadian children must be taught in both languages, and all federal government documents, road signs, and so forth must be bilingual.

Since World War II especially, the schools of most industrialized Western European countries have had to cope with a new crop of difficult linguistic and related problems arising from the great influx of "guest workers" and their families from lower income countries of southern Europe, North Africa, and the Middle East. A majority of the primary-school children in Amsterdam and Rotterdam, for example, fall into this category. In the United States over the past two decades many major urban school systems have become heavily populated by the enormous wave of monolingual Spanish-speaking (and some French-speaking) immigrant children from Latin America, particularly Puerto Rico, Mexico, Cuba, and Haiti, and by more and more non-English-speaking children from Asia. To further complicate this linguistic problem of schools, the U.S. courts have ruled that any child—in principle even a third- or a fourth-generation American-born child of Italian, French, German, Polish, Russian, Japanese, or Chinese extraction—has the right to be taught the language of his or her forebears as a means of preserving his or her cultural heritage and identity. With respect to the mass of new arrivals from Latin America and elsewhere, the public schools have no real choice but to engage in some form of bilingual education, although the actual form of that education, for how many grades, and whether it should be limited to the new immigrants or imposed on native-born English-speaking children as well, remains a matter of vigorous pedagogical and public controversy.

The Quest for Cultural Identity

Compounding the already difficult linguistic problems confronting the schools of the world, a growing hunger and demand for cultural identity arose in the 1970s. In developing countries, the spirit of nationalism grew and political leaders and the people became increasingly anxious to reduce their nations' dependency on powerful industrialized nations and to revitalize their own culture and identity. Thus pressures increased on the schools to adhere to the "national" language as the medium of instruction. But this undertaking posed several practical difficulties. First, as already indicated, the offical national language was often little known in many areas of the country. Second, a European language, usually French or English, was already deeply entrenched in the education system. And third, especially crucial at the university level, the great bulk of the world's most up-to-date scholarly literature, scientific reports, and other important documentation is available only in English or in French, German, Spanish, or Russian.*

Thus, the very understandable and indeed imperative efforts of developing countries to preserve and enhance their own cultural heritage and identity, and to extend their declaration of independence to their education system, have inevitably been fraught with practical difficulties and contradictions, stemming in no small measure from the "language problem." Their universities found themselves in the ambiguous position of being prime rescuers and promoters of the indigenous cultural heritage, while at the same time being principal importers and disseminators of political ideologies, cultural values, and modes of thinking and behavior from the Western democracies or the Eastern socialist countries. The ambiguity has been especially evident in returning young scholars, researchers and faculty members who have undertaken collegiate level and postgraduate studies in the North.

The education systems of various industrialized countries also felt the impact of a strong upsurge of cultural identity movements among various subgroups in their populations, reflecting both a heightened pride and interest in their particular cultural heritage and a desire to mobilize and exert greater influence on the local and national political scene. This phenomenon was especially widespread in the United States—"a nation of immigrants" from all parts of the world with an extraordinary diversity of nationality, racial, and ethnic roots. The vigorous black civil rights movement of the 1960s blossomed educationally into "black studies" in the schools and colleges and legitimized "black history" and "black English" (with its own unique vocabulary and syntax) as subjects worthy of serious scholarly investigation. Spurred in part by this movement and the racial pride it inspired, Americanized descendants of earlier immigrant groups from various European countries and other parts of the world, along with the newer Hispanic immigrants, displayed a greatly heightened pride and interest in their original ethnic and cultural roots. Today the educational and political ramifications of this heightened quest

---

*Even these "modern" international languages frequently borrow technical terms as well as everyday jargon from each other (such as computer, television, sputnik, and silicon chip) to fill gaps in their own language. In 1982 the French government, in its latest move in a long battle to preserve the purity of the French language, began imposing fines on any French publisher who included "franglaise" or other corrupt foreign terms in a newspaper article or other publication. But it is probably a losing battle, for it seems unlikely that even the most patriotic of the French would stop going to "Le Drugstore" or taking a "weekend" trip to the countryside. Their neighbors across the channel are far less concerned over the corruption of the "Queen's English" that goes on daily.

for cultural identity continue to plague the education system of almost every city in the United States.

Western Europe has also witnessed cultural identity movements during this recent period, including some very convulsive ones tied to separatist movements—the Basques in Spain, the Catholic Irish in Northern Ireland, the Welsh and Scots in the United Kingdom, and the Bretons in France. These movements have inevitable educational repercussions on the emotional and political atmosphere of the schools and higher education institutions and sometimes on the curriculum itself.

PROSPECTS

Our purpose in this chapter has been to call attention to the powerful influences exerted on education in all countries in recent times by sweeping worldwide cultural changes and scientific advances, by controversial moral issues and concerns, by the pedagogical and political dilemmas posed by language differences, and by a host of other societal changes on the march. All of these dynamic environmental changes have confronted those involved in education—from policymakers to classroom teachers and managers of nonformal education programs—with a formidable array of everyday problems often ignored by critics who tend to view schools as if they existed in a social vacuum. Often these upsetting environmental changes are seen only vaguely and in piecemeal by busy educational administrators whose thinking is imprisoned in outmoded educational doctrines, folklore, and habitual methods. The net effect has been for educational institutions to become increasingly at odds with the changing needs of their clients and society.

As we cast our eye to the future, we expect that the accelerated pace of these cultural, scientific, tehnological, and other environmental changes will continue apace. This means that educational leaders will have no choice but to try to come to grips with these changes with all the imagination, courage, and force they can muster. Clearly the implications for curriculum reform, for the training and retraining of teachers, and for educational planning, management, and finance, are staggering. To sit back in the hope that things will eventually straighten themselves out is a sure way to allow an already serious crisis of disharmony to worsen.

Alert educational leaders in both developed and developing countries and at the international level are far more aware of these problems today than they were 10 or 20 years ago, and many have been trying to tackle them in innovative ways. In the process they have learned at least two important things: First, there are no quick, simple, standardized international solutions to fit all such problems in all situations. Although countries can learn valuable lessons from one another's experiences, each must devise its own best solutions to fit its own particular environment, and each will have to work intensively, continuously, and patiently to apply these chosen solutions, for they will all be shooting at a moving target. Second, educators cannot do the job alone; they must have cooperation and help, the constructive criticisms and ideas, and the strong support of many others, both in their society and beyond. Even the perennial critics of education can play a valuable role in this process, but only if they, too, become more aware of the dynamic societal forces bearing in on educational systems these days, often with crushing power.

NOTES

1. Peter J. Fensham, "An Introduction to Out-of School Science Education in Asia and the Pacific," *Bulletin of UNESCO Regional Office for Education in Asia and the Pacific* (Bangkok, Thailand), Special Issue, December 1982, p.5
2. John Vaizey, "The Dinosaur and the Child in the New Environment," an unpublished paper prepared for the International Council for Educational Development, Essex, Conn., 1979.
3. Joseph Lauwerys, "Some Thoughts on Moral Education. A 'Think Paper,'" prepared for the International Council for Educational Development, Essex, Conn., July 1978.
4. Melvin J. Fox, "Language as a Factor in Education and Development," an unpublished paper prepared for the International Council for Educational Development, Essex, Conn., 1980. Much of the factual information on languages presented in this chapter is drawn from this paper.
5. Ibid.

CHAPTER 9

THE TARNISHED LITERACY MYTH

THE DISCUSSION of language problems in the previous chapter brings us inexorably to the issue of literacy and the emotion-packed "literacy doctrine" that emerged in the early 1950s and swept around the world like a new universal religion. The underlying article of faith of the doctrine was that learning the mechanics of reading and writing was the touchstone that could liberate poor and uneducated people everywhere from the bonds of ignorance, disease, and hunger. By giving them access to the wide world of modern knowledge and skills, literacy would enable children and adults alike to pull themselves up by the bootstraps, whoever and wherever they were and whatever their environmental circumstances and life-style. It followed from this reasoning that the priority learning need of the poorest people in developing countries, whether they lived in an urban slum or a remote rural village, was to learn to read and write. All other good things would follow: better health, nutrition, housing, improved employment opportunities, higher productivity and income. Moreover, the spread of literacy would not only improve the lot of the needy but work wonders for each nation's overall social and economic development. Literacy, in short, was the hallmark of, and the "open sesame" to, modernization.

This reasoning was embraced by many high-minded, well-educated, and well-intentioned people, especially compassionate urban dwellers in the Western world who were looking for shortcuts to relieve the misery of poverty-stricken masses in the Third World. The literacy doctrine also had strong appeal for political leaders in developing countries, especially those newly elevated to power who were anxious to show the common people, by launching a new literacy campaign, that their new government was committed to improving their lot. The people themselves usually welcomed the opportunity to acquire literacy skills, for to them literacy was a prestigious symbol of modernity, a means of new power and self-protection, and a way to get ahead.

At the international level, UNESCO from its beginning became the leading world advocate of spreading literacy skills on a massive scale. Its "fundamental education" approach in the 1950s (an offspring of the earlier League of Nations campaign for fundamental education) combined literacy training with activities to meet other basic learning needs—for example, in agriculture, health, child-rearing, and occupational training. But because this was regarded by other United Nations specialized agencies as an intrusion into their jurisdictions, UNESCO was forced to retreat from its "integrated" approach and was left only as the guardian of schools and pure adult literacy. In the early 1960s, as noted earlier, UNESCO's landmark regional conferences set bold targets for achieving universal primary schooling within two decades or less, and UNESCO simultaneously led the movement for achieving universal adult literacy within the same period. To help implement the latter target, the organization gave encouragement and technical assistance over the years for adult literacy classes and campaigns in numerous developing countries. Also at the international level, development agencies such as the World Bank indirectly lent credibility to the literacy doctrine by regularly citing national literacy statistics as a key proxy measure of a nation's social and economic development progress.

THE LITERACY BALANCE SHEET

The questions to be asked in the early 1980s are the following: Where does the matter now stand, and what are the prospects? What does the literacy balance sheet show after three decades of worldwide adult literacy campaigns and dramatic expansion of school enrollments?

The answers are both encouraging and discouraging, depending on one's angle of vision and expectations. An optimist will find solace in the figures presented in Table 9.1 and Figure 9.1. The table shows marked increases in all regions of the world between 1970 and 1980 in the percentage of literates (age 15 and over), and projected further increases up to 1990. Figure 9.1 shows that the actual number of literate people in this age-group increased impressively between 1970 and 1980, especially in the less developed regions, and is projected to increase substantially more by 1990.

The more worrisome side of the story, however, is brought out in Figure 9.2, which shows that the absolute number of *illiterates* in the world

Table 9.1 Growth in the Percentage of Literates (Age 15 and older), 1970–90

	1970	1980	1990
World total	67.5	71.1	74.3
Developing countries	43.2	52.3	60.9
Developed countries	97.5	98.2	98.5

Source: UNESCO, *Estimates and Projections of Illiteracy* (Paris: UNESCO, Division of Statistics on Education, Office of Statistics, September 1978), Table 4, p. 111.

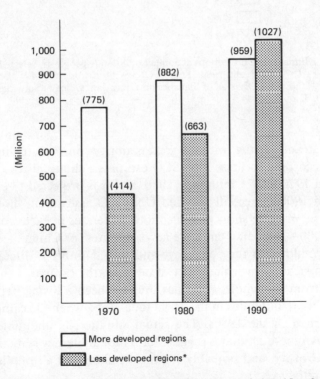

Figure 9.1. Estimates and projections of number of literate people (age 15 and older), 1970, 1980, 1990 (not including China, Democratic People's Republic of Korea, and Vietnam). [Source: UNESCO, *Estimates and Projections of Illiteracy* (Paris: UNESCO), Division of Statistics on Education, Office of Statistics, September 1978), Table 4.]

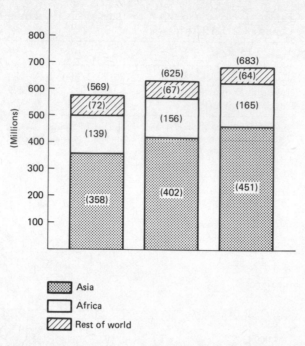

Figure 9.2. Estimates and projections of number of illiterate people, by selected regions (age 15 and older), 1970, 1980, and 1990. [Source: UNESCO, *Estimates and Projections of Illiteracy* (Paris: UNESCO, Division of Statistics on Education, Office of Statistics, September 1978), Table 4.

has been steadily rising, with the great majority concentrated in Asia and Africa. According to these UNESCO estimates, the total rose from 569 million in 1970 to 625 million in 1980, and it is projected to exceed 680 million in 1990. A recently revised UNESCO assessment, not yet published, is reported to show projected total illiterates in excess of 900 million by 2000—including tentative new estimates for China.

In short, although the percentage and total number of literate people has grown steadily over the past two decades, the campaign to eradicate illiteracy from the whole world has thus far been a losing battle. There are many more illiterates in the world today than when the campaign was first launched in the 1950s. The actual situation is undoubtedly even bleaker than these estimates suggest, for national literacy statistics are the least trustworthy, and probably the most inflated, of all published educational statistics.*

---

*National literacy statistics are usually based on the most recent census data (if the country has had a census). But census data on literacy are ambiguous at best. Depending on the particular country, respondents may be automatically classified

What went wrong? Why after all these efforts to make adults literate, and after more than 20 years of dramatic expansion of primary schooling, are there substantially more illiterates in the world today than two decades ago? One possible explanation, of course, is that the widely heralded literacy doctrine was a myth, resting on spurious assumptions. A second possibility, however, is that the appealing rhetoric of the doctrine was largely lip service that was never backed up by enough action and ample resources. Yet another possible explanation is that, although the objective of the doctrine was sound, its implementation suffered from lack of appropriate know-how on the part of the planners and implementers. Or again, perhaps the main explanation is that all of the promoters of the doctrine—in particular UNESCO—were heroically but naively "shooting for the moon"; they grossly underestimated the complexities involved and thus set targets that simply were not feasible within the specified time period.

There is truth in all of these explanations. But two other major factors must be added: first, the enormous population increase that has been going on in developing countries, which has outpaced the literacy efforts, and second and most important, elementary education. This factor was vividly analyzed by Ingvar Werdelin, a former UNESCO staff member and now a professor of education in Sweden, in a paper for an international seminar on education in developing countries held in 1982. Pointing out that the available statistics do not enable us to measure the exact size of the "nonschooling" problem in developing countries, Professor Werdelin suggested the following:

A crude estimate seems to indicate, however, that in all developing countries as a group, as many as one-half of all children never enter school. . . . Of those who enter . . . at least one-third, perhaps many more, drop out before having completed the whole cycle. This means that only about one-third of all children in developing countries can count on being able to graduate from elementary school.

as "literate" if they declare to the census taker that they have attended four years or more of primary school or can sign their own names or simply can read and write. No test of literacy is given. In addition, many people who acquired rudimentary literacy skills some years earlier may have lapsed back into illiteracy for lack of using these skills. The literacy estimates are even more suspect for countries that have never had a national census, such as Ethiopia. China, with about one third of the developing world's total population (age 15 or more), undertook its first census in 1982, but the tabulations were not yet available at the present writing.

He then went on to draw the implications for illiteracy:

If it is true [as many experts now agree] that about six years of schooling is necessary to make a pupil permanently literate, it is evident that most children of school-age in these countries will, in fact, join the cadre of illiterates in spite of the efforts invested in education.[1]

In examining the record, we seek not to put the blame in any particular place but rather to identify important lessons of past experience that can be helpful in solving the literacy problem.

HISTORICAL ROOTS

It is important to ask first where the literacy doctrine originated. UNESCO did not create it out of whole cloth; its roots can be traced back to vigorous religious and ideological movements active long before UNESCO was founded.

From the time of Gutenberg on, Protestant ministers in the West, and Protestant missionaries in less developed regions, have promoted literacy with great fervor so that members of their flocks could read the Bible and be inspired by the "Word." In Sweden, for example, because of the strong efforts and sanctions of the Lutheran church, "By mid-1800s . . . the overwhelming majority [of adults] had achieved literacy in reading [though not in writing] long before provisions for elementary schooling were made compulsory by legislation in all the parishes."[2] In the nineteenth and early twentieth centuries, European and North American missionaries to Africa transcribed indigenous tribal languages into written form, printed Bibles in these tongues, and taught the "natives" to read them. It was largely these missionaries who established and ran the first common schools in Africa, and many also in Asia and Latin America. To this day, in the South Indian State of Kerala—the most Christianized (and also the most strongly communist) state—literacy rates are the highest in the nation, notwithstanding Kerala's very low per capita income level.

Christian churches have not been the only religious promoters of literacy. A similar literacy phenomenon occured in the vast areas penetrated by Islam, ranging from West and North Africa to Indonesia and the southern Philippines. Islam also had a Holy Book to be read, and the Koranic schools, with mullahs as teachers, taught millions of young men to read it (generally in Arabic script). This goes on today, side by side with secular government schools.*

One hears repeatedly about the dramatic increase in literacy rates in the Soviet Union, China, and Cuba in the wake of their respective political revolutions. Though the statistical claims may be somewhat exaggerated, as some observers believe, there is nevertheless much truth to them. The point to be stressed is that these political revolutionary movements, just as Islam and Christianity, had their own inspirational tracts to be read by the people—the writings of Marx and Lenin, the *Thoughts of Mao,* and numerous other revolutionary messages, instructions, and directives from the ideological leaders. Popular literacy and broader forms of education were consciously adopted and promoted by these leaders as crucial instruments for achieving the goals of their revolutionary doctrines, just as literacy was employed by the Christian missionaries and Islamic clergy to spread their respective gospels.

Literacy, in short, in the context of all these vigorous religious and political movements, was not just literacy in the currently popular sense of mastering the mechanical rudiments of reading and writing; it was *functional* literacy—literacy with an inspired purpose, a means to what was seen to be a better life.

MORE RECENT EXPERIENCES

There is a fundamental difference between the foregoing religious and revolutionary functional approach to literacy and most literacy campaigns conducted in developing countries over the past three decades. This campaign brand of literacy resembles the smile on the face of the Cheshire cat, whose body disappeared while the smile lingered on. In similiar fashion, the purely mechanical approach to literacy tends to be

---

*In the early 1970s, ICED researchers in Senegal, examining the large files of letters written by listeners to the adult education radio station, discovered a surprisingly high rate of literacy among presumably illiterate male listeners. From their Koranic school background they had learned to write the local language, Bambera, in Arabic script. Yet they were officially classified as illiterate because they could not read or write in French, the colonial language. A similar condition was found in heavily Islamic northern Nigeria in the wake of British rule; parents stoutly resisted sending their children to modern Western schools where English was taught, preferring to send them to Koranic schools.

detached from practical cultural realities and from any inspiring movement or ideology, other than a vague international secularized ideology of "development." That ideology exists mainly in the minds of well-educated urban people who are often unaware of what life is really like for people living in extreme poverty in remote rural areas. The drive for literacy has become detached not only from any Great Book to be read, but from any other reading matter related to the real-life needs and interests of illiterates.

Many rural areas are utterly devoid of reading materials; they are essentially oral societies. The point can be illuminated with an example from Bangladesh in the late 1970s. A commission of distinguished educators and elder statesmen, appointed to recommend national policies and priorities on the use of nonformal education, had just about agreed to recommend that first priority should be given to yet another literacy campaign aimed at rural adults. At the last minute some visiting researchers freshly returned from the countryside informed the commission members, to their astonishment, that there was nothing available to read in most villages of Bangladesh—not even an old newspaper or agricultural or health bulletin, much less a book of Bengali poems and short stories. One notable exception the researchers had found was a pile of adult literacy primers from a previous failed campaign, stashed in a warehouse gathering dust. The content of these old primers, similiar to primers for primary school children, bore no apparent relation to the needs and interests of the local adults. Not surprisingly, after the first few meetings of the literacy class, when it became clear that learning to read and write required much time and hard effort, the local adults lost their enthusiasm and stayed away. They found little reason or motivation to make the investment, the more so since the only things available to read in their village were these dull primers. This state of affairs is by no means unique to Bangladesh; similiar conditions can be found on a vast scale in rural areas thoughout most of the developing world.[3]

LESSONS OF A MAJOR UNESCO EXPERIMENTAL PROGRAM

In the early 1960s, UNESCO's director general, René Maheu, sought to mobilize political and financial support for an all-out World Literacy Campaign aimed at eradicating illiteracy in all nations. The cost, as estimated by a reputable economic consultant, would be feasible, it was believed, when spread over a decade or so. But when the major funding agencies—the United Nations Development Programme (UNDP), the World Bank, U.S. Agency for International Development (USAID), and others—were unconvinced and declined to provide the requested funds, UNESCO put forth a more modest proposal for an Experimental World Literacy Program (the EWLP), designed to lay the foundations for a later full-blown campaign. After much discussion and negotiation, UNDP agreed to underwrite the external costs of the experiment, but only on two conditions. The first condition was that the aim of the experiment should be to demonstrate whether or not literacy training for selected groups of urban and rural workers, *integrated with pertinent occupational training,* would increase their productivity and income and thus contribute significantly to national economic development. The second condition was that the experimental program would be objectively and rigorously evaluated. This experiment, in short, would put the literacy doctrine to an acid test.

For UNESCO, with its broad humanistic commitment to social, cultural, and intellectual development, not simply economic development, to accept the terms of this narrow economic focus was, as some saw it, like consorting with Mammon. But, confident that the challenge could be met, thus opening the door to a much broader approach, the agency accepted. After all, this was an unprecedented opportunity to tailor-make, apply, and evaluate a more selective and intensive approach to literacy training, drawing not only on past experience but on sophisticated social science concepts and methods—with more literacy funds than UNESCO had ever been able to muster before.

What actually happened to this unique experiment over the next several years is too lengthy and complex a story to tell here. Suffice it to say that, despite a lengthy period of intensive preparations in Paris, little went as planned in the field. Virtually everything that could go wrong did. The story is told with perception and candor in an official assessment of the EWLP published jointly by UNESCO and UNDP in 1976.[4] This even-handed assessment highlighted both the positive and negative aspects. Though diplomatically phrased, it left little doubt that the overall performance and accomplishments of the EWLP had fallen far short of UNESCO's expectations and that the failures were traceable in no small measure to the limited vision, misconceptions, and false assumptions of the central planners and directors of the EWLP. The general tone and view of the assessment report was that the experiment had in all events generated some valuable lessons as guides to future actions, and it put its main emphasis on bringing these lessons out into the open. Four warrant special mention here.

First the realities in the field proved to be far more complex than had been anticipated from the distant vantage point of UNESCO's Secretariat in Paris.

> The degree of complexity encountered was quite unexpected at the programme's outset and daunted a good many participants, instructors and administrators, not to mention analysts and evaluators. The complexity was all the greater since the present generation of specialists in industrialized countries—who were expected to provide much of the expertise for designing, implementing and assessing EWLP—simply does not have personal experience of literacy as a chronic national problem.[5]

The second lesson was that the successful promotion of literacy is not simply, or even primarily, a matter of employing the "right" pedagogical techniques. The architects of the EWLP plans had assumed that the main reason many previous literacy programs had gone poorly was that they lacked appropriate methods of instruction. Thus viewed, the problem was seen as mainly a technical one whose solution called for a "techno-scientific" approach, constructed from rather esoteric social science concepts and methodologies. As it turned out, however, the problems encountered in the field were far less technical than social, cultural, psychological, and political. The assessment concluded as follows:

> It is a mistake to design overwhelmingly technical solutions to literacy problems that are only partly technical. . . .
> A broad, multidimensional approach to both development and literacy is required. Indeed, it would seem that literacy programmes can only be fully functional—and development contexts can only be fully conducive to literacy—if they accord importance to social, cultural and political change as well as economic growth.[6]

A third major lesson, tied to the second, was addressed especially to UNESCO but had relevance for all international agencies. It was a counsel of modesty and one of realism with respect to the inherent limitations of international models and experts. The planners of the EWLP had assumed at the outset that developing countries had not made better progress in literacy because they lacked the necessary competence. Thus, the obvious solution was to bring joint international competence to bear in these countries under the leadership of UNESCO. This conclusion was tied to a further conclusion, instinctive among specialized international agencies, that there must therefore be international standards and specifications and a duly sanctified universal model for getting things done right, in any and all situations. Once the model was designed (at head-quarters) the main task would then be to market it to individual countries and to recruit and brief experts who would be dispatched to the willing buyers.

> This unfortunate logic ignored the wishes of at least certain of what the pro-gramme itself called "clients." Certain countries wanted national literacy campaigns and seem to have "bought" the [selective, intensive, and integrated] EWLP "product" in part because they were not aware of all its implications, and in part because they saw no prospect for obtaining inter-national aid in any other way. Predictably, national and international EWLP staffs of these countries' projects tended to work at crosspurposes—one cause of the severe problems encountered there. To a degree EWLP may even be said to have delayed progress toward mass literacy in these cases.[7]

The fourth lesson concerns the important question of whether literacy can best be taught to adults as a separate subject (as it is in school) or rather in conjuction with the teaching of other things of more direct and immediate concern to the adult learners (as the EWLP set out to do). Unfortunately, this EWLP integrated approach was never given a real test in most projects, except negatively. This was because the literacy part of the instruction was turned over in most cases to schoolteachers or vol-unteers who were not sufficiently familiar with the related occupational field concerned (such as agriculture, sugar refining, metalwork, and so forth) to be able to integrate the two kinds of training. Thus, contrary to the original intention, in the majority of instances either the two matters were handled by two instructors and became divorced from each other or the project in effect abandoned the occupational training component altogether and slid back into being a conventional "pure literacy" program.

However, in one country, Mali, the integrated literacy approach was relatively successful. The whole job was turned over to knowledgeable experts running an integrated regional agricultural development pro-ject—experts who were never trained to be literacy teachers. As one of the ablest of UNESCO's literacy experts later observed, "It is far easier to make a good literacy instructor out of an agricultural expert than to make an agricultural expert out of a school teacher." The difficulty in finding willing instructors who could play two quite different instruments in harmony was just one of the many practical complications not ade-quately anticipated by the planners of the EWLP.

The EWLP experience also underscored a number of other important findings from many other adult literacy efforts (such as that mentioned earlier in Bangladesh). A few of these lessons, drawn from many sources, may be briefly summarized:

- *Lesson 1.* In selecting audiences for literacy training, planners should give preference to people who will be able to make important use of literacy in their daily lives and who, once they have learned how to read, will have ready and continuing access to relevant, useful, and interesting reading matter (such as local newspapers, magazines, "how-to" agricultural and health bulletins, and entertaining stories). If the local environment does not already contain such materials, provision for creating a continuing supply should be built into the literacy program; otherwise it is almost sure to be a waste of everybody's time. (Curiously, few literacy programs seem to have paid attention to this obvious requirement; all their efforts and resources have been concentrated on teaching people to read and virtually none on making sure they would have something pertinent to read. Presumably this was regarded as "somebody else's worry.")
- *Lesson 2.* Literacy training materials for adults should be tailored to their environment and their interests, way of thinking, and style of learning. This means that the designers of such materials must be understanding and sensitive observers, capable of looking through the eyes of those they seek to serve. Such people are admittedly hard to find, but anything less is likely to result in inert, school-like primers that will bore the adult learner. Most literacy materials for rural adults have been prepared at a distance by well-educated urban experts who did not appreciate the real interests and concerns of the rural audience.
- *Lesson 3.* Teaching literacy to adults as a discrete subject, divorced from other learning needs of strong immediate interest and concern to the particular learners, carries a high risk of failure. Teaching it in a primary school classroom with a primary teacher as instructor compounds that risk.

PUTTING THE LESSONS TO GOOD USE

In our view the EWLP, despite its disappointing immediate outcomes, was a well-justified investment in terms of the important down-to-earth lessons it yielded. It was a good investment, that is, *provided* these lessons are taken seriously and put to good use by UNESCO itself, by ministries of education, and by all others concerned with literacy and basic education.

Thus, the key questions is whether the useful lessons of EWLP and of many other literacy training experiences have been and are being applied in real-life situations. The bright side of the answer, supported by extensive evidence, is that they are indeed being applied in certain countries—by government ministries, individual UNESCO advisers, and nongovernmental organizations pursuing an integrated approach to rural development. Numerous examples could be cited, but one from Thailand will suffice to make the point.[8]

An Example from Thailand

In the early 1970s the Adult Education Division of Thailand's Ministry of Education, with technical assistance from World Education, Inc., mounted an innovative Functional Literacy and Family Life Education Program that has since spread far beyond the initial pilot area. This program focuses on a critical examination by the participants themselves of possible ways to solve everyday problems in their local area—problems relating, for example, to farming practices, nutrition, family health, and child care. To prime the discussion at each meeting, locally produced loose-leaf sheets were distributed containing hand-drawn graphic illustrations, individual words, questions, and statements relating to the particular problem or practice to be explored. As if by osmosis, the participants began to absorb these written words and store them away for future use. Their motivation to learn, which was strong, came not from some abstract desire to be literate, but from the opportunity afforded all the members to discuss openly and more deeply, and on equal terms, the everyday problems and practices that directly affected their own family life. The literacy was almost incidental, yet it took hold far better than it had in a succession of earlier unsuccessful conventional literacy programs tried in Thailand. The follow-up to this new approach has included the establishment and servicing of a network of village reading centers containing newspapers, magazines, "how-to" bulletins, and other reading matter of interest to local people. Thus, their initial literacy skills, rather than evaporating for lack of use (as so often happens with regular literacy programs), continued to broaden and deepen.

Four Basic Principles

This Thai program, and a number of other relatively successful ones elsewhere in the developing world, have adopted and adhered to four basic principles. The first principle, which the EWLP experiment had intended to follow but for the most part did not, is that of integrating literacy with the simultaneous learning of subjects of immediate interest and utility to the particular learners. Second is the principle of participation by the learners in deciding what their most urgent concerns are and what they would most like to learn about. Third is the related principle of creating on the spot simple learning materials directly geared to local conditions and interests rather than using mass-produced "readers," sent from afar, which usually have little local relevance and spark little local interest. The fourth principle is to follow up the initial literacy skills acquired with a continuing flow of easily accessible reading matter of interest to the new literates.

This integrated, locally based approach to developing literacy skills, in concert with other useful knowledge and skills, is likely to require a larger investment of competent personnel and patience, at least initally, than is usually provided for in conventional literacy programs. But its ultimate cost-effectiveness is so much greater that it is a much more productive investment. This approach, however, should not be entered into lightly and superficially, or with promises of quick and spectacular results. By now it should be clear that there are no cheap shortcuts to spreading and perpetuating functional literacy skills in areas unaccustomed to the written word as an everyday staple of life.

Unrealistic Targets

Although the growing acceptance and application of the foregoing principles and innovative approaches to literacy are certainly encouraging, a more disconcerting side of the story is that, in apparent disregard of the clear lesson taught by the EWLP and by many other literacy undertakings that ended in disappointment, little seems to have changed at the level of international rhetoric. When ministers of education gather at UNESCO conferences, the old rhetorical drums continue to beat out the familiar call for the total eradication of illiteracy from the face of the earth (these days by the year 2000) with no reference to how it can be done. To cite one recent example, a UNESCO-sponsored conference of Latin American and Caribbean ministers of education convened in Quito, Ecuador, in 1981 to formulate goals and plans for a new regional "major project," set as one of the priority objectives "the eradication of [adult] literacy by the end of the century." A companion goal was to provide "all children of Latin America and the Caribbean [with] a minimum of eight to ten years of general education" by 2000. These goals and deadlines, it should be noted, were formulated not by UNESCO but by the ministers themselves, speaking for their respective countries. No one can doubt that they are laudable goals, but that is not the issue. The real issue is whether they are realistically attainable goals within the specified time-frame.

By now it is much clearer than it was in the 1950s and early 1960s, when virtually anything seemed possible within a decade or two, that spreading adult literacy and good-quality primary schooling throughout the developing world is, by its very nature, a far more complicated, difficult, and expensive undertaking than it was first thought to be. Yet inflated rhetorical resolutions and targets, known to be unrealistic, continue to be adopted and promoted, not only in education but in other areas of major human need. Similar unrealistic international slogans are currently being promoted by other United Nations specialized agencies, trumpeting, for example, "health for all by 2000" and "food for all by 2000."

One wonders what good purpose can possibly be served by such admittedly unattainable targets. The justification sometimes given in private conversations is that they serve to spur individual countries to move faster than they otherwise might toward these goals and to stimulate greater external assistance to help countries on their way. There was undoubtedly a measure of truth in this thesis in earlier times when the international development movement was just getting started and there was much still to be learned about the realities of implementation. But this argument has worn thin by now, when even the poorest peasants in rural isolation have had their fill of inflated and unfilled promises. Unattainable targets and implied promises repeatedly issued under the imprimatur of prestigious international or national agencies can only spread a contagion of disillusionment and cynicism on all sides—and especially among the people in greatest need of help. For the habit of broadcasting rhetorical dreams works in its own way to divert energies from what actually needs to be done, namely, to formulate concrete plans based in hard realities, to recognize the obstacles to their attainment, to assess the means available for overcoming the obstacles, and then to proceed to do what can actually be done within the confines of real possibilities. We are convinced that if international conferences addressed these down-to-earth tasks, rather than indulging in rhetorical flourishes, the participants would return home much better informed and with a greater resolve to get on with the job of doing what can, in fact, be done.

AMBIGUITIES

This discussion would be incomplete without facing up to the thorny question of just what is meant by literacy, for the lack of agreement on this matter is itself an important part of the problem.

Literacy is often thought of as simply a certain minimum level of mastery of the mechanics of reading and writing in a particular language—

plus, some would add, a minimum competence in numeracy. Starting at that minimum level, it is tacitly assumed, the individual will attain greater mastery through continuous use of these skills. This would seem to be the implicit definition that underlies most literacy campaigns and published national literacy statistics.

This narrow mechanical concept was considerably broadened by the World Conference of Ministries of Education on the Eradication of Illiteracy, which met in Tehran in 1965 to lay the groundwork for UNESCO's Experimental World Literacy Program and gave wide currency to the term *functional literacy* defined as follows:

> Rather than an end in inself [functional literacy] should be regarded as a way of preparing man for a social, civic and economic role that goes far beyond the limits of rudimentary literacy training consisting merely in the teaching of reading and writing. The very process of learning to read and write should be made an opportunity for acquiring information that can immediately be used to improve living standards. Reading and writing should lead not only to elementary general knowledge but to training for work, increased productivity, a greater participation in civil life and a better understanding of the surrounding world, and should ultimately open the way to basic human culture.[9]

The productivity-connected concept of functional literacy, however, even though broader than the old simplistic mechanical view, soon came under fire from various quarters for being too limited and rigid. Humanist critics saw it as narrowing the focus of education to a limited and basically utilitarian role. Disciples of Paulo Freire's psychosocial approach to literacy critized it for ignoring the need of illiterates for greater political awareness. As a French scholar observed, "There is risk that functional literacy [EWLP style] will supply the economy with individuals tailormade to fit specific job requirements instead of enabling each individual to understand, control and dominate progress."[10]

As time went on, UNESCO's own leadership, mindful that UNESCO's mission included cultural development and not merely economic development, became increasingly uncomfortable with the narrow utilitarian concept of functional literacy underlying the EWLP. At an International Conference on Adult Education in Tokyo in 1972, UNESCO's new director general, Amadou M'Bow, sought to allay the fears of humanists in this regard while at the same time affirming the important role of education in economic development:

> We do think that the idea of functional purpose ought to be kept in education since education is not an end in itself, and by insisting on its functional pur-

pose we emphasize the relationship which exists between education and society's needs and between education and the motivations and aspirations of the individual which, as you know, have been too long disregarded.

But he hastened to add the following concerning the strongly economic focus that EWLP had initially given to functionality:

There should be no misunderstanding on this point, even if other organizations sometimes use the idea of the functional nature of education in general, and of literacy work in particular, in a much too narrow, strictly economic sense which UNESCO itself rejects.[11]

The debate over the meaning of functional literacy, both outside and within UNESCO, has not been settled to this day and probably never will be, for the simple reason that no dictionary-type international definition can possibly fit all cultures and all times. In any event, the key issue is whether literacy as commonly conceived fits into the present cultural context of a particular society and how it relates to other forms and media of communication. Clearly, in any culture where the written word is still a total stranger and there are few if any written words available to read in the local environment, most adults can hardly be expected to summon up the necessary motivation and effort to learn to read. Nor is this at all their most immediate learning need, which may be to learn things that will help them survive. In other cultural contexts in which the written word is an integral part and necessity of daily life, it becomes an urgent necessity and powerful tool for a great many people.

CRITICAL QUESTIONS FOR FUTURE STRATEGY

Three crucial questions should be posed in planning future literacy efforts—questions that have too often been glossed over by the enthusiastic and well-intentioned advocates of the literacy doctrine. First, for whom is literacy crucially important? When and under what circumstances? Second, what kind of literacy, in what language, what form, and how broad and deep? Third, what are the most effective ways to motivate and assist people in acquiring such literacy?

Finding and applying better answers to these questions is now more important than ever, for the unfinished business of literacy is enormous and growing steadily larger. The enormity of the need is greatest, of course, in the Third World. Again, however, there are wide differences between individual countries. The reported literacy rate in 1977 was only

5 percent in Upper Volta and Niger and 15 percent or less in Chad, Ethiopia, Afghanistan, and Mali—compared to 80 percent or higher in Nicaragua, Sri Lanka, Thailand, and Vietnam. Taken by themselves, however, such statistics can be a misleading gauge of the *real* literacy needs of these countries and a dubious basis for planning future literacy efforts. For as indicated previously, many of the people in the low-literacy countries live in cultural settings that are simply not conducive to learning and using literacy skills and are not likely to be for some time to come. The important task in such countries is to identify the people who *are* ready for literacy skills and who will be strongly motivated to acquire them because they can make immediate, effective use of them.

One might assume from their published literacy rates of 99 or 100 percent that the Western industrialized countries, after generations of universal primary education, no longer have a literacy problem. This is another statistical illusion. Recent surveys in the United States, the United Kingdom, France, and the Scandinavian countries—presumably among the most highly educated nations of the world—have revealed a shockingly high proportion of native-born adults and older youth who are unable to cope with the routine functional literacy demands of daily life. A recent UNESCO periodical observed the following, with reference to industrialized countries:

> [One] need only stand at the counter of a post office, bank, tax office or social security office or even in a [bus or railroad] station to realize that functional illiterates are legion. They may have more or less mastered the rudiments of reading and writing because these have been drummed into them, but in the jungle of bureaucracy they are lost, entangled in the red tape and incapable of understanding the instructions or filling in forms.[12]

This observation suggests that the need for literacy training is not limited to developing countries. It also suggests that the "literary" literacy conventionally taught in the schools is not the same as the functional literacy required to cope with everyday life in a changing world.

On the bright side, thanks to the extensive experience acquired in the intervening years, we have today a much larger stockpile than 20 or 30 years ago of practical lessons on how and how not to go about propagating literacy in the world. The most urgent need at this point is to ferret out, interpret, and synthesize these practical lessons; to disseminate them in comprehensible form to all who can use them; and to provide such assistance as they may need and desire to put these lessons to work in a manner appropriate to each situation and each set of learners. Meeting this need must be the work of many hands and minds and many organizations all over the world at every level. But at the international level, no organization is better positioned than UNESCO to take the lead in this matter. And soaring rhetoric aside, UNESCO is doing just that in some practical operational ways—through its special studies, expert meetings, and publications; through its advisers in developing countries; through the research and analytical work and country training courses conducted by the International Institute for Educational Planning, and through the stimulation and encouragement that UNESCO provides to many independent scholars and organizations in many countries.

To give them their due, the enthusiastic promoters of the literacy doctrine were quite right in stressing the importance of literacy. Where they went wrong was in attaching a special mystique to mechanical literacy skills as such, in failing to differentiate between different cultural situations, and in grossly underestimating the practical obstacles to making the whole world literate within a single generation.

NOTES

1. Ingvar Werdelin, "The Elementary School: Responsible for Causing Illiteracy?" mimeographed, paper presented at a seminar organized by the Nordic Association for the Study of Education in Developing Countries, University of Oslo, October 1982.
2. Torsten Húsen, *The School in Question: A Comparative Study of the School and Its Future in Western Societies* (New York: Oxford University Press, 1979), p. 44.
3. For a useful assortment of specific examples and a perceptive summary of difficulties encountered in adult literacy programs, see Abdun Noor, "Managing Adult Literacy Training," in *Prospects,* Vol. XII, No. 2 (Paris: UNESCO, 1982).
4. UNESCO, *The Experimental World Literacy Programme: A Critical Assessment* (Paris: UNESCO Press/UNDP, 1976). The principal (though anonymous) author was Seth Spaulding, an able former member of the UNESCO Secretariat, who by then had returned to being a professor of education at the University of Pittsburgh. Spaulding took on the professionally and politically difficult task of writing the final evaluation after earlier attempts by others had failed.
5. Ibid., p. 11.
6. Ibid., p. 122.
7. Ibid., p. 125.
8. "Thailand: An Innovative Approach to Functional Literacy, " in ICED, *Edu-*

cation for Rural Development: Case Studies for Planners, ed. Manzoor Ahmed and Philip H. Coombs (New York: Praeger, 1975), pp. 293–329.

9. *World Conference of Ministers of Education on the Eradication of Illiteracy. Final Report* (Paris: UNESCO, 1965).

10. Quoted in UNESCO, *The Experimental World Literary Programme,* p. 40.

11. *Third International Conference on Adult Education. Final Report* (Paris: UNESCO, 1972), address by UNESCO director general Amidou M'Bow, quoted in UNESCO, *The Experimental World Literacy Programme,* p. 121.

12. *Literacy 1981* (Paris: UNESCO, 1981).

CHAPTER 10

INTERNATIONAL COOPERATION (I): EDUCATIONAL DEVELOPMENT ASSISTANCE

THE SUBJECT matter of this and the next chapter impinges on all of the critical issues examined in earlier chapters and poses the question of how, with cooperative action, nations can cope more effectively with those issues. It also impinges on the awesome dilemma confronting humankind at this point in history—a dilemma succinctly put by Soedjatmoko, the eminent Indonesian rector of the United Nations University. In his recent address to a gathering in Canada of North American social scientists, he spoke of "a mutation in the human condition" and the lack of sociocultural models to help explain the dynamics of the global transformation now in progress. He continued with the following statement:

> The whole international system itself is in a state of crisis. The many cohesions—political, economic, social and otherwise—which have held that system together are coming unstuck at a frightening rate and there are no signs of any replacement at hand. Worse than this there is increasingly the growing realization that we don't seem fully to understand, and have lost control over the international or global processes of change now under way. . . .
>
> At the global level, these problems have added to the fragmentation and drift in international relations—the uncertainty and unpredictability of political behaviour of individual countries as well as of alliances. The incapacity to undertake the concerted international efforts to overcome the global recession, the continuing international economic disarray and the most urgent international or regional security problems and simultaneously the inclination to look for national solutions in isolation.[1]

The creative spirits of our time must be foremost in facing the challenge of this new kind of international crisis and in laying the conceptual basis for more secure and equitable conditions in the interests of all humankind. With this in mind, and also with a view to drawing together

285

the main strands of our discussion in previous chapters, we mean to examine in these final two chapters what has happened of late to the multifaceted international intercourse in education and cultural affairs.

Broadly perceived, this intercourse constitutes a worldwide "common market" for educational, intellectual, and cultural goods and ideas that flow daily across national boundaries through books, newspapers, and magazines, by means of the revolutionary new electronic communications media and by way of performing artists, concert groups, and exhibitions. It also includes the vastly increased number of students studying abroad; foreign experts and advisers working in developing countries; the literally hundreds of international professional meetings held annually throughout the world; and the untold number of dialogues and exchanges that go on informally and incessantly between scholarly, scientific, and artistic colleagues in different parts of the world through letters, reports, and personal encounters. It includes as well the hordes of international tourists, whose number has grown phenomenally in recent years despite adverse economic conditions and whose purpose in most cases, especially among students and other young people, is at least partly educational and cultural.*

From among the flourishing range of daily interchanges that make for this kind of worldwide common market, we will focus on four categories of primary importance to the present report. All are frequently interwoven, but for analytical purposes the categories will be dealt with separately, under the following headings: (1) educational development assistance, (2) foreign students, (3) intellectual, scientific, and cultural exchanges, and (4) studies of foreign areas and languages and other international affairs. Together, these four topics constitute too heavy a load for a single chapter to carry; therefore, we will divide them, dealing with educational development assistance in the present chapter and with the remaining three topics in the next one. We can better appreciate the recent dramatic changes within each of these if we first briefly note some recent significant changes in the broader environment.

---

*As but one example, the number of Americans traveling overseas totaled 1.6 million in 1960, 5.3 million in 1970, and 7.8 million in 1979. In 1981, more U.S. passports were issued to travelers under 30 years than in the entire decade of the 1970s (based on data in Francis X. Sutton, "The Funding of International Cooperation in Higher Education Scholarship and Research," an unpublished paper prepared for an international conference at the University of Hawaii and East–West Center in April 1982).

THE ALTERED CLIMATE OF COOPERATION

The remarkable growth of intercountry educational cooperation in the immediate postwar years went beyond anything previously dreamed of. The initial focus was mainly on cooperation among the developed nations in the Northern Hemisphere that had borne the brunt of battle in World War II. But by the early 1960s the focus had expanded to include cooperation between the developed nations of the Northern Hemisphere and the newly independent and older developing nations to the South. Hundreds of governmental, intergovernmental, and nongovernmental organizations the world over became involved in cooperative educational activities, especially in connection with student and faculty exchanges and with material and technical assistance to Third World countries to spur educational and other forms of development. The specific missions of these cooperative organizations varied, but nonetheless they shared the same basic objective—namely, to advance understanding among nations and to build the foundations for a new world order in which all peoples could live in peace.

This unprecedented upsurge of international cooperation in education, and in many allied fields, reached a high point in the late 1960s and early 1970s. Thereafter, the animating spirit of hope, enthusiasm, adventure, and friendship that had marked the earlier period seemed to wane. Of the many causes, the first was the deterioration in the political relations between countries and blocs of countries, which, among other things, increasingly transformed international technical cooperation agencies (such as UNESCO) into arenas for divisive political struggles. A second important cause was the sharp and prolonged worldwide recession, beginning in 1973, which constricted national budgets everywhere and prompted leading donor nations of Western Europe and North America to become increasingly preoccupied with deepening domestic problems.

Also in the 1970s, some of the key governmental and private agencies that had done so much in their youthful days to pioneer international cooperation in fresh directions began to show signs of premature aging and fatigue, and in some cases flagging public interest and support. Though most of them continued to do important and useful work, they were becoming increasingly bureaucratized, to the growing frustration of both their own staffs and the countries and people they were created to serve. Their administrative and "project" procedures tended to grow increasingly elaborate and rigid, impairing their innovative capacity and their ability to respond promptly to changing needs and conditions.

These negative aspects, however, are not the whole story, as there were also important bright spots in the record of international cooperation during the 1970s. Not least of these was the way the industrial nations of the North, despite their own serious economic and budgetary problems, collectively increased their development assistance to the less developed nations, whose economic troubles were far more serious. It can be, and has frequently been, argued that considerably more should have been forthcoming from the richer nations; but in view of the deteriorating economic and political conditions of the period, perhaps the surprising thing is that the volume of their assistance held up as well as it did. Further, various official bilateral and multilateral development assistance agencies, despite their growing infirmities, managed in close cooperation with various developing countries to blaze some important new trails that hold considerable promise for the future.

Many developing countries, for their part, began to come to terms with their own complex and deep-rooted economic, social, and educational problems. They started to reach out toward more realistic solutions to them, and by means that frequently involved unconventional approaches.

Meanwhile, many voluntary agencies operating in Third World countries not only increased the level and geographic scope of their activities, but shifted from their traditional emphasis on transitory relief and social welfare to more basic development measures that could have a more enduring impact on improving the lives of disadvantaged people. Most of these new development measures included a high educational content, particularly in the realm of nonformal education, and in many developing countries voluntary organizations and official government agencies increasingly tended to cooperate more closely to achieve common objectives, each doing what it could do best.

All this went hand in hand with two other matters that marked the field of educational cooperation in the 1970s. One was the marked growth of interest in science and technology, the cultural and qualitative aspects of education, and extensive reforms and innovations in conventional educational arrangements. The other was the increased recognition of the potential benefits of "horizontal cooperation" between countries of the South.

Perhaps the most significant advance in the 1970s, though it had its prickly aspects, was the increased sense of independence and self-reliance exhibited by many developing countries, including their determination to make their own development decisions and plans and reduce their reliance on foreign experts. As one official put it, "We want to be free to make—and learn from—our own mistakes." This did not mean, he hastened to add, that his country no longer needed outside help. "We still need help, but not of the kind we have been getting."

But there is a question to be asked. How did the negative and positive changes in the overall environment and mechanisms of international development cooperation during the 1970s affect *educational* cooperation in particular? Even more to the point, how did they affect (for better or worse) the critical issues discussed in previous chapters? In seeking an answer to this question, a good place to start is with the changes that occurred during the 1970s and early 1980s in external assistance for educational development in Third World countries.

CHANGES IN EDUCATIONAL DEVELOPMENT ASSISTANCE

From the late 1940s onward, external assistance—from bilateral and multilateral cooperation agencies and from private foundations—played a major role in shaping and developing the formal education systems of developing countries, in helping them create a diversity of development-related nonformal education and training activities, and in enlarging and improving their supply of high-level manpower, through both their own new secondary and higher educational institutions and the advanced education and training of their people in the institutions of more developed countries.

During the 1960s especially, when dozens of newly independent nations (especially in Africa) were just making their start, education was given priority by most external assistance agencies and by developing countries themselves. Educational assistance increased steadily in this period and in most years up to the early 1970s the so-called education sector topped all other development sectors in the share of total development assistance it received. The major part of this educational assistance was concentrated on formal education, mainly secondary and higher education including teacher training, although some of it also went into building agricultural and health services, adult literacy programs, and other out-of-school activities that were later to become classified as nonformal education. Significantly, most external assistance agencies in the 1950s and 1960s steered clear of elementary education for two reasons. First, they regarded it as a bottomless pit, best left to the developing countries to deal with on their own. Second, despite the priority given to universal primary education at the UNESCO regional conferences of ministers of education, these agencies and many leaders in developing countries believed that the greatest immediate need was to strengthen the supply of high-level manpower to provide expert skills and leadership for government and all major fields.

The bulk of this external assistance was in the form of technical assistance, particularly the supplying of advisers, teachers, and grants for overseas study. In addition to technical assistance, however, sizable amounts of capital assistance were provided for constructing and equipping educational facilities and obtaining textbooks and other supplies. Assistance to formal education was generally handled by a separate education bureau in each external assistance agency, working in conjunction with the ministry of education of the recipient country or, in many cases, working directly with officials of universities and other higher educational institutions beyond the immediate jurisdiction of the ministry of education. Apart from this, however, considerable assistance (how much is unknown) took the form of nonformal education and training components of sectoral proejcts under the jurisdiction of other ministries. This is one of the major reasons (discussed later) why it is so difficult to assess the quantitative trends in educational assistance. Most bilateral and multilateral agencies only report under "Education" the assistance channeled through their education bureau or department. All other educational assistance is hidden in the accounts of other sectoral bureaus under such categories as agriculture or health or industry.

Problems of Measurement

We come now to some questions about educational assistance since 1970: Did the overall volume continue to increase or did it decline? What were the main sources of such aid and how did they change? How did the policies and patterns of educational aid change? Were there any significant changes in the modes of negotiating, providing, and utilizing such aid?

In trying to determine what happened to the volume of educational development assistance over the past decade, we immediately encounter five problems. First, no international agency or other organization has assumed responsibility for monitoring and annually reporting significant trends and changes in this field, in the way, for example, that the World Bank Group and OECD monitor international financial flows and fluctuations in great detail, in some cases from week to week. The most recent attempt to construct an overall picture of trends in educational assistance, covering the period 1970–75, was undertaken by H. M. Phillips for the Rockefeller Foundation.[2] His study provided important insights and was widely appreciated, but no organization has since tried to update the picture.

The second problem, related to the first, is one of definition and accounting. Different development assistance agencies define education differently, and most of them do not include or even keep track of the many educational and training components in projects outside the education sector. The World Bank is one of the few organizations that tried during the 1970s to dig out and add up the missing pieces. The results, shown later in these pages, considerably altered the profile of the Bank's record of performance with respect to education. If certain of the larger bilateral agencies, particularly the U.S. Agency for International Development, were to do the same thing, their educational assistance record for the 1970s would look considerably better than it now does.

The third problem affects developed countries as well. Educational assistance data, if reported at all, are reported in current prices. In a period of rampant inflation, such as the 1970s and early 1980s, these inflation-loaded figures greatly exaggerate the reality. To convert current price figures into reasonably accurate real terms, however, would require a "deflator" especially tailored to the peculiar cost components and structure of educational assistance. But no such deflator exists. There is good reason to believe, however, that technical assistance costs, which constitute some 80 percent of total educational assistance, rose substantially faster than the general price level since 1970. The Phillips study found this to be the case for the period of 1970–75.

The fourth problem, closely connected to the third, is that because of time lags, there is often a sizable discrepancy in any one year between the allocation of resources by assistance agencies and the actual disbursement of these resources to developing countries. Thus, in tracking the trend over a period of years, it is important to use one set of figures or the other and not get them mixed.

The fifth problem is that the monetary value of educational assistance often looks substantially larger from the vantage point of the sending country and agency than from that of the recipient. It may cost a bilateral or multilateral agency more than $60,000 a year to provide for an expert educational adviser or visiting professor, including salary (based on prevailing industrial country standards) and travel and living expenses, and often those of the expert's family as well. But the going market value for a comparable expert in the receiving country, assuming one were available, might be well below half this amount. All the officially reported figures for educational assistance, however, are based on the costs to the sending agencies. Again, there is no available satisfactory way to translate them into the recipient country's terms. Still, despite these substantial technical difficulties and information gaps, the evidence at hand supports at least an impressionistic picture of recent trends and changes in overall educational assistance.

Growth of Total Official Development Assistance

Official development assistance (ODA), refers to assistance funds for all purposes appropriated by donor country governments. The major portion of these funds is distributed directly through their own bilateral agencies, and the rest through multilateral and regional development cooperation agencies—primarily the United Nations Development Programme (UNDP), various United Nations specialized agencies, the World Bank and regional development banks, and the European Economic Community. We can take an initial cut at estimating what happened to the volume of educational assistance between 1970 and 1982 by looking first at trends in overall ODA, itself the source of roughly 85 percent of all assistance funds, with the remainder coming from private nonprofit voluntary organizations and philanthropic foundations.

Troubled world economic conditions made the 1970s and early 1980s difficult times for development assistance. Yet surprisingly, and contrary to the popular impression, the overall volume of ODA grew substantially. The total—stated in current prices that reflected high inflation—more than quadrupled between 1970 and 1980. But even in real terms, measured in constant 1981 prices with allowance for exchange rate fluctuations, total ODA from all sources grew from U.S. $21.4 billion in 1970 to $37.4 billion in 1980, an increase of more than 62 percent. The details are shown in Table 10.1.* The total declined substantially from 1980 to 1981 (mainly because of time lags in the replenishment of multilateral funds); but in 1981 it bounced back and resumed its upward course, at least in the case of the members of OECD's Development Assistance Committee (DAC).

In the early 1960s, the OECD/DAC group provided virtually 100 percent of all ODA, but as the Council for Mutual Economic Assistance (CMEA) countries and then the Organization of Petroleum Exporting Countries (OPEC) joined in, the OECD/DAC share of the increasing total declined to 84 percent in 1970 and 71 percent in 1980. The indications are that relatively little of either the OPEC or CMEA assistance went into education.**

---

*It is debatable whether the GNP deflator used by OECD to convert ODA from current to constant (1981) prices takes sufficient account of the inflation in external assistance costs, particularly the special costs of technical assistance, which some analysts believe have risen more rapidly than the general structure of prices reflected in the GNP deflator. There seems little doubt, however, that total ODA did experience a substantial real increase in the 1970s, but it may not have been as much as 62 percent.

**The OPEC contribution rose rapidly between 1970 and 1979, but fell off in

Table 10.1 Official Development Assistance in Real Terms, 1970–82 (billions of U.S. dollars, 1981 prices)

	1970	1975	1980	1981	1982
OECD/DAC countries[a]	17.9	21.2	26.4	25.6	28.4
OPEC countries[b]	1.0	9.5	8.9	7.8	n.a.
CMEA countries[c]	2.5	1.1	2.1	2.1	n.a.
Total	21.4	31.9	37.4	35.6	
GNP deflator for OECD countries	38.8	65.4	103.1	100.0	
			Index: 1981 = 100		

[a]The members of the OECD/DAC include Australia, Austria, Belgium, Canada, Denmark, Finland, France, the Federal Republic of Germany, Italy, Japan, Netherlands, New Zealand, Norway, Sweden, Switzerland, the United Kingdom, and the United States.
[b]About three quarters of all Organization of Petroleum Exporting Countries (OPEC) assistance came from Saudi Arabia and the bulk of the rest from Kuwait and the United Arab Emirates.
[c]The Council for Mutual Economic Assistance (CMEA) includes the U.S.S.R. (nearly 80 percent of CMEA's total official development assistance), Bulgaria, Czechoslovakia, the German Democratic Republic (second largest contributor), Hungary, Poland, and Romania.
Source: 1982 Annual Review, (Paris: Organization for Economic Co-operation and Development, Development Assistance Committee, 1982), pp. 18–21; *OECD Observer,* No. 123 (July 1983), pp. 18–21; and *OECD Observer,* No. 129 (July 1984), pp. 26–29.

All along the OECD/DAC group has been by far the largest contributor to the multilateral agencies. During the 1970s, this group sharply increased the proportion of its total ODA allocated to multilateral agencies, from 16 percent in 1970 to nearly 32 percent in 1978. This increase in multilateral funds had the desirable effect of channeling an increased proportion of total ODA funds from OECD/DAC countries into the low-income countries—desirable because the multilateral agencies generally direct a larger percentage of their available funds to these countries than the OECD bilateral agencies. Many of the latter agencies, because of historical ties and national economic, political, and strategic considerations, have tilted strongly toward middle-income developing countries. What this means can be seen by contrast: the World Bank's International Development Association (IDA), the Bank's "soft loan window," now

---

1980 and 1981 as oil prices and revenues weakened. A high proportion of OPEC aid has been extended bilaterally, mainly in the form of general support assistance to the Arab "Confrontation States." In 1980, CMEA assistance constituted about 6 percent of the total world ODA and was heavily concentrated on three countries: Vietnam, Cuba, and Afghanistan. [See *1982 Annual Review [of] Development Cooperation.* Efforts and Policies of the Members of the Development Assistance Committee (Paris: OECD, 1982), and *OECD Observer,* No. 122 (May 1983).]

channels virtually 100 percent of its loans and credits into low-income countries, whereas the corresponding average figure for the OECD bilaterals is only 50 percent.[3]

Trends in Educational Assistance

These recent trends in overall ODA provide the basis for the question most pertinent to the present study: What happened to the volume of *educational* aid between 1970 and the early 1980s?

The available evidence points to three conclusions. First, most (though not all) of the external assistance agencies that accorded education a priority in earlier years reduced that priority after the early 1970s, but continued to provide substantial support. In many instances this diminished priority reflected the joint views of the external agency and developing country authorities; that is, although both continued to attach great importance to education, both felt compelled to increase attention to competing urgent needs. Second, the overall volume of assistance to formal education, measured in real terms, declined after the early 1970s, though not drastically—which is to say that the education sector, as defined by most bilateral and multilateral agencies, received a declining percentage share of total ODA. Third, external assistance for (largely nonformal) education and training components "hidden" in projects outside the education sector, increased substantially during the 1970s (although by how much is unknown).

These conclusions should not be interpreted to mean that the recent levels of external assistance are adequate to meet the pressing educational needs of developing countries, especially the poorest of them. Far from it; they need considerably more educational assistance. Yet, given the increasingly tight constraints on overall development assistance since the early 1970s and the powerful competing demands from other sectors, it seems fair to say that education's share held up better than might have been expected. The more important question—one dealt with later—is how appropriately and efficiently this educational assistance was allocated and utilized.

In reaching the preceding conclusions, we assessed a great variety of evidence and testimony, some of which was conflicting. We took as our starting point the estimates presented in the previously mentioned Phillips report—undoubtedly the best available for the first half of the decade.[4] Two key points stand out in Figure 10.1, based on that report. One is the sizable *apparent* increase in total educational assistance between 1970 and 1975; the other is the significant change in the shares of the total provided by the different categories of assistance organizations.

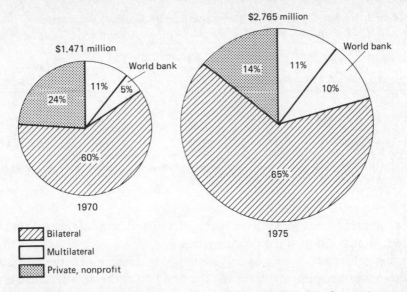

Figure 10.1. Sources of external aid to education, 1970 and 1975. (The figures shown apply largely to grants and loans, mainly for formal education, classified by aid agencies under the education sector. Thus, they do not include assistance for largely nonformal education and training components hidden in the accounts of other sectors.) [Source: World Bank, *Education Sector Policy Paper, 1980;* based on H. M. Phillips, *Higher Education: Cooperation with Developing Countries* (New York: The Rockefeller Foundation, February 1978).]

As to the first point, much of the large increase in educational assistance (shown in current prices of each year in Figure 10.1) was wiped out by general price inflation. This was especially true, as Phillips points out, because the costs of technical assistance, which account for about 80 percent of all educational aid, rose more rapidly than the general level of prices. He notes, for example, that the cost of sending an educational expert to a developing country doubled between 1970 and 1975 and suggests that this helps explain the sharp decrease between 1969 and 1975, shown in Table 10.2, in the number of educational experts and teachers furnished by the OECD/DAC countries.* Phillips also observed that

*A further explanation for this decline is that many developing countries had by then made sufficient progress in improving their own supply of teachers and experts that they no longer needed or desired as many imported ones as earlier. Moreover, in view of the high cost of outside experts (and their unsatisfactory quality and performance in some cases), given a choice, they much preferred to use available educational assistance in less costly alternative ways, such as sending more of their promising young people abroad for advanced education and training.

Table 10.2 Technical Assistance Exchanges Under Bilateral Programs of
OECD/DAC Countries, 1969 and 1975

Type of Technical Assistance	Number of Persons		Percentage Change
	1969	1975	
Teachers	59,400	35,700	−41
Educational advisers and experts	6,700	2,400	−64
Students assisted	39,700	43,700	+10
Trainees assisted	33,300	34,600	+4

Source: H. M. Phillips, *Higher Education: Cooperation with Developing Countries* (New York: Rockefeller Foundation, February 1978).

these "people figures" are often a more reliable indicator of the real trends in educational aid than the dollar figures.

At best, therefore, there was only a modest real increase in overall assistance to the education sector during the first half of the decade, and quite possibly an actual decrease.

The marked changes between 1970 and 1975 in the percentage shares of total educational assistance provided by different sources (Figure 10.1) are especially significant. Similar changes evidently continued into the second half of the decade, to which we now shift our attention.

The World Bank's Record. A clear case in point is the much expanded role of the World Bank, including both the International Bank for Reconstruction and Development (IBRD) and the International Development Association (IDA), in the overall educational assistance picture. As shown in Figure 10.1, the Bank's share of total assistance doubled between 1970 and 1975—from 5 to 10 percent. As shown by the data in Appendix Table 10.1, the Bank's educational support continued to expand up to 1982. Loans and credits to the education sector (that is, projects administered by the Bank's Education Department and the education subdivisions of its geographic bureaus) increased from an annual average of $163 million between 1970 and 1974 to an average of $523 million in the 1979–82 period, thereby keeping in step with the substantial increase in the Bank's overall lending. Especially striking, however, is the sharp and steady increase in the Bank's lending for project-related education and training programs in other sectors of the Bank's overall program. Total annual lending for these types of educational activities grew from a minimal level (probably under $10 million per year) in the 1970–74 period to more than $300 million in the 1979–82 period. Thus, total World Bank lending for all educational purposes grew from an annual average of $170 million in 1970–74 to an average of $859 million in 1979–82—or from 5.5 percent of the Bank's total lending in the earlier period to 7.3 percent in the more recent period. Although the figures are in current prices, they clearly reflect a large real increase in the Bank's educational lending during this period, after discounting for inflation.

The Record of Other Multilateral Agencies. The combined share of total educational assistance provided by all the other multilateral agencies, according to the Phillips study, remained at 11 percent between 1970 and 1975. The indications, however, are that for the decade as a whole virtually all of these agencies substantially reduced their real support to the education sector (though some of them probably increased assistance for education and training activities in other sectors, especially agriculture, rural development, health, population, and occupational training). The UNDP's total real resources declined during this period, and the percentage of the total allocated to the education sector (administered mainly by UNESCO) also declined. The Inter-American Development Bank, largest of the regional banks, had played a leading role in providing assistance to formal education (especially higher education) in Latin America and the Caribbean during the 1950s and 1960s but virtually abandoned this field in the 1970s. Even UNICEF, which had devoted 20 percent of its total program budget to education in the 1960s and 1970s and which in 1973–74 had declared its intention to step up its support for primary and nonformal education, reduced the proportion of its resources going to education after 1975 to between 14 and 15 percent.

The Record of the Bilateral Agencies. As shown in Figure 10.1, the bilateral agencies increased their share of total educational assistance from 60 percent in 1970 to 65 percent in 1975, the great bulk of which came—and still comes—from the members of OECD/DAC. Their record since 1975 is difficult to interpret. On the one hand, their combined commitments to the education sector (in current prices) fell from $1.5 billion in 1975 to below $1.3 billion in 1976, and then increased steadily to a peak of nearly $3.4 billion in 1980, only to drop sharply the next year to $2.6 billion.[5] On the other hand, the proportion of total OECD/DAC bilateral aid allocated to the education sector declined from 16.6 percent in 1976 to 13.9 percent in 1980, and 11.3 percent in 1981.

The first problem encountered in interpreting these figures is that roughly half of these dollar amounts came from the French aid program alone, which has regularly devoted over one third of its total bilateral aid to education, mostly to provide teachers and, increasingly, teacher training, to its former colonies in Africa and its current overseas departments and territories.

The second problem is how best to convert these amounts in current prices into real amounts in constant prices. As shown on Appendix Table 10.2, if one applies the OECD GNP deflator, the total OECD/DAC allocation to the education sector (in 1981 prices) for the period 1976 through 1981 averages U.S. $2.57 billion per year, compared to U.S. $2.36 billion in 1975—a modest real increase. On the other hand, if one uses as a deflator the International Monetary Fund's index of consumer price movements in industrial countries, the average allocation to education from 1976 through 1981 would be U.S. $1.50 billion (in 1975 prices)—a modest *decrease* from the U.S. $1.55 billion in 1975.

Either way, it seems clear that there was no substantial *real* increase in bilateral aid to the education sector between 1975 and 1981. Because neither deflator reflects the greater increase in educational technical assistance costs than in the general level of prices, our conclusion is that there was probably a significant decrease.

Two further points should be made about the OECD/DAC record of performance in education. First the preceding composite figures mask wide differences between individual countries, in the percentage of their total bilateral aid allocated to education and in how these percentages have changed from year to year. One can get an idea of these differences from Appendix Table 10.3. The figures for individual donor countries reflect a whole complex of factors, including former colonial and other traditional ties, language similarities and differences, and considerations relating to geographic proximity and current national economic, political, and security interests.

The second point is that the foregoing OECD/DAC figures include only allocations to the education sector (hence mainly to *formal* education). For the most part they exclude outlays for educational and training elements under the labels of other sectors. There is reason to believe that the latter educational outlays increased substantially in real terms during the 1970s and early 1980s, especially for those bilateral agencies, such as the American, British, and Scandinavian agencies, that gave serious attention after the early 1970s to meeting the needs of the rural poor, to integrated community-based rural development, and to nonformal education.

The Record of Private Nonprofit Organizations. This is the most difficult group to assess because its members are so numerous and diverse. Phillips estimated (Figure 10.1) that this group's share of total educational assistance declined sharply from 24 percent ($353 million in current prices) in 1970 to 14 percent ($387 million) in 1975. Clearly that is a substantial real decline when allowance is made for inflation.

What happened to this group's contribution after 1975 is difficult to establish, but this much we know. First, the major U.S. foundations—Ford, Rockefeller, and Carnegie—that had played key roles in the 1950s and 1960s in helping to develop new universities and to train high-level specialists in a number of Asian, African, and Latin American countries largely terminated these programs in the 1970s, as did several European foundations. A notable exception is the Bernard Van leer Foundation in The Hague, which continued to give strong support to educational and social experiments in dozens of developing (and developed) countries designed to benefit deprived preschool-age and young school-age children.

During the 1970s many voluntary organizations based in North America and Western Europe and operating in developing countries, financed mainly by private contributions but to some extent also by grants from official bilateral agencies, endeavored to expand the scope of their activities (most of which included substantial nonformal as well as formal educational components). Some of them clearly succeeded, but whether as a group they were able to attract sufficient additional real resources to expand significantly remains an open question. Clearly, however, their fund-raising efforts encountered increasing difficulties after 1975. Our best guess—and it can only be a guess—is that, excluding government grants already accounted for under bilateral aid agencies, the overall educational assistance provided by these voluntary organizations to developing countries increased very little in real terms between 1975 and 1982, and may actually have declined.

Adding the Pieces Together

In summing up the findings discussed so far, we turn full circle to our original conclusions. First, the strong priority widely accorded to the education sector in the 1950s and 1960s by many official agencies and major private foundations diminished visibly in the 1970s and early 1980s. There were some notable exceptions, however, the most conspicuous one being the World Bank.

Second, in a reversal of the previous 20-year upward trend, the overall volume of assistance to formal education, in real terms, appears to have declined after the early 1970s. This decline is reflected especially in the much reduced number of teachers and educational advisers sent by OECD/DAC countries.

Third, an opposite trend became apparent with respect to assistance for (largely nonformal) education and training components in programs and projects outside the customary province of the education sector, as traditionally defined by most external assistance agencies. If this is true, then we must modify our previous conclusions to say that, including these hidden forms, total education assistance probably increased somewhat during the 1970s, though still not as much as total ODA. To reiterate an earlier caveat, however, because of the shortage of hard evidence and the difficulty of making accurate conversions of current price data into real terms, these conclusions are necessarily impressionistic.

In any event, trends in overall external assistance to education do not by themselves provide a sufficient basis for evaluating the efficacy of educational aid since the early 1970s. For such an assessment, it is essential also to know how the aid was used—where it went, for what specific purposes, how efficiently it was applied, and whether there were significant improvements in the aid process itself. To help answer these questions it will be useful to refer back to the drastic changes in development and educational concepts and policies in the early 1970s that were outlined in Chapter 1 and to ask an overarching question: To what extent were these new policies actually implemented during the second half of the 1970s and early 1980s?

THE NEW DIRECTIONS

It will be helpful at this point to recall briefly the main objective of these new strategies and policies. On the general development front they called for the following: (1) well-aimed measures to increase economic output, but in ways consistent with the need to engage the entire population in the development process and to achieve a more equitable distribution of the benefits; (2) a large-scale, *integrated* effort to accelerate rural development and to transform rural societies, with local people and communities themselves playing a central role; (3) a coordinated frontal attack on the roots of mass poverty (in both rural and urban areas), designed to meet the basic needs of disadvantaged families and individuals, including such needs as education, health, food, employment, and increased income, housing, and family planning; and (4) special efforts to improve the status and welfare of especially vulnerable and disadvantaged subgroups—in particular, girls and women, young children, and ethnic minorities.

Within the framework of these new development strategies, the newly declared educational policies called for the following: (1) a shift of emphasis from secondary and especially higher education to expanding access to primary education in unserved areas and improving its quality and effectiveness; (2) a corresponding increasing emphasis on providing appropriate kinds of basic education—largely in a nonformal mode—for out-of-school youth and adults; (3) efforts to reduce gross educational disparities and inequalities, particularly those affecting people in rural areas and urban slums, girls and women, and ethnic minorities; and (4) concerted efforts to improve the relevance, quality, and efficiency of formal education at all levels and, to this end, carefully aimed and sustained efforts to enable developing countries to strengthen their basic informational, analytical, planning, and management capacities in the whole field of education.

Problem of Implementation

In approaching the question of how well these new strategies and policies have actually been implemented, three crucial realities should be kept in mind. First, statements of general policies and priorities by external assistance agencies can only offer a broad framework through which to view the widely varying needs, circumstances, and self-determined priorities of individual developing countries. This framework can help guide negotiations with each country, but such policies and priorities cannot, and should not, be imposed on or uniformly applied to each and every country. They must in the nature of things be flexibly adapted, and in special circumstances even departed from, to accommodate the practical conditions and preferences of each individual country. This being the case, one should not expect to find a perfect fit between the avowed general policies and priorities of an external agency and the pattern of actions that flow from them.

The second important reality concerns the organizational mechanisms, at the international, national, and subnational levels, responsible for implementing the new policies and strategies. Each of these organizations has a personality and pattern of behavior all its own—shaped by its prescribed mission, its established doctrines, precepts, and procedures, and its traditions and practical experience. No one voice speaks for all these organizations, and even the same organization may speak with multiple voices. The larger and more complex the organization is and the more specialized subdivisions it has, the more diverse the points of view within it will be and the greater the tensions and rivalries between these points of view. Generally the top administrator, standing above the fray, inspires and enunciates major changes in the organization's overall strategies and policies, sometimes with the concurrence of a governing body. But as strongly committed as an administrator may be to these avowed new policies, it does not follow that all the operators at lower levels in the organization will necessarily accept and willingly carry them out.

The third reality is that, even if all the people in all the subdivisions of each organization willingly accept new strategies and policies in principle, they may not know how to go about implementing them. Relatively little attention was given to these knotty implementation questions before the formulation and announcement of the new strategies and policies in the early 1970s.

For all the foregoing reasons, turning around any established organization and heading it in new and unfamiliar directions is a slow and difficult process at best, and even more so when it involves upsetting established jurisdictions and modes of operation. Further complications may exist, such as the degree of centralization or decentralization of the particular organization (for example, the highly centralized World Bank or the much more decentralized UNICEF or WHO) or the extent to which one organization may be partly dependent on one or more other organizations in shaping its program actions (for example, UNICEF and the World Bank are partly dependent in educational matters on the technical support and advice of UNESCO).

Of all the new strategies and emphases, three in particular created the greatest confusion and natural resistance in the 1970s, primarily because they required the most drastic changes in conventional thinking and customary operational behavior. The first was the new emphasis on a more integrated approach. Under this approach, specialized organizations and the subdivisions of complex organizations that had long been firmly wedded to a particular sector and were accustomed to "going it alone" were in effect required to surrender some of their autonomy and to begin working in concert with various other specialized groups. The difficult challenge this presented to top management was comparable to that of de-Balkanizing and unifying a loose collection of rival Balkan states.

The second set of prickly problems arose from the new emphasis on community participation and community-based development. This entailed a wrenching departure from the prevailing top-down approach. The problem there was not so much one of resistance to the idea; no one could deny its obvious good sense. The problem was rather the lack of know-how in going about it, for these top-down organizations, including not least of all most ministries of education, had little previous experience with working in equal partnership with individual communities and groups within them.

The third complicating strategy—one that, as noted earlier, at least initially created the greatest confusion, misunderstanding, and resistance on the part of many educational experts and authorities—was the new stress on nonformal education. Many education ministries and educators welcomed this new emphasis insofar as it applied to the types of nonformal education with which they were familiar, such as adult literacy programs and "second chance" school-type programs for out-of-school youth. But it was difficult for them to recognize that such programs, closely allied to formal education, were only a small segment of all nonformal education and that the other segments involved numerous other specialized ministries and a vast assortment of voluntary organizations. Thus, a perplexing question came to haunt those who were preoccupied less with the learners and their needs than with keeping things neat and tidy, well planned and coordinated, and above all under control. The question was: Who would be in charge of this bewildering assortment of nonformal educational activities?

The pragmatic answer to this question soon became apparent. By the nature of these nonformal education activities, no one organization—least of all the ministry of education—could be in charge in the sense of controlling, planning, and managing all of them. A more realistic solution would have to be found to each country's particular circumstances and traditions.

Progress on the New Policies

In light of all these factors it is hardly surprising that the new policies adopted in the early 1970s had been only fractionally translated into action by the early 1980s, leaving the bulk of the job still to be accomplished. The progress that was actually made, however, should not be underestimated.

In developing countries such as Bangladesh, India, and Indonesia, to mention only a few, new organizational arrangements were made in the ministry of education, and increased staff and funds were provided to promote broader and more concerted actions (often unconventional ones) to enlarge "basic education" for unserved needy people—including primary education for children and nonformal education for out-of-school youth and adults. Among others, Kenya, Nigeria, and Tanzania launched major campaigns to expand access to primary school in rural areas. Beyond the customary boundaries of the education sector, many countries, with the support of external agencies and in conjunction with basic needs programs, for example, in small-scale farming and industry, health, water supply, and family planning, gave increased attention to the inclusion of stronger educational and training components.

Several bilateral agencies turned their attention to encouraging and supporting experimental community-based integrated rural development programs of various kinds, invariably with substantial educational and communication components. Some of them, such as USAID and the

Netherlands' cooperation agency, invested more heavily in research aimed at uncovering useful knowledge about the nature of rural community development problems and how to attack them more effectively. The Canadian-supported International Development Research Centre (IDRC) and its Swedish counterpart, the Swedish Agency for Research Cooperation (SAREC), also moved in this direction, with special emphasis on helping developing countries to build their own research capacity.

The World Bank moved with unprecedented speed toward trying to practice what its president, Robert McNamara, had been preaching. By the second half of the 1970s the Bank had mounted a spate of new-type integrated agricultural and rural development projects and urban site development projects, an enlarged health and population program, and new efforts to assist small farmers and businesses. Many of these new efforts included substantial education and training components. In addition, the Bank's education sector shifted the pattern of its program to give increasing emphasis to the new policy directions. As indicated in Appendix Table 10.4, the combined percentage of the Bank's total education sector lending for elementary and nonformal education rose from 10 percent in 1970–74 to 33 percent in 1979–82. Increased emphasis was also given to general institutional development (as distinct from specific schools and institutions), particularly for developing learning materials and media and strengthening educational planning and management that could serve a wider purpose. In a precedent-setting move, loan provisions for technical assistance, which the Bank had previously shied away from, rose from only 3 percent of total education sector lending in 1963–69 to 17 percent in 1972–82. Some of these technical assistance funds were earmarked for research and experimentation associated with particular projects or to lay the foundations for future projects.

UNESCO, always a vocal friend of adult education (especially literacy) but with a long-standing and overwhelming program emphasis on formal primary and secondary education and teacher training, took steps in the 1970s and early 1980s to strengthen its staff and program in adult education and rural development and encouraged its member states to do likewise. UNESCO's actual financial allocations for these purposes, however, remained very modest.

All in all, considering the many bureaucratic, political, and other obstacles, some real progress had been made by 1983 toward converting the rhetoric of the new policies into real action. Still, no one close to the scene had any illusions that all this was more than a good start in the right direction. Many internal bureaucratic problems remained at both the national and international level, and much was yet to be learned from research and practical experience about how to pursue the stated objectives more efficiently and effectively. The greatest remaining puzzle was how to reach and assist the poorest of the poor. As the World Bank's 1982 Annual Report candidly confessed:

> Neither donors nor borrowers have been particularly adept at bringing about benefits to those without productive assets—the rural landless, the urban jobless, most adult illiterates, and many female-headed households, for example. The Bank will intensify its efforts to understand how to increase the productivity and employment of such people.[6]

THE FUTURE OF EDUCATIONAL ASSISTANCE

Three main questions arise concerning the future of educational assistance. First, what is likely to happen to the overall amount? Second, how can future educational assistance, whatever its quantitative scale, be put to the most effective use? And third, how can the assistance process itself be improved?

Quantitative Prospects

The answer to the first question (the overall amount) must necessarily be highly speculative. Moreover, it will be strongly conditioned by the breadth of one's concept of education and optimism or pessimism about the general world outlook.

Our own conjecture is relatively optimistic—at least compared to the forecasts of professional doom-sayers. But it is qualified by two important "ifs." *If* the world economy gets back on its feet and stays there and *if* the level of overall development assistance resumes its upward course, the future volume of aid to education (broadly defined) will increase more or less in step with total development assistance.

This forecast is based on the conviction that, despite mounting criticisms of education and the disenchantment that have lately been expressed, most people the world over including political leaders will continue to attach great importance of education, in all its many forms. The critics, we believe, at least the constructive ones, can play a crucial role in the improvement of education. If they were not convinced of its importance, they would not take so much trouble to criticize it. They are not opposed to education per se but to poor education, education that is irrelevant, inefficient, and ineffective, and education marked by gross socioeconomic inequities. Whether their criticisms and remedies are right or wrong is of secondary importance. Of prime importance is that their criticisms help to focus public attention, discussion, and debate on the profound importance of education to everyone's life, and on the compelling need to change, improve, and broaden the educational status quo.

Most Effective Uses of Educational Aid

Even if the financial volume of educational aid increases in the future, the total will surely fall far short of meeting all of the enormous educational needs of developing countries. It is even more imperative, therefore, to make the most effective use of whatever assistance is available. This brings us to our second question: How can this be done?

The responsibility for shaping the decisions on priorities and allocations must reside primarily with the developing countries themselves, not the external agencies. However, in negotiating assistance agreements, and in other ways, these external agencies—because they are likely to have a broader comparative view of education in a variety of developing countries—can often help the authorities of individual countries to see their own situation and options more clearly and in a broader perspective. But they cannot unilaterally impose their judgments and preferences and expect successful results.

Without venturing any fail-safe formula, we believe the following guidelines could be of help to any country in sizing up its own best uses of external assistance. The guidelines themselves spring from the previous analytical chapters of this report and their essence is suggested by the words *balance, leverage, program support* (as distinct from projects), *innovation,* and *analytical and management capacity.*

1. Balance. All developing countries have serious gaps and imbalances within what we have called their overall lifelong learning network. To begin with there are evident imbalances within their formal education systems. One of the most serious is typically the underdevelopment of first-level education in relation to the secondary and tertiary levels. There are also serious imbalances and gaps between their formal education provisions for children and youth and their nonformal education provisions for preschool children, older youths, and adults. There are gross imbalances in educational opportunities between rural and urban areas, males and females, and people of different socioeconomic status. And there is a whole series of imbalances and maladjustments between the learning outputs of these various educational provisions and the realistic learning and development needs of both the learners and their society.

The first requirement for formulating the most fruitful proposals for external assistance, therefore, is to develop a broad overview and assessment of these imbalances and to identify those that merit first attention. If this overview and the identification of priorities is itself to be balanced and even-handed, it must be done by people of broad analytical vision and with no vested interest in any particular level, type, or institution of education.

2. Leverage. External assistance, even if the total increases, will never be more than a small fraction of the total educational expenditures of developing countries. The countries themselves must provide for the great bulk of these expenditures from their own public and private resources. This being the case, the second requirement for formulating the most fruitful proposals for external assistance is to identify those priority needs for which external assistance has a substantial comparative advantage— namely, those that the country is least able to provide by itself because of the unavailability of appropriate human resources, equipment, supplies, and funds for acquiring them. Because the resulting list will inevitably exceed the amount of external aid likely to be available, it is important to select those things that can ultimately have the greatest leverage in broadening and strengthening the nation's overall learning network. The items discussed below will generally rank high in this category.

3. Program Aid versus Project Aid. External assistance agencies have been afflicted for years by a disease known as "projectitis." The typical project is characterized by (1) a relatively narrow focus on some particular educational element or institution and geographic area, (2) a project plan with a list of required human and physical inputs and a timetable indicating when various activities are supposed to occur, and (3) a budget based on the projected input costs. The underlying premise is that the designers of the project have an uncanny ability to foresee and provide for all contingencies and that if the implementers stick faithfully to the plan, timetable, and budget, all will go well and the objectives will be achieved. If things do not in fact go as expected and some midcourse corrections are called for, getting clearance for such deviations from the plan may prove to be more trouble than it is worth. The time schedule usually provides three to five years for the "completion" of the project, and unless an extension is negotiated, an automatic time bomb goes off and the external assistance terminates abruptly, leaving the country, ready or not, to carry on by itself.

This project approach has several distinct advantages from the external assistance agency's point of view. A project has the appearance of something very concrete—something the people back home can visualize and appreciate; it offers a neatly wrapped package; it can be tailored to fit a limited budget, thus enabling the donor agency to support more projects in more countries (each represented by a colorful pin on a world map); it puts a clear limitation on the size and duration of the agency's financial commitment; and not least of all, it wears the agency's own identification, enabling it to point to "our project." External agencies themselves have their own problems of securing funds from sometimes very critical and reluctant providers, such as national legislatures, which in turn are very sensitive to public opinion; therefore, these advantages are not inconsequential.

From the point of view of the recipient country, however, these advantages are often disadvantages. For one thing, the project, particularly if it is a so-called pilot project, is frequently the brainchild of a visiting expert or of some ingenious designer back in the agency's headquarters, thousands of miles away. Thus, the country itself tends to regard it as somebody else's project, not its own, and may feel no great commitment or enthusiasm for keeping the project alive at its own expense after the external assistance has dried up—especially if it was not too keen on this project in the first place and would have much preferred a different type of assistance fitted to its own ideas and priorities. In addition, these pilot projects have a way of being impossibly expensive, so that even those that are successful in their own limited terms cannot be replicated on a large scale by the country within the limits of its own resources. All this explains why the landscape of the Third World today is littered with the carcasses of pilot projects that failed to pilot anybody anywhere.

Not all projects, of course, fit this description. Many have been well designed and very useful, especially when the country's own people have participated fully in the choice of the project and in its design and management. The real problem does not lie in projects as such but in the mentality that insists that all foreign assistance must always be packaged in discrete projects.

In recent years external agencies have begun to cure themselves of this disease and become more amenable to providing broader program support, not linked to a specific school or higher institution or locality but to strengthening infrastructural elements and processes that can contribute in a broader and more lasting way to the improvement of many individual institutions. One example would be external assistance over a substantial period of time, perhaps taking a variety of forms, aimed at strengthening a country's educational information base and its analytical, planning, evaluation, and management capacity. Another example would be assistance to develop and strengthen certain common services that could be beneficial to a wide variety of nonformal education activities. Yet another would be assistance over a substantial period designed to strengthen a country's educational research capabilities. There are a number of important advantages to these types of broader program support: first, they can yield enduring benefits to the country's whole educational effort; second, they can steadily reduce the country's dependence on outside experts; and third, they can help the country to spend its own educational funds more efficiently and effectively.

Few things could enhance the efficiency and effectiveness of external assistance as much as releasing developing countries from the straightjacket of the conventional project approach. Given this broader flexibility and range of choices, many would undoubtedly come up with fresh types of proposals of assured lasting value that external agencies would find attractive and worthwhile.

4. Reforms and Innovations. There is no lack of conviction in most developing countries today that major changes are needed in education and no lack of good ideas about possible alternative approaches. One major reason that these promising ideas seldom get off the ground is the lack of funds and personnel to try them out. By the time the annual education budget is approved, it is already virtually all committed to keeping the existing system operating, however poorly. Hence there is little or nothing left in the budget for significant research and experimentation to lay the groundwork for much-needed major reforms and innovations.

This is precisely where external assistance can have its maximum comparative advantage—in providing any country that has a serious commitment to introducing major educational reforms and innovations, and some promising ideas on how it wants to go about it, with some resources to help put some of these ideas into action. It is important to recognize, however, that *major* reforms and innovations, to have any real chance of success, require extensive preparation, often including preliminary experimentation over a considerable period of time. This means that in all prudence and fairness, any external assistance agency (and it could be several) willing to assist in the venture must be prepared to stay with it for considerably more than the usual time of only three to five years. These outside agencies will also be well advised not to try to dominate the process of reform and innovation with their own pet ideas and personnel, for unless the country's own personnel, including its teachers, have the major voice in shaping and managing any major reform or innovation, it almost certainly will not go well.

This does not mean, of course, that external agencies should mindlessly agree to support whatever proposal a country comes up with. They must have their own criteria and general priorities and must satisfy themselves by their own hard-nosed assessment that the country's proposal makes good sense in its particular context. If in the preliminary negotiations the country and the particular agency find themselves too far apart to possibly reach agreement without seriously compromising either the country's proposed approach or the agency's basic principles and policies, then it is far better to terminate that particular negotiation and look for some other kind of proposal in a different area where their respective thinking is more in harmony.

There is nothing really new about any of these suggested guidelines; they have been expressed many times before, and here and there actually put into action. What *is* new is that the atmosphere of the 1980s, both in the developing countries and in the external agencies, is much more conducive to moving in these directions than it was in previous decades. The decade of the 1970s was an important period of transition, when many conventional educational and aid dogmas were critically reexamined, challenged, modified, or rejected. It was also a time when many important new and alternative educational approaches were given a serious hearing, and in some instances an initial start. These occurrences in the 1970s created the essential conditions, including the change of attitudes and perceptions, for a substantial acceleration of much-needed educational changes in the 1980s and 1990s and for far-reaching improvements in the whole process of educational assistance. Whether full advantage will be taken of these favorable new conditions remains to be seen, but in all events, the opportunity exists.

NOTES

1. Soedjatmoko, *The Social Sciences and Global Transformation,* address to the International Symposium on the Fundamental Problems and Challenges of the Social Sciences in North America, 3 May 1983 (Ottawa: Canadian Commission for UNESCO, 1983).
2. H. M. Phillips, *Higher Education: Cooperation with Developing Countries* (New York: Rockefeller Foundation, February 1978).
3. *1982 Annual Review [of] Development Cooperation,* Efforts and Policies of the Members of the Development Assistance Committee (Paris: OECD, 1982); and *OECD Observer,* No. 122, May 1983.
4. Phillips, *Higher Education.*
5. Derived from Organisation for Economic Co-operation and Development, Development Assistance Committee, *Annual Reviews.*
6. *1982 Annual Report* (Washington, D.C.: The World Bank, 1982).

Appendix Table 10.1 World Bank Lending for Education and Training, 1970–82 (current prices in millions of U.S. dollars)

	Annual Averages for the Periods Indicated			
	1970–74 (actual)	1975–78 (actual)	1979–82 (actual)	1979–83 (projected)
Total Bank/IDA lending	3,076.0	6,846.0	11,699.8	11,580.0
Loans and credits to education sector	163.0	281.0	522.5	600.0
(As percentage of total lending by World Bank/IDA)	(5.3)	(4.0)	(4.7)	(5.2)
Education and training components in other sectors	6.5	131.0	306.9	305.0
Total lending for education and training	169.5	412.0	859.4	905.0
(As percentage of Total lending by World Bank/IDA)	(5.5)	(6.0)	(7.3)	(7.8)

Source: World Bank, Education Department, Washington, D.C., 1983.

Appendix Table 10.2 OCED/DAC Bilateral Allocations to Education Sector, 1975–81 (in current and constant prices, alternative methods, in billions of U.S. dollars)[a]

Year	(A) In Current Prices	(B) Constant 1981 Prices (OECD/GNP Deflator)	(C) Constant 1975 Prices (IMF Consumer Price Changes)
1975	1.55	2.36	1.55
1976	1.28	1.89	1.17
1977	1.72	2.36	1.44
1978	2.09	2.49	1.59
		$2.57	$1.50
1979	2.66	2.89	1.79
1980	3.40	3.29	1.88
1981	2.60	2.60	1.18

[a]Columns B and C show the results of two alternative methods of converting current prices into constant prices (real amounts).

Source: (Column A) OECD/DAC, *Annual Reviews,* 1977 through 1982; (Column B) OECD/DAC, *1982 Annual Review,* Table II, G.2, p. 252; (Column C) "Changes in Consumer Prices, 1963–82," Industrial Countries, *World Economic Outlook, 1982* (Washington, D.C., International Monetary Fund, 1982), Appendix B, Table 7, p. 148.

Appendix Table 10.3 Percentage of Total Bilateral
Aid Allocated to Education Sector by OECD/DAC
Members

Country	1975–76 Percent	1980 Percent	1981 Percent
Australia	13.8	5.8	5.8
Austria	8.6	14.3	7.2
Belgium	1.7	3.7	4.7
Canada	5.1 (1976)	0.3	4.7
Denmark	2.6	5.2	6.0
France	33.9	39.4	25.9
Germany	15.2	12.5	14.0
Japan	1.5	2.7	2.6
Netherlands	13.1	8.8	12.5
New Zealand	3.6	16.9	15.4
Norway	4.5	2.3	2.1
Sweden	9.8	4.4	10.4
Switzerland	4.4	6.0	9.2
United Kingdom	10.6 (1976)	15.6	18.8
United States	2.5	6.1	5.4
Total DAC	16.6 (1976)	13.9	11.3

Source: OECD/DAC, *Annual Reviews,* 1977, 1978, and 1982.

Appendix Table 10.4 Distribution of World Bank Lending for the Education Sector, 1963–82[a] (percent)

Distribution	1963–69	1970–74	1975–78	1979–82
By level				
Primary	b	5	14	19
Secondary	84	50	43	34
Higher	12	40	26	33
Nonformal	4	5	17	14
Total	100	100	100	100
By curricula				
General and diversified	44	42	34	23
Technical and commercial	25	30	41	49
Agriculture	19	15	11	8
Teacher training	12	12	12	15
Management	b	b	1	4
Health and population	b	1	1	1
Total	100	100	100	100
By outlay				
Construction	69	49	48	37
Equipment	28	43	39	46
Technical assistance	3	8	13	17
Total	100	100	100	100
By scope				
General institutional development				
Learning materials and media	c	2	2	7
Curriculum development	c	1	2	1
Planning and management	c	1	3	5
Specific schools and training institutions	c	96	93	87
Total	c	100	100	100

[a]Excludes project-related training and education components in multisectoral projects.
[b]Zero or negligible.
[c]Data not available.
Source: World Bank Education Department, Washington, D.C., 1983.

CHAPTER 11

INTERNATIONAL COOPERATION (II): PEOPLE, IDEAS, AND KNOWLEDGE

WE SHIFT our attention now to the three remaining categories of international educational cooperation mentioned earlier: foreign students; intellectual, scientific, and cultural exchanges; and the study of foreign areas and languages and broader international affairs. Although these categories, as well as educational development assistance, overlap considerably, it is worth repeating for emphasis that there is value in focusing on each one separately.

CHANGES IN FOREIGN STUDENT FLOWS AND POLICIES

By far the most dynamic sector of international educational cooperation in the 1970s was the exchange of students. Despite adverse world economic conditions, the total number of foreign students around the world doubled between 1970 and 1980, reaching a total of about 1 million. There were also significant changes in the pattern of flow and in the policies of several major host countries bearing on foreign students.

This portion of our discussion addresses the following questions: Where did all these students come from and where did they go to study? How were they financed? What did they study, and at what levels? How did the receiving countries react? What new factors entered the picture in the 1970s that are likely to influence the size and pattern of foreign student flows in the future? What policy issues and options now face sending countries and host countries? The available evidence for the answers to

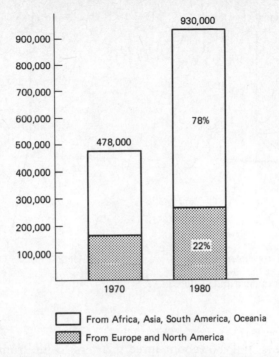

Figure 11.1. Increase in foreign students by region of origin. North America, as defined by UNESCO, includes Central America and the Caribbean. The numbers shown are incomplete. A reasonable estimate of the actual world total in 1979 would be close to 1 million. [Source: Based on data from UNESCO, *Statistical Yearbook, 1983* (Paris: UNESCO, 1983).]

these question is limited, but there is enough to provide a fairly good indication of the important trends.*

Where They Came From and Where They Studied

The extraordinary increase in the world's total of foreign students between 1970 and 1980 is shown graphically in Figure 11.1. A summary picture of the regions they came from and the regions where they were studying in 1980 is portrayed in Figure 11.2. The great majority of all

*We found three sources especially useful: first, UNESCO's annual *Statistical Yearbooks,* which, although incomplete, provide the only available worldwide picture of the magnitude and changing geographic pattern of foreign student flows; second, the yearly census reports—*Open Doors* (published annually since 1955 by the nongovernmental Institute of International Education in New York)—which provide a remarkably detailed picture of the changing foreign stu-

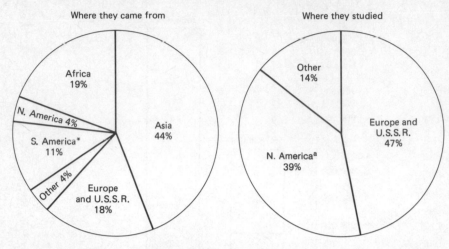

Figure 11.2. Foreign students, 1979. [*Source:* Data from UNESCO, *Statistical Yearbook,* 1982 (Paris: UNESCO, 1982).]
[a]Includes Central America and Caribbean

foreign students in 1980 (about three quarters) came from developing countries, but over 8 out of every 10 of them were studying in North America, Europe, and the U.S.S.R. The proportion of the total represented by students from developing countries had increased substantially from 15 to 20 years earlier, when student exchanges within and between Europe and North America constituted a much higher proportion of the total than they do today.

The leading countries of origin, with 10,000 or more students studying abroad in 1980, are listed in Appendix Table 11.1. The top five, in descending order, were Iran, Greece, Malaysia, China (including Taiwan), and Nigeria. The five leading host countries, with 50,000 or more foreign students each in 1980, are listed in Appendix Table 11.2. They include the United States, France, the U.S.S.R., the Federal Republic of Germany, and the United Kingdom, which together hosted more than

---

dent situation in the United States (which hosts nearly one third of all foreign students in the world); and third, a recently published study in the United Kingdom (Peter Williams, ed., *The Overseas Student Question: Studies for a Policy,* sponsored by the Overseas Student Trust [Suffolk: Chaucer Press, Ltd., 1981]) that focuses primarily on the United Kingdom but also provides useful comparative information on other important host countries, as well as an unusually penetrating discussion of critical policy issues and options relating to foreign students.

two thirds of the world total in 1980. All five had more than twice as many foreign students in 1980 as in 1970.

The mix of foreign students in these host countries from different countries of origin is strongly influenced (as seen earlier in the case of foreign aid flows) by such factors as language, former colonial and other traditional ties, and current political and economic relations and interests. Thus, for example, over half of the foreign students in France in recent years have come from former French colonies in Africa (mainly North Africa), whereas students from Commonwealth countries are predominant in the United Kingdom's total. The mix in the United States is much more of a hodge-podge; in 1981–82 they came from 192 different countries and territories from all corners of the earth. A general picture of the various mixes of foreign students among the five major host countries by 1978, by regions of origin, is presented in Appendix Table 11.3.

The Changing Geographic Pattern

Changing economic and political conditions during the 1970s prompted some marked changes in the geographic flows of foreign students. The most striking of these, in regional terms, were the greatly increased influxes of students from OPEC countries, mainly in the Middle East and Africa, into the Western industrial countries. South and Southeast Asia continued to dominate the world total, but its percentage share declined significantly. We can illustrate some of these changes in terms of specific countries of origin by examining the changing foreign student picture in the United States and the United Kingdom during this period. In the United States, as shown in Appendix Table 11.4, major changes occurred between 1969–70 and 1981–82 in the list of the 15 leading countries of origin of foreign students, which accounted in 1981–82 for 60 percent of the U.S. total. Six new countries had joined the list by 1981–82, replacing six that were on the 1969–70 list. The newcomers included Nigeria, Japan, Saudi Arabia, Malaysia, Lebanon, and Jordan. Those no longer among the leading 15 included Cuba, the United Kingdom, the Philippines, the Federal Republic of Germany, Israel, and Colombia. (Most of these "drop-off" countries, however, still had a sizable number of students in the United States in 1981–82, but to qualify as one of the leading 15 that year meant having more than 6000 students, compared to only 2000 in 1969–70.) The number of students in the United States from OPEC countries (primarily Iran, Nigeria, Venezuela, and Saudi Arabia) increased sevenfold during the 1970s, boosting their percentage of total foreign students from 9 percent in 1970 to 35 percent in 1980.[1]

Changes in the foreign student picture in the United Kingdom between

1969–70 and 1978–79 are portrayed in Appendix Table 11.5, which shows the sending countries with more than 1000 students in the United Kingdom in each of these years. The countries are listed in rank order as of 1978–79, which is a quite different order from that of 1969–70. In the meantime, the list had increased from 11 to 18. All but one country (Pakistan) in the earlier group were still on the list in 1978–79, and most had expanded somewhat their number of overseas students in the United Kingdom. But the really gigantic increases involved Malaysia (up from 1713 to 13,308), Iran (up from 1074 to 9095), Nigeria (up from 1473 to 5896), and Hong Kong (up from 1053 to 5133). The newcomers to the list, in rank order, are Greece, Iraq, Jordan, Singapore, Rhodesia (Zimbabwe). Turkey, Canada, Federal Republic of Germany, and Libya. Significantly, 9 of the 18 countries on the list in 1978–79 were not members of the British Commonwealth, compared to only 2 of the 11 countries on the list in 1969–70.

In 1978, France was host for 14 percent of all foreign students, totaling 108,000. The countries of origin with more than 2000 students that year, listed in rank order, were Morocco, Algeria, Lebanon, Greece, Iran, the United States, Federal Republic of Germany, and the United Kingdom— all countries with strong traditional ties to France.

Academic Preferences

An important question to be asked is what all of these overseas students study, and how useful it is likely to be to their future careers and their countries' needs. Unfortunately, UNESCO does not collect this type of information, so we must again fall back on data from the United States and the United Kingdom.

One significant academic change during the 1970s in both of these host countries was the substantial rise in the proportion of undergraduate foreign students and the corresponding percentage decline (though not in actual numbers) of graduate students. In the United States the undergraduate proportion increased from 52 percent of the total in 1969–70 to nearly 65 percent in 1979–80. In the United Kingdom a similar trend was observed. During the five years from 1973–74 to 1978–79, the ratio of overseas undergraduate students in the universities rose from 40 to 50 percent. However, if all overseas students in the United Kingdom are included in the calculation, including those enrolled in nonuniversity institution, then two thirds were studying at an undergraduate level in 1978–79—roughly the same percentage as in the United States.

In both of these countries, however, despite this increase the proportion of overseas undergraduates remained much lower than that of home students. Nevertheless, many educators and officials feel that young people, particularly from developing countries, should complete their undergraduate studies at home if at all possible and only then go abroad for advanced study, especially if the subject they seek is not available at home. One consideration behind this view is that younger students are most easily uprooted from their own culture when they stay abroad in a different culture for an extended period. Another is that younger students are less likely to return home than more mature ones, and even if they do return they are less likely to find a satisfactory job. Most students from developing countries, however, hold a quite different view, based on very practical considerations. Even if their own country has one or more universities, their degrees do not carry as much prestige and economic value as a degree from a well-known university in an industrial country. Moreover, in a number of their countries the universities are frequently shut down by strikes, civil disturbances, or political fiat, leaving serious students high and dry.

This lure of foreign degrees, however, is also a cause of concern among many educators and others in developing countries. Felipe Herrera, the distinguished Chilean who served as president of the Inter-American Development Bank for many years and was a staunch supporter of Latin American universities, observed recently that few of these universities would ever achieve excellence as long as European and North American degrees were considered more prestigious than local degrees, and thus continued to attract many of the best Latin American students abroad for both their undergraduate and post-graduate education.

Apart from this rise in the proportion of undergraduates, what did the foreign students actually study when they came to the United States or the United Kingdom? The answer for the United States is illustrated in Figure 11.3, which shows changes between 1969–70 and 1980–81 in the distribution of foreign students by subject fields. As will be seen, the outstanding favorites have been engineering and business management—both of which gathered further strength during the 1970s. Not surprisingly, enrollments in mathematics and computer sciences also grew substantially in the 1970s. The most striking declines, on the other hand, were in the humanities, social sciences, and natural and life sciences. Strangely, agriculture—a subject of extreme importance to most developing countries, and one in which the United States is strong—enrolled less than 3 percent of all foreign students throughout the decade.

The nearest comparable figures for the United Kingdom, for the academic year 1977–78 only, are contained in Appendix Table 11.6. They

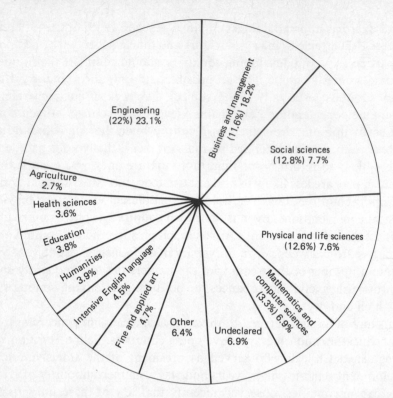

Figure 11.3. Distribution of U.S. foreign students by major fields of study, 1969–70 versus 1981–82 (percentages in brackets are for 1969–70). [Source: Redrawn from *Open Doors, 1981/82* (New York: Institute of International Education, 1983).]

combine university undergraduates and postgraduate students with those attending nonuniversity postsecondary institutions. As in the United States, engineering and technology were the favorites, with social, administrative, and business studies a strong second. Enrollments in science, however, are significantly higher in the United Kingdom than in the United States (though this may reflect in part differences in classification).

These changes in the popularity of different subject fields among foreign students undoubtedly reflect their changing expectations about future employment opportunities. Far fewer of them today, compared to 15 or 20 years ago, confidently expect to get a high-level government post or a university teaching position when they return home. Hence more and more of them are looking to the private sector, which helps explain the growing interest in technology and business administration and management. Their academic choices are also related to their sources of finance, to which we now turn.

The Financing of Foreign Students

In the area of financing, the picture also appears to have changed since 1970, mainly in the direction of a higher proportion of self-financed foreign students. This seems quite clearly to be the case in the United States. Not only did the number of foreign students double, but so did tuition fees and other college and university costs, whereas the number of scholarships and fellowships for foreign students, if anything, declined. The *Open Doors* census of foreign students in 1981–82 revealed that two thirds of them were financed by their own or family resources. The next largest primary sources of finance were the home governments (for 13.4 percent of foreign students) and the host college or university (9.4 percent). Surprisingly, the U.S. government was the primary source of support for only 2.3 percent of foreign students. We have found no comparable figures for Western European countries but suspect that the majority of their guest students are also self-financed, although the central government of the host country in most cases provides financial assistance to a larger proportion of students than the U.S. government.

Apart from the out-of-pocket costs incurred by foreign students—for such things as travel, tuition fees, books, and board and room—there are substantial hidden costs borne by the host institution (or the host government), mainly in the form of instructional costs that substantially exceed tuition fees. These instructional subsidies tend to run much higher for foreign students than domestic students because a much higher proportion of them enroll in high-cost courses at both the undergraduate and graduate level, such as engineering and science, which involve extensive laboratory work and equipment and often a much lower student/faculty ratio. In the United Kingdom in 1977–78, for example, overseas students constituted only 7 percent of total undergraduate students in the universities but 21 percent of enrollments in engineering and technology. At the graduate level their proportions were much higher. There they constituted 37 percent of all students, but 57 percent of total enrollments in engineering and technology, 56 percent in agriculture and forestry, and 44 percent in medicine. In the United States there has been a similar concentration of foreign students in higher cost undergraduate and graduate fields. This pattern applies not only to students from developing countries, but even more to those from high-income industrial countries, many of whom go abroad for specific graduate studies and higher degrees.

New Restrictions on Foreign Students

During the second half of the 1970s, growing concern over these high hidden costs of foreign students, coupled with the continuing upsurge in their total number, prompted most Western European governments to institute new measures aimed at curbing the inflow of foreign students and their cost to the public treasury. These restrictive measures warrant special attention here because they have major implications for the future and pose serious policy questions.

In the heady atmosphere of goodwill and cooperation that prevailed during the first two decades after World War II, the welcome mat was out in virtually all the developed nations of the North for foreign students, especially from the newly independent nations of the South. By and large, wherever they came from, these foreign students received a warm welcome in their host institutions and communities. Indeed, colleges and universities took pride in the number and geographic diversity of their guest overseas students and often found ways to assist them financially. Host governments also encouraged this flow of students from the Third World. Although it was recognized that significant costs were involved, in both overt and hidden subsidies, it was generally accepted that they were substantially outweighed by the resulting benefits, though ill-defined and largely unmeasurable.

What had begun as a trickle, however, eventually turned into a torrent—at least by any previous standard. By the end of the 1960s, a half-million foreign students were at large in the world, a large majority concentrated in the countries of Western Europe and North America that made up the world's great "open classroom." And by the mid-1970s it was clear that this half million was well on its way to doubling by 1980. This disturbing prospect galvanized treasury officials—and in turn top education policymakers—of Western European countries. Faced with severe budget stringencies stemming from the worst economic recession in 40 years, they suddenly became more cost-conscious about foreign students and began doubting whether the great "benefits" that had long been taken for granted actually justified the high and mounting costs involved. There was also concern that this growing influx of foreign students, including many from fellow members of the European Community, might both impair educational quality and place their own students at a disadvantage in gaining admission to such expensive and oversubscribed fields as medicine, dentistry, science, engineering, and technology.

These anxieties soon gave rise to a variety of restrictive measures calculated to control a situation that was seen, especially by finance officials, as having gotten out of hand. In devising these restrictive measures, each country went its own way, generally giving priority consideration to its own national problems and its own economic, political, and educational interests. One gets the impression that the particular restrictions were often framed in a hurry, with little effort to assess their likely impact on different categories of students and countries, or even on the higher institutions of the host country.

Some of the Western European countries, in keeping with their particular traditions and philosophy of government, adopted a "direct regulation approach," whereas others took a "free market, price approach."[2] Either way, the net effect was that for the first time since World War II the great Western European open classroom which had so generously welcomed qualified students from all corners of the world, suddenly began to be less open. France, for example, adopted a classic regulatory approach. As early as 1974 it introduced a system of pre-inscription whereby foreign students desiring to study in France were required to submit their application for approval before they left home. This pre-inscription system was greatly tightened in 1979 by the so-called Imbert Decree, which required intending foreign students to pass a French-language proficiency test in their home country and to give proof of having a bank account with sufficient funds to carry them through their first cycle. Moreover, this decree replaced the previous system, under which a foreign student had been able to apply for admission to a particular university that would then make its own decision, with a central commission that would receive and decide on external applications and then allocate the successful applicants to a specific university of its own choosing.

In 1979, the United Kingdom, in keeping with the free market philosophy of its ruling Conservative government at the time, adopted a "market price" approach whereby most foreign students would be obliged to pay a full-cost tuition. Under the minimum recommended fees for overseas students, effective in 1980–81, shown in Appendix Table 11.7, newly entering foreign students would pay fees ranging from almost double to over six times as great as those for home students.*

Several other Western European countries approached the matter by reinstituting the old *numerus clausus* limitations in certain oversubscribed fields of study, applicable to their own students as well as foreign

---

*Actually, these so-called full-cost tuition fees, calculated by the government on the basis of average current costs per student, were considerably less than the true real cost per student, as demonstrated by Professor Mark Blaug in his chapter on "The Economic Costs and Benefits of Overseas Students" in Williams, *The Overseas Student Question*.

students. In deference to foreign students, however, Germany (F.R.) and Norway, reserved a portion of each quota for outside students (though there was no assurance that those from the poorest countries would get an equitable share). Two other countries—Austria and Switzerland—with long-standing reputations for generosity to foreign students, particularly in such fields as medicine, dentistry, and veterinary medicine, began imposing severe restrictions on them in the mid-1970s aimed in part at protecting their own students against excessive competition. In 1975, foreign students (primarily from other Western European countries) constituted over 14 percent of all higher education enrollments in Austria, and over 22 percent in Switzerland. But by 1980–81 there were reportedly no places at all open in any Swiss university for a foreign student desiring to pursue a full course in medicine, dentistry, or veterinary science. Austria was reported in 1979–80 to have imposed a complete ban on foreign students in the University of Veterinary Medicine in Vienna. The Universities of Graz, Innsbruck, and Vienna had similar prohibitions in medicine, certain natural sciences, journalism, and psychology but more moderate restrictions in other fields.[3]

Belgium, whose universities had traditionally charged virtually no tuition fees, adopted an ingenious two-price system for foreign students expressly calculated to favor students from the poorest developing countries while at the same time curbing the influx of neighboring European students escaping the *numerus clausus* restrictions in their own countries. The new tuition fees, introduced in 1980–81, were set at roughly 50 percent of the previous year's government subsidy in each field. They applied to students from any country with an average per capita income above $600, but students from poorer countries were exempt. This fair-minded treatment of the poorer countries, however, left the French-speaking Belgian universities vulnerable to a heavy spillover of students from low-income Francophone countries who were unable to make it through the tightened restrictions in France.

An overview of this assortment of new curbs in Western Europe designed to retard or even reverse the large inflow of foreign students was reminiscent of an economic battle of mercantilistic national trade barriers. It remained to be seen what the ultimate (and unanticipated) repercussions and reactions would be on the part of neighboring European countries, the developing countries, and the universities of the countries imposing the barriers. As far as the poorer developing countries were concerned, this new restrictive environment was clearly bad news, for it unquestionably placed their students, and the countries themselves, at a serious disadvantage. The first conference of the Commonwealth Ministries of Education after the announcement of the new U.K. policy of full-cost tuition for foreign students expressed deep concern over the move.

The meeting of Commonwealth Heads of Government in 1981 took note of this new development, and in their final communiqué they called on member governments to give "early and sympathetic consideration" to proposed steps for dealing with the problem. Later, the secretary-general set up a Commonwealth Standing Committee on Student Mobility to consider ways to alleviate the problems created by increased fee levels imposed by "some member countries." In France there were great student demonstrations against the new restrictions. In Britain many university people and opposition members of Parliament expressed grave misgivings about the new tuition policy. Though they readily conceded that there was a real problem, they challenged the wisdom and fairness of the particular solution the government had adopted.

Meanwhile, across the Atlantic in the United States and Canada, the traditional free-market academic pricing system was busily at work—not as the result of any newly imposed central government policy (since the central governments in these federal systems were not concerned with higher education admission requirements, instructional budgets, and tuition fees), but simply as a matter of long practice. Tuition charges in both public and private colleges and universities moved sharply upward during the 1970s, creating increasingly serious barriers for aspiring students, both domestic and foreign, with slim resources. Though many received at least partial scholarships from their institution—and practically all received substantial hidden subsidies in the form of tuition fees well below the real costs of instruction—available scholarship funds could not keep pace with the rapidly increasing charges.

State colleges and universities in the United States, whose tuition fees had generally been well below those of private institutions, though somewhat higher for out-of-state students (including foreign students), now began to widen the spread between in-state and out-of-state students. Increasing fears were expressed by many academics that parochially minded state legislators and budget officers would follow the course of some European countries and impose prohibitive restrictions on foreign students in the interest of economy. Even without such restrictions, however, the combination of sharply rising tuition fees and the greatly increased price of the U.S. dollar in terms of foreign currencies, served increasingly to ration college and university places to those foreign students who had the greatest personal means or could obtain a scholarship from their home country.

Perplexing Policy Issues

Some grave policy dilemmas have been left in the wake of these new restrictive measures against foreign students that took shape in the 1970s and early 1980s. Ironically, they came at the very time when domestic student enrollments in higher education in these countries, after years of rapid expansion and strain, were beginning to stagnate and in some cases even decline. Hence, for some years to come the colleges and universities of the Western industrial nations will be in a better position, in terms of available capacity, to absorb more foreign students than ever before. But this was not the central question on the mind of the financial authorities in these countries who carried heavy weight in these policy decisions. Their central question was, and remains: *Who will pay the costs?* National authorities in developing countries are equally concerned with the same question, but they view it from a quite different angle. From their angle, nothing less than their nation's continuing development is at stake.

There can be no doubt that the host countries and their educational institutions are indeed faced with troublesome educational financing problems, quite apart from foreign students. Nor is there any doubt that these problems have been aggravated somewhat by the sharp increase in the number of foreign students—at least to the extent that their overseas education is partly or wholly subsidized by the host government or institution. Some argue that the marginal cost of adding a few more foreign students is lower than the average cost per student. This is only true, however, where economies of scale are available, and even then the added marginal cost can still be substantial. But consider what happens to both the average and marginal cost when large and increasing numbers of foreign students are concentrated in the highest cost fields of study, which has been the case in many host countries. Then there is reasonable cause for concern.

The size of the costs, and who pays them, are not the only important questions, however, although they have dominated much of the debate. There are also serious questions concerning benefits and fairness, which have tended to be swept aside by the advocates of greater restrictions on foreign students. In his recent attempt to assess the purely economic benefits accruing to the United Kingdom—such as future trade advantages—from its public investment in foreign students, Mark Blaug, a professor of the economics of education at the University of London Institute of Education, attempted to bring the benefits side of the equation into the open. His conclusion was that the economic benefits of foreign students to the United Kingdom were substantially outweighed by the costs they imposed on the public treasury.[4] He may well be right, although admittedly any such calculation of current and future national economic benefits is highly speculative at best and could prove to be wide of the mark. Blaug was careful, however, to point out that there were presumably other *noneconomic* benefits that cannot be quantitatively measured and that were excluded from his calculations. But, the fact that these more intangible benefits cannot be fed into a computer makes them no less real and important. They include, for example, international goodwill and constructive foreign relations; the undoubted contribution that many foreign students make to research and teaching in their host institution and to broadening and deparochializing the education and outlook of home students; and, not least of all, the important role that some foreign students play in the later development and stability of their own nation—a matter in which the United Kingdom and all other industrial countries have a large future stake.

The obvious difficulty, of course, is that the extent of these intangible benefits (and this is true as well of the seemingly more tangible economic benefits) varies greatly from student to student, depending on such factors as their personal characteristics and talents, what country they come from, whether they actually return to it, and if so what kind of position they will eventually occupy. Still, a national policy aimed not simply at minimizing the costs of foreign students to the host government, but also at maximizing the benefits they can bring to it (including benefits to their own country's future development and stability that can indirectly benefit the host country) ought to give serious weight to these imponderables. Granted, it is impossible to predict the future careers of individual students and the kind of contributions each will make. But it is certainly possible to identify their country of origin, and there are long-standing academic mechanisms for judging their basic abilities and qualifications and the extent of their financial needs. These factors and perhaps other relevant ones could be carefully taken into account in the admission of applicants and the assignment of scholarships. From all appearances, however, most of the hurriedly contrived new restrictive measures in Western Europe were aimed singlemindedly at minimizing the immediate financial burden on the host countries, with little regard to these longer term benefits or damaging fallout. By and large they are based on a standardized formula that applies indiscriminately to a mixed assortment of aspiring foreign students, coming from widely differing countries and having widely differing financial means.

That brings up the fundamental fairness question, which in the long run could be the most important one, for even to *appear* to disregard fairness can do great damage to the climate of international cooperation. The new regulatory and tuition-boosting measures in their present form not only have the appearance but the clear practical effect of being highly discriminatory. They discriminate against the impecunious but able student in favor of the affluent one. They discriminate against the poorer countries, most in need of well-educated people, in favor of countries that can far better afford the high cost of sending their students overseas. The same is true, of course, of the sharply increased tuition fees and other essential student costs in the great open academic marketplace of North America, although they were not intentionally directed against foreign students. (Indeed, they are having the same discriminatory impact on able but indigent domestic student.) In both situations the negative impact is all the greater in the absence of adequate and well-directed scholarship and student loan funds (which in the early 1980s were cut back by the Reagan Administration in a fit of economizing on everything—save the military budget).

In short, from the point of view of outsiders, and many insiders as well, something serious and sad happened in the late 1970s to the great tradition of generosity and evenhandedness the Western nations had always shown toward qualified foreign students, whatever their means or origin. Access to the great open classroom of the Western world, which so many had counted on for so long, was now strewn with new obstacles and could no longer be counted on with assurance. It was well understood that these host nations had serious educational financing problems they needed to do something about and that foreign students were part of that problem. What was so disappointing was the particular solutions they chose to adopt. For these solutions, as viewed by both developing countries and domestic critics, including many devoted internationally minded educators, appeared not only to be shortsighted and grossly unfair to the disadvantaged but smacked of an excess of narrow national self-interest.

Sympathetic well-wishers of all the countries concerned are fervently hoping that able university people on both ends of the partnership will apply their creative minds in the immediate future to examining alternative ways of achieving the desired objectives without creating so many damaging educational, political, and human side effects and that their counsel will be heeded by top policymakers. It is by no means an easy problem to solve, but there must be better solutions than those now in place.

One also hopes that more attention and assistance will be given to encouraging a large horizontal flow of foreign students between the developing countries themselves. That flow did increase somewhat in the 1970s, but not nearly as much as the enormous increase from South to North that helped bring on the restrictions. In addition it is vitally important to enlarge the present relative trickle of students and scholars between the Western democracies and the Eastern socialist countries, if only to correct the superficial and distorted images that each still has of the other's way of life. There is a similar urgent need for an increased two-way interchange of students and scholars between the West and China.

THE EXCHANGE OF TEACHERS, SCHOLARS, AND RESEARCH

It is generally acknowledged that international exchanges of teachers, scholars, and scientists, as well as cooperation in research, have played, and continue to play, a vital role in the generation, sharing, and diffusion of knowledge among nations and in elevating the quality of education everywhere. It is important to ask, therefore, what happened to these kinds of international traffic during the decades of the 1970s. The available evidence, though much too limited to answer this question definitively, suggests some basic trends and changes.

Teachers

During the 1950s and 1960s when many developing countries were not yet able to supply sufficient trained teachers of their own to meet their rapidly expanding needs, especially in secondary and higher education, large numbers of temporary teachers were provided by developed countries to help fill the gap. A large proportion of these teachers were financed under official aid programs, but many were also provided by voluntary organizations or came on their own as individual volunteers. In the meantime, parallel steps were taken to increase the capacity of developing countries to train their own teachers and to train many abroad, especially at the postsecondary level.

This combination of actions clearly achieved far-reaching results. By the early to mid-1970s most countries of Asia and Latin America—except for some of the smaller and poorer ones that got a late start on educational development (such as Nepal and Afghanistan)—were able to meet their own teacher requirements at all levels, except for selective shortages at the postsecondary level. By this time a good number of African countries had also sharply reduced their earlier heavy dependence on expatriate teachers. For example, in 1964 only 44 percent of secondary teachers in Kenya were native Kenyans, whereas in 1976, despite a large increase in secondary enrollments in the interim, this figure had grown to 73 percent.[5] In Malawi, the proportion of expatriate teachers declined from 80 percent in 1965 to 32 percent in 1976.[6] In some African countries, however, there is still a serious shortage in higher education in certain subject areas. In Botswana—one of the "late starters"—only one quarter of all secondary teachers in 1975 were locals.[7] In Senegal in the same year, more than half the faculty at the University Technology Institution were foreigners.[8] The 1970s were also notable for a large buildup of foreign professors in the rapidly expanding new higher institutions in Middle East oil-producing countries—most dramatically in the case of

Saudi Arabia. There was also a marked increase in the number of foreign professors and teachers, especially of English, in the People's Republic of China, and a substantial reverse flow of Chinese students and scholars to Western nations.

Overall, however, it seems clear that the number of foreign teachers in developing countries sponsored by official development agencies declined sharply in the 1970s. As we saw earlier, the total number from OECD countries (by far the largest suppliers) dropped off 40 percent between 1969 and 1975 (from nearly 60,000 to less than 36,000). In those years and since, France has been by far the largest supplier of teachers, mainly to its former colonies in Africa and its present overseas territories. There are still many volunteer foreign teachers, especially in Africa where the need remains the greatest, but their total number has undoubtedly dwindled since 1970.

Scholars and Research

There are even fewer firm facts about recent trends in university scholars going abroad to teach or do research. No organization keeps score on such exchanges any longer, but the general indications are that the flow of university scholars from North to South peaked in the 1960s and has since fallen off sharply. One reason, in the case of the United States, was the sharp cutback in the university contract system extensively used by USAID throughout the 1960s to assist developing countries in establishing their higher education institutions. The indications are that the number of officially sponsored scholars exchanged between OECD countries also diminished during the 1970s, although the number of unsponsored or privately sponsored exchanges may have held up somewhat better. The number of foreign scholars teaching in U.S. colleges and universities, which grew steadily up to the late 1960s, is reported to have declined substantially in the 1970s. The number of Fulbright scholars (which was never more than a small fraction of the total, but a very symbolic one) declined sharply in the 1970s and early 1980s when the allocation of U.S. government funds for this purpose failed to keep pace with inflation.

On a brighter note, the interest in development-related research on the part of bilateral and international agencies appears to have increased during the 1970s. The World Bank, for one, substantially increased its expenditures on both internal staff research and commissioned research, and more and more of its loan contracts with developing countries included a provision for research. With a view especially to building research capabilities in the Third World, the Canadian government provided strong support to IDRC in Ottawa; the Swedish government created its counterpart SAREC; and USAID continued to support a sizable and wide-ranging research program. The new United Nations University based in Tokyo strongly encouraged the formation of interdisciplinary research consortia across national lines to tackle major development problems common to many countries. Only a small fraction of all this fresh research in the 1970s and since has been directed at education per se, although much of it has extensive implications for education, especially nonformal education.

It is also evident that sizable international networks of cooperative research linkages have grown up over the years between individual institutions and scholars and through scholarly and scientific nongovernmental associations. Such linkages exist not only between university researchers but on a large scale also through commercial businesses that are heavily involved in technical and even basic scientific research, such as the Bell Laboratories. It would be literally impossible to keep track of all these interchanges, but the scattered evidence suggests that this expanding worldwide common market of high-level intellecutal exchanges is probably doing a more thriving business today than ever before, especially in the areas of advanced scientific and medical research and in the high-tech fields.

THE WORRISOME DECLINE IN INTERNATIONAL STUDIES

Following World War II, there was wide recognition among educators and national authorities in many countries that the first requirement for a peaceful and cooperative world in the future was for all nations, old and new alike, to learn a great deal more about each other's backgrounds, customs, and current developments, and to be able to communicate with the people of other countries in their own language.

This need was especially keenly felt in the United States, which had emerged from the war with heavy leadership responsibilities for which it was poorly prepared in these respects. The number of American scholars and experts with substantial knowledge about many of the newly independent countries of Asia and Africa could be counted on the fingers of one hand. National competence in relation to Latin America, the Soviet Union, Japan, and China was only slightly better. The European countries, especially those with experience as colonial powers, were relatively less ignorant about some of these distant parts of the world, but mainly the parts they had colonized. Thus, they too recognized the need to learn much more, not only about areas unfamiliar to them but about the fast-moving events and changes in their recently liberated former colonies.

These extensive and continuing knowledge needs presented an enormous challenge to the education systems of all countries, big and small, old and new, from the graduate universities right down to the elementary schools. It also presented a special challenge to the new international agencies—particularly UNESCO, whose mandate put heavy emphasis on promoting mutual understanding among nations.

With respect to languages, there was an immediate brisk and spontaneous demand throughout the developing world for learning French and English, which was widely catered to by the Alliance Française, the British Council, and the U.S. Information Service. A strong interest also developed in Western and Eastern Europe in learning English, which was rapidly emerging as the prime international lingua franca in science, commerce, various academic disciplines, diplomacy, and even air transport.

The heart of the problem, however, was not with these two widely known and widely used Western languages, but with the less known languages of other regions, parochially referred to in the West as exotic languages (although they were often the mother tongue of many millions of people). The problem also centered on the development and dissemination of basic knowledge of Asian and African countries and to a lesser extent, Latin American countries, which was often sparse even in the scholarly literature of the West. Knowledge in the West about the Soviet Union, Japan, and China was also surprisingly limited in view of their obvious great importance in the postwar world.

The United States, being especially ignorant considering the heavy worldwide responsibilities it had inherited, mounted a major effort—first through the initiative of major private foundaitons and later with government support—to establish new foreign area and language institutions and new programs of international studies in leading research universities. By the late 1960s enough of these institutes were present at universities to blanket all regions of the world several times over. Hundreds of graduate students were emerging with MA and Phd degrees in specialized studies relating, for example, to India and the subcontinent, Indonesia, East and West Africa, Latin America, the Middle East, Eastern Europe, Japan, and China. During this same period the study of foreign languages and international affairs was strongly promoted in the schools and undergraduate colleges and through adult education programs. The United States was at last reaching out from its continental isolation to get to know the rest of the human family.

There was a simultaneous upsurge of scholarly interest in many of the universities of Western Europe in studying less known regions and languages of the world, though the upsurge was less dramatic and extensive than across the Atlantic. The Soviet Union, for its part, feeling the same urgent need to acquire greater knowledge and competence in international affairs, created special schools in which selected children and youth were given intensive long-term training in the cultures, customs, and languages of particular foreign countries in order to groom them for various types of future careers involving international relations. Also, a series of specialized institutions was established within the framework of the Soviet Academy of Science to do continuous high-level research and analysis on current economic, political, social, scientific, and other significant developments in countries in all major regions of the world. One of the best known of these is the Institute for the Study of the United States and Canada.

Judging from the available indications, Soviet research and training in international affairs has continued to receive priority. In Western Europe and the United States, however, the earlier interest and enthusiasm rapidly waned in the 1970s. Among the prime reasons in the case of the United States were the drying up of government and foundation funds for graduate studies and for overseas travel and research; the sharp contraction of job opportunities for area and language specialists; and the shift of public and scholarly interests from overseas affairs to increasingly serious domestic issues.

By the late 1970s, there was sufficient concern in high places in the government of the United States that President Carter appointed a Special Commission on Foreign Languages and International Studies, headed by James A. Perkins, chairman of the International Council for Educational Development, to evaluate the situation and make recommendations for improving it. The commission's final report, based on a year of intensive investigation and nationwide meetings and consultations with knowledgeable academic, government, business, labor, and civic leaders, and with a number of able observers from foreign countries, came to the following conclusion:

> We are profoundly alarmed by what we have found: a serious deterioration in this country's language and research capacity, at a time when an increasingly hazardous international military, political and economic environment is making unprecedented demands on America's resources, intellectual capacity and public sensitivity.[9]

Documenting its conclusions with concrete examples from the education system, the diplomatic service, and other government agencies, from business, journalism, labor, and other facets of national life, the commission went on to observe the following:

> The problem extends from our elementary schools, where instruction in foreign languages and cultures has virtually disappeared, to the threatened imminent loss of some of the world's leading centers for advanced training and research on foreign areas. Such specific educational neglect, moreover, is reflected in public uncertainty about the relationship between American interests and goals and those of other peoples and other cultures.

One of the commission's main recommendations, which shortly materialized, opened the way to a promising avenue of international education cooperation. The recommendation was that an independent nonprofit organization be established, sponsored by various interested academic associations, business and labor groups, and civic organizations and funded by private foundations, for the purpose of stimulating public interest in, and support for, international and language studies, monitoring progress (or the lack of it) in this whole area, and taking initiatives to encourage studies on neglected problems. Soon after the report was released this new nongovernmental organization came into being, known as the National Commission on Foreign Language and International Studies. The commission promptly established a liaison with a newly formed group of Western European academic leaders who shared the same concerns. These two groups have since been meeting annually to exchange information, experiences, and ideas.

Both groups would undoubtedly agree that major and sustained effort will be required to recover the momentum and ground that was lost in this field during the 1970s. Even more, they would undoubtedly agree that, with the whole world in an unstable, rapidly changing, and precarious condition, no countries—least of all those carrying sizable international leadership responsibilities—can long afford to allow their educational and research institutions to lag behind the critical and fast-moving field of international affairs.

A similar but broader conclusion applies to all four of the interconnected sectors of international education cooperation we have sought to examine and put in perspective in these last two chapters: (1) assistance to developing countries for educational and human resources development; (2) the exchange of higher education students between countries; (3) international intellectual and cultural intercourse involving teachers, scholars, scientists, and creative artists; and (4) cooperation in strengthening international and foreign language studies in all countries.

In our attempts to peer into the cloudy and uncertain future we have found some reasons for alarm and other reasons for encouragement and hope. This much seems clear. International cooperation in education and research cannot be expected to alleviate overnight the immediate problems, but with determincd and well-directed efforts it can be expected to contribute significantly in the long run to a saner and more secure world in which all people, in all countries, can with greater confidence aspire to and work toward a better quality of life.

NOTES

1. *Open Doors 1981–82* (New York: Institute of International Education, 1983).
2. For a more detailed discussion of these different approaches, see Peter Williams, ed., *The Overseas Student Question: Studies for a Policy,* sponsored by the Overseas Student Trust (Suffolk: Chaucer Press, Ltd., 1981).
3. Ibid.
4. Mark Blaug, "The Economic Costs and Benefits of Overseas Students", in *The Overseas Student Question.*
5. Audrey C. Smock, "Education and Career Patterns in the Public Service Sector in Kenya" (Paris: International Institute for Educational Planning/UNESCO, 1978), pp. 17, 19.
6. World Bank, unpublished report, 1977.
7. Report of the National Commission on Education, *Education for Kagisano* (Gaborone, Botswana, April 1977), pp. 36–37.
8. World Bank, unpublished report, 1977.
9. Report of the President's Commission on Foreign Language and International Studies, *Strength Through Wisdom: A Critique of U.S. Capability* (Washington, D.C.: U.S. Government Printing Office, 1979).

Appendix Table 11.1 Foreign Students: Major Countries of Origin (with over 10,000 Abroad in 1980–81)

Developed Countries	Number of Students Abroad	Developing Countries	Number of Students Abroad
1. Greece	31,509	1. Iran	65,521
2. United States	19,843	2. Malaysia	35,693
3. Japan	18,066	3. China*	30,127
4. Canada	17,714	4. Nigeria	26,863
5. Federal Republic of Germany	16,983	5. Morocco	20,876
6. United Kingdom	15,776	6. Hong Kong	20,625
7. Italy	13,848	7. Venezuela	17,755
8. France	11,159	8. Jordan	17,030
		9. India	15,238
		10. Lebanon	15,117
		11. Turkey	14,606
		12. Syria	13,701
		13. Algeria	12,661
		14. Vietnam	12,403
		15. Saudi Arabia	11,701
		16. Sudan	11,008
		17. Indonesia	10,957
		18. Mexico	10,452
		19. Cyprus	10,127

*Includes Taiwan
Source: UNESCO, *Statistical Yearbook, 1983* (Paris: UNESCO, Office of Statistics, 1983).

Appendix Table 11.2 Foreign Students: Major Host Countries, in 1970 and 1980

Five Leading Countries	Number of Foreign Students	
	1970	1980
1. United States	144,708	311,880
2. France	34,500	114,181
3. U.S.S.R.	27,918	62,942 (1978)
4. Federal Republic of Germany	27,769	61,841
5. United Kingdom	24,606	56,003
Total	281,764	606,847
Percentage of world total	63	69

Source: UNESCO, *Statistical Yearbook, 1983* (Paris: UNESCO, Office of Statistics, 1983).

Appendix Table 11.3 Percentage Distribution of Foreign Students from Major World Regions among Leading Host Countries, 1978

Host Country	Region of Origin							
	Africa	Asia	Europe	U.S.S.R.	North America	South America	Oceania	TOTAL
United States	21.3	39.6	13.3	11.9	45.0	46.7	51.9	31.3
France	34.9	5.5	11.8	5.9	7.5	12.6	2.0	12.8
U.S.S.R.	8.6	5.8	11.0	—	7.1	9.4	0.0	7.5
United Kingdom	8.1	7.8	4.3	1.3	6.8	4.7	13.2	7.1
Federal Republic of Germany	2.6	5.8	13.4	3.1	5.4	4.5	1.8	6.6
TOTAL (5 largest countries)	75.5	64.5	53.8	22.2	71.8	77.9	68.9	65.3
TOTAL (15 next largest countries)	15.4	25.8	39.1	9.2	23.1	18.5	22.8	26.3
TOTAL (25 next largest countries)	9.1	9.7	7.1	68.6	5.1	3.6	8.3	8.4
GRAND TOTAL	100.0	100.0	100.0	100.0	100.0	100.0	100.0	100.0

aIncludes Bermuda, Canada, the Caribbean, Central America, Puerto Rico, and the United States.
Source: Open Doors, 1981–82 (New York: Institute of International Education, 1983), p. 5. Based on data from UNESCO Statistical Yearbook, 1981 (Paris: UNESCO, Office of Statistics, 1981).

Appendix Table 11.4 15 Leading Countries of Origin of All Foreign Students in the United States in 1981–82, Compared to Their Ranks in 1969–70

Country of Origin	1969–70		1981–82	
	Number of Students	Percentage of Total	Number of Students	Percentage of Total
Iran	5,175	3.8	35,860	11.0
Taiwan	12,029	8.9	20,520	6.3
Nigeria	a	—	19,560	6.0
Canada	13,318	9.9	14,950	4.6
Japan	a	—	14,020	4.3
Venezuela	a	—	13,960	4.3
India	11,327	8.4	11,250	3.4
Saudi Arabia	a	—	10,220	3.1
Malaysia	a	—	9,420	2.9
Hong Kong	7,202	5.3	8,900	2.8
Korea, Republic of	3,991	3.0	8,070	2.5
Mexico	2,501	1.9	7,890	2.4
Lebanon	a	—	6,800	2.1
Thailand	4,372	3.2	6,730	2.1
Jordan	—	—	6,180	1.9
TOTAL				59.7

aFewer than 2000.

Source: Open Doors, 1981–82 (New York: Institute of International Education, 1983).

Appendix Table 11.5 Countries with More than 1000 Students in the United Kingdom, 1969–70 and 1978–79

Country	Number of Students	
	1969–70	1978–79
Malaysia	1,713	13,308
Iran	1,074	9,095
Nigeria	1,473	5,896
Hong Kong	1,053	5,133
United States	2,360	3,720
Greece	a	3,148
Iraq	a	2,482
Sri Lanka	1,153	2,068
Jordan	a	1,875
Singapore	a	1,786
Cyprus	1,179	1,587
Rhodesia (Zimbabwe)	a	1,534
Turkey	a	1,463
Kenya	1,275	1,166
India	1,668	1,162
Canada	1,057	1,061
Germany (F.R.)	a	1,032
Libya	a	1,014

aFewer than 1000.

Source: Peter Williams, ed., *The Overseas Student Question: Studies for a Policy* (Suffolk: Chaucer Press, Ltd., 1981), p. 31, Table 2.4.

Appendix Table 11.6 Distribution of Overseas Students in the United Kingdom by Subject Fields, 1977–78

Subject Group	Percentage of All Classified Students
Education	4.3
Medicine, dentistry, and health	4.5
Engineering and technology	36.4
Agriculture, forestry, and veterinary science	1.3
Science	14.6
Social, administrative, and business studies	24.6
Architecture and other professional and vocational subjects	4.8
Language, literature, and area studies	3.7
Arts other than languages	5.5

Source: Peter Williams, ed., *The Overseas Student Question: Studies for a Policy* (Suffolk: Chaucer Press, Ltd., 1981).

Appendix Table 11.7 Minimum Recommended Fees for Overseas Students in the United Kingdom, effective 1980–81 (£ per annum)

	Home Students Undergraduate	Postgraduate	New Overseas Students	
Universities				
Arts	740	1105	2000	
Science	740	1105	3000	
Clinical years of medicine, dentistry, and veterinary medicine	740	1105	5000	
Nonuniversity maintained and voluntary institutions	Advanced	Nonadvanced	Advanced	Nonadvanced
Laboratory and workshop-based courses	740	595	3300	800
Classroom-based courses	740	595	2400	1380

Source: Peter Williams, ed., *The Overseas Student Question: Studies for a Policy* (Suffolk: Chaucer Press, Ltd., 1981), p. 39, Table 2.8.

INDEX

N.B.: The letters f and t following page numbers refer to figures and tables, respectively.

ACPO (Accion Cultural Popular), 89
Adiseshiah, Malcolm, 206
Adult education
  attitudes toward nonformal, 87–88
  International Council for, 98
  new organizational arrangements, 303
  Tokyo International Conference, 280
  unanswered questions, 87
Afghanistan, 51, 282
Africa. See also individual countries
  educational costs and expenditures, 144t,
    158t, 167t, 168t
  enrollment projections to year 2000, 42,
    43f
  female enrollments, 225t, 227
  foreign teachers, 329
  increase in enrollment ratios (1960–80),
    80t, 100t
  preschool enrollment, 236
  projected growth of urban and rural
    population, 49, 50f
  projected population by year 2100, 40
  sex disparities, 227, 231
  socioeconomic disparities, 231
  sub-Saharan, 199, 258
Agriculture
  decline of farmers in Europe, 47
  decline of food production, 51
  graduates in U.K., U.S., and developing
    countries, 56–57
  share of labor force and GNP, 11
Ahmed, Manzoor, 32, 63, 98, 135, 284
Aims of education, 67–69, 69–71, 112

Anderson, Arnold, 205
Anwar, A. A., 205
Arab States, 225t
Araujo Oliveira, J. B., 135
Aristotle, caution about precision, 35
Arkleton Trust, 56, 62
Asia. See also East Asia; South Asia;
    individual countries
  educational costs and expenditures, 144t,
    158t, 159f, 167t, 168t
  female enrollments, 227
  foreign students, 317
  foreign teachers, 329
  preschool enrollment, 236
  socioeconomic disparities, 231
Austin, Jane, 224
Australia, 56, 71, 185, 219
Austria, 324
Avakov, R., 205

Bangladesh, 10, 12, 58, 89, 272
Basic education, 26. See also Learning
    needs; Nonformal education; Primary
    education
Beier, George, 62
Belgium, 324
Bell Laboratories, 331
Benin, 237
Bernard Van Leer Foundation, 299
Blaugh, Mark, 206, 323, 326, 335
Bolivia, 200, 223
Borders, William, 206

Botkin, James W., 33n
Botswana, 90, 131, 329
Bowen, Howard, 152–54, 167
Bowles, Samuel, 240
Bowman, Mary Jean, 205
Brazil, 45, 78–79, 200, 225–26
Bronte, Charlotte, 224
Brumberg, S. F., 135
Bulgaria, 193, 207t, 208t
Burma, 225

Cameroon, 225
Canada
  foreign students, 318, 325
  increase in labor force and employment,
    184
  meeting rural learning needs, 56
  rising cost per student, 146–47, 169t
  women in higher education, 225
  youth unemployment, 185
Carnegie Commission on Higher
  Education, 71
Carnegie Corporation, 299
Carnoy, Martin, 240
Carron, Gabriel, 240
Carter, President Jimmy, 333
Castro, Claudio de Mauro, 241
Caveats concerning study, 28–29
C-Bird (Community-Based Integrated
  Rural Development), 89, 90
Cerych, L., 135, 205
Chad, 282
Chau, Ta Gnoc, 240, 241
Chile, 12
China
  foreign students, 316, 330
  foreign teachers and scholars, 330
  knowledge about, 332
  new learning needs, 59
  new UNESCO enrollment estimates, 73n
  projected population by year 2025, 40
  projected population of Peking and
    Shanghai, 45
  reemergence, 12, 13
  Thoughts of Mao and, 271
Chupronov, D., 205
Churchill, Anthony, 62
Churchill, Winston, 33
Club of Rome, 33n
CMEA (Council for Mutual Economic
  Assistance), 292–93
Cohen, Michael, 62
Colombia, 88, 89, 317

Commonwealth countries, 317, 318, 324,
  325
Commonwealth South Asia Symposium,
  206
Coombe, Trevor, 205, 240
Coombs, Philip H., 32, 63, 98, 135, 284
Cornell University, Center for
  International Studies, 52t
Court, David, 241
Cuba, 317
Culture and education. *See also*
    Educational environment; Language;
    Religion; Science education; Social
    change
  broad concept of culture, 244
  impact of sociocultural changes on
    schools, 111–13
  influence of Western education models,
    112
  interaction of cultures, 244–45
  quest for cultural identity, 261–63
  recent cultural upheavals, 244–46
Curriculum
  challenge of computers, 248
  efforts to strengthen science and math,
    115, 246
  growing obsolescence, 5
  impact of rapid technological change,
    248
  modification of colonial legacies, 70–71
  need to adapt to diversified students,
    116
  UNESCO advocacy of new subjects, 116
  urban-oriented curriculums in rural
    areas, 56
Czechoslovakia, 69, 193, 207t, 208t, 260

DAC (OECD's Development Assistance
  Committee), 292, 293n
  record of educational assistance, 293t,
    296, 297–98, 311t, 312t
Denmark, 118, 186
Developed nations. *See individual regions
  and countries*
Developing nations. *See individual regions
  and countries*
Development assistance. *See also*
    Educational development;
    International understanding and
    cooperation
  focus of World Bank's IDA on poorest
    countries, 293–94
  growth of ODA in 1970s, 292, 293t

horizontal cooperation, 288
increased support for research, 303–4
membership of OECD/DAC, CMEA,
  and OPEC, 293
new directions and priorities in 1970s,
  300, 301
problems of implementing new
  strategies, 301–3
project aid versus program aid, 307–9
sources of funds for multilateral
  agencies, 293
support for integrated, community-based
  programs, 303
World Bank's new priorities, 304
Development assistance for education
decline of aid to formal education, 299
decline of teachers and advisers from
  OECD countries, 295, 296t
earlier priority for high-level manpower,
  289–90
increased costs per expert, 295
most effective uses of external assistance,
  306–10
new strategies and priorities in 1970s,
  300, 301
nonformal components of sectoral
  projects, 290
Phillips report for Rockefeller
  Foundation, 294, 295f
problems of implementing new
  strategies, 301–3
problems of measurement, 290–91
prospects for future volume, 305–6
record of bilateral agencies, 295f, 297–
  98
record of private nonprofit
  organizations, 298–99
rise in aid to nonformal education, 299,
  300
shifting sources of educational aid, 295f
trends in dollar volume, 294–96
trends of OECD/DAC bilateral
  allocations to education sector, 311t,
  312t
Diebold de Cruz, Paulo, 242
Disparities and inequalities. *See also*
  Poverty; Rural schools; Women
approaches to reducing inequalities, 233
attacking disparities, 233–35
built-in social bias of schools, 212
early hopes to eradicate, 211
five general propositions, 217–18
geographic disparities, developed
  countries, 218–20

geographic disparities, developing
  countries, 222–23
greatest disparities in higher education,
  225
IIEP research, 218, 240
Latin American example, 230, 242t
living examples of disparities, 213–15,
  216
obstacles to eradicating, 211–13, 216–17
qualitative disparities, 223–24
sex disparities, 224, 225t, 226–28
socioeconomic disparities, 230–32
voices of criticism, 215
Dominica, 224
Dore, Ronald, 110, 135, 205
Dropouts. *See* Wastage
Dubbeldam, Leo, 240
Durkheim, Emile, 215

East Asia, 50f
Economic development. *See also* World
  economy
awakening to realities in early 1970s, 16–
  18
early simplistic theories, 14–15
"growth with equity," 19
lopsided, inequitable pattern, 16
Marshall Plan and postwar
  reconstruction, 14
new concepts (priorities and strategies),
  18–19
new consensus on rural development, 19
progress of developing countries, 16
prospects for, 161–65, 170t
relation to educational development
  strategy, 15
urban-rural gap, 15, 16
Economists, 15–16
Ecuador, 200, 278
Education
budgets. *See* Educational costs
Faure Commission report, 21
progress achieved by developing
  countries, 18
reform of, 20
Education and employment. *See also*
  Employment markets; Manpower;
  Youth unemployment; World
  economy
early assumptions of economists, 172–
  73
historic symbiotic relationship, 172–73
OECD studies, 171–87

Educational costs. *See also* Educational
  productivity; Teacher salaries
  Bowen's "Five Laws on Higher
    Education Costs," 153–54
  budget impact of upgrading teacher
    qualifications, 151
  consequences of replacing foreign
    teachers, 151
  differentials by education levels, 157,
    158t
  differentials per student by region, 159f
  illusory cost reductions, 156
  implications of enrollment stagnation,
    152
  insufficient knowledge, 145–46
  need to improve internal efficiency, 155
  rising real cost per student, 146–47, 169t,
    170t
Educational development. *See also*
  Economic development; Population;
  World economy
  handmaiden to economic strategy, 15
  initial aims of developed countries, 67–
    69
  initial aims of developing countries, 69–
    71
  intention of building from ground up,
    213
  lopsided, inequitable pattern, 16
  new emphasis on basic education, 26
  progress over past three decades, 9
  shift of priorities in 1970s, 26, 72
  strategy of linear expansion, 6, 96
Educational environment
  demographic changes, 13
  economic and technical changes, 9–11
  impact of science, 246–50
  political forces, 11–13
  social and cultural changes, 244–46,
    250–55
Educational gaps. *See also* Disparities and
  inequalities; Maladjustments
  approaches to closing, 132–35
  major current and prospective, 131–32
  many individuals beyond reach of
    schools, 132
  quantitative and qualitative, 35
  view of 1968 report, 33–35
Educational planning
  complicating factors, 173–74
  cost-benefit (rate of return) approach, 67,
    174–77
  evolution in 1960s, 173
  experience of U.S.S.R., 176

incentive structures incompatible with
    national needs, 178
  manpower-planning approach, 174–77
  more an art than a science, 177
  needed changes and improvements, 177
  role of IIEP and OECD, 173
  social-demand approach, 174–77
  suggested alternative approach to
    preparing a plan, 165–66
Educational priorities, 26, 73. *See also*
  Development assistance for education;
  Educational development
Educational productivity. *See also*
  Educational costs; Educational
  technologies; Teacher supply and
  demand
  automatic promotion, 123–24
  contrast with other professions, 148
  inhibiting factors, 123
  lack of textbooks and equipment, 123
  need to reorganize teaching-learning
    system, 148–51
  schools overloaded with too many
    functions, 114
  static technologies, 147–48
  teachers given little time for in-service
    training, 121–22
  team teaching approach, 149–51
  textbooks and teacher manuals, 116
Educational pyramids, 68–73
Educational technologies. *See also*
  Educational productivity; Reforms
  and innovations
  ACPO in Colombia, 131
  available inventory of new technologies
    for developing countries, 133–34
  computers, 133
  distance learning, 71, 130–31
  IIEP evaluation study of new media,
    128–29
  imported technologies, 71
  International Extension College, 131
  labor-intensive, static technologies, 147
  little media, 129–30
  MPATI, 127
  narrow and broader concepts, 125–26
  need for radical educational change, 135
  neglect of software, 128, 133
  open colleges and universities, 131
  radio and TV, 71
  radiophonic schools in Central America,
    131
  revolution in communications
    technology, 133

Socrates disdained the book, 133
teaching-learning systems, 125–26
unfulfilled promise of instructional TV,
    126–29
Egypt, 179, 259
Eicher, J. C., 167
Elmandjra, M., 33n
El Salvador, 12, 129, 224, 233
Emerson, Ralph Waldo, 3
Employment markets. *See also* Manpower;
    Youth unemployment
conjectures, 203–4
impact of changing technologies, 11
impact of population trends, 184, 190,
    195
modern and informal sectors, 11, 17
more women working in OECD
    countries, 59–60, 65t
segmentation, 11, 188
urban modern sector, 11
Enrollment trends. *See also* Learning
    needs; Population
comparison of different ratios, 80t
developed countries' stagnation, 80–81,
    101t, 102t
estimating completers in Brazil, 78–79
gross enrollment ratios, 75, 76t, 77–79
higher education in Eastern socialist
    countries, 193, 206t, 208t, 209t
lack of data on school completers, 77–
    79
numerical growth, 73, 74f, 75, 99t
outlook for developed countries, 83
outlook for developing countries, 84,
    85f, 86
overreporting to UNESCO, 75
ratios by age groups, 79, 80, 100t, 101t,
    102t
reimposition of *numerus clausus* in
    Europe, 155
slowdown in 1970s, 80–83
UNESCO projections to year 2000, 84,
    85f
Ethiopia, 12, 91, 123, 222, 282
Europe
aging population, 60
enrollment projections to year 2000, 42,
    43f, 64t
foreign students, 316
preschool enrollment, 236
ratio of women enrolled, 225t
rise in job qualifications, 180
rural population, 219
European Community, 322

Fensham, Peter J., 264
Ferge, Zsuzsa, 241
Ford Foundation, 127, 257, 299
Foreign students. *See also* Development
    assistance for education; International
    understanding and cooperation
changing geographic pattern, 317, 338t
concern about undergraduates, 318–19
costs versus benefits of, 326–27
distribution by level and fields of study
    (U.S. and U.K.), 318–19, 320f
financing, 321
future policy issues, 325–28
hidden costs and subsidies, 321–22
leading countries of origin, 316, 336t
leading host countries, 316–17, 336t
lure of foreign degrees, 319
major source of in France, 318
new European restrictions, 322–25
sharp increase in 1970s, 314, 315f
where they came from, 315, 316f, 337t
where they studied, 316, 337t
Formal education systems. *See also*
    Educational costs; Learning needs;
    Reforms and innovations
colonial, 6, 17, 70, 71, 243–44
diversified in U.S. and U.S.S.R., 68–69
elitist in Western Europe, 68
imported elitist structures, 6
imports from noncolonial countries, 71
need for overhauling and updating, 21–
    22
outlook in developed countries, 83
outlook in developing countries, 85
postwar democratization in Europe, 68
separate urban and rural, 214–15
Foster, Philip, 181, 205
Fox, Melvin J., 257, 264
France
Alliance Française, 332
baccalaureate in colonies, 214
efforts to preserve language's purity,
    262
foreign students, 316, 317
Imbert Decree, 323
Instituts Universitaires de Technologie
    (IUTs), 68
population of Paris, 45
replacement of auxiliary teachers, 118
socioeconomic disparities, 230
Université du troisième age, 60
youth unemployment, 185
Fredriksen, Birger, 98, 241
Freire, Paulo, 280

Gambia, 221–22
Germany (G.D.R.), 69, 193, 206t, 208t
Germany (F.R.G.)
  Fachhochschule, 68
  foreign students, 316–18
  socioeconomic disparities, 230
  University of Constance, 68
  women in higher education, 225
  young poets, 255–56
  youth unemployment, 186
Ghana, 18, 196
Gintes, Herbert, 240
Greece, 316, 318
Guatemala, 237
Gurgulino de Souza, Heitor, 167

Handicapped, 61. *See also* Learning needs
Harbison, Fred, 201
Haub, Carl, 62
Health. *See also* Learning needs;
    Nonformal education; Women
  basic indicators, 64t
  external assistance for health education,
    303
  infant mortality in poorest countries, 51,
    64t
  relation to productivity and learning, 52
  shocking rural conditions, 16, 51–52, 64t
Herrera, Felipe, 318
Higher education. *See also* Educational
    costs; Formal education systems;
    Reforms and innovations
  admission policies in Eastern Europe, 69
  budgetary curtailment of programs in
    West, 114
  children of affluent subsidized by less
    affluent, 214
  enrollment stagnation in developed
    countries, 83
  expansion of programs in developing
    countries, 114
  growth of nontraditional students, 83
  lack of faculty research opportunities,
    125
  new models of in Western Europe, 68
  overcrowding in India and Latin
    America, 124
Honduras, 200, 237
Hong Kong, 318
Hornick, R. C., 135
Houvasi, Evan, 241
Humphreys, John, 205
Hungary, 193, 206t, 208t, 223, 260
Husen, Torsten, 242, 283

IDA (International Development
    Association). *See* World Bank
IDRC (International Development
    Research Center), 304, 330
Illich, Ivan, 23, 32
India
  "basic education," 303
  Department of Nonformal Education, 90
  directory of nonformal education, 88
  educated unemployed, 198–99
  export of skilled manpower, 10
  Ghandian basic school, 237
  Kerala State, 270
  language problems, 260
  motor vehicle repairs, 58
  overcrowded universities, 124
  overreporting of local enrollments, 75
  projected populations of Bombay and
    Calcutta, 45
  studies of, 332
  university student protests, 12–13
  urban population, 46
  woman as head of state, 224
Indochina, 12
Indonesia, 59, 89, 90, 303, 332
Industrial Revolution, 228
Infants and preschool-age children. *See
    also* Educational gaps; Learning needs
  educational needs, 61
  existing programs, 61
  Head Start program in U.S., 235
  infant mortality. *See* Health
  need to increase provisions, 235–36
  new approach in Netherlands, 236
  primary education and, 236
Inflation. *See* World economy; Educational
    costs
Informal education
  definition, 24
  expanding newspaper circulation, 94,
    103t
  gross regional disparities, 91–95
  impact of communication satellites, 95
  increased access to radio, TV, and films,
    94–95, 103t, 104t
  increased publication of books, 93–94,
    102t
  influence of increased parental
    education, 93
  informal learning environments, 92
  potential policies for strengthening, 92
Institute of International Education
  Open Doors, 315, 320n, 337
Inter-American Development Bank, 230,
    297, 319

International Council for Adult Education, 98

International Institute for Educational Planning, 8, 128, 173, 218n, 283

International Labor Office, 195–96, 200

International understanding and cooperation. *See also* Development assistance; Foreign students
common market for educational and cultural goods, 286
decline in foreign area and language studies, 331–34
deterioration of political climate in 1970s, 287
increased "horizontal cooperation," 288
increased sense of independence, 288
international system in state of crisis, 285
new trails blazed in 1970s, 288
premature aging and politicization of agencies, 287

Iran, 12, 316–18, 336t

Iraq, 318

Islamic societies, 226

Israel, 317

Italy, 60, 230

Ivory Coast, 129, 225

Jallade, Jean-Pierre, 167

Jamaica, 223

Jamison, D. T., 135

Januszkiewicz, Franciszek, 98

Japan, 71, 184, 185, 227, 317, 332

Jeria, Maximo, 242

Jervier, Wills S., 241

Jiltsov, E., 205

Jordan, 317–18

Kahnert, F., 135

Kenya, 81, 196, 200, 201, 220, 329

Kinyanjiu, Kabiru, 241

Kluczynski, Jan, 98

Korea, Republic of, 10, 89, 90

Kwiatkowski, Stefan, 98

Landsheere, Gilbert de, 234, 242

Language. *See also* Migration; Rural schools; Urbanization
contact languages, 258
decline of foreign-language studies in West, 331–34
difficulty of choosing a national language, 259–60
European languages in higher education, 259
importance of language to ethnicity, 257
language problems in developed countries, 260–61
linguistic fragmentation in Africa and India, 257–59
problems arising from language differences, 256–57
staggering educational implications, 256–63
Towers of Babel everywhere, 257
unwritten languages, 256
use of mother tongue in early schooling, 256

Latin America and Caribbean. *See also individual countries*
educational costs and expenditures, 144t, 158t, 159t, 167t, 168t
enrollment projections, 42, 43f, 64t
enrollment ratios, 79, 80t, 100t
female enrollments, 225, 227
foreign teachers, 329
overcrowded universities, 124
population, 40, 46, 49, 50
preschool enrollment, 236
primary school dropouts, 77
qualitative disparities, 223
rural inequalities, 215
socioeconomic disparities, 231
unemployment, 179, 200

Lauwerys, Joseph, 250–55, 264

Layard, P. R. G., 206

Learning needs
of elderly, 60
of handicapped, 61
of infants and preschool-age children, 61
of rural children and youth, 53–55
of rural populations, 49–57
of working women, 59–60

Learning needs, causes of rapid growth in. *See also* Infants and preschool-age children; Migration; Population; Urbanization; Women
development, 57–61
economic and technological change, 57–59
energy shortage, 59
explosion of knowledge, 57
increase in number of learners, 36–40
migration and urbanization, 44–49
more women entering labor force, 59–60
social changes, 59–61

348 / *Index*

Learning network, national lifelong, 27–28
Lebanon, 317–18
Lenin, V. I., 216
Liberska, Barbara, 205
Libya, 318
Literacy and illiteracy. *See also* UNESCO
  ambiguities of meaning, 279–81
  eradication targets, 70, 278–79
  functional illiteracy in Europe and
    America, 282
  functional literacy, 271–72, 280
  Fundamental Education, 266
  growth of adult illiterates, 86, 268f
  historical roots of literacy doctrine, 270–
    71
  innovative approach in Thailand, 277
  lack of reading material in rural areas,
    272
  linkage to primary-school weaknesses,
    269–70
  literacy balance sheet, 266, 267f, 267t,
    268f
  questions for future strategy, 281–83
  underlying assumptions of literacy
    doctrine, 265
  UNESCO's Experimental World
    Literacy Programme, 272–76, 280–81
  unreliability of statistics, 268–69

Maheu, René, 272
Maladjustments
  between education and employment, 204
  causes, 35
  education geared only to modern sector,
    178
  essence of educational crisis, 5
  incentive structures versus national
    needs, 178
  on increase since 1960s, 131
  student choices, 178
Malawi, 329
Malaysia, 316–18
Mali, 214, 275, 282
Malica, John R., 169t
Malitza, M., 33n
Management, 145–46, 163. *See also*
  Educational planning
Manpower. *See also* Employment markets;
  Population; Women; Youth
  unemployment
  brain drain, 10
  effect of population changes, 184, 185f,
    190–91, 195

future supply and demand, 202–3
  more women entering labor force, 59–
    60, 65t
  transition from shortages to surpluses,
    10
Marga Institute (Sri Lanka), 206
Marshall Plan, 14
Marx, Karl, 217, 271
Marxism, 249, 291
Marxism and neo-Marxists, 216, 249, 260
Mass education, 71, 109, 181
Mayo, J. K., 135
Mazrui, Ali A., 240
M'Bow, Ahmadou, 280, 284
McAnany, E. G., 135
McNamara, Robert, 16, 32, 304
Methods. *See* Educational technologies;
  Reforms and innovations
Mexico, 45, 47–48, 200
Middle East, 10, 12, 59
Migration. *See also* Language; Learning
    needs; Urbanization
  between nations, 44
  "guest workers" in Western Europe, 47
  Hispanics and Asians in U.S., 44–45
  impact on learning needs, 44–45, 48–49
  internal within U.S., 47
  learning needs of migrants, 48–49
  patterns in developed world, 46–48
  refugees, 12, 44
  rural to urban, 16, 44
  rural-urban migration in Europe, 47
Moral education. *See also* Social change
  confused with religious education, 251
  debate will remain lively, 255
  "old values" preached but not practiced,
    251, 255
  "powerful and dangerous nonsense," 253
  resurgence of interest in, 250, 253
Morocco, 214, 318
Murphy, Elaine, 62

National Council for International Health,
    63
Nepal, 329
Netherlands, 225, 304
New Zealand, 71, 219
Nicaragua
  literacy, 282
  political upheaval, 12
Niger, 282
Nigeria, 81, 128, 220, 257–58, 316–18
Noah, Harold J., 169t

Nonformal education. *See also* Agriculture; Educational costs; Health; Literacy and illiteracy; Occupational education
  definition and misconceptions, 23–25
  diverse sources of support, 25–26
  diversity of sponsorship and management, 24–25
  existing programs, wealth of, 88
  growth in 1970s, 88, 89
  ICED research reports, 29, 32, 89, 90
  measurement difficulties, 29
  national inventories, 88
  need for technical support services, 91
  NFE in industrialized countries, 25
  not a separate "system," 23
  organizational obstacles, 91
  prospects for future growth, 97
  shortcomings and practical problems, 90–92
  support from aid agencies, 23, 90
  upsurge of interest in early 1970s, 22–23
North America
  aging population, 60
  enrollment projections, 42, 43f, 64t
  foreign students, 316
  percentage increase of women in enrollments, 225t
  rise in job qualifications, 180
  rural population, 219
Norway, 68, 324

Occupational education. *See also* Education and employment; Learning needs; Youth unemployment
  ancient forms, 171
  early obsolescence, 247
  impact of increased specialization, 172
  lifelong process, 172
  multipurpose schools, 115
  preemployment versus on-the-job training, 172
  "vocational school fallacy," 181
ODA (Official Development Assistance). *See* Development Assistance
OECD (Organization for Economic Cooperation and Development)
  important source of data for present study, 8
  member countries, 201, 215, 219
  OECD Observer and special studies, 167, 205–6
OPEC (Organization of Petroleum Exporting Countries), 292, 293, 317

Out-of-school youth, 84, 85, 238–39. *See also* Learning needs; Nonformal education; Youth unemployment

Pakistan, 10, 198, 205
Panama, 220, 225, 233, 237
Passow, A. Harry, 169t
Perkins, James A., 333
Peru, 200
Philippines, 179, 198, 225, 317
Phillips, H. M., 290, 291
Platt, William J., 98
Poland, 12, 60, 69, 192–93, 206t, 208t, 260
Political forces and upheavals, 11–13, 244–46
Poole, Millicent, 205
Population. *See also* Employment markets; Learning needs; Poverty; Manpower
  age distribution and dependency ratios, 38, 39f, 40
  analysis in *World Development Report 1984,* 62n
  birth rates declining except in Africa, 36
  continuing rural growth in developing countries, 49, 50f
  contrasting trends, 36, 38, 39f
  demographic reversal in developed countries, 13
  developing world's increasing share in, 38, 39f, 63t
  educational implications, 41–42, 43f
  expanding world of learners (1950–2000), 38f
  growth since the Old Stone Age, 37–38
  impact on poverty, 50–51
  impact on primary enrollment ratios, 43
  long-range projections of developing regions, 40
  postwar explosion, 13
  pressure on education in developing countries, 195
  trends in school-age populations, 63t
  uneven geographic distribution, 38–41
  UN world projections to year 2000, 39f
Poverty. *See also* Health; Population; Rural schools
  absolute poverty defined, 16
  declining food production per capita, 51
  examples from Gambia, Sudan, Ethiopia, 221–22
  on increase in Africa, Asia, and Middle East, 49–52
  landless and near-landless, 16, 51, 52f

link with population growth, 16
measure of wasted human resources, 197
problem of reaching the poorest, 305
rural in OECD countries, 57
seamless web, 221–23
World Bank projection of in year 2000,
161
Prieur, M., 205
Primary education, 71–80, 213–15. *See
also* Disparities and inequalities;
Rural schools; UPE; UNESCO
Production schools, 237
Prosser, Roy C., 32, 63

Qualitative dimensions of education. *See
also* Educational technologies; Teacher
supply and demand
critics of schools, 107
difficult mandate of democratic mass
systems, 109
diploma disease, 110
false comparisons of quality, 108–9
five influential school factors, 113–31
impact of sociocultural changes in
schools, 111
quality and standards viewed as relative
matters, 107
quality versus quantity, 109, 123
relevance (fitness) a major factor, 105
two views of "standards," 107–8

Ratinoff, Luis, 242
Recession. *See* World economy
Reforms and innovations. *See also*
Educational technologies;
Maladjustments; Teacher salaries
Faure Commission findings, 21
important use for external assistance,
309
largely piecemeal, 113
more fundamental changes needed, 113,
166
open colleges and universities, 131
radiophonic schools in Central America,
131
rigidities imposed by teacher contracts,
121
Tanzania's approach to UPE, 220–21
teacher training essential for success, 116
in Zambia, 213

Religion. *See also* Culture and education;
Moral education
Bible in various tongues, 270
Christian-Democratic values, 255
Christianity, 249
Christian missionaries and literacy, 270
education of girls in Islamic societies,
226
ethical codes of major religions, 251
Islam and Koranic schools, 270–71
Lutheran church and literacy in Sweden,
270
New Testament and Talmud, 171
spread of Buddhism, Christianity, Islam,
244
Repeaters. *See* Wastage
Research in developing countries, 125,
330–31. *See also* Science and
technology; Science education
Rhodesia (Zimbabwe), 318
Rickover, Admiral Hyman, 108
Rio de Janeiro, projected population, 45
Rockefeller Foundation, 289, 290
Robinson, Brandon, 241
Rodrigues da Cunha Filho, Gladstone, 167
Romania, 193, 206t, 208t
Rural development. *See* Economic
development; Learning needs; Rural
schools
Rural schools. *See also* Disparities and
inequalities; Learning needs
access to rural professional careers, 238
contrast with urban, 16–18, 72
disparities reduced in developed
countries,, 218–20
foreign medium of instruction, 124
poor conditions concealed by statistics,
17, 223–24
semiarid educational deserts, 124
ways to attack geographic disparities,
233–34

SAREC (Swedish Agency for Research
Cooperation), 304, 331
Saudi Arabia, 226, 317, 329–30
Scandinavian countries, 56
Schramm, Wilbur, 129, 135
Schumacher, E. F., 129
Science and technology, 247–50
Science education, 115–16, 246–48
Scottish Outer Hebrides, 56
Secondary education, 115, 224, 236–37

SENA (National Apprenticeship Program), 89
Senegal, University of Technology, 329
Sierra Leone, 51
Singapore, 318
Smith, Abigail Adams, 224
Social change, 48, 111–12, 211–13, 232
Social demand. *See* Educational planning
Socialist countries, Eastern Europe, 69, 176, 192–93, 215, 219, 260. *See also* U.S.S.R.
Soedjatmoko, 285
South Africa, University of Stellenbosch, 259
South Asia
  increase in enrollment ratios (1960–80), 79, 80t, 100t
  projected population by year 2100, 40
  projected urban and rural population growth, 49, 50f
  UNESCO enrollment projections to year 2000, 42, 43f, 64t
Spain, 185
Spaulding, Seth, 283
Spencer, Herbert, 254
Sri Lanka, 51, 89, 198, 224, 282
Standards. *See* Qualitative dimensions of education
Stanford University, School of Education, 119
Statistics, educational
  excellent work of UNESCO statisticians, 83
  inadequate national information systems, 83
  main sources used, 8
  recommendation to aid agencies, 83
Strategies. *See* Economic development; Educational development
Students. *See also* Population; Enrollment trends
  behavioral problems, 251
  curriculum choices, 178
  more diversified, 116
  nontraditional, 83, 96, 193, 208t, 209t
  protests, 12–13, 180
Sub-Saharan Africa, 157
Sudan, 225, 259
Sudaprasert, Kamal, 241
Sweden, 67, 146, 169, 225, 230
SWRC (Social Work and Research Center), 89
Systems analysis, 27
Szalai, Julia, 241

Tabah, Leon, 38, 62
Taiwan, 316
Tanzania, 81, 201, 220, 221
Teacher organizations, 120–21, 145. *See also* Teacher salaries
Teacher salaries. *See also* Educational costs; Teacher supply and demand
  contrasted with other professions, 148, 150
  effects of uniform salary schedules, 120, 148
  illogical structuring, 147
  impact of higher qualifications on budget, 123
  inflationary erosion, 121
  pros and cons of merit pay, 149
Teacher supply and demand. *See also* Employment markets; Population; Qualitative dimensions of education; Teacher salaries
  declining demand in 1970s, 118–19, 122
  eroding status, 20–21
  influence of on quality, 113
  in-service training, 121–22
  pupil-teacher ratios, 118
  reduction of expatriates, 124
  shortage of in science and math, 119, 120, 247
  qualifications, 118, 119
  worldwide growth of staff, 117t
Technological change. *See* Curriculum; Educational environment; Educational technologies; Learning needs
Thailand
  adult education, 87
  educational disparities, 215, 223
  functional literacy and family life, 277
  literacy, 282
  National Social and Economic Board, 206
  nonformal education programs, 89
  unemployed graduates, 198
Timar, Janos, 240
Tunsiri, Vichae, 241
Turkey, National Institute of Education, 90, 318

UNDP (United Nations Development Programme), 273, 292, 297
U.N. Economic Commission for Europe, 167

UNESCO
  Experimental World Literacy
    Programme, 272–76, 280–81
  International Commission for the
    Development of Education (Faure
    Commission), 21, 32
  Quito, Ecuador, conference, 278
  Regional conferences (Addis Ababa,
    Karachi, Santiago-de-Chile, Tripoli),
    70, 73–74
  Teheran International Conference on
    Eradication of Illiteracy, 280
  Tokyo International Conference on
    Adult Education, 280–81
UNICEF, 23, 221–22, 297
United Kingdom
  British Council, 332
  curtailment of teacher training, 118
  Greater London population, 45
  International Extension College, 131
  modern school, 67
  Open University, 130
  overseas students, 316–23, 326, 338t,
    339t
  sandwich programs, 237
  Sussex University and various
    polytechnics, 68
  youth unemployment, 185, 186
United Nations
  Commission on the Status of Women,
    223
  Fund for Population Activities, 241n
  population estimates and projections,
    62–63
United Nations University, 285, 331
United States
  "Black studies," 262
  College Entrance Examination Board,
    109
  Committee on Refugees, 62
  diversified education system, 68
  extra resources for "problem
    neighborhood" schools, 118
  foreign area and language studies, 331–
    34
  foreign students, 316–21, 325, 338t
  Fulbright program cutbacks, 330
  "graying" of the nation, 60
  increase in labor force and employment,
    184
  MPATI, 127
  multilingualism, 260–61
  National Academy of Education, 119,
    135

  National Center for Educational
    Statistics, 135, 206
  National Council on Foreign Language
    and International Studies, 334
  new female careers, 227–28
  New York City's population in 1980, 45
  Presidential Commission on Education,
    109
  Presidential Commission on Foreign
    Languages and International Studies,
    333–34
  Reagan administration, 328
  recent influx of Hispanics and Asians,
    47–48
  rising expenditure per student, 146,
    170t
  saturation of academic market for
    Ph.Ds, 119
  shortage of science and math teachers,
    119
  storefront schools, 237
  teacher unions and strikes, 121, 145
  U.S. Information Service, 332
  upgrading of labor force, 201
  women in higher education, 225
  youth employment, 185, 186
USAID (United States Agency for
    International Development), 23, 291,
    303
UPE (Universal Primary Education). *See
    also* Disparities and inequalities;
    Rural schools; UNESCO
  consequences of rapid population
    growth, 48
  deviation from adopted goals, 213–15
  differing definitions, 77n
  failure to achieve 1980 targets, 72, 213–
    14
  initial strategy and targets, 213
  progress on Addis Ababa target, 81–82
  Tanzanian unconventional approach,
    220–21
  UNESCO 1982 assessment, 214
University of London, Institute of
    Education, 326
University of Moscow, 216
University of Nairobi, 201
Upper Volta, 51, 214, 282
Urbanization, 17, 45–46, 49–50f. *See also*
    Economic development; Migration;
    Population; Youth unemployment
Urban-rural gap. *See* Disparities and
    inequalities; Economic development;
    Rural schools

Urban schools, 17–18, 72. *See also* Disparities and inequalities; Rural schools

U.S.S.R. (Soviet Union). *See also* Socialist countries, Eastern Europe
  diversified education system, 69
  foreign area and language training, 333
  foreign students, 316
  graduates in the economy, 201
  higher education enrollments, 190, 193, 206t
  knowledge about, 332
  language diversity, 260
  postsecondary institutions, 69
  socioeconomic disparities, 230
  Soviet Academy of Sciences, 333
  Universities of Leningrad and Moscow, 216
  women in higher education, 225

Vaizey, John, 249–50, 264
Van der Tak, Jean, 62
Venezuela, 200, 317
Vietnam, 214, 282
Vocational education. *See* Occupational education; Secondary education
Voluntary agencies (N.G.O.s), 288, 298–99. *See also* Development assistance; Educational development; Nonformal education; Poverty

Wastage (dropouts and repeaters), 75, 77n, 237–38
Wells, H. G., 254
Werdelin, Ingvar, 269, 283
West, Peter, 205
Western Europe, 67, 68, 230
Women. *See also* Disparities and inequalities; Employment markets; Poverty; Youth unemployment
  children of working mothers, 111
  common features of sex disparities, 226–29
  customs and taboos, 228
  education as key to transforming societies, 224–25
  girls in Islamic societies, 226
  increasing percentage of enrollments, 225t
  more entering labor force in OECD area, 59–60, 65t
  new career opportunities in U.S., 227–28
  preference for male children, 228–29

  prospects for reducing sex disparities, 229
  reasons for not sending girls to school, 229
  sex discrimination in employment, 186, 227–28
  sexual liberation movements, 252
  writers and political leaders, 224
Woodhall, Maureen, 206
World Bank
  basic needs programs, 304
  record of educatonal assistance, 296–97, 299, 304–5, 311t, 313t
World economy. *See also* Economic development; Educational costs; Educational development
  accelerated inflation, 10, 143–45, 168t
  future prospects, 161–65, 170t
  GNP projections to year 1995, 170t
  impact of oil price rises, 10
  New International Economic Order, 58–59, 252
  world recession, 10–11, 181
World Education, Inc., 277
World educational crisis
  continuing, 14
  disparity and maladjustment, 4–5
  new crisis of confidence, 9
  summarization of thesis of 1968 report, 4–7
  Williamsburg International Conference, 4

Youth unemployment. *See also* Educational employment; Employment markets; Manpower; Students; Women
  attitudes and morale, 189–90
  causes, 186–88
  contrast between industrial and developing countries, 194
  educated unemployed in 1960s, 179
  experience of developing countries, 194–200
  experience of U.S.S.R. and Eastern European Socialist countries, 190–93
  impact of recession, 181
  obstacles in employment markets, 188
  outlook for employment, 200–204
  selective shortages, 179
  spread of in 1970s, 10, 179
  uneven impact on different groups, 185–88
Zambian father's advice to son, 181